The One Show · Volume 27

Advertising's Best Print, Design, Radio and TV

president
David Baldwin

executive director
Mary Warlick

editor
Yash Egami

designer
Joy Robles

editorial assistants
Jose Alvarado
Noelle Carbone
Joel Fischer
Jacqueline Kynoch

creative and art direction
Oliver Voss
Götz Ulmer
Jung von Matt / Hamburg
www.jvm.de

art buyer
Bianca Winter

one show sponsors
Adobe
Adforum
Getty Images
Mediatemple
Yahoo!
Sony BMG Music Entertainment
Domino Foods

published by
One Club Publishing
21 E. 26th Street, 5th Floor
New York, NY 10010

isbn
0-929837-27-4

production
AVA Book Production Pte. Ltd.
production@avabooks.com.sg

distributed in the US and internationally by
Rockport Publishers
3 Commercial Street
Gloucester, MA 01930
www.rockpub.com
978-282-9590

Board of Directors	iv
President's Message	v
One Show Judges	vi
One Club Members	vii
Best of Show	1
Gold, Silver, Bronze	4
Gold on Gold - Judge's Choice	113
Print Merit	145
Public Service Merit	241
Television and Radio Merit	275
Innovative/Integrated Merit	327
Design Merit	347
College Merit	435
Illustration Credits	455
Index	457

Contents

Board of Directors

David Baldwin, President
McKinney/Durham

Tod Seisser, Vice President
Freelance/New York

Earl Cavanah, Treasurer
Lowe/New York

Kevin Roddy, Corporate Secretary
BBH/New York

Rick Boyko
VCU AdCenter/Richmond

Brian Collins
Ogilvy & Mather - Brand Integration Group /New York

John Doyle
Labyrinth Worldwide

Joe Duffy
Duffy & Partners/Minneapolis

Kara Goodrich
BBDO/New York

Gerry Graf
TBWA\Chiat\Day/New York

Jan Leth
Ogilvy Interactive/New York

José Mollá
la comunidad/Miami

Deborah Morrison
University of Oregon/Portland

Jim Mountjoy
Loeffler Ketchum Mountjoy/Charlotte

Steve Sandstrom
Sandstrom Design/Portland

Ernie Schenck
Freelance/Boston

Luke Sullivan
GSD&M/Austin

Joyce King Thomas
McCann Erickson/New York

The One Club is the world's foremost non-profit organization for the recognition and promotion of creative excellence in advertising through awards shows, educational programs, exhibitions and scholarships.

David Baldwin
One Club President

This show is revered around the world because of one thing.

The work.

Not the parties, not the client hookups, not the tans.

The One Show is still the greatest show on the planet. It honors the best work in the world, done by the best people in the world, judged by the best creative people in the world.

Maybe the coolest thing about this year's One Show Festival is that for the first time ever we held the One Show and the One Show Interactive at the same time. On the same night. In the same venue. Across the hall from each other.

It's a great sign of what's going on in the business. Our job is to reflect the great work you're doing and maybe, if we get it right, even the way you're doing it.

So we started with a cocktail reception, we went into our respective shows and then at the end we got together for a party afterwards.

One thing I find interesting is that some of the same pieces were entered into both shows. That's because advertising today cannot be parsed so easily into what media it ran in.

Sure, it's still all about a great idea. It will always be about a great idea. But there are so many different ways to express ideas these days that it's pretty exhilarating to see them all in one place.

It sure makes judging tough, but then that's why we go out and get the best creative people in the world to judge our shows. This year we saw judges from 13 countries who slogged their way through 17,000 entries over one week in Manhattan. Work from 34 different countries, mind you.

It starts out pretty easy in the first few days. It's not so tough to winnow out the usual. But then in the finals there is a lot, and I mean a lot, of work that's pretty good. But as we all know, good enough, ain't. So that's when the real work starts. A judge's job is to separate out the great from the good.

Getting a merit in this show isn't easy. So if you did something awesome, and I mean awesome in the traditional Ceasar staring at his legions way, or Moses parting the Red Sea sense of the word, and you won a Pencil, congratulations, you've truly had to beat the world to do it.

President's Message

One Show Judges

2005 One Show Jury

Olivier Altman
Publicis / Paris

Rose Bardales
Mother / London

Eugene Cheong
Ogilvy & Mather / Singapore

Harry Cocciolo
Tool of North America / Santa Monica

David Crawford
GSD&M / Austin

Sean Doyle
Campbell Doyle Dye / London

Andy Fackrell
180 Amsterdam / Amsterdam

Laura Fegley
Cliff Freeman & Partners / New York

Kara Goodrich
BBDO / New York

Ian Grais
Rethink / Vancouver

Tay Guan-Hin
Grey Worldwide / Kuala Lampur

Ann Hayden
Y & R / New York

Porky Hefer
Lowe Bull / Cape Town

Mike Hughes
The Martin Agency / Richmond

John Jay
Wieden + Kennedy / Tokyo

Margaret Johnson
Goodby, Silverstein & Partners / San Francisco

Paul Keister
Crispin Porter + Bogusky / Miami

Marcos Medeiros
DDB Brazil / Sao Paulo

Joaquin Mollá
la communidad / Miami

Bob Moore
Publicis / Seattle

Piyush Pandey
Ogilvy & Mather India / Mumbai

Joe Shands
TBWA\Chait\Day / Los Angeles

Calvin Soh
Fallon / Singapore

Kirk Souder
Granite Pass / San Francisco

Monica Taylor
Wieden + Kennedy / Portland

Jureeporn Thaidumrong
Saatchi & Saatchi / Bangkok

Oliver Voss
Jung von Matt / Berlin

2005 One Show Design Jury

Laurie DeMartino
Laurie DeMartino Design / Minneapolis

Charles Anderson
Charles Anderson Design / Minneapolis

Kit Hinrichs
Pentagram / San Francisco

Jason Schulte
Jason Schulte Design / San Francisco

Hal Wolverton
Johnson & Wolverton / Portland

Allison Williams
Design: MW / New York

J.P. Williams
Design: MW / New York

2005 One Show Radio Jury

William Gelner
Bartle Bogle Hegarty / New York

Adam Chasnow
Goodby, Silverstein & Partners / San Francisco

Erik Fahrenkopf
davidandgoliath / Los Angeles

Dave Holloway
Euro RSCG Worldwide / New York

Jim Le Maitre
BBDO / New York

Mike Lescarbeau
Freelance / Hopkins

Dan Morales
Cliff Freeman & Partners / New York

Ian Reichenthal
TBWA\Chiat\Day / New York

Rob Reilly
Crispin Porter + Bogusky / Miami

Eddie Van Bloem
Lowe / New York

a

David Abbott
Jeffrey Abbott
Tara Adams
Lisa Albano
Joe Alexander
Shari Alexander
Burcin Alici
Olivier Altmann
Ali Alvarez
Dr. Patricia Alvey
Gideon Amichay
Ralph Ammirati
Charles Anderson
Keith Anderson
Daniel Anderson
Magnus Andersson
Monica Andralliski
Daniel Andréani
David Angelo
Anthony Angotti
Asif Ansari
Marcelo Aragao
Maryah Arangio
Gil Arevalo
Michael Arkin
Linda Artemchuk
Michael Asphar
Brian Austin
David Ayscue

b

Kristina Backlund
Ron Bacsa
Neylan Bagcioglu
Chris Baier
Rob Baiocco
Larry Baisden
Dennis Bajec
David Baldwin
Jeanine Ball
Lisa Balser
Jimi Bankole
Rudy Banny
Shameka Brown Barbosa
Rosie Bardales
Keate Barker
Aileen Barrameda
Ann Barrick
Bob Barrie
Ben Bartholomew
Lars Bastholm
Allan Beaver
Chris Becker
Beelzebub
Paul Belford
Brian Bellanca
Gregg Benedikt
Benjamin Bensimon
Thomas Berger
Meredith Bergman Apicella
David Bernstein
Ethan Besser
Vikas Bhalla
Bruce Bildsten
Craig Bing
Samantha Birchard
Andy Blood
Michael Blore
Helen Boak
Alex Bogusky
Eddie Booth
Reynaldo Bosque
Dr. Courtney Bosworth
Rit Bottorf
Michael Boulia
Jeroen Bours
Mark Braddock
Tim Braybrooks
Brad Brinegar
John Brockenbrough
Bill Brokaw
Robert Brothers
Mark Brown
David Bryant
Gayle M. Budd
Alex Bunch
John Burr
Robert Burt
John Butler

One Club Members

One Club Members

c

Larry Cadman
Michael Calienes
Marianne Camarda
Bridget Camden
Jason Campbell
Jennifer Campbell
Tommy Campbell
William Campbell
David Canning
Josephine Carey
Christopher Caro
Karen Carroll
Christopher Cashdollar
Gary Caulfield
Pierre Chan
Joanne Chan
Lu-Lyn Chang
Daniel Charron
Lisa Chase
Matthew Chen
Andy Cheng
Eugene Cheong
Brian Chin
Jeremy Chin
Young-hee Choi
Dana Choi
Meng Leong Chong
Aaron Chown
David Christiansen
Kevin Christie
Thomas Christmann
Guilherme Chueire
David Cid
Lee Clow
David Coats
Harry Cocciolo
David Cohen
Scott Cohen
Peter Cohen
Kemal Colakel
Rick Colby
Christopher Cole
Marco A. Colin
Anna Coll
Leighton Collis
Vasco Condessa
Brian Connaughton
Sara Corenzwit
Lawrence Corwin
Fabio Costa
Susan Cotler Block
Niko Courtelis
Jeremy Craigen
Elizabeth Craine
Jay Cranford
David Crawford
Tom Crimp
George Curi
Hal Curtis

d

Sonal Dabral
Prince of Darkness
Trish Daley
Michael Dambra
Billy D'Ambrosio
Celeste Dang
Keith Darby
Kimberly Daulton
Joanna D'Avanzo
Craig Davies
James Davis
Joshua Davis
Mateus de Paula Santos
Jay Deegan
Rich Degni
Laura DeGraff
Tom DelMundo
Charles DeMarco
Laurie DeMartino
Toni Deramo
Chris Desalvo
Sal DeVito
Sasima Dharagul
Samantha Digennaro
Lisa Diller
Greg DiNoto
Joe Dobbin
Jim Doll
Michael Donovan
Steve Doppelt
Icaro Doria
Kristine Dorman
Alicia Dotter
Nigel Douglas
Juliet Dowsey
Brian Doyle
Sean Doyle
Aurelia Drackett
Danny Drexler
Katie Dropick
David Drucker
Anja Duering
Joe Duffy
Jim Durfee
John Durham

e

Lee Earle
Matt Eastwood
Vanessa Eckstein
Jackie End
Shirley Epps
Marcelo Ernelindo
Dirk Eschenbacher
Marcella Estes
Anne Louise Etgen Reitz

f

Michele Fabrizi
Andy Fackrell
Dave Fagin
Perry Fair
Dana Farbo
Jordan Farkas
John Fayard
Laura Fegley
Jason Feirman
David Felton
Matt Ferrin
Alison Fetten
Daniele Fiandaca
Jane Field
Ricardo Figueira
Monique Fikar

Stan Fineman
Leo Fiorica
Beryl Firestone
Brooke Fisher
Tim Fisher
Kevin Flatt
Mike Flegle
Michael Folino
David Foote
Brian Fouhy
Karen Francis
Roger Frank
Eugenio Franyutti
Chris Franzese
Gregory Frassetti
Charlie Frazer
Cliff Freeman
Robert Fremgen
Kellie French
Glen Fruchter
Javier Fuentes
Tracey Fuller

g

Tom Gabriel
Sarah Galluzzo
Mauricio Galvan
Mark Ganton
Bertrand Garbassi
Steven Garcia
Lee Garfinkel
Amil Gargano
Robert Gaxiola
Joel Gehman
Danny Gellert
Elliot Gerard
Richard Gerdes
Monica Giardina
Vivienne Gibson
John Gilbert
Keith Gillespie
Maria Gitto
Kenneth Gleason
Max Godsil
George Goetz
Kevin Goff
Dan Goldgeier
Cristian Gomez
Emiliano Gonzalez De Pietri
Jeff Goodby
Kara Goodrich
Mitch Gordon
Folkert Gorter
Ian Grais
Tony Granger
Chris Graves
Doug Green
Ali Greenwell
Jason Gregory
Norm Grey
Aaron Griffiths
Philip Growick
Tay Guan-Hin
David Guerrero
Ted Guidotti
Sonia Gulian
Sean Patric Gunann

h

Noel Haan
Christian Haas
Emily Haas
Lori Habas
Nathan Hackstock
Jennifer Hahs
Stephen Hall
Robin Haller
John Halliday
Matthew Hallock
Rhea Hanges
Lee Hanson
Steve Harbour
Penny Hardy
Roy Wisnu Hariadi
Linda Harless
Justin Harris
Jessica Hartmann
Heidi Hartz
Mike Hasinoff
Ann Hayden
Mary Healy
Devin Heatley
Tim Heckman
Porky Hefer
John Hegarty
Brent Heindl
Weitzer Helmut
Brendan Hemp
Roy Herbert
Armando Hernandez
Taylor Hersh
Rony Herz
Ralf Heuel
Ana Hidalgo
Heather Higgins
William Hillsman
Adrian Hilton
Helmut Himmler
Woody Hinkle
Kit Hinrichs
Paul Hirsch
Troy Hitch
Brian Ho
Rob Hoffman
John Hofmeister
Sally Hogshead
Bill Hollister
Dave Holloway
Tricia Holman
Jodie Holmes
Robert Holtzer
Emily Honigsfeld
Kelly Hood
Jim Hord
Ryan Hose
Jonathan Huang
Rob Hudak
Ellen Huffman
Mike Hughes
John Hunt
Mark Hurst
John Hynes

One Club Members

i

Hyun Ho Im
Juri Imamura
Brenda Innocenti
Vladislav Ivangorodsky

j

Ermalee J.
Rob Jackson
Harry Jacobs
Erwin Jansen
John Jay
Bob Jeffrey
Lee Jennings
Lance Jensen
Andrew Jeske
Nick Jibben
Emily Johnson
Anthony Johnson
Marcus Johnson
Margaret Johnson
Ed Jones
Stephen Jones
Melanie Juaner
Rick Julian
William Jurewicz
Elizabeth Kallstrom

k

Stephen Kamsler
Bong (Kalvin) Kang
Seijo Kawaguchi
Gareth Kay
Kevin Kearns
Paul Keister
Carol Lee Kelliher
Ramona Kelly
Tom Kelly
Susanne Kelly
Thomas Kemeny
Daniel Kenneally
David Kennedy
Elizabeth Kerin
Janet Kestin
Jeffrey Keyton
Jean Kim
Lily Kim
Joanne Kim
Eugina Rae Kim
Tony King
Liz Kintz
Takyoshi Kishimoto
Joe Knezic
Bob Kochuk
Kristen Koop
Jerry Kopec
Maya Kopytman
Hitomi Kosumi
Philip Koutsis
Dennis Koye
Tom Kraemer
Joe Kreisberg
Paul Kruger
Adam Kruvand
Ken-ichi Kubo
Kim Kullmann
Ben Kunz
Sasha Kurtz
Michael Kutschinski
Hye Jin Kwon

l

Robin Landa
Jesus Lada
Ming Lai
Fatemah Laleh
John LaMacchia
Jake Lancaster
Robin Landa
Bryan Landaburu
David Landis
Richard Lao
Eric Larkin
Adam LaRocca
Amber Lashmett
David Laskarzewski
Jonathan Laughlin
Alice Laussade
Ron Lawner
Eun-Jung Lee
Cary Lemkowitz
Dany Lennon
Jon Leon
Christian Lester
Kate Levin
Hank Levine
Maryah Lewis
Ted Lim
Jessica Lin
Stewart Logan
George Lois
Giovanna Lopez
Myriam Lopez
Maria Pilar Anne Lopezbanos
Frank Lopresti
Helga Loser
Eileen Lovern
Attila Lovey
David Lubars
Lucifer
Bonnie Lunt
Mike Lupariello
Ernest Lupincacci
Michael Lynch
Zach Lyon

m

Shayne Mackey
Sam Maclay
Vanessa Maganza
Joel MaHarry
Rania Makarem
Karen Mallia
Patricia Malone
Jeff Mancini
Michael Manning
John Mannion
Steve Mapp
Sarah Marden
Marcin Markiewicz
Lawrence Marks
Sasha Martens
Christine Martin

Maqui Martinez
Michael Mastrullo
Stuart Matz
Gabrielle Mayeur
Jeff Maynard
Scott McAfee
Cal McAllister
Ed McCabe
Brian McCarthy
David McCarty
Todd McCracken
Joe McDonagh
Joseph McDonough
Emily McDowell
Tom McFarlane
Peter McHugh
D. McReynolds
John McVicker
Marcos Medeiros
Chris Mello
Christopher Mellon
Alex Melvin
Mark Mendelis
Mephistopheles
Lucy Meredith
Ari Merkin
Tom Mescall
Melinda Mettler
Philippe Meunier
Kindra Meyer
G. Andrew Meyer
Bogdan Migulski
Kevin Andrew Miles
Mark Millar
Kari Miller
Renee Miller
Simon Milliship
Laurence Minsky
Jerry Mlekoday
Joaquín Mollá
José Mollá
Sakol Mongkolkasetarin
Ty Montague
Bill Montgomery
Younghwa Moon
Beverly Ann Moore
Bob Moore
Ami Morakhia
Kevin Moriarty
Deborah Morrison
Nicholas Moser
Jim Mountjoy
Stanford Moy
Zak Mroueh
Jonathan Mueller
Alexander Muk
David Muldoon
Ned Munson
Jayant Murty
Jason Musante
Anthony Musmanno
Rick Myers

n

Michael Nadeau
Yugo Nakamura
Seigo Nakanishi
Gaitan Namouric
Jesus Navarro Saracibar
Jeff Neely
Arun K. Nemali
David Noot
Travis Nuckolls
Toke Nygaard
Michael Nyrop-Larsen

o

Stephanie O' Connell
David Oakley
Patrick O'Brien
Naoto Oiwa
Yasumichi Oka
Frank Oles
Martin Olinger
Jeff Olsen
Dan Olson
Takashi Omura
Hollie Ontrop
Asli Ors
Mike Ortega
Reuben Orter
Sandra Ortiz
Mikio Osaki

p

Paula Pagano
Patricia Palma
Matias Palm-Jensen
Piyush Pandey
Stephen Papageorge
Joe Paprocki
Charles Parr
Richard Parubrub
Babita Patel
Michael Patti
Tina Paul
Lance Paull
Mike Payer
Stan Pearlman
Richard Pels
Steve Penchina
Anthony Perullo
Marianne Pillsbury
Christopher Pinckney
Joe Pistone
Owen Plotkin
Demir Karpat Polat
Valerie Ponte
Wayne Posthumus
Belinda Pruyne
Lynn Pulsifer
Andreas Putz

q

Keith Quesenberry

One Club Members

r

Vincent Raffray
Suzanne Raitt
Anselmo Ramos
Robert Rasmussen
Vidur Raswant
Sean Reaves
Brett Reese
Hal Reeves
Julia Regan
Gina Reif
Robert Reitzfeld
Nancy Rice
Stan Richards
Hank Richardson
Tonya Rinehart
Hal Riney
Peter Risafi
Adrian Riyadi
Tim Roan
Nigel Roberts
John Robertson
Phyllis Robinson
Sherese Robinson
Ed Robinson
Carlos Rocca
Kevin Roddy
William Roden
Scott Rodgers
Alberto Rodriguez
Jason Rogers
Fernanda Romano
Nick Roope
Tom Roope
Brad Roseberry
Jonathan Rosman
Sebastian Royce
Melody Rozsa
Roger Ruegger
Dr. Bill Ryan

s

Laurenne Sala
Steve Sandstrom
Paulo Sanna
Yukimo Sano
Emmanuel Santos
Keiichi Sasaki
Yasuharu Sasaki
Ann Saulnier
Robert Sawyer
Robert Saxon
Dennis Scheyer
Scott Schindler
Chris Schlegel
Robert Schnabel
Serena Schonbrun
Jason Schulte
Danny Schuman
Michael Schwabenland
Jaime Schwarz
Heinz Schwegler
Sally Schweitzer
Joe Sciarrotta
Tom Sebanc
Eric Segal
Tod Seisser
Ben Seldon
Burl Seslar
Christopher Sewing
Joe Shands
Denise Shearer
Mike Sheehan
Glen Sheehan
Peter Sheldon
Geoffrey Sheldon
Bill Shelton
Jennifer Shoop
Alon Shoval
Dana Sickles
Mark Silber
Rich Silverstein
Tonia Simon
Steve Simpson
Richard Singer
Dalbir Singh
Liz Sivell
Pat Sloan
Michelle Smith
Randy Snow
Calvin Soh
Mo Solomon
Kirk Souder
William Spencer
Michael Spriggs
Catherine St. Jean
Russ Stark
David Steinke
Eric Stephens
Jaclyn Steudtner
Mike Stocker
Lorna Stovall
Emily Strand
Thomas Stringham
Alan Stuart
Brett Stuckel
Wade Sturdivant
Amy Su
Luke Sullivan
Steve Swan
Steve Swartz
Matthew Szymczyk

t

Masaaki Takizawa
owolabi Talabi
Monica Taylor
Rob Taylor
Jessica Terlizzi
Mike Tesch
Larry Thacker
Jureeporn Thaidumrong
Patrick Thiede
Greg Thomas
Jeff Thompson
Justin Tindall
Kristina Tjahjono
Tina Toda
Chris Torrens
Domingo Torres
Brian Torsney
Patricia Totzke
Vincent Tozzi
Daniel Treichel
Anthony Trimpe
Megan Trinidad
Shek Tso
Roman Tsukerman
Mark Tutssel

U

Kathy Umland

V

Stephan Valter
Novi van Baak
Peter Van Regenmorter
Paul Venables
Sterling Vernon
Carol Vick-Bynum
John Vitro
Michael Volkmer
Brigitte von Puttkamer
Nancy Vonk
Oliver Voss
Ted Voss
Steve Vranakis

W

Wayne Waaramaa
Peter Wadsworth
Christopher Wagner
Elaine Wagner
Adam Ward
Melinda Ward
Regan Warner
Bob Warren
Graham Warsop
Timothy Wassler
Pei Hsiu Wei
Joe Weismann
Craig Welsh
Robert Shaw West
Scott Westerlaken
Brian Wheeler
Mara White
Dan Wieden
Aaron Wiggan
Scott Wild
Bradley Wilkerson
Peggy Willett
Alison Williams
JP Williams
Tim Williams
Michael Winslow
Stewart Winter
Lloyd Wolfe
Hal Wolverton
Sean Womack
David Wong
Rena Wong
Leslye Wood
Doug Worple
Nick Worthington
Bill Wright

Y

Fadi Yaish
Betsy Yamazaki
Lo Sheung Yan
Dennis Yang
Joan Yhun
Kam Ying
Seo Young

Z

Chantel Zapata
Richard Zeid
John Zilly
Shareif Ziyadat

Best of Show

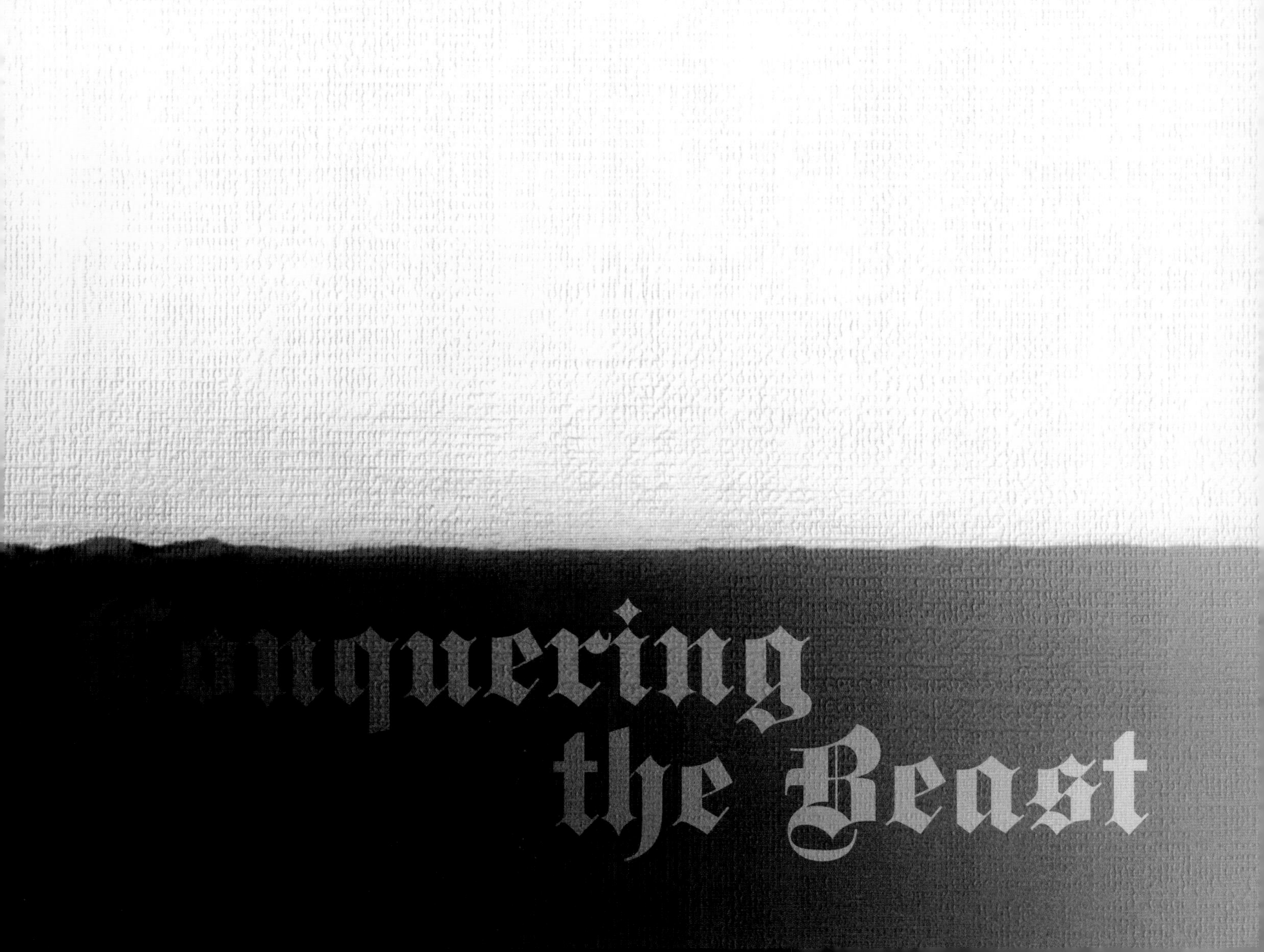
Conquering
the Beast

Best of Show

Client:
Honda

Agency:
Wieden+Kennedy/London

After sweeping the award shows in 2003 with their impressive "Cog" TV spot for Honda, what does Wieden+Kennedy/London do for a follow-up? Flying motors, dancing animals and rainbows, of course.

"Grrr," which features an animated cast of wildlife gleefully "hating" noisy diesel engines, wowed our judges and was the overwhelming favorite for this year's "Best of Show."

For W+K and Honda, it meant top honors for the second year in a row.

Who knew hate could be so good?

"Grrr"

GARRISON KEILLER: (spoken)
Here's a little song for anyone who's ever hated.
In the key of Grrr...

Can hate be good? Can hate be great?
Can hate be good? Can hate be great?
Can hate be something we don't hate?
(whistling)

We'd like to know...why it is so.
That certain diesels must be slow
and thwack and thrum...and pong and hum...
and clatter clack (whistling).

(Chorus)
Hate something. Change something.
Hate something, change something,
make something better-r-r-r...(whistling)

Oh isn't it just bliss......
when a diesel goes like this?
...(silence...then whistling)

Hate something. Change something.
Hate something, change something,
make something better-r-r-r...
(whistle)

(spoken) Sing it like you hate it!

Hate something. Change something.
Hate something, change something,
make something better-r-r-r...(whistle)

SUPER: Honda
The Power of Dreams
www.honda.co.uk

Gold · Silver · Bronze

Out from the Darkness

One Show

CONSUMER NEWSPAPER : OVER 600 LINES — SINGLE

Gold

art director
David Mously

writer
Mirko Stolz

creative director
Burkhart von Scheven

client
DHL

agency
Jung von Matt / Berlin

05001A

No size limits.

SUZUKI
Go Anywhere. Do Anything
4x4
Don't forget to write.

Silver

art director
Jonathan Santana

writer
James Cloete

creative director
Mike Schalit

client
General Motors

agency
Net#Work BBDO /
Hyde Park

05003A

Also Awarded:
merit
One Show Design
P.O.P. and In-Store:
Single

TABORA 50c
TANZANIA
ZIMBABWE
SUZUKI
Go Anywhere. Do Anything
4x4
Don't forget to write.

CONSUMER NEWSPAPER : OVER 600 LINES — SINGLE

Silver

art director
Nick Allsop

writer
Simon Veksner

illustrator
Paul Slater

creative directors
Jeremy Craigen
Ewan Paterson

client
Volkswagen

agency
DDB / London

05002A

Also Awarded:
merit
Consumer Magazine
Color: Full Page: Single

merit
Outdoor: Single

www.volkswagen.co.uk
Small but tough. Polo.
Official fuel consumption in mpg (litres/100km) for the Polo range: urban 49.6 (5.7)–27.2 (10.4), extra urban 68.9 (4.1)–47.1 (6.0), combined 61.4 (4.6)–37.2 (7.6). CO2 emissions 182–124g/km.

Gold

art director
Ralf Nolting

writers
Thies Schuster
Reinhard Patzschke

photographer
Emir Haveric

creative directors
Ralf Nolting
Patricia Pätzold
Ralf Heuel

client
Volkswagen

agency
Grabarz & Partner / Hamburg

05004A

CONSUMER NEWSPAPER : 600 LINES OR LESS — SINGLE

Silver

art directors
Marcus Rebeschini
Derrick Song

writer
Robert Kleman

illustrators
Weng Foong
Yang Young Soon

creative directors
Marcus Rebeschini
Robert Kleman

client
MINI

agency
TBWA \ Singapore

05006A

Also Awarded:

merit
Collateral P.O.P.
and In-Store: Single

merit
Collateral P.O.P.
and In-Store: Campaign

THINGS TO DO
BEFORE YOU DIE.
ATM
ATM
ROUTE
66
GAS STATION
ROUTE
#12
SEE ROUTE 66 IN A MINI.

THINGS TO DO
BEFORE YOU DIE.
#6
TEST DRIVE A MINI.

Silver

art directors
Marcus Rebeschini
Derrick Song

writer
Robert Kleman

illustrators
Weng Foong
Yang Young Soon

creative directors
Marcus Rebeschini
Robert Kleman

client
MINI

agency
TBWA \ Singapore

05007A

Also Awarded:

merit
Collateral P.O.P.
and In-Store: Single

merit
Collateral P.O.P.
and In-Store: Campaign

CONSUMER NEWSPAPER : 600 LINES OR LESS — SINGLE

Bronze

art directors
Marcus Rebeschini
Derrick Song

writer
Robert Kleman

illustrators
Weng Foong
Yang Young Soon

creative directors
Marcus Rebeschini
Robert Kleman

client
MINI

agency
TBWA \ Singapore

05008A

Also Awarded:
merit
Collateral P.O.P. and
In-Store: Campaign

THINGS TO DO
BEFORE YOU DIE.
#8
RAISE A FAMILY IN A MINI.

Gold

art director
Jamie Mietz

writer
Vincent Raffray

creative directors
Vincent Raffray
Khaled Gadallah

client
Sony

agency
Tonic Communications / Dubai

05011A

CONSUMER MAGAZINE : COLOR : FULL PAGE OR SPREAD — SINGLE

Silver

art directors
Richard Johnson
Kelly Dickinson

writer
Simon Jenkins

photographer
Jimmy Fok

creative directors
Richard Johnson
Matt Cullen
Gary Tranter

client
The Economist

agency
Ogilvy & Mather / Singapore

05012A

Also Awarded:
merit
Collateral
Posters: Single

Bronze

art director
Chris Garbutt

writer
Matthew Branning

photographer
Dimitri Daniloff

creative director
Erik Vervroegen

client
Sony Playstation

agency
TBWA \ Paris

05013A

…ectors
L… …iva Dias
Du…rte Pinheiro De Melo

client
Grande Reportagem
Magazine

agency
Foote Cone and Belding / Lisbon

05014A

ZINE : COLOR : FULL PAGE OR SPREAD — CAMPAIGN

Silver

art directors
John Parker
Alex Burnard
Mike del Marmol

writers
Evan Fry
Dave Schiff

photographers
Sebastian Gray
Getty Images

illustrator
Pres Rodriguez

creative directors
Alex Bogusky
Bill Wright

client
Molson

agency
Crispin Porter + Bogusky / Miami

05015A

WALLET-SIZED PROOF THAT YOU'RE A MAN WITH A SENSITIVE SIDE.
IN CASE SHE'S INTO THAT.

Step 1 — DISPLAY SENSITIVE PHOTO OF YOUR CHOICE INSIDE WALLET.
Step 2 — POSITION WALLET SO HOTTIES NOTICE PHOTO WHEN YOU BUY A MOLSON.
Step 3 — YOU'RE IN, BIG FELLA. NOBODY'S MORE SENSITIVE THAN YOU.

SEXY GALS CAN'T RESIST SENSITIVE GUYS. BUT SINCE YOU'RE WAY TOO BUSY TO FIND THAT PICTURE OF YOUR GRANDMA, YOUR FRIENDS AT MOLSON HAVE YOU COVERED. SIMPLY CHOOSE AN IMAGE FROM THE INSERT ACCOMPANYING THIS AD, AND THE NEXT TIME YOU BUY SOME HOTTIE AN EASY DRINKING MOLSON, LET THE PHOTO DO THE WORK FOR YOU. WE'RE SURE YOU'LL FIND THAT THERE'S NOTHING LIKE A PICTURE OF "BOOTSIE," YOUR BELOVED LITTLE DACHSHUND, TO SEND HER SENSITIVITY RADAR INTO THE RED ZONE AND START A CONVERSATION THAT REALLY GOES SOMEWHERE.

MAKING "FRIENDS" SINCE 1786
WWW.MOLSONUSA.COM/TOOLS

IN 1786, JOHN MOLSON BEGAN BREWING BEER USING THE FINEST CANADIAN WATER AND BARLEY FROM A LAND WE NOW CALL SASKATCHEWAN. WE LEFT WELL ENOUGH ALONE.

LADIES FREAK FOR GUYS WITH EXPENSIVE HOBBIES.
AND NOW YOU'VE GOT SOME.

Step 1 — KEEP SOME PRESTIGIOUS BUSINESS CARDS AT THE READY.
Step 2 — WRITE YOUR DIGITS ON THE BACK OF ONE AT NUMBER-EXCHANGE TIME.
Step 3 — NOW YOU'RE A MAN OF WEALTH AND INTRIGUE. AND THAT AIN'T BAD.

REAL HOTTIES GET TONS OF PHONE NUMBERS FROM ALL SORTS OF GUYS. SO YOUR COMPADRES AT MOLSON HAVE DEVISED A WAY TO HELP YOUR INFO RISE ABOVE THE REST. PRESTIGIOUS BUSINESS CARDS. JUST CARRY SOME IN YOUR WALLET TO WRITE YOUR DIGITS ON, AND PRESTO! – NOW YOUR NAME GETS ASSOCIATED WITH THOROUGHBRED HORSES AND EXOTIC CARS. AND WHO SAYS IT SHOULDN'T? AFTER ALL, YOU'RE THE KIND OF GUY WHO DRINKS MOLSON. THE WORLD IS YOUR OYSTER. WRITE YOUR NUMBER ON A BUSINESS CARD THAT BROADCASTS THAT FACT LOUD AND CLEAR.

MAKING "FRIENDS" SINCE 1786
WWW.MOLSONUSA.COM/TOOLS

IN 1786, JOHN MOLSON BEGAN BREWING BEER USING THE FINEST CANADIAN WATER AND BARLEY FROM A LAND WE NOW CALL SASKATCHEWAN. WE LEFT WELL ENOUGH ALONE.

GALS WANT A GUY WHO'S INTERESTED IN MORE THAN SPORTS AND NUDIE MAGS.
AND NOW YOU ARE.

Step 1 — SELECT THE ACTIVITY STICKER THAT SPEAKS TO YOU.
Step 2 — DISPLAY STICKER AT OPTIMAL HOTTIE EYE-LEVEL.
Step 3 — "WOW. I HATE HATE TOO. WANNA GO SOMEPLACE AND TALK?"

LADIES DON'T WANT A GUY – THEY WANT A GIVER. AND IF YOU HAD TIME, WE KNOW THAT YOU'D BE GIVING BLOOD OR CARING FOR THE ENVIRONMENT YOURSELF. SO HERE'S A WAY TO SHOW ALL THE HOTTIES WHAT YOU'RE REALLY ABOUT. SIMPLY WEAR ONE OF THE ACTIVITY STICKERS INCLUDED ON THE PRECEDING PAGE. WHEN THEY ASK ABOUT IT, PLAY COY. "SILLY ME. DID I FORGET TO TAKE THAT THING OFF AGAIN?" AFTER AN ICE BREAKER LIKE THAT, JUST KEEP THE CONVERSATION FLOWING WITH AN EASY DRINKING MOLSON. BECAUSE THAT'S WHAT GIVERS DO.

MAKING "FRIENDS" SINCE 1786
WWW.MOLSONUSA.COM/TOOLS

IN 1786, JOHN MOLSON BEGAN BREWING BEER USING THE FINEST CANADIAN WATER AND BARLEY FROM A LAND WE NOW CALL SASKATCHEWAN. WE LEFT WELL ENOUGH ALONE.

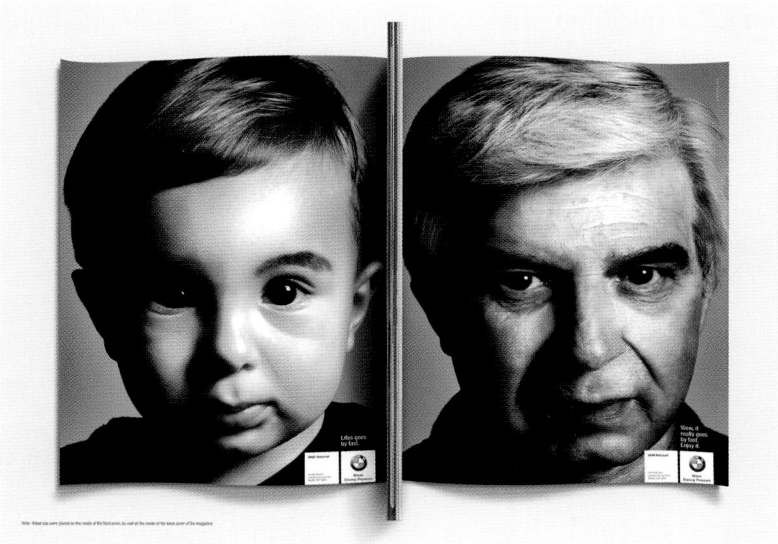
Lifes goes by fast.
Wow, it really goes by fast. Enjoy it.

Lifes goes by fast.
Wow, it really goes by fast. Enjoy it.

Lifes goes by fast.
Wow, it really goes by fast. Enjoy.

Bronze

art director
Silvio Medeiros

writer
Thiago Carvalho

photographer
Alan Nielsen

creative directors
Fernando Campos
Valdir Bianchi

client
BMW

agency
Giovanni, FCB /
São Paulo

05016A

Gold

art director
Paul Belford

writer
Nigel Roberts

creative directors
Paul Belford
Nigel Roberts

client
The Economist

agency
Abbott Mead Vickers
BBDO / London

05017A

Silver

art director
Molly Sheahan

writer
Marty Senn

creative director
Ari Merkin

client
TIME Magazine

agency
Fallon / New York

05018A

Gold

art director
Menno Kluin

writer
Menno Kluin

designer
Joanna Switowski

creative directors
Bettina Olf
Timm Weber

client
Smith & Wesson

agency
Springer & Jacoby /
Hamburg

05020A

Also Awarded:

silver
Consumer Newspaper
Over 600 Lines:
Campaign

silver
Collateral
P.O.P. and In-Store:
Campaign

Bronze

art directors
Tony Hardcastle
Roy Hyndman
Paul Belford
Matt Doman

illustrator
John Tisdall

writers
Mark Tweddell
Tim Riley
Nigel Roberts
Ian Heartfield

creative directors
Paul Belford
Nigel Roberts

client
The Economist

agency
Abbott Mead Vickers
BBDO / London

05022A

Stop having to remind people who you are.

You can so tell the people who like don't read The Economist.

TRADE : COLOR : FULL PAGE OR SPREAD — CAMPAIGN

Gold

art director
James cé Cruickshank

illustrator
James cé Cruickshank

creative directors
Andreas Geyer
Ulrich Zünkeler
Ursus Wehrli

client
Bisley Office Equipment

agency
Kolle Rebbe / Hamburg

05023A

Also Awarded:
silver
Outdoor: Campaign

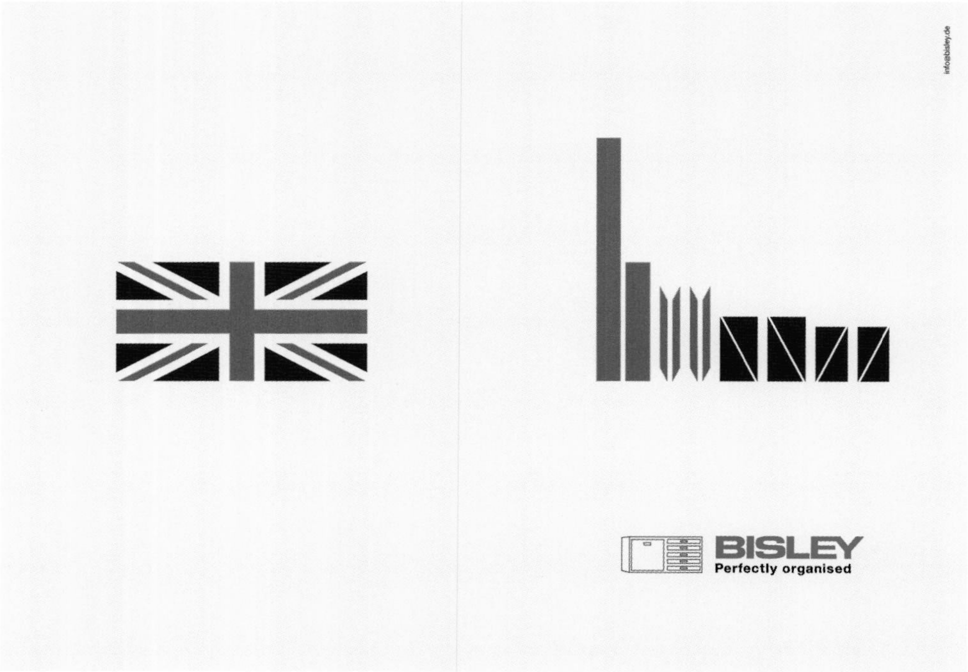

Silver

art directors
Thirasak Tanapatanakul
Kittitat Larppitakpong
Jon Chalermwong

writer
Nutchanun
Chiaphanumas

photographers
Anuchai
Sricharunputong
Nok

creative directors
Thirasak Tanapatanakul
Prangthip Praditpong

client
Tamiya Assembly Toys

agency
Creative Juice\G1
(a TBWA company) /
Bangkok

05024A

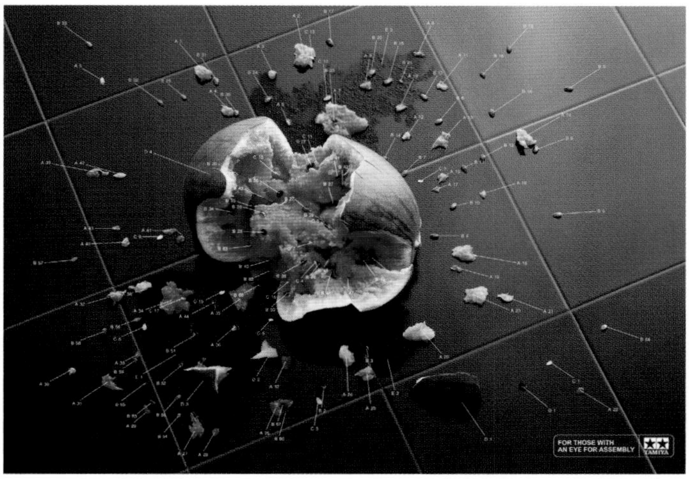

One Show

TRADE : COLOR : FULL PAGE OR SPREAD — CAMPAIGN

Bronze

art directors
Adam Staples
Paul Miles

writers
Adam Staples
Paul Miles

photographer
Paolo Milez

creative director
Tony Granger

client
BMX Rider Magazine

agency
Saatchi & Saatchi /
London

05025A

Gold

art directors
Kenny Choo
Jane Yang

writers
Stephen Kong
Kenny Choo

photographer
Alex Kaikeong

creative directors
Eddie Booth
Ruth Lee
Kenny Choo
Stephen Kong

client
Y+ Yoga Center

agency
Leo Burnett / Hong Kong

05026A

One Show

COLLATERAL ADVERTISING : P.O.P. AND IN-STORE — SINGLE

Silver

art director
Johannes Hicks

writer
Stuart Kummer

designer
Paul Etzel

creative directors
Jan Leube
Matthias Speatgens

client
Berlitz

agency
Scholz & Friends / Berlin

05027A

Also Awarded:

merit
Consumer Magazine
Color: Full Page: Single

merit
Outdoor: Single

merit
One Show Design
Posters: Single

Silver

art director
Philippe Taroux

writer
Benoît Leroux

photographer
Dimitri Daniloff

creative director
Erik Vervroegen

client
Sony Playstation

agency
TBWA\Paris

05028A

Also Awarded:
merit
Consumer Magazine
Color: Full Page: Single

Bronze

art director
Naoki Ga

photographer
Jonathan Tay

creative director
Craig Smith

client
Nike

agency
Ogilvy & Mather / Singapore

05029A

COLLATERAL ADVERTISING : P.O.P. AND IN-STORE — CAMPAIGN

Gold

art director
Kay Luebke

writer
Michael Haeussler

photographer
Ralph Baiker

creative directors
Matthias Spaetgens
Jan Leube

client
Weru

agency
Scholz & Friends / Berlin

05030A

Also Awarded:
merit
Outdoor: Campaign

merit
Trade: Color: Full Page: Campaign

< Merit >

< Merit >

Bronze

art directors
Philipp Boettcher
Marco Weber
Christian Mommertz

writers
Philipp Boettcher
Dr. Stephan Vogel

photographer
Heinz Wuchner

creative directors
Christian Mommertz
Dr. Stephan Vogel

client
Intertool

agency
Ogilvy & Mather / Frankfurt

05032A

Also Awarded:

merit
Consumer Magazine
Color: Full Page: Single

merit
Consumer Magazine
Color: Full Page: Single

COLLATERAL ADVERTISING : POSTERS — CAMPAIGN

Silver

art director
Liam Wielopolski

writer
Michael Blore

photographer
Michael Meyersfeld

creative director
Graham Warsop

client
Reckitt Benckiser

agency
The Jupiter Drawing Room (South Africa) / Johannesburg

05035A

Also Awarded:

silver
Collateral: Posters: Single

bronze
Collateral: Posters: Single

merit
Consumer Newspaper: Over 600 Lines: Single

merit
Consumer Newspaper: Over 600 Lines: Single

< Silver, Merit >

< Bronze, Merit >

Pizza Hut
PART OF HOME-MOVIES. FOR DELIVERY CALL 62-35-35-35

< Silver, Merit >

Pizza Hut
PART OF HOME-MOVIES. FOR DELIVERY CALL 62-35-35-35

< Silver >

Pizza Hut
PART OF HOME-MOVIES. FOR DELIVERY CALL 62-35-35-35.

< Merit >

Bronze

art directors
Alex Lim Thye Aun
Ali Shabaz

writers
Ali Shabaz
Alex Lim Thye Aun

designers
Sin Eng Lee
Alex Lim Thye Aun
Ali Shabaz

photographers
Teo (Teo Studio)
Nick (Corbis)

illustrator
Wishing Well

creative director
Francis Wee

client
Pizza Hut Singapore

agency
BBDO / Singapore

05036A

Also Awarded:

silver
Consumer Magazine:
Black and White:
Full Page: Single

silver
Consumer Magazine:
Black and White:
Full Page: Single

merit
Consumer Magazine:
Black and White:
Full Page: Single

merit
Collateral: Posters: Single

One Show

COLLATERAL ADVERTISING : POSTERS — CAMPAIGN

Bronze

art director
Bradley Wood

writer
Ryan Ebner

photographers
David Emmite (Garage)
Howard Cao (Sleeping)

creative directors
Mark Figliulo
Dave Loew

client
Miller Brewing Company

agency
Y&R / Chicago

05037A

Also Awarded:
merit
Consumer Magazine:
Color: Full Page:
Campaign

merit
Collateral: Posters:
Single

Sleeping on Concrete Hurts less than sitting in Crappy seats
HERE'S TO 50 YEARS OF ROCK AND THE GREAT TASTE OF MILLER
Miller
Good call.

< Merit >

WORLD TOUR
DOOMRAIDERS
TOM'S BASEMENT 7/3/04
DAVE'S GARAGE 7/9/04
DAVES GARAGE 7/21/04
ED'S HOUSE 7/24/04
Miller
Good call.

I DON'T MEASURE WEALTH IN DOLLAR BILLS
HERE'S TO 50 YEARS OF ROCK AND THE GREAT TASTE OF MILLER

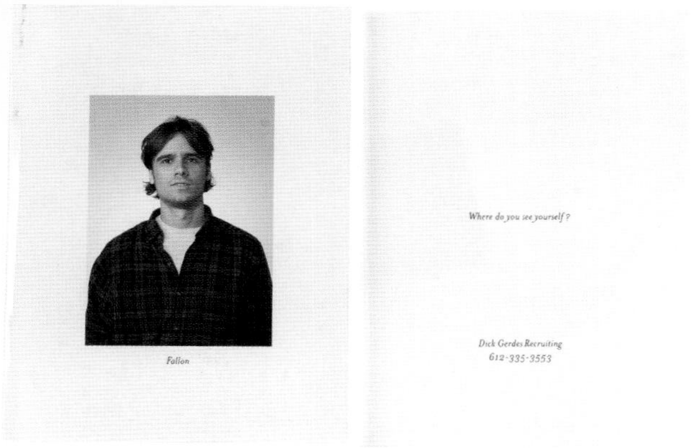

Silver

art director
Cody Spinadel

writer
Joe Alexander

photographer
Dwight Loew

creative director
Joe Alexander

client
Dick Gerdes

agency
The Martin Agency /
Richmond

05038A

PUBLIC SERVICE / POLITICAL–PRINT : NEWSPAPER OR MAGAZINE — SINGLE

Silver

art director
Marcus Kawamura

writer
Marcio Juniot

photographer
Mario Daloia

creative director
Ruy Lindenberg

client
The Akatu Institute for Conscious Consumption

agency
Leo Burnett / São Paulo

05039A

ARE YOU SO INDIFFERENT
THAT YOU DIDN'T EVEN NOTICE THAT
THIS PHOTO IS UPSIDE DOWN?
CARE
AKATU.ORG.BR

Silver

art director
Passakorn Chantrawan

writers
Passakorn Chantrawan
Vituwat Rongkavongs

photographer
Remix Studio

creative director
Nopadol Srikieatikajohn

client
National Park Wildlife and Plant Conservation Dept.

agency
Ogilvy & Mather / Bangkok

05040A

Keep chopping
National Park, Wildlife and Plant Conservation Department

Appearing on consecutive double page spreads of boating magazines, this ad dramatises how quickly weather conditions can change in New Zealand waters. As you turn the page, a wave breaks over the boat.

Bronze

art director
Josh Moore

writer
Seymour Pope

photographer
Chris Lewis

illustrator
The Lounge

creative director
Nick Worthington

client
New Zealand Coastguard

agency
Publicis Mojo / Auckland

05041A

PUBLIC SERVICE / POLITICAL–PRINT : NEWSPAPER OR MAGAZINE — CAMPAIGN

Gold

art directors
Tham Khai Meng
Claire Chen

writer
Eugene Cheong

illustrator
Agathe de Bailliencourt

creative directors
Tham Khai Meng
Eugene Cheong

client
Anglican Welfare Council

agency
Ogilvy & Mather / Singapore

05042A

Also Awarded:

merit
Public Service/Political Newspaper or Magazine: Single

merit
Outdoor: Single

In 1939, the world thought Churchill was insane to take on the massive Nazi war machine. He was.
KEEP AN OPEN MIND. DON'T SHUT OUT THE MENTALLY ILL.

‹ Merit ›

WHAT SORT OF MIND DOES IT TAKE TO DISCOVER THE LAW OF GRAVITY?
A TOTALLY DERANGED ONE.

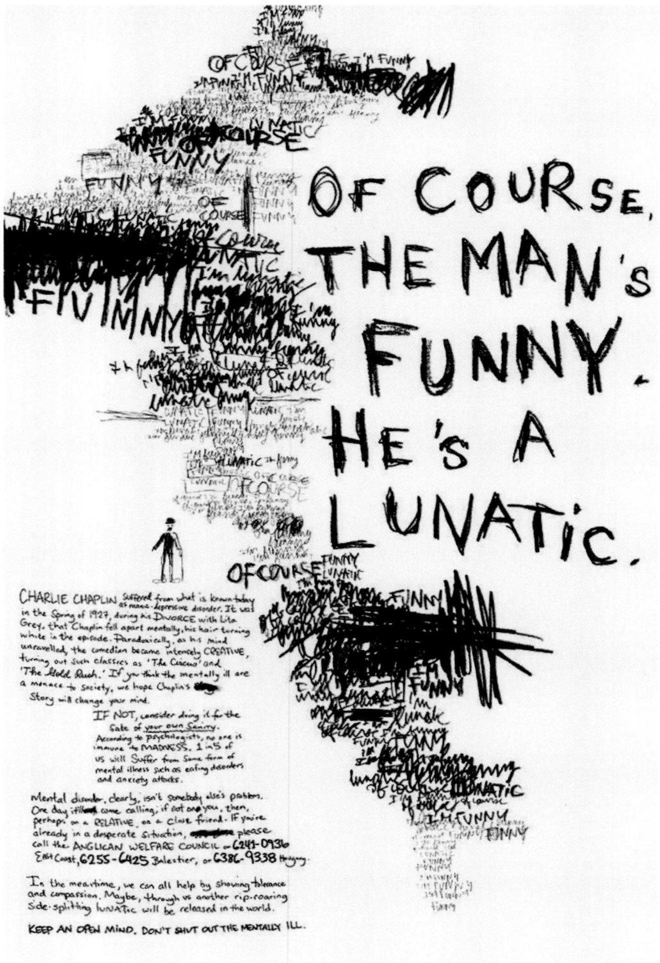
OF COURSE, THE MAN'S FUNNY. HE'S A LUNATIC.
CHARLIE CHAPLIN suffered from what is known today as manic-depressive disorder. It was in the Spring of 1927, during his DIVORCE with Lita Grey, that Chaplin fell apart mentally, his hair turning white in the episode. Paradoxically, as his mind unravelled, the comedian became intensely CREATIVE, turning out such classics as 'The Circus' and 'The Gold Rush.' If you think the mentally ill are a menace to society, we hope Chaplin's story will change your mind.
IF NOT, consider doing it for the sake of your own Sanity. According to psychologists, no one is immune to MADNESS. 1 in 5 of us will Suffer from Some form of mental illness such as eating disorders and anxiety attacks.
Mental disorder, clearly, isn't somebody else's problem. One day it'll come calling, if not on you, then, perhaps on a RELATIVE or a close friend. If you're already in a desperate situation, please call the ANGLICAN WELFARE COUNCIL on 6241-0936 East Coast, 6255-6425 Balestier, or 6386-9338 Hougang.
In the meantime, we can all help by showing tolerance and compassion. Maybe, through us another rip-roaring side-splitting lunatic will be released in the world.
KEEP AN OPEN MIND. DON'T SHUT OUT THE MENTALLY ILL.

‹ Merit ›

Welcome to
CRAZYWORLD
CRAZYWORLD
Redeem this ticket anywhere. Because you're already in Crazyworld.
In 1995, a major tobacco company voluntarily recalled eight billion of its own cigarettes because, according to the company, the cigarettes could cause temporary discomfort. Like wheezing and dizziness. And yet no cigarette company has ever recalled cigarettes because they kill 440,000 people every year. In Crazyworld, it seems dizzy is worse than dead.
ADMIT ONE
ADMIT ONE
truth

Welcome to
CRAZYWORLD
FREE
ADMISSION
00001997
00001997
CRAZYWORLD

CRAZYWORLD
CRAZYWORLD
Present this ticket anywhere. You're already in Crazyworld.
Secondhand smoke kills 50,000 people a year. But in 1996, a major tobacco company ran an ad campaign claiming that milk and cookies are actually more dangerous than secondhand smoke. In Crazyworld, we don't make this stuff up.
ADMIT ONE
ADMIT ONE
truth

Silver

art director
Kat Morris

writer
Ronny Northrop

photographer
David Harriman

producers
Barrie Bamberg
Jessica Hoffman

creative directors
Ron Lawner
Alex Bogusky
Pete Favat
Tom Adams
Roger Baldacci

client
American Legacy Foundation

agencies
Arnold Worldwide / Boston and Crispin Porter + Bogusky / Miami

05043A

One Show

PUBLIC SERVICE / POLITICAL-PRINT : NEWSPAPER OR MAGAZINE — CAMPAIGN

Bronze

art directors
Wisit Lumsiricharoenchoke
Gumpon Laksanajinda

writers
Kulvadee Doksroy
Sirilak Chitpanvong

illustrator
Gumpon Laksanajinda

creative director
Wisit Lumsiricharoenchoke

client
WWF Thailand

agency
Ogilvy & Mather / Bangkok

05044A

Also Awarded:
merit
Public Service/Political
Newspaper or Magazine:
Single

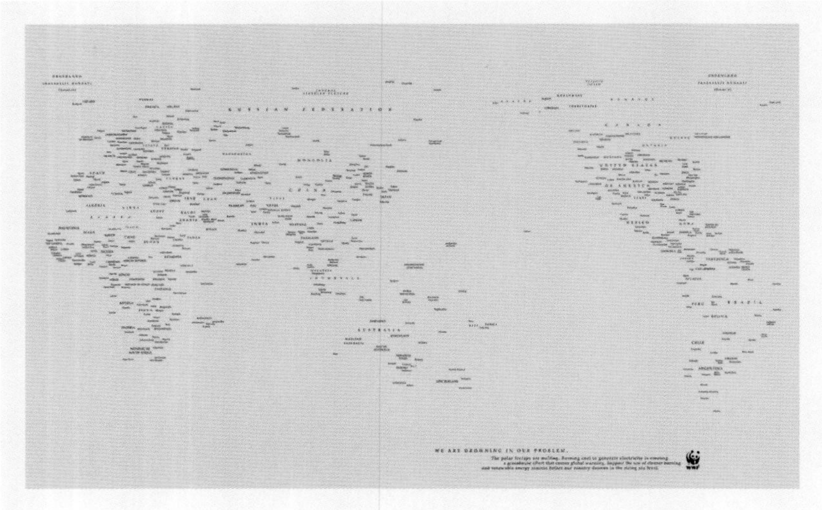
WE ARE DROWNING IN OUR PROBLEM.
WWF

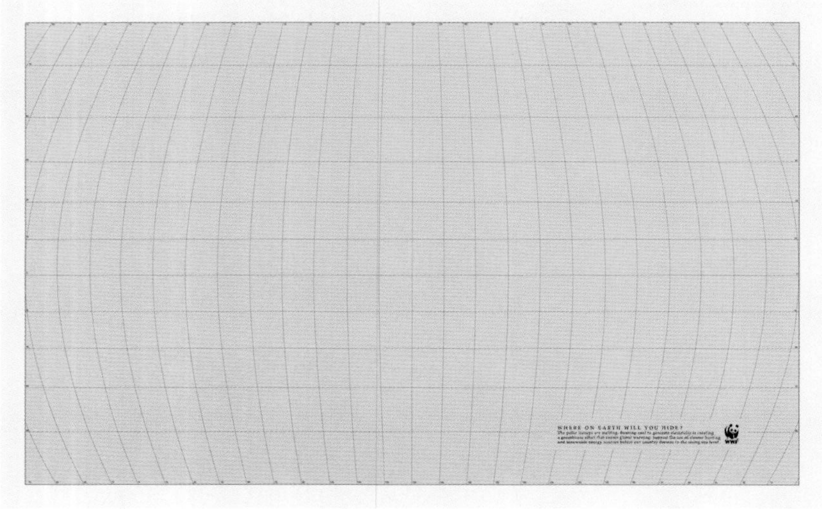
WHERE ON EARTH WILL YOU HIDE?
WWF

< Merit >

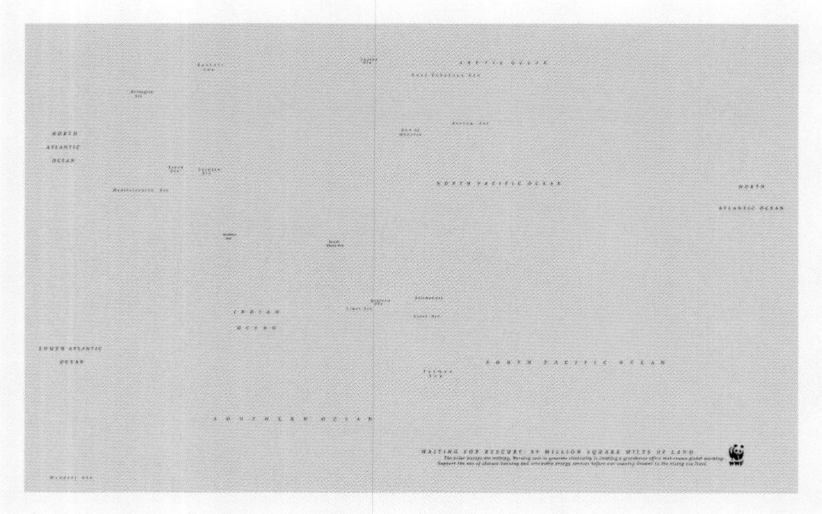
NORTH PACIFIC OCEAN
INDIAN OCEAN
SOUTH PACIFIC OCEAN
SOUTHERN OCEAN
WWF

ADSHEL
At 60km/h
you'd stop
about here.
At 65km/h
you'd stop
about here.
DROP 5. SAVE LIVES.

Silver

art director
Levi Slavin

writer
Dave Govier

creative director
Andrew Tinning

client
Office of Road Safety

agency
Marketforce / West Perth

05045A

PUBLIC SERVICE / POLITICAL-PRINT : OUTDOOR AND POSTERS — CAMPAIGN

Silver

art director
Liu Yi-ping

writers
Daming Zheng
Miu Miao

illustrator
May

creative directors
Daming Zheng
Leo Zou

client
WWF

agency
CC&E Advertising / Guangzhou

05046A

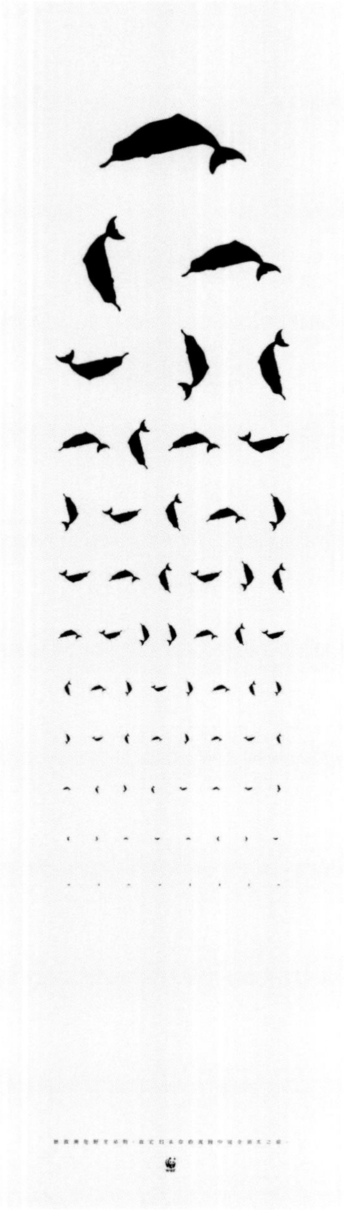

PUBLIC SERVICE/ POLITICAL-RADIO: SINGLE

gold

writers
Mike Howard
Marc Einhorn
agency producer
Carron Pedonti
production company
Bartradio
director
Bart Smith
creative directors
Ron Lawner
Pete Favat
Alex Bogusky
Roger Baldacci
Tom Adams
client
American Legacy Foundation
agency
Arnold Worldwide / Boston and Crispin Porter + Bogusky / Miami

05001R

silver

writer
Mike Howard
agency producer
Carron Pedonti
production company
Bartradio
director
Bart Smith
creative directors
Ron Lawner
Pete Favat
Alex Bogusky
Roger Baldacci
Tom Adams
client
American Legacy Foundation
agency
Arnold Worldwide / Boston and Crispin Porter + Bogusky / Miami

05002R

PUBLIC SERVICE/ POLITICAL-RADIO: CAMPAIGN

silver

writer
Clint! Runge
agency producer
Joe Goddard
production company
Archrival
director
Clint! Runge
creative director
Clint! Runge
client
Nebraska Domestic Violence Council
agency
Archrival / Lincoln

05003R

silver

writers
Cesar Sastre
Nacho Guillo, Pablo Gonzalez De La Peña
Victor Aguilar
agency producer
Manuela Zamora
production company
Rafa Arnau
Jingle Box
creative director:
Juan Nonzioli
client
Save the Children
agency
Shackleton / Madrid

05014R

CONSUMER RADIO: CAMPAIGN

gold

writers
Daniel Giachetti
John Clement
Brad Emmett
Lee Seidenberg
Erik Fahrenkopf
Anthony DeCarolis
agency producer
Barbara Michelson
production company
McHale Barone
creative director
Sal DeVito
client
National Thoroughbred Racing Association
agency
DeVito/Verdi / New York

05005R

Also Awarded:
{Gold}
Consumer Radio: Single
{Merit}
Consumer Radio: Single
{Merit}
Consumer Radio: Single

silver

writers
Adam Alshin
Marcus Woolcott
agency producer
Zarina Mak
production company
Kamen Entertainment Group
creative director
Ari Merkin
client
Virgin Mobile USA
agency
Fallon / New York

05006R

bronze

writer
Paul Little
agency producer
Sue Bell
production company
GGRP
director
Peter Clarke
creative director
Alan Russell
client
Insurance Corporation of British Columbia (ICBC)
agency
DDB / Vancouver

05007R

PUBLIC SERVICE/POLITICAL-TELEVISION : SINGLE

Gold

art director
Rob Sweetman

writer
Rob Tarry

agency producer
Jacqueline Burgmann

production company
Radke Films

director
Michael Downing

creative directors
Ian Grais
Chris Staples

client
Science World

agency
Rethink / Vancouver

05002T

SHAKING HANDS
SPREADS MORE GERMS
THAN KISSING.

(We see a boardroom where people are walking up to each other to introduce themselves. Except instead of shaking hands, they kiss one another on the mouth.)

SUPER: Shaking hands spreads more germs than kissing. Science World. We can explain.

Bronze

art director
Jan Jacobs

writer
Leo Premutico

agency producer
Manuela Franzini

production company
large

director
Danny Kleinmann

creative director
Tony Granger

client
NSPCC

agency
Saatchi & Saatchi / London

05005T

(We see a man with a ventriloquist dummy of a young girl in a classroom. The teacher asks her a question while the man holding the dummy is looking at it. She's afraid to answer. Then we see a playground where a child asks her if she wants to come to her house after school and she says "no." Next we see her on a bus while the other kids are making fun of her and she sits alone in the back looking sad. Then we see her at the dinner table.)

MOTHER: Sally, you're not eating again. What's wrong?

GIRL: I'm fine, can I go now?

SUPER: Abused children can't speak up. Find out how you can help us be there for them.

Call 0800 801 837.

Cruelty to children must stop.

NSPCC logo.

(We see a sparsely furnished classroom. On the wall of the room is a blackboard with: "Short film actor's workshop – love scene" written on it. A group of students sit cross-legged on the floor, their backs to us - watching the scene. The teacher is standing before the group with two students.)

TEACHER: Steve, John... make passionate love to each other.

(The two students look at one another, they then begin to move in closer together – beginning to hug. The teacher stops the students.)

TEACHER: Enough! That was terrible, sit down.

TEACHER: It's a short film, okay.

(The teacher calls up another student to help him demonstrate.)

TEACHER: Ron, please come up here.

(The student hurries to the front of the class. The teacher begins to take off his shirt.)

TEACHER: The love scene technique I'm about to show you will allow you to make love effectively, in less than three seconds. Pay attention – this is going to happen very fast.

SUPER: Worldwide Short Film Festival logo.

< Silver >

< Silver >

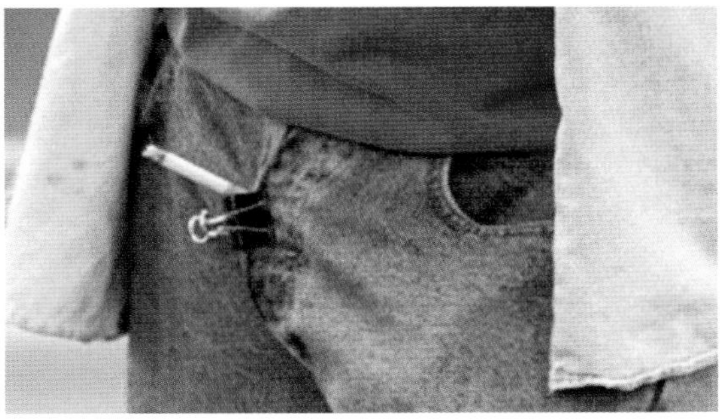

< Merit >

Gold

art director
Dave Douglass

writer
Pete Breton

agency producer
Sam Benson

production company
untitled

director
Tim Godsall

creative director
Zak Mroueh

client
Canadian Film Centreís Worldwide Short Film Festival

agency
Taxi / Toronto

05006T

Also Awarded:

silver
Public Service/Political Television: Single

silver
Public Service/Political Television: Single

merit
Public Service/Political Television: Single

Silver

art director
Lara Palmer

writer
Paul Little

agency producer
Janice Crondahl

production company
Circle (Hungry Man)

director
David Shane

creative director
Alan Russell

client
BC SPCA

agency
DDB / Vancouver

05007T

Also Awarded:
gold
Public Service/Political Television: Single

merit
Public Service/Political Television: Single

Some things you can only do with a pet.

< Gold >

(We see a man sleeping on the couch. His roomate comes over and sits down and then puts the man on his lap belly up. He begins to rub the man's belly while watching TV. The man wakes up and is confused to find himself on his roommate's lap.)

SUPER: Some things you can only do with a pet.
BC SPCA. Adopt soon.
www.spca.bc.ca

Some things you can only do with a pet.

Some things you can only do with a pet.

< Merit >

GARRISON KEILLER: (spoken)
Here's a little song for anyone who's ever hated.
In the key of Grrrr...

Can hate be good? Can hate be great?
Can hate be good? Can hate be great?
Can hate be something we don't hate? (whistling)

We'd like to know...why it is so.
That certain diesels must be slow
and thwack and thrum...and pong and hum...
and clatter clack (whistling)

(Chorus)
Hate something. Change something.
Hate something, change something,
make something better-r-r-r...(whistling)

Oh isn't it just bliss......
when a diesel goes like this?
...(silence...then whistling)

Hate something. Change something.
Hate something, change something,
make something better-r-r-r...(whistle)

(spoken) Sing it like you hate it!

Hate something. Change something.
Hate something, change something,
make something better-r-r-r...(whistle)

SUPER: Honda
The Power of Dreams
www.honda.co.uk

Gold

art directors
Sean Thompson
Michael Russoff
Richard Russell

writers
Sean Thompson
Michael Russoff
Richard Russell

agency producers
Charlie Tinson
Rob Steiner

production company
Nexus

director
Smith & Foulkes

creative directors
Tony Davidson
Kim Papworth

client
Honda

agency
Wieden + Kennedy / London

05009T

CONSUMER TELEVISION : OVER : 30 — SINGLE — MAX. : 90

Silver

art director
Hal Curtis

writer
Mike Byrne

agency producer
Jennifer Smieja

production company
Smith & Jones Films

director
Ulf Johansson

creative directors
Carlos Bayala
Mike Byrne
Hal Curtis

client
Nike

agency
Wieden + Kennedy / Portland

05010T

(We see a boxing ring and a large crowd. A man in a yellow-hooded robe enters the ring and takes off the hood. We see that it's cyclist Lance Armstrong. Then we see tennis player Andre Agassi playing shortstop for the Boston Red Sox. The next scene shows runner Marion Jones about to do a vault, then football-players Michael Vick and Brian Urlacher playing ice hockey, baseball-pitcher Randy Johnson at a bowling championship and tennis-star Serena Williams playing beach volleyball.)

SUPER: Just do it. Nike logo.

Bronze

art director
Philip Ireland

writer
John Davenport

agency producer
Caroline Switala

production company
Velocity

director
Greg Grey

creative director
Mike Schalit

client
Virgin Atlantic Airways

agency
Net#Work BBDO / Hyde Park

05011T

(We see a young, good-looking guy and his sweetheart in clichéd romantic settings. They have a picnic in a meadow, they row a boat across a lake, they run hand-in-hand along a beach at sunset, they ride bicycles, and share a kiss in front of a roaring log fire. Finally we cut to them in a church, about to get married. But his sweetheart is not a young pretty girl...it is the huge, sweaty, unattractive man sitting next to him on the plane. We cut to a shot of him sitting next to the guy, who is fast asleep and drooling on his shoulder.)

VOICE OVER: If you wanted to sleep with him you would have married him. Rather fly Virgin Atlantic Upper Class and get your own flatbed suite.

SUPER: Virgin Atlantic Upper Class Suite logo

< Gold >

(We see basketball player Tracy McGrady practicing on the basketball court. We then see a whole miniature army try to stop him from going to the hoop. They use helicopters with ropes and nets to try and keep him down. He then charges for the hoop and makes a slam-dunk.)

SUPER: Impossible is nothing. adidas logo.

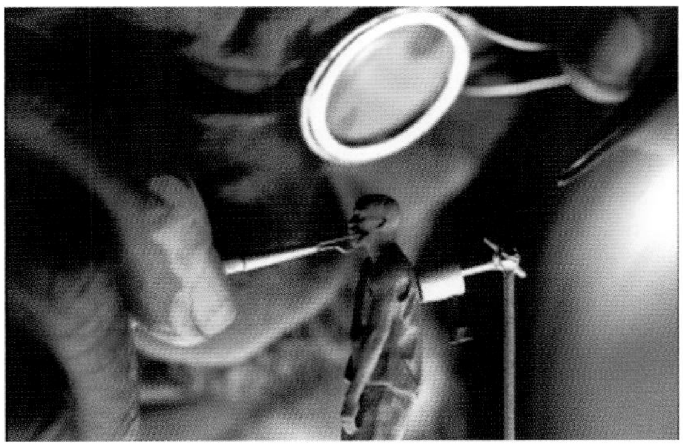

Gold

art director
Geoff Edwards

writers
Scott Duchon
(Carry & Unstoppable)
Scott Duchon
John Patroulis
(Made to Perfection)

agency producers
Jennifer Golub
Andrea Bustabade

production company
Biscuit Filmworks
(Carry)
Smuggler (Unstoppable)
Omaha Pictures
(Made to Perfection)

directors
Noam Murro (Carry)
Brian Beletic
(Unstoppable)
Rupert Sanders
(Made to Perfection)

creative directors
Chuck McBride (Carry)
Chuck McBride
Geoff Edwards
Scott Duchon
(Unstoppable)
Chuck McBride
Geoff Edwards
Scott Duchon
John Patroulis
(Made to Perfection)

client
adidas

agency
TBWA\Chiat\Day / San Francisco (180\TBWA)

05012T

Also Awarded:
gold
Consumer Television
Over :30 – Single – Max. :90

Silver

art directors
Luke Williamson
Yan Elliott

writers
Luke Williamson
Yan Elliott

agency producer
Hayley Irow

production company
Hungry Man

director
Bryan Buckley

creative directors
Robert Saville
Mark Waites

client
Orange Consumer

agency
Mother / London

05013T

(We open in boardroom of The Orange Film Funding Board. We see a calendar on the desk and then we find out that this is the Verne Troyer pitch meeting.)

BRENNAN: Mr. Troyer – your film pitch, please.

VERNE: Born into a cruel society, a misfit tries to survive in a prejudiced world. People, this is a story about a man trying to find a voice.

BRENNAN: Wow, I mean we deal with voices every day and your story needs to be heard.

VERNE: Thank you.

BRENNAN: No, Verne, thank you.

OTHER BOARD MEMBER: I've got it! He could find his voice on his very own voice mail.

ALEX: Yes and he can leave himself messages like in that tattoo movie.

JACK: Climaxing in a conference call.

VERNE: NO !

BRENNAN: No, this is much bigger than that, people. Am I right?

VERNE: Yes, much bigger.

BRENNAN: Yes, we need to put pictures to that voice. This is about video messaging. No, think about it—less widescreen, more phone screen.

VERNE: ...Come on guys. This film needs...needs stature.

JACK: No, this film needs funding.

BRENNAN: Yes, what he said...

BRENNAN: (Raising his finger in a mock Dr. Evil voice) About one million pounds.

VERNE: You did not.

BRENNAN: Yes I did.

(Verne gives the board the finger and starts to exit the room.)

BRENNAN: Throw me a frikkin phone here.

(We hear everyone laughing hysterically like megalomaniacs.)

SUPER: Don't let a mobile phone ruin your movie. Please switch it off. Orange logo.

(We see two office workers talking next to the water cooler.)

MAN: Hi! Bob, I bought "Kill Bill" DVD yesterday. Have you seen it before? Oh! It's so exciting. I like the scene that gangsters are trying to kill the heroine while she is holding...(Freeze)...Then she sta...sta...sta...stabs one of the gangsters...suddenly suddenly suddenly suddenly...

VOICE OVER: Soken...plays smoothly.

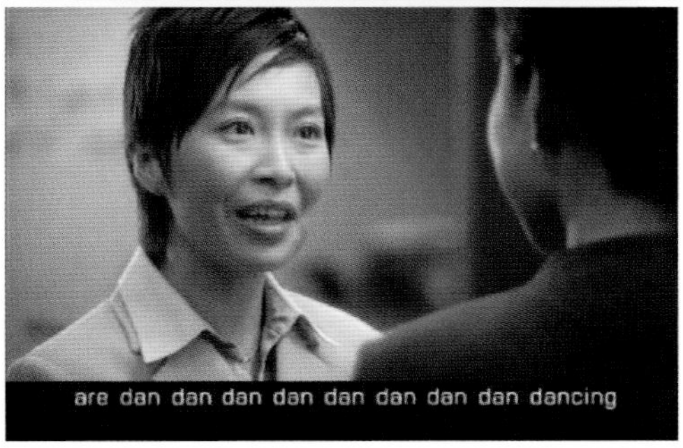

Bronze

art directors
Nimit Songsri
Wiboon Leepakpreeda

writers
Sittichai Okkararojkij
Passapol Limpisirisan

agency producer
Phunyawee Intamas

production company
Matching Studio

director
Suthon Petchsuwan

creative directors
Chukiat Jaroensuk
Wiboon Leepakpreeda
Passapol Limpisirisan

client
Soken Electronics

agency
Euro RSCG / Bangkok

05014T

CONSUMER TELEVISION : 30/:25 — SINGLE

Gold

art director
Ian Grais

writer
Andy Linardatos

agency producer
Christine Pacheco

production company
Spy Films

director
Trevor Cornish

creative directors
Ian Grais
Chris Staples

client
BC Lions

agency
Rethink / Vancouver

05015T

(Open on a woman putting money in a vending machine. The candy bar gets stuck and doesn't fall. Disappointed, she turns to leave. A man stops her.)

MAN: You're not just going to walk away and give up are you?

WOMAN: It's stuck.

MAN: You can get that. It's yours, nobody else's. Get in there and give it some heat. Give it some heat.

(The woman gives the machine a little tap. As the man's cheering intensifies, her taps turn into hard slaps and kicks. Another co-worker gets in on the cheering.)

MAN: Give it some heat. You get in there and you get it. You go in there, baby, and you get it hard. You get it. You get it. That's the one right there. You get it. Yes! Alright, yes!

(The woman body-checks the machine. The bar drops. She holds it up for all to see, wondering what just got into her.)

SUPER: Cheering works.

(We hear roar of stadium crowd.)

SUPER: B.C. Lions logo.
Up next Toronto, July 4th. Tickets 604-280-4400

Silver

art director
Stephen Leps

writer
Aaron Starkman

agency producer
Janet Woods

production company
Reginald Pike

director
The Perlorian Brothers

creative directors
Elspeth Lynn
Lorraine Tao

client
Vim

agency
ZiG / Toronto

05016T

(We see a woman in an orange shirt behind what appears to be prison glass. Her daughter is on the other side.)

DAUGHTER: When are you gonna get outta here?

MOTHER: In a while.

(The daughter puts her hand on the glass and the mother does, too.)

MOTHER: I gotta get back.

DAUGHTER: I love you, mama!

MOTHER: I love you too, baby.

(We see a much wider view and we discover that the woman is actually in a bathtub with a sliding glass shower door. We see that there is some really nasty grime in the tub. The woman sprays a cleaner on it and she proceeds to scrub the grime really hard. It's not coming off and it looks like she's going to be there a while.)

SUPER: Spend less time cleaning.
Vim Cream. Cleans the tough stuff. Easily.

(We see a sneaker on a playground basketball court that continually morphs from one shoe to the next.)

SUPER: Nike logo.
nikebasketball.com

Silver

art director
Brad Trost

writer
Jason Bagley

agency producer
Jennifer Fiske

production company
The Embassy

director
Neill Blomkamp

creative directors
Mike Byrne
Hal Curtis

client
Nike

agency
Wieden+Kennedy / Portland

05018T

Gold

art directors
Feh Tarty
Michael Mittelstaedt

writers
Pat McKay
Josh Fell

agency producers
Vanessa MacAdam
David Zander
Lisa Rich
David Glean
Darlene Gorzela

production company
MJZ

director
Craig Gillespie

creative directors
Mark Monteiro
Hélène Côté

client
Ameriquest

agency
DDB Direct /
Los Angeles

05019T

Also Awarded:
merit
Consumer Television
:30/:25: Single

DON'T JUDGE TOO QUICKLY

< Merit >

XXX VIDEO

(We see a man walking into his girlfriend's apartment carrying a bag of groceries and flowers. He goes into the kitchen and it becomes apparent he is making a surprise dinner. He takes out a large kitchen knife and begins chopping vegetables and lights some candles, apparently in a hurry. A white, fluffy cat enters the kitchen and jumps up on the stove. Suddenly, the cat tips over a pot of tomato sauce and spills it on the floor. The cat is covered in sauce. Frustrated, the man picks up the cat from the floor and the sauce while holding the kitchen knife in the other hand. Then the girlfriend walks into the apartment and encounters the messy scene. She stares in shock.)

SUPER: Don't judge too quickly. We won't.

VOICE OVER: Ameriquest. An open-minded, equal opportunity lender.

SUPER: Ameriquest logo. NFL logo.

Silver

art director
Marcus Woolcott

writer
Adam Alshin

agency producers
Erika Best
Tammy Auel

production company
Morton Jankel Zander

directors
Tom Kuntz
Mike Maguire

creative director
Ari Merkin

client
Virgin Mobile USA

agency
Fallon / New York

05020T

Also Awarded:
merit
Consumer Television
:30/:25 Single

(Open on a young couple, awkwardly standing side-by-side on a gritty urban street. They face straight ahead, and belt out a phone conversation a cappella.)

MAN: Hello?

WOMAN: Hey, Baby. Are you at John's house?

MAN: Yeah.

WOMAN: Did you ever talk to him about that thing?

MAN: Chicken sounds delicious.

WOMAN: He's in the room, isn't he.

MAN: Yeah.

WOMAN: OK, call me later

MAN: Alright.

SUPER: For the love of music.
Virgin mobile logo.
Get free real music ringtones
on the Vox 8610.
Now $20 off.

‹ Merit ›

Bronze

art director
Dean Maryon

writer
Richard Bullock

agency producers
Peter Cline
Cedric Gairard

production company
Park Pictures

director
Lance Acord

creative directors
Peter McHugh
Lee Clow
Richard Bullock
Dean Maryon

client
adidas

agency
180 Amsterdam
(180\TBWA)

05021T

Also Awarded:
bronze
Consumer Television
:30/:25: Single

< Bronze >

(The 13-year-old gymnast, Nastia Liukin, literally follows in the path of the legendary Nadia Comaneci, the first gymnast ever to score a perfect "10".)

(Open on a man in an office walking and talking to camera.)

MAN: It's so easy to use GEICO-dot-com a caveman could do it! Ha, ha, ha!

CAVEMAN: What?

(We see a caveman holding the boom off set. He storms off.)

CAVEMAN: Not cool!

MAN: I did not know you were there. I didn't know. I can ch...

SUPER: GEICO logo.

VOICE OVER: GEICO. Fifteen minutes could save you fifteen percent or more on car insurance.

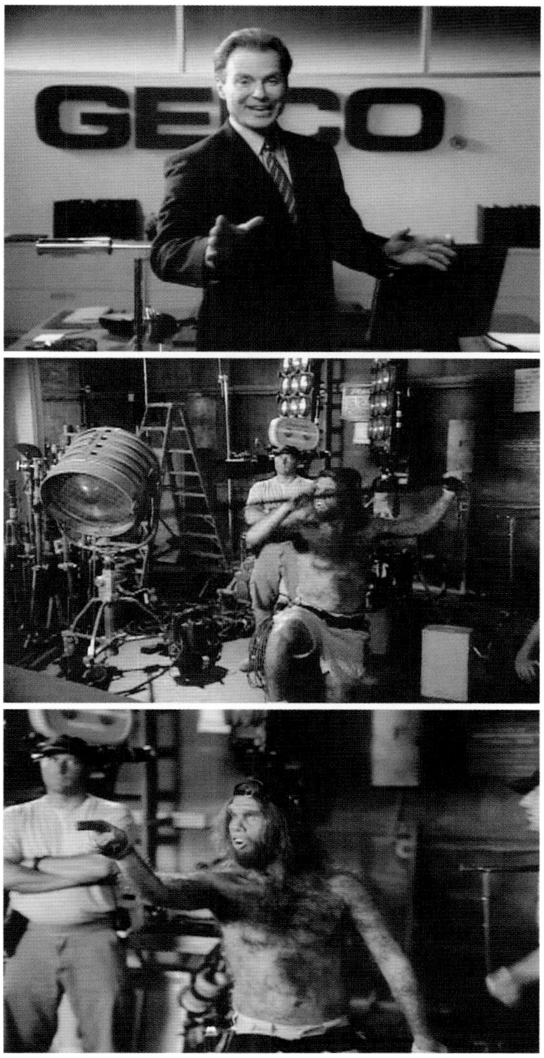

Silver

art director
Noel Ritter

writer
Joe Lawson

agency producers
Brad Powell
Emily Moore

production company
Omaha Pictures

directors
Will Speck
Josh Gordon

creative director
Steve Bassett

client
GEICO

agency
The Martin Agency / Richmond

05022T

CONSUMER TELEVISION : COMMERCIALS : VARIOUS LENGTHS — CAMPAIGN

Gold

art directors
Julian Montessano
Ricky Vior

writers
Leonardo Pratt
Martin Jalfen

agency producer
Facundo Perez

production company
Landia

directors
Andy Fogwill
Agustin Alberdi

creative directors
José Mollá
Joaquín Mollá
Ricky Vior

client
VH 1

agency
la comunidad / Miami Beach

05023T

Also Awarded:
merit
Consumer Television : Over : 30 – Single – Max. : 90

A musician's life is more than just videos.

< Merit >

(Opens in a classroom setting.)

TEACHER: My name is Mary and I'm your children's teacher. Umm, If you can have a look at the program, paragraph one please you will notice...

ROCKSTAR FATHER: Excuse me, Miss.
Hi everybody, I'm Jenny's father (Guitar strikes long, loud chord). I don't understand the French subject really.

TEACHER: What exactly are your concerns?

ROCKSTAR FATHER: Aren't they too young to learn another language? (Guitar strikes two long, loud chords and smoke shoots out from seat).

FATHER IN BACKGROUND: Yeah, I agree with him.

TEACHER: Don't worry, recent studies have shown that the younger they start learning, the easier it will become for them.

ROCKSTAR FATHER: Is French really a...

TEACHER: They can actually choose between three languages: French, Spanish and German...

ROCKSTAR FATHER: German also? (Guitar strikes two long, loud chords and smoke and lights shoot out from seat).

TEACHER: Yes, however, let me clarify again that they must choose between one of the three languages.

ROCKSTAR FATHER: Oh, that's great because I always wanted Jenny to grow up without pressure in a normal environment (Guitar begins playing heavily in the background and pyro shoots up from his seat).

SUPER: A musician's life is more than just music videos.

VH1 logo. Beyond the Music.

A musician's life is more than just videos.

< Merit >

Gold

art directors
Paul Silburn
Tony McTear

writers
Paul Silburn
Tony McTear

agency producer
Diane Croll

production company
Large

director
Daniel Kleinman

creative director
Trevor Beattie

client
Playstation2

agency
TBWA\London

05024T

Also Awarded:

merit
Consumer Television
Over :30/: Single

merit
Consumer Television
Over :30/: Single

SUPER: Life on Playstation.

[We open on the vast plains of Africa where we see a group of Lycra-clad athletes. Some are doing a series of stretches and warm ups, like they would do at the track.]

VOICE OVER: The athlete's control of the Playstation is under threat. The ventriloquists are planning a challenge.

[We see long grass where we see the head and neck of a ventriloquist's dummy pop up and look around. We see several other ventriloquists hiding in the long grass. Suddenly the young ventriloquist makes a solo run at the athletes, screaming loudly as they advance.]

VOICE OVER: This youngster has yet to discover how to overcome a faster opponent on the Playstation. But later he will learn from his elders...

[Soon the ventriloquist and his dummy are among the scattered athletes chasing one, then another but actually getting nowhere. In no time the young man and his dummy are panting and wheezing for air. We now see some of the older ventriloquists throwing their voices.]

VENTRILOQUISTS: Gottle of Geer.

[This causes total panic amongst the athletes who think the voice is coming from another direction and drives them, in their confusion, straight towards the waiting ventriloquists.]

VOICE OVER: For some, life on the Playstation can be brief.

SUPER: Fun, anyone?
PS2 logo.

< Merit >

Bronze

art director
Molly Sheahan

writer
Marty Senn

agency producer
John Cline

production company
Biscuit Filmworks

director
Tim Godsall

creative director
Ari Merkin

client
Virgin Mobile USA

agency
Fallon / New York

05025T

ROSS: I wouldn't say I...I chose to become a ringtone composer.

SUPER: Ross Widmoyer
Ringtone Composer

ROSS: You don't choose your gifts. That's why they're gifts.

SUPER: Virgin Mobile logo.

(We hear music by D12.)

VOICE OVER: Real music ringtones are finally here.

ROSS: What are ringtones if not modern symphonies...that are short.

SUPER: Virgin mobile logo. Live without a plan.
The Vox 8610.

(Two employees watch a customer play a vintage guitar. The customer finishes and returns the guitar to its stand. He waves goodbye and exits. The employees begin clapping.)

EMPLOYEE 1: Whoooooo Hooooooo!

(After several beats, the surprised customer peer through the window and returns to the store. The employees settle down and the customer begins playing again.)

VOICE OVER: Chicago Music Exchange. For the guitar obsessed.

SUPER: Chicago Music Exchange. Clark and School.

Gold

art director
Matt Spett

writer
Rick Hamann

agency producer
Craig Jelniker

production company
Chelsea Pictures

director
Evan Bernard

creative directors
Dennis Ryan
Danny Schuman

client
Chicago Music Exchange

agency
Element 79 Partners / Chicago

05026T

(Two employees watch a customer furiously play a vintage guitar. The customer wildly plays the finishing chords and smashes the guitar into bits on the store floor. Employee 1 cautiously approaches the customer who holds the mangled neck of the guitar.)

CUSTOMER: I'll take it.

EMPLOYEE 1: Good choice.

VOICE OVER: Chicago Music Exchange. For the guitar obsessed.

SUPER: Chicago Music Exchange. Clark and School.

Silver

art director
Matt Spett

writer
Rick Hamann

agency producer
Craig Jelniker

production company
Chelsea Pictures

director
Evan Bernard

creative directors
Dennis Ryan
Danny Schuman

client
Chicago Music Exchange

agency
Element 79 Partners / Chicago

05027T

Gold

art director
Andrew Keller

writer
Bill Wright

agency producer
Rupert Samuel

production company
Arden Sutherland Dodd

director
Harry Enfield

creative directors
Alex Bogusky
Bill Wright
Andrew Keller

client
Virgin

agency
Crispin Porter + Bogusky / Miami

05028T

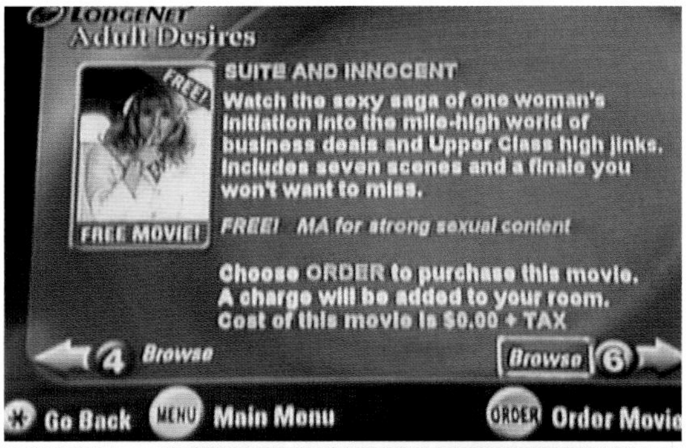
LODGENET
Adult Desires
FREE!
FREE MOVIE!
SUITE AND INNOCENT
Watch the sexy saga of one woman's initiation into the mile-high world of business deals and Upper Class high jinks. Includes seven scenes and a finale you won't want to miss.
FREE! MA for strong sexual content
Choose ORDER to purchase this movie. A charge will be added to your room. Cost of this movie is $0.00 + TAX
4 Browse
Browse 6
Go Back
MENU Main Menu
ORDER Order Movie

(We see what appears to be a porn film, but is actually a commercial for Virgin Airline's Upper Class Service.)

SUPER: Go jet set, go! Virgin Atlantic.
Virgin Atlantic logo.

(We see two kids on steps playing. They are making car noises and pretending to be driving. One kid stops while the other keeps going higher in pitch until he is red in the face.)

SUPER: Shift gears without interruption.
The Direct Shift Gearbox DSG.
Volkswagen logo.

Silver

art directors
Bart Kooij
Scott Smith

writers
Nico Akkermann
Vinny Warren

agency producer
Marion Lange

production company
Cobblestone Hamburg Filmproduktion

director
Sebastian Strasser

creative directors
Amir Kassaei
Wolfgang Schneider
Mathias Stiller

client
Volkswagen

agency
DDB / Berlin

05114T

Also Awarded:
bronze
Consumer Television Under $50,000 Budget: Single

merit
Consumer Television :30/:25: Single

Bronze

art directors
David Nobay
Scott McBurnie

writers
Scott McBurnie
David Nobay

agency producer
Scott McBurnie

production company
Revolver Films

director
Steve Rogers

creative director
David Nobay

client
Toyota

agency
Saatchi & Saatchi / Sydney

05029T

(We see a man walking through the woods. He sees a pair of shoes tied up in a tree and he gets them and puts them on. We hear music playing. He then walks and slips down a hill. He looks up to see a donkey standing there and gets on and begins riding on it. The donkey stops after a while and he sees a wheelbarrow and has the donkey pull it. But then he crashes and walks with the donkey again. He then finds a tractor, then a pickup truck, then a sportscar that runs out of gas. Finally, he sees a Prius.)

SUPER: The petro-electric Toyota Prius.
Keep moving forward.

(Two men are jogging down the street. One says goodbye to the other and then he jogs across the street. He then runs into a parked Mercedes and falls down, startled.)

SUPER: It actually exists. The SLR. Mercedes-Benz logo. The future of the automobile.

Bronze

art director
Nikolaus Ronachen

writer
Norman Störl

agency producer
Hermann Krug

production company
Markenfilm

director
Marc Schölermann

creative directors
Tobias Ahrens
Frank Bannöhr

client
Mercedes-Benz

agency
Springer & Jacoby / Hamburg

05030T

One Show

EXCEPTIONAL INNOVATION IN MARKETING : SINGLE

Gold

art directors
Shintaro Hashimoto
Hirofumi Nakajima

writer
John Merrifield

production company
Media Concierge

creative director
John Merrifield

client
adidas

agency
TBWA\Japan / Tokyo
(180\TBWA)

05001G

Also Awarded:
bronze
Outdoor - single

Silver

writers
Sean Vij
Court Crandall

agency producer
Heidi Hawkings

production company
Headquarters

director
Laurence Thrush

creative director
Court Crandall

client
ESPN/Miller Brewing
Company

agency
Ground Zero /
Los Angeles

05002G

(This was a six-minute short film featured online entitled "The Squeeze," about three guys from South Boston whose uncle has a fatal heart attack while watching Boston win game six of the World Series. Suddenly, they're forced to speculate as to what their uncle would want them to do — bury him or watch game 7.)

To promote the fact that air conditioning comes as standard on the Volkswagen Polo Twist, a life-size, exact replica of the car was sculpted from ice and installed on a busy London street.

Bronze

art directors
Gavin Siakimotu
Graeme Hall

writers
Graeme Hall
Gavin Siakimotu

designer
The Ice Box

creative directors
Jeremy Craigen
Ewan Paterson

client
Volkswagen

agency
DDB / London

05003G

Bronze

art directors
Chee-Wee Choo
Ean-Hwa Huang

writer
Ajay Bakhshi

designer
Sie-Yang Tan

photographers
Adam Seow

agency producer
Jimmy Ong

creative directors
Szu-Hung Lee
Ean-Hwa Huang

client
Sony

agency
McCann Erickson / Kuala Lumpur

05004G

Also Awarded:
merit
Outdoor: Single

Gold

art directors
Ben Callis
Justin Barnes

writers
Justin Barnes
Ben Callis

agency producer
James Brook-Partridge

production company
The Viral Factory

director
The Viral Factory

creative directors
James Sinclair
Malcolm Poynton

client
Ford

agency
Ogilvy & Mather /
London

05005G

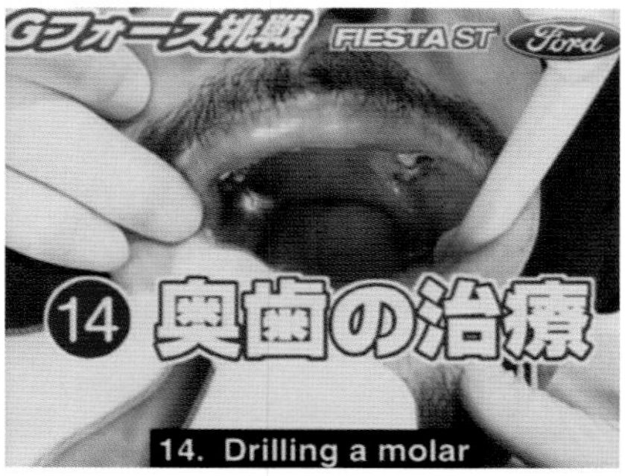

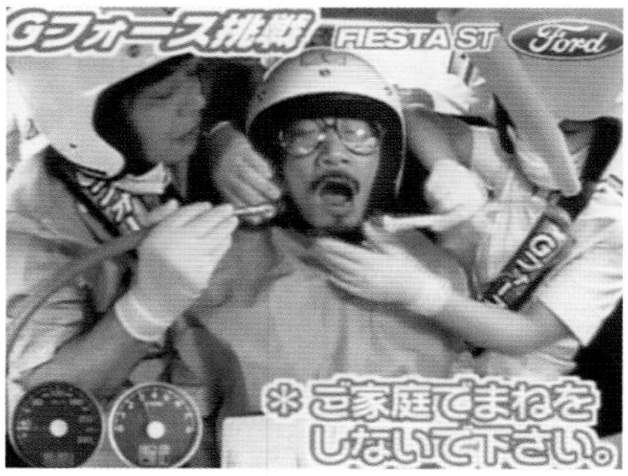

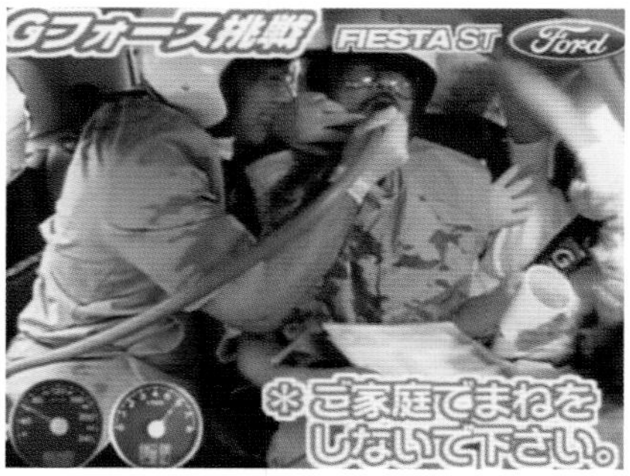

BURGER KING® PRESENTS
CHICKEN SANDWICH WORLD
CHAMPIONSHIP
"TC"
AKA TENDERCRISP® Chicken
VS
"Spicy"
AKA Spicy TENDERCRISP® Chicken
¡YOU DECIDE!
CHICKENFIGHT.COM

Don "The Dragon" Wilson
Carlos Del Valle

Silver

art directors
James Dawson-Hollis
Michael Ferrare

writer
Rob Strasberg

photographer
Kyla Kuhner

illustrators
Mike Koelsch
James Dawson-Hollis

programmer
WDDG

digital artist/multimedia
Brand New School

agency producers
Rupert Samuel
David Rolfe
Corey Bartha
Paul Sutton

production company
Radical Media

directors
Jonathan Kneebone
Gary Freedman

creative directors
Alex Bogusky
Andrew Keller
Jeff Benjamin
Rob Reilly

client
Burger King

agency
Crispin Porter + Bogusky / Miami

05006G

Bronze

art director
Joachim Silber

writer
Paul Fleig

designer
Andreas Jeutter

photographer
Steffen Müller

creative director
Joachim Silber

client
ITS Travel

agency
Jung von Matt / Stuttgart

05007G

SCIENCE WORLD
We can explain.
Day

CAT Pee
glows under
black light
SCIENCE WORLD
We can explain.
Night

Gold

art directors
Rob Sweetman
Hylton Mann

writers
Rob Tarry
Bob Simpson

illustrator
Rob Sweetman

agency producers
Jacqueline Burgmann
Christine Pacheco

production company
Radke Films

director
Michael Downing

creative directors
Ian Grais
Chris Staples

client
Science World

agency
Rethink / Vancouver

05008G

AN OWL'S
EYES ARE BIGGER
THAN ITS BRAIN
SCIENCE WORLD
We can explain.
Real stuffed owl attached to transit shelter

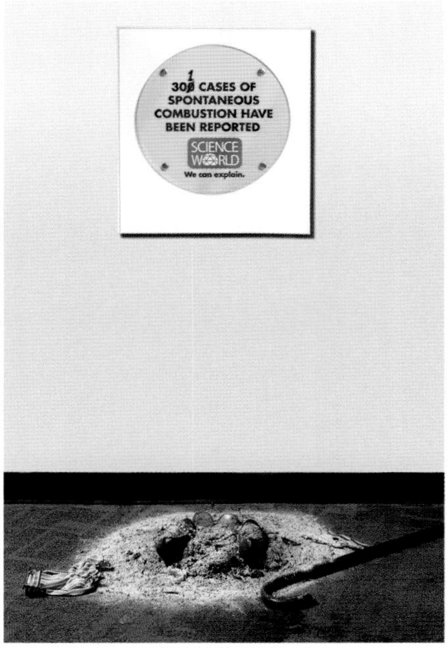
1
300 CASES OF
SPONTANEOUS
COMBUSTION HAVE
BEEN REPORTED
SCIENCE WORLD
We can explain.
3D POP at Science World

SHAKING HANDS
SPREADS MORE GERMS
THAN KISSING.

PLANTS
GROW FASTER
UNDER GLASS
SCIENCE WORLD
We can explain.
Transit shelter filled with living plants

PLANTS
GROW FASTER
UNDER GLASS
SCIENCE WORLD
We can explain.
Week eight

One Show

INTERGRATED BRANDING : CAMPAIGN

Silver

art director
Mike Hughes

writer
Charlie Gschwend

programmer
Andreas Tagger

digital artist/multimedia
Nei Caetano da Silva/
Andreas Tagger

agency producers
Tracy Kurtz
Francesca Prada

production company
Zaaz

directors
Alastair McKeviit
(Charles &
Arorah's Garage)
Peter Craig (Gary)

creative directors
John Butler
Mike Shine

content strategist:
Ed Cotton

client
Converse

agency
Butler, Shine, Stern &
Partners / Sausalito

05009G

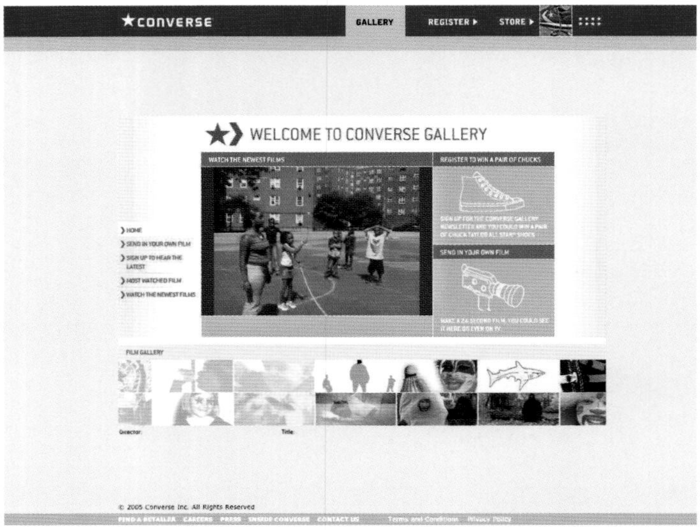

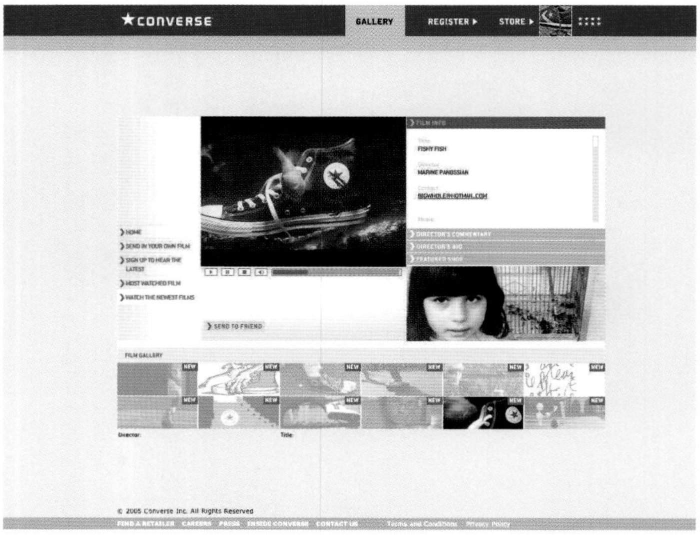

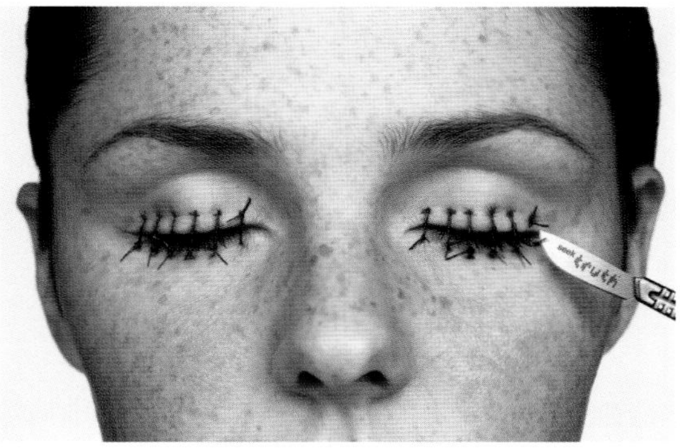

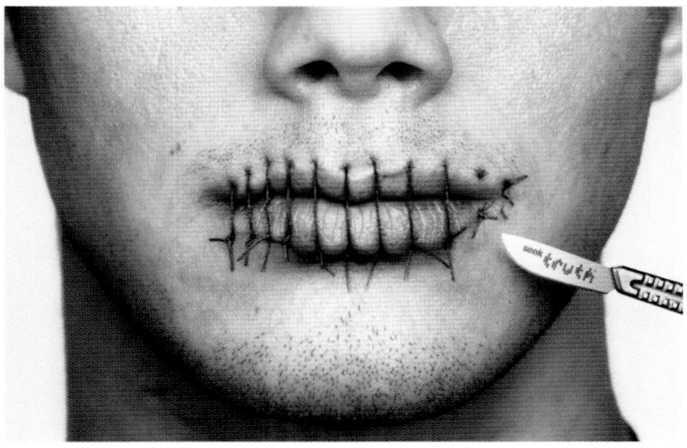

Bronze

art directors
Phil Covitz
Brandon Sides
Tricia Ting
Meghan Siegal

designers
Meghan Siegal
Chris Valencius
Max Pfennighaus
Suzanne McCarthy

writers
John Kearse
Marc Einhorn
Jackie Hathiramani
Annie Finnegan
Bill Hollister

photographer
Hans Gissinger

programmers
Ebbey Mathew
Adam Buhler

agency producers
Carron Pedonti
Barry Frechette
Linda Donlon
Kathy McMann

production company
Redtree Productions

director
Christian Hoagland

creative directors
Ron Lawner
Pete Favat
Alex Bogusky
Tom Adams
John Kearse

client
American Legacy Foundation

agency
Arnold Worldwide / Boston and Crispin Porter + Bogusky / Miami

05010G

BRAND AND CORPORATE IDENTITY DESIGN : BOOKLET BROCHURE

Gold

designer
Mark Stead

art director
Mark Stead

writer
Livio Tronchin

illustrator
Jared Barbe

creative director
Jenny Ehlers

client
Research Surveys

agency
King James RSVP / Cape Town

05001D

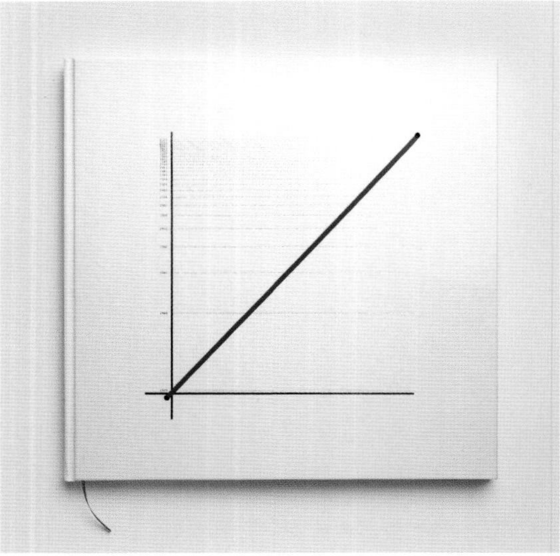

Silver

designers
Leng Soh
Roy Poh
Pann Lim

art directors
Leng Soh
Roy Poh
Pann Lim

writer
Alex Goh

photographer
Jeremy Wong

illustrator
Leng Soh

creative director
Kinetic

client
Pulling String

agency
Kinetic / Singapore

05002D

Also Awarded:
silver
Direct Mail: Single

Bronze

art directors
Andreas Kittel
Lisa Careborg

photographer
Jäger Arén

creative director
Anders Kornestedt

client
Arctic Paper

agency
Happy Forsman &
Bodenfors / Gothenburg

05003D

Also Awarded:
merit
One Show Design
Direct Mail: Single

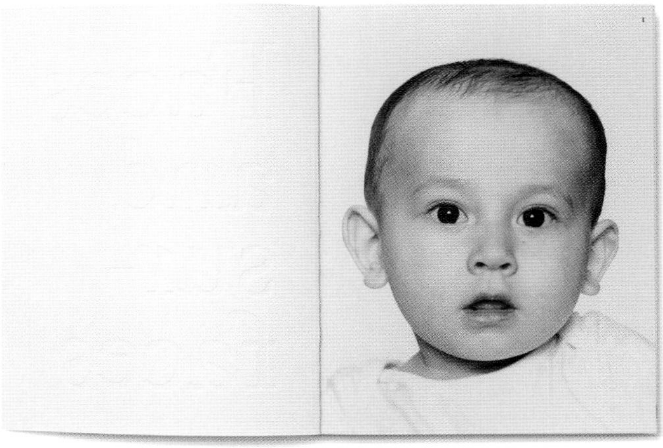

Gold

designers
Toshihiro Hyodo
Minoru Fuwa
Megumu Kasuga
Mari Kobayashi

art director
Seijo Kawaguchi

photographer
Shoji Uchida

creative director
Yasumichi Oka

client
Sanyo Shokai

agency
Tugboat / Tokyo

05004D

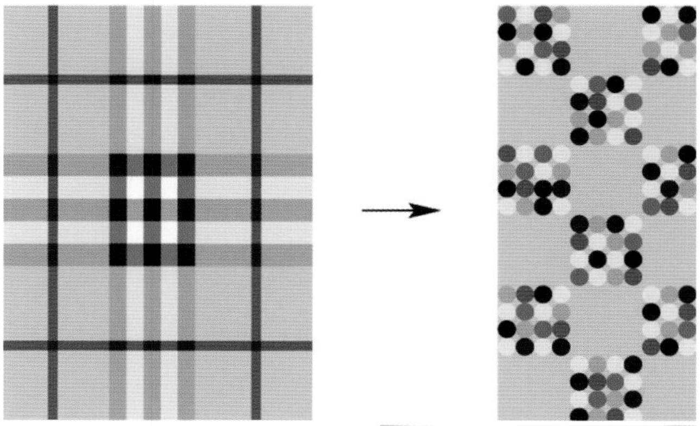

Bronze

designer
Joan Jacobs

art director
Joan Jacobs

writer
Livio Tronchin

creative director
Jenny Ehlers

client
Atmosphere PR

agency
King James RSVP / Cape Town

05006D

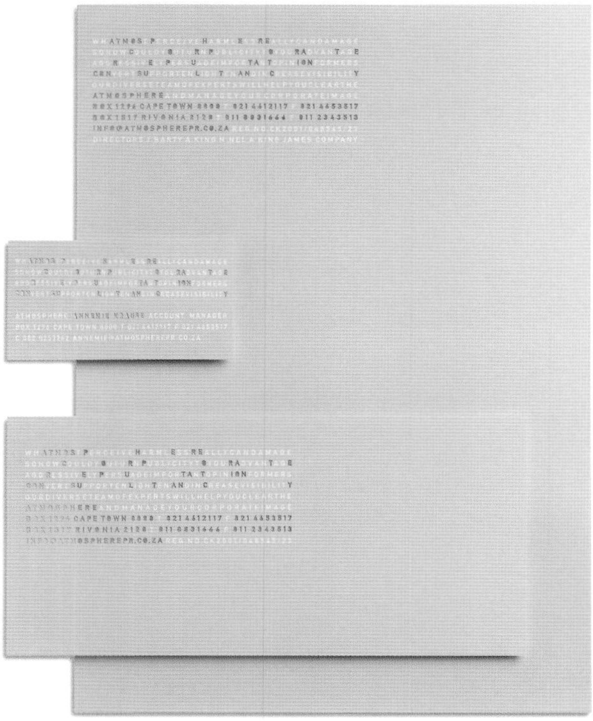

DUFFY &
PARTNERS

Silver

designer
Ken Sakurai

creative directors
Joe Duffy
Dan Olson

client
Duffy & Partners

agency
Duffy & Partners / Minneapolis

05007D

Bronze

designer
Jesse Kaczmarek

creative director
Bill Thorburn

client
City of Minneapolis

agency
Carmichael Lynch Thorburn / Minneapolis

05008D

Silver

designers
Go Takahashi
Yui Takada

art director
Manabu Mizuno

writer
Hideki Azuma

creative directors
Hideki Azuma
Manabu Mizuno

client
Kirin

agency
Good Design Company / Tokyo

05010D

Silver

designer
Martin Reintz

art directors
Nicke Bergström
Mattias Brodén

creative director
Matias Palm Jensen

client
Galatea Spirits

agency
Farfar / Stockholm

05009D

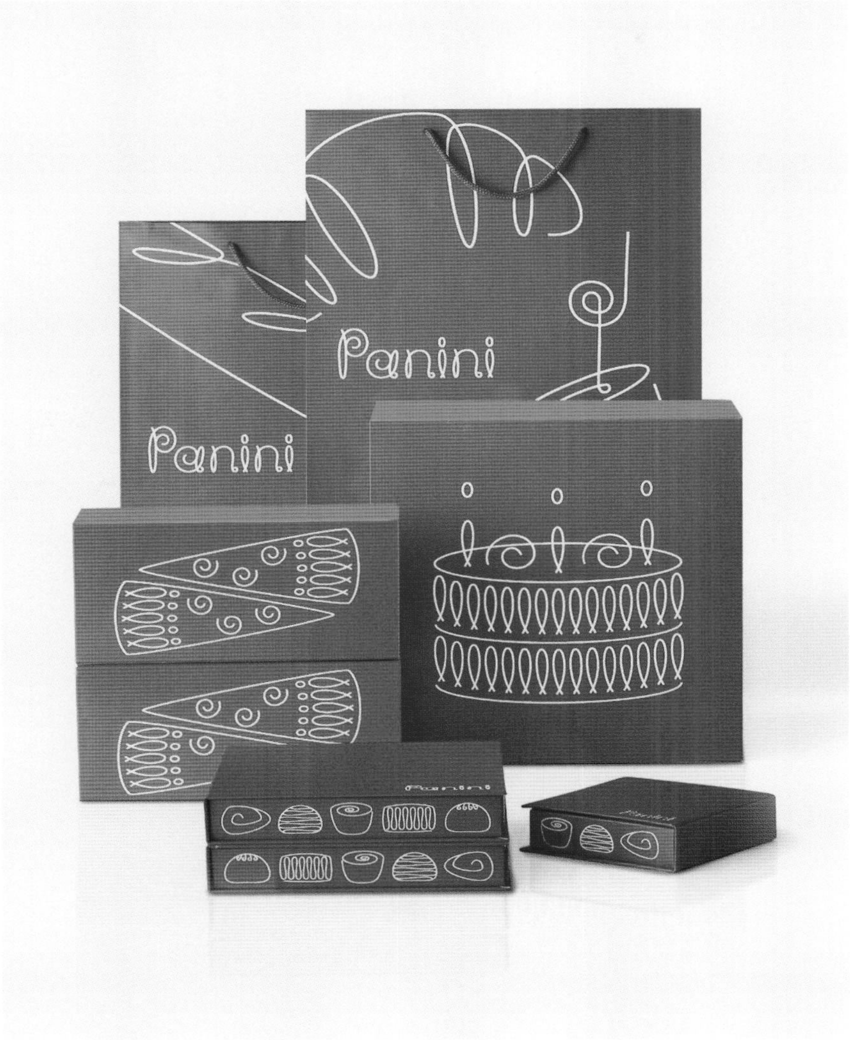

Bronze

designers
Hideo Akiba
Fiona Verdon-Smith

illustrators
Hideo Akiba
Fiona Verdon-Smith

creative director
Mary Lewis

client
Grand Hyatt Dubai

agency
Lewis Moberly / London

05011D

PACKAGE DESIGN : CAMPAIGN

Gold

designers
Roy Poh
Pann Lim

art directors
Roy Poh
Pann Lim

writers
Roy Poh
Pann Lim
Alex Goh

illustrators
Roy Poh
Pann Lim

creative director
Kinetic

client
Wong CoCo

agency
Kinetic / Singapore

05012D

Silver

art director
Dustin Black

writer
Kara Connolly

photographers
Vern Grove
Jack Revoir

creative directors
Yves Roux
Mark Andeer

client
Hormel Foods
Corporation-DiLuso
Genoa

agency
BBDO / Minneapolis

05013D

Silver

designer
Go Takahashi

art director
Manabu Mizuno

creative director
Manabu Mizuno

client
Twinkle Corporation

agency
Good Design Company / Tokyo

05014D

Bronze

art director
Lee O'Brien

illustrator
Lee O'Brien

creative director
Keith Borshak

client
Tiffany O'Brien

agency
The Woodbine Agency / Winston Salem

05015D

COLLATERAL DESIGN : POSTERS — CAMPAIGN

Gold

designers
Charles S. Anderson
Sheraton Green
Jovaney Hollingsworth

art director
Charles S. Anderson

client
French Paper Company

agency
Charles S. Anderson
Design / Minneapolis

05016D

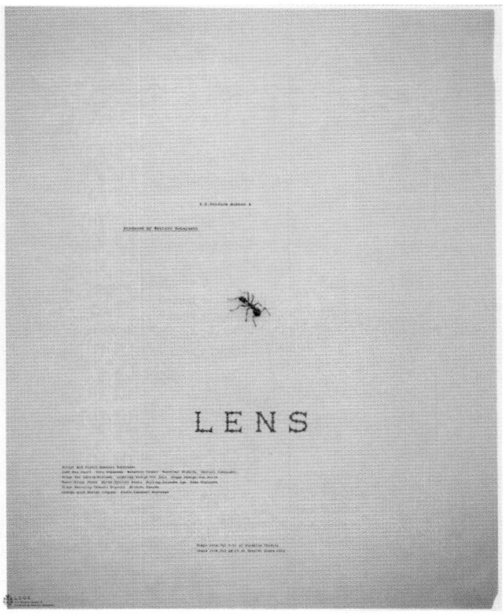

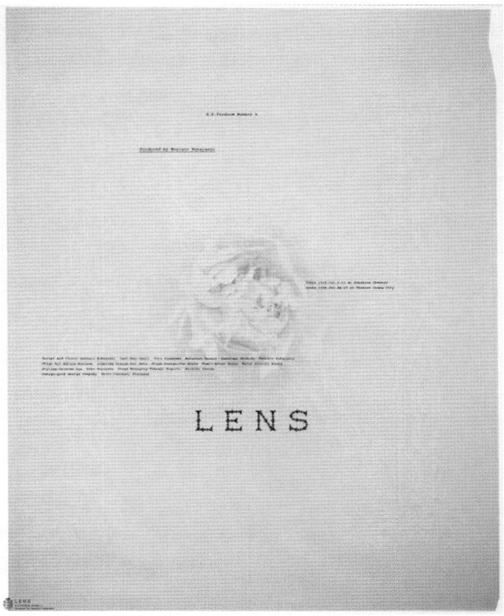

Silver

designers
Go Takahashi
Yuta Akimoto

art director
Manabu Mizuno

photographer
Yasunari Kurosawa

creative director
Manabu Mizuno

client
Twinkle Corporation

agency
Good Design Company / Tokyo

05017D

COLLATERAL DESIGN : POSTERS — CAMPAIGN

Bronze

designers
Ken Goh
Jann Lim

art director
Ken Goh

writer
Monica Chen

photographer
Melvin Lee (Untold Images)

illustrator
Monica Lee

creative directors
Yap Pow Hoong
Kit Ong

client
RayTan Florist

agency
Foote Cone & Belding / Kuala Lumpur

05018D

Also Awarded:
merit
One Show
Collateral
Posters: Campaign

Silver

art director
Menno Kluin

writer
Menno Kluin

creative directors
Bettina Olf
Timm Weber

client
Smith & Wesson

agency
Springer & Jacoby / Hamburg

05019D

Also Awarded:
merit
Collateral Design
Posters: Single

COLLATERAL DESIGN : P.O.P. AND IN-STORE — CAMPAIGN

Silver

art directors
Gang Hu
Paul Yu
Hai Liang
Bamboo Zhuang

writers
Thomas Zhu
Joe Wu

photographer
JianXin Liu

illustrators
Ning He
Hong He

creative directors
SheungYan Lo
Nick Lim
Bill Chan
Gang Hu
Thomas Zhu

client
Nike

agency
JWT / Shanghai

05020D

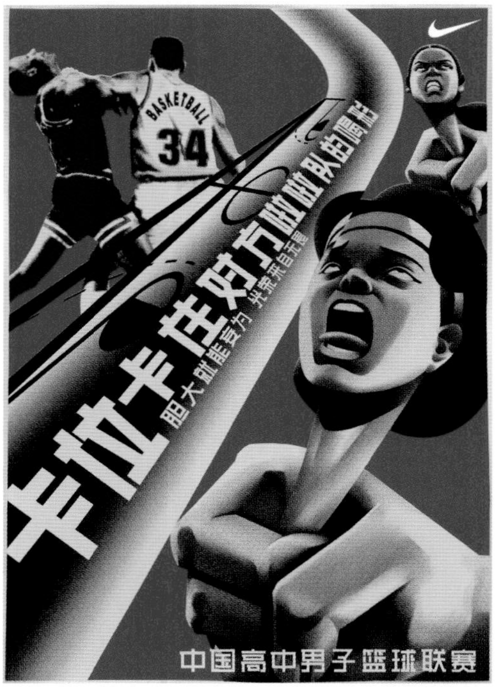
BASKETBALL
34
胆大就能妄为 光荣来自无畏
中国高中男子篮球联赛

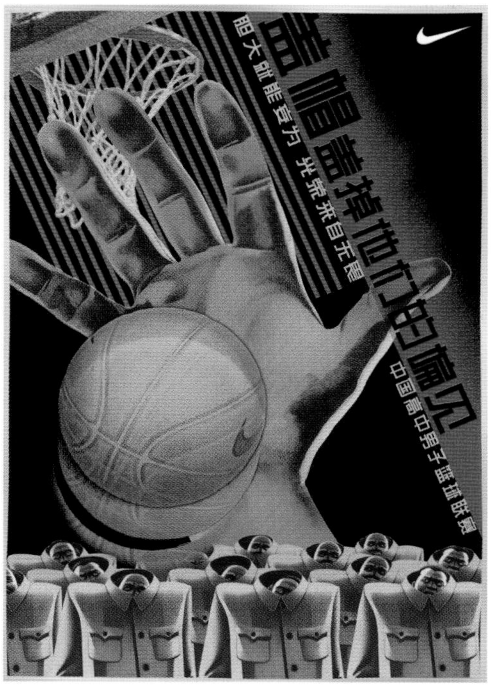
盖帽盖掉他们的偏见
胆大就能妄为 光荣来自无畏
中国高中男子篮球联赛

补篮 帮对手补补谦虚这节课
胆大就能妄为 光荣来自无畏
中国高中男子篮球联赛

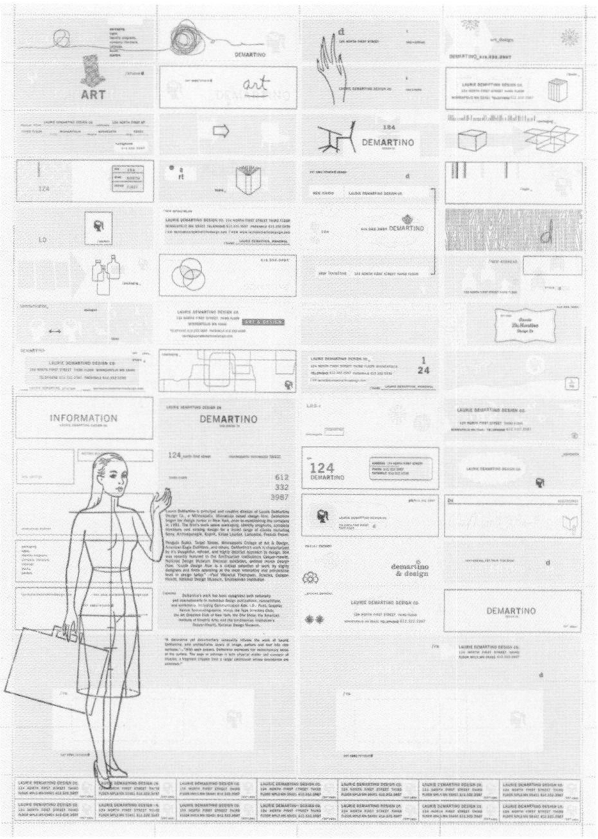

Gold

designer
Laurie DeMartino

art director
Laurie DeMartino

client
Laurie DeMartino Design

agency
Laurie DeMartino Design / Minneapolis

05021D

Also Awarded:
silver
One Show Design
Brand and Corporate Identity Design
Corporate Identity

wisdom
More or less

Karen —nike talent
life's too short, have fun

Danica —expense Accountant
True Happiness comes from within

Bill —Art Director—
Everything happens for a reason, and its usually not the reason you think it is.

Silver

art director
W+K 12

writer
W+K 12

illustrator
Ryan Alexander-Tanner

creative director
W+K 12

client
W+K 12

agency
Wieden + Kennedy / Portland

05022D

Bronze

art director
The Glue Society

writers
JWT
The Glue Society
Assignment Group

creative director
Craig Davis

client
JWT

agency
JWT / London

05023D

THE WORLD
NOW
LOOKS AT US
DIFFERENTLY.
WE NEED A
NEW WAY
TO LOOK AT
OURSELVES.

I'D RATHER SPEND TIME AT THE DENTIST THAN WITH THIS IDEA.
01
I'D RATHER SPEND TIME WITH MY PARENTS THAN WITH THIS IDEA.
02

HOLD
my
SKATEBOARD
while I KISS
your
Girlfriend

Your suitcase will soon get out again. A chicken is stuck here all its life.
Hen batteries are cruelty to animals. We fight that. www.vier-pfoten.de

Gold

art director
Melanie Mertens

writer
David Leinweber

creative directors
Bettina Olf
Timm Weber

client
Vier Pfoten e.V.
Foundation for Animal Welfare

agency
Springer & Jacoby / Hamburg

05024D

Also Awarded:
merit
Exceptional Innovation in Marketing: Single

Silver

art director
Jan Knauss

writer
Thies Schuster

creative directors
Ralf Nolting
Patricia Pätzold
Ralf Heuel

client
Volkswagen

agency
Grabarz & Partner /
Hamburg

05025D

Klosters
Graubünden
Graubünden

Normal condition
The Touareg V10 TDI®. From 0 to 100 km/h in 7.8 seconds.

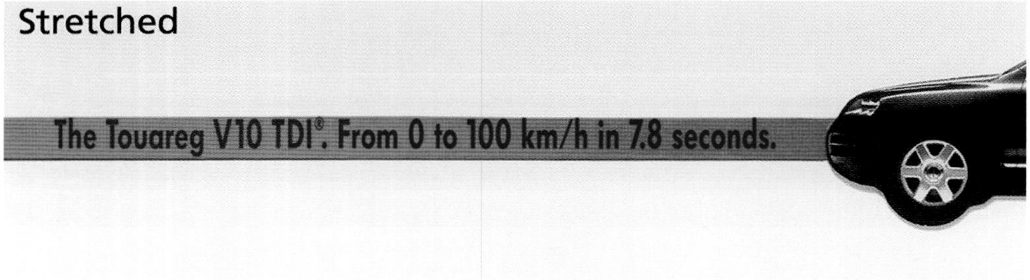
Stretched
The Touareg V10 TDI®. From 0 to 100 km/h in 7.8 seconds.

Bronze

art director
Ali Alvarez

writer
Ali Alvarez

illustrator
Erik Sandberg

creative directors
Richard Flintham
Andy McLeod

client
United Airlines

agency
Fallon / London

05026D

Gold

designers
Shigeto Akiyama
Seymour Chwast
Alexander Isley
Michael Bierut
Alexander Gelman
Stefan Sagmeister
Sam Potts
Aimee Sealfon-Eng
Woody Pirtle
Paula Scher
James Victore
Michael Ian Kaye
Carin Goldberg
David Schimmel
Scott Stowell
Steff Geisbuhler
Mirko Ilic
Chip Kidd
Steven Brower
Kent Hunter
Emily Oberman
Bonnie Sigler
Todd St. John
Robert Valentine
Marcos Chin
Roberto de Vicq de Cumptich

art director
David Schimmel

writer
Walter Thomas

creative director
David Schimmel

client
Neenah Paper

agency
And Partners / New York

05027D

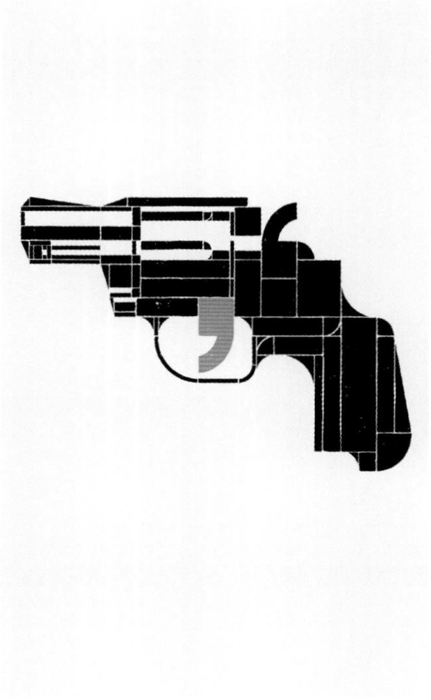

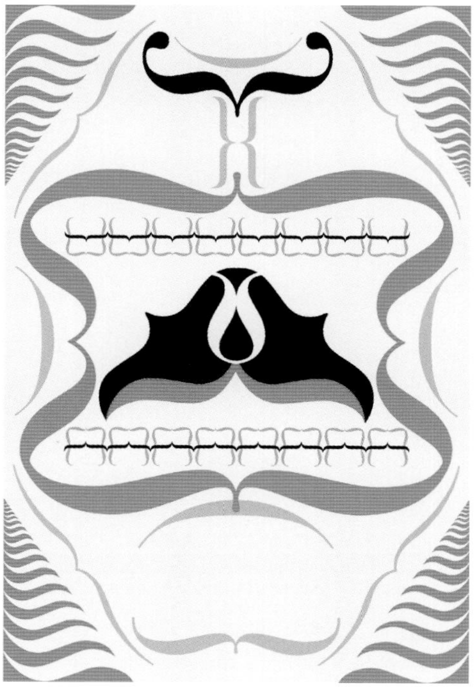

Gold

designer
Neil Powell

art director
Neil Powell

writer
Josh Rogers

illustrators
Various

creative director
Neil Powell

client
Rheingold Beer

agency
Powell / New York

05028D

ENVIRONMENTAL DESIGN : CAMPAIGN

Silver

art directors
Selena McKenzie
Toby Moore

writers
Toby Moore
Selena McKenzie
Darren Spiller

photographer
Richard Giles

illustrators
Andrew Trevillian
Alison Colpoys

creative director
Darren Spiller

client
Tourism Victoria

agency
Publicis Mojo /
Melbourne

05029D

• 94 •

BEYONDcompare
BEYONDcompare
Beauty for me is self-acceptance.

Bronze

designers
Leigh Okies
Helena Fruehauf
Satian Pengsathapon
Nathalie Hennequin

creative directors
Brian Collins
David Israel

client
Dove

agency
Ogilvy & Mather /
New York

05030D

Gold

designer
Paul Sahre

art director
Paul Sahre

writer
Richard Wilde

client
School of Visual Arts

agency
School of Visual Arts/
Advertising & Graphic
Design Dept. / New York

05031D

Silver

designer
Shereen Peterson

art directors
Hans Seeger
Shereen Peterson
Brian Shembeda

writers
John Condon
Avery Gross

photographer
Magnus Magnusson

creative director
Mark Tutssel

client
Chicago Creative Club

agency
Leo Burnett / Chicago

05032D

Gold

designer
Misugi Yokoo

art director
Chie Morimoto

writer
Tomoyuki Makita

photographers
Hiroki Nakashima
Mikiya Takimoto
Orie Ichihashi

illustrator
Ichio Otsuka

production company
Robot Communications

creative director
Chie Morimoto

client
Pie Books

agency
Hakuhodo / Tokyo

05033D

One Show Design

PUBLICATION DESIGN : CONSUMER MAGAZINE — FULL ISSUE

Gold

designer
John Hobbs

art director
John Hobbs

writers
Robert Ourlian
Michael Poris
Harry Russell
Christy Wood
Nancy Barr
Hobey Echlin
Maria Kovac
Mike Rehfus
Liz Copeland
Tamara Warren

photographers
Various

illustrator
John Hobbs

creative director
Toni Torres

client
BIG magazine

agency
Bartle Bogle Hegarty / New York

05034D

Silver

art director
Studio Von Birken

creative director
Douglas Lloyd

client
BIG Magazine

agency
Lloyd and Company / New York

05035D

Gold

designers
Heidi Chisholm
Peet Pienaar

art directors
Heidi Chisholm
Peet Pienaar

writer
Mirjam Asmal

illustrators
Heidi Chisholm
Peet Pienaar

creative director
Peet Pienaar

client
Pro Helvetia (Swiss Arts Council)

agency
Daddy buy me a Pony
(a 9November Union Company) / Cape Town

05036D

Bronze

designer
Mike Brandt

art director
Mike Brandt

writers
Jens Ringena
Stefanie Thul

illustrators
André Roesler
Springer & Jacoby Design

creative director
Uli Guertler

client
Raffles Hotel Vier Jahreszeiten Hamburg

agency
Springer & Jacoby / Hamburg

05038D

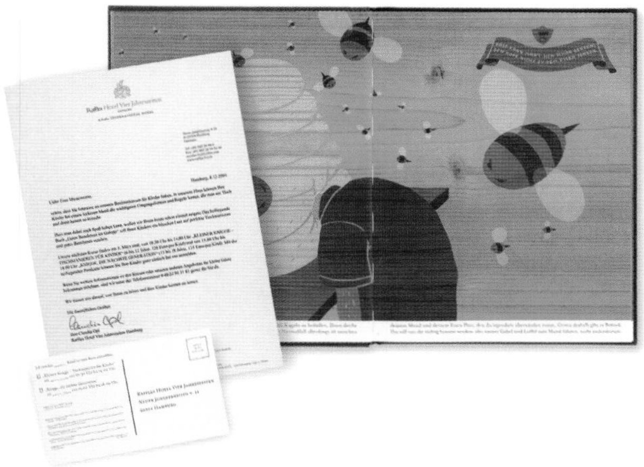

Silver

designers
Steve Sandstrom
Kristin Anderson
Kristy Adewumi

art director
Steve Sandstrom

photographer
Mark Hooper

creative director
Steve Sandstrom

client
Mark Hooper

agency
Sandstrom Design / Portland

05039D

BROADCAST DESIGN : SINGLE

Gold

designers
Cadu Macedo
Rafael Grampá
Paula Nobre
Guilherme Marcondes
Diogo Kalil
Carlos Béla
Mario Sader
Rogério Marmo
Will Broadbent
Luís Blumenfeld

agency producers
Loic Dubois
Joao Tenorio
Sabine Teerink

production company
lobo

creative director
Mateus de Paula Santos
Dave Bell

client
Diesel

agency
Lobo / São Paulo

05040D

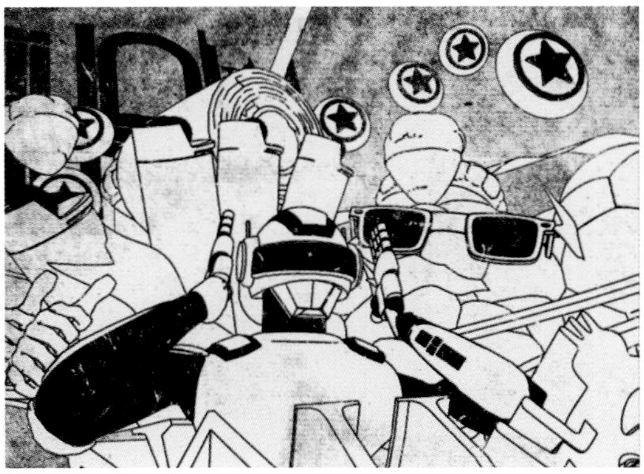

Silver

designer
WOOG

art director
+CRUZ
John Jay

writers
+CRUZ
John Jay
WOOG

production companies
Wieden+Kennedy Tokyo
Lab / Oceanmonsters /
Triton Films (BKK)

director
+CRUZ

creative director
John Jay

client
Wieden+Kennedy/Tokyo

agency
Wieden+Kennedy/Tokyo

05042D

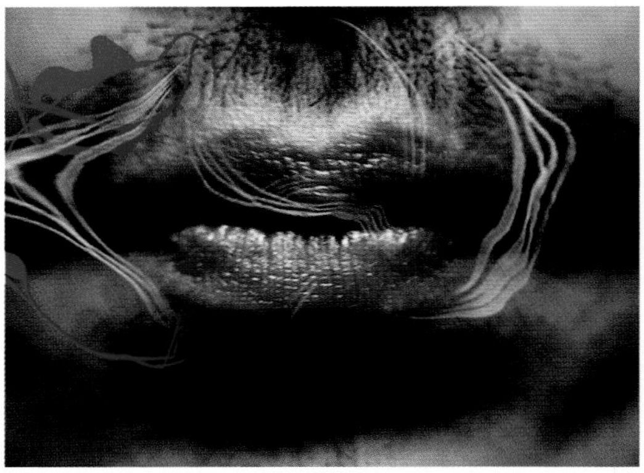

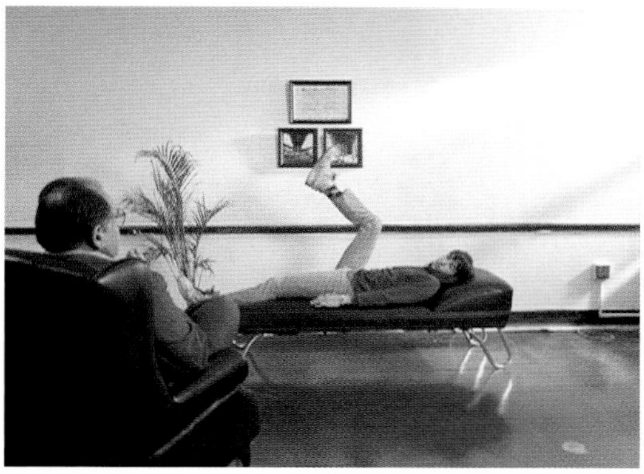

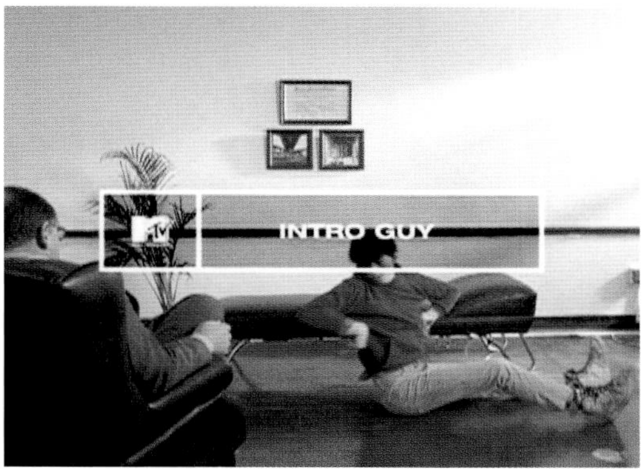

Silver

designer
Dave Skinner

producers
Leslie Legare
Owen Plotkin

directors
Lena Beug
Kip Bogdahn

art director
Lena Beug

writer
Clay Weiner

creative directors
Jeffrey Keyton
Romy Mann

client
MTV Design

agency
MTV Networks / New York

05041D

Bronze

designer
Dave Skinner

producers
Leslie Legare
Owen Plotkin

directors
Lena Beug
Kip Bogdahn

art director
Lena Beug

writer
Clay Weiner

creative directors
Jeffrey Keyton
Romy Mann

client
MTV Design

agency
MTV Networks / New York

05043D

Gold

designer
Dave Skinner

producers
Leslie Legare
Owen Plotkin

directors
Lena Beug
Kip Bogdahn

art director
Lena Beug

writer
Clay Weiner

creative directors
Jeffrey Keyton
Romy Mann

client
MTV Design

agency
MTV Networks /
New York

05044D

ASTOUNDING
TALES!
AMPUTATED HAND CRAWLS 900 MILES TO PUT CIGARETTE BACK IN MOUTH!!!
RESEARCH SHOWS THAT MOST STUDENTS WHO SAY THEY'LL GIVE UP CIGARETTES AFTER COLLEGE CAN'T.

Silver

designer
Aesthetic Apparatus

art director
Steve Mitchell

writer
Doug Adkins

creative directors
Doug Adkins
Steve Mitchell

client
American Cancer Society/Blue Cross Blue Shield

agency
Hunt Adkins / Minneapolis

05046D

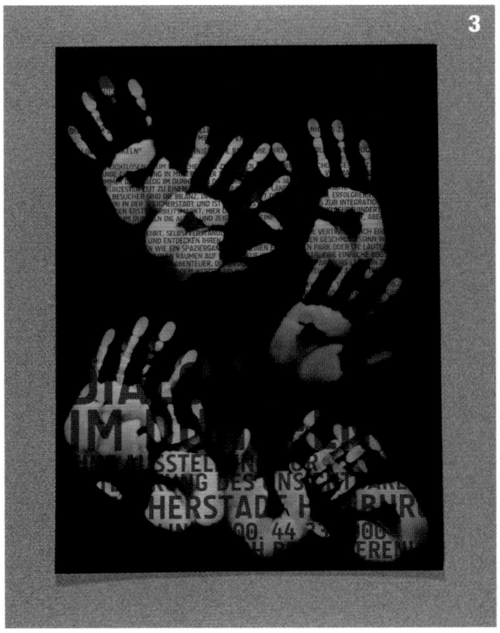
3

4
DIALOG
IM DUNKELN®
EINE AUSSTELLUNG ZUR
ENTDECKUNG DES UNSICHTBAREN
SPEICHERSTADT HAMBURG
BOOKINGLINE 0700. 44 33 2000
BITTE TELEFONISCH RESERVIEREN!

Silver

designer
Mitoh

art director
Mitoh

creative director
Michael Hoinkes

client
Dialogue in the Dark

agency
He Said She Said / Hamburg

05045D

PUBLIC SERVICE/NON-PROFIT/EDUCATIONAL : POSTERS — SINGLE

Bronze

designers
Nobuya Mochinaga
Hitoshi Miyamoto
Nanae Sega

art directors
Nils Andersson
Keiichi Sasaki

writers
Keiichi Sasaki
Nils Andersson

illustrators
Minoru Nakahama
Tomoko Higuchi

creative directors
Nils Andersson
Keiichi Sasaki

client
Animal ID Promotion Organization

agency
Hakuhodo\TBWA\G1 / Tokyo

05047D

WHERE IS TAMA?
You have 2 minutes.
If not it's the end for TAMA.
That's the sad truth. As every
2 minutes in Japan, a lost cat has
to be put to sleep.
A simple microchip would
have helped TAMA find
his way home.
Animal ID Promotion
Organization
AIPO

1 = black
Help us keep life colourful. Oro Verde. The Rainforest Foundation

1 = black
Help us keep life colourful. Oro Verde. The Rainforest Foundation

1 = black
Help us keep life colourful. Oro Verde. The Rainforest Foundation

Gold

art directors
Till Schaffarzcyk
Helmut Himmler

writers
Ales Polcar
Lars Huvart

creative directors
Helmut Himmler
Lars Huvart

client
OroVerde Rainforest Foundation

agency
Ogilvy & Mather / Frankfurt

05048D

One Show Design

PUBLIC SERVICE / NON-PROFIT / EDUCATIONAL : POSTERS — CAMPAIGN

Silver

designers
Kum-jun Park
Joong-gyu Kang

art director
Kum-jun Park

writer
Jong-in Jung

photographers
Seung-youn Nam
Jae-hee Park

illustrator
Kum-jun Park

creative director
Kum-jun Park

client
VIDAK (Visual Information Design Association of Korea)

agency
601Bisang / Seoul

05049D

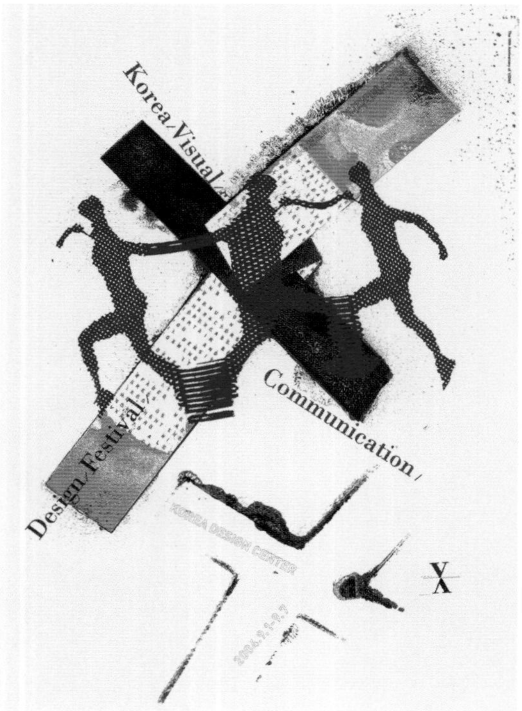

nice prize
POLAR MUSIC PRIZE
THE ROYAL SWEDISH ACADEMY OF MUSIC AWARD

Silver

art director
Andreas Kittel

creative director
Anders Kornestedt

client
Polar Music Prize

agency
Happy Forsman &
Bodenfors / Gothenburg

05050D

Also Awarded:
merit
Environmental Design:
Single

COME AND SEE
NEW SWEDISH
PHOTOGRAPHY
AT HASSELBLAD
CENTER
14.5–6.6 2004
SARA APPELGREN / NYGÅRDS KARIN BENGTSSON
ALBIN BIBLOM / KAJSA DAHLBERG / BEATA FRANSSON
SUSANNA HESSELBERG / ANDERS KRISÁR / JENNY KÄLLMAN
ANNEÉ OLOFSSON / LARS WALLSTEN / PERNILLA ZETTERMAN
14.5
THE EXHIBITION OPENS ON FRIDAY 14 MAY AT 4–6 P.M. AT 4.30 P.M.
BO MYHRMAN, MANAGING DIRECTOR, WILL ANNOUNCE THE 2004
HASSELBLAD FOUNDATION FELLOWSHIP FOR POSTGRADUATE
STUDIES IN PHOTOGRAPHY. THE EXHIBITION WILL THEN BE
OFFICIALLY INAUGURATED BY HASSE PERSSON, CURATOR.
HASSELBLAD CENTER, GÖTAPLATSEN, GOTHENBURG, SWEDEN.
OPENING HOURS: TUE, THU 11 A.M.–6 P.M. WED 11 A.M.–9 P.M.
FRI–SUN 11 A.M.–5 P.M. WWW.HASSELBLADCENTER.SE

Bronze

art directors
Lisa Careborg
Pontus Höfvner

creative director
Anders Kornestedt

client
Hasselblad Center

agency
Happy Forsman &
Bodenfors / Gothenburg

05051D

Also Awarded:
merit
Direct Mail: Single

Gold

art director
Michael Bae

writer
Francisco Garcia-Tunon

school
Miami Ad School /
Miami Beach

CCA01

Domino
SUGAR

Silver

art director
Emily Honigsfeld

writer
Tom Sebanc

school
Miami Ad School/
Minneapolis

CCA02

ANIMALS
HAVE BEEN TESTING IT
FOR CENTURIES.
Domino
SUGAR
PURE BY NATURE.

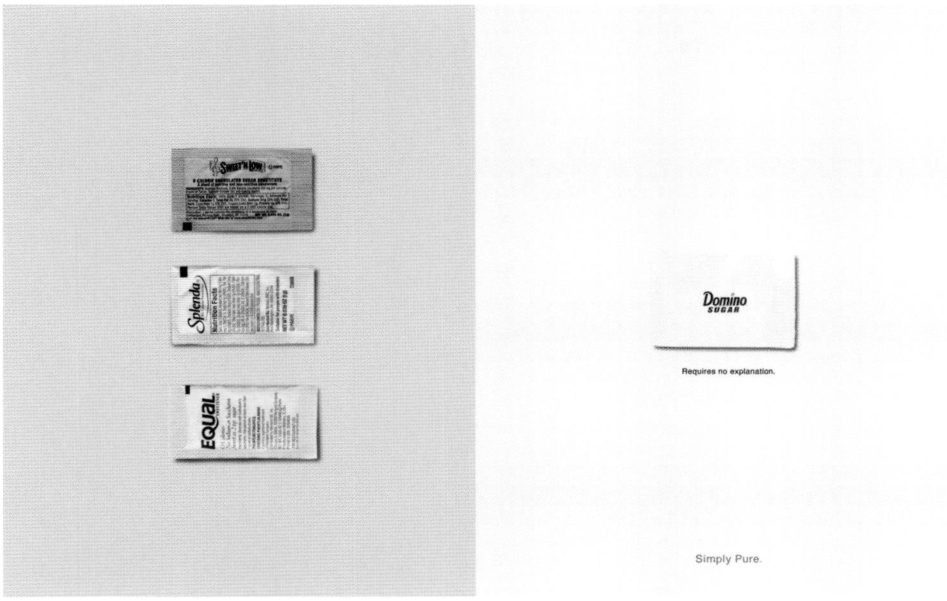
Requires no explanation.
Simply Pure.

Bronze

art director
Lisa Hee Yuen Chun

writer
Lisa Hee Yuen Chun

school
Art Center College
of Design/Pasadena

CCA03

Silver

designer
Rebecca Zerilla

school
University of Mississippi / University

CCD01

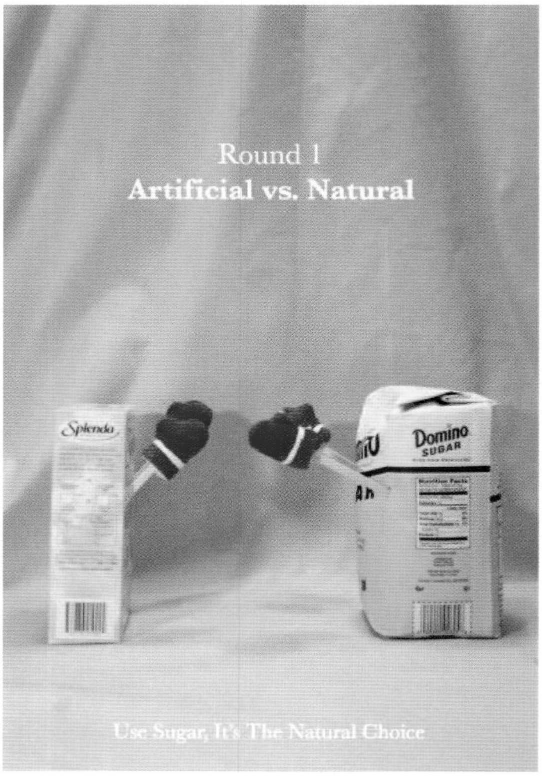

Bronze

art directors
Emily Rawitsch
Leah Wilson

writers
Emily Rawitsch
Leah Wilson

school
The College of Saint Rose/Albany

CCD02

Splendidly
bad for your health
ARTIFICIAL SWEETENER
Domino
SUGAR
There's no substitute.

Bronze

art director
Angela Mosera

designer
Angela Mosera

writer
Angela Mosera

school
Texas A&M University-Commerce / Commerce

CCD03

Gold on Gold

◆

Judge's Choice

Master of Your Destiny

Gold on Gold

client
DHL

agency:
Jung von Matt / Berlin

05001A

Mirko Stolz
David Mously
The attempt to reach one's own limits and go beyond them is DHL's most profound motivation: limits of speed, of size, of reach, of service, etc. This ad also follows this motivation. It is the attempt to reach the limit of branding and of a double-page spread in a daily newspaper. We were not able to overcome it. But then, we're only an advertising agency, not DHL.

Burkhart von Scheven
Our communication strategy was to put full personal pressure on our best team in order to get me into the books.

client
Volkswagen

agency:
Grabarz & Partner / Hamburg

05004A

Ralf Heuel
Ralf Nolting
The former gas stations in our ads are all located between Hamburg and Wolfsburg. Since working for Volkswagen, we drove past them exactly 432 times. Suddenly, during ride number 433, someone had an idea. Who says that taking the train pays? Thank you for this extraordinary prize.

client
Sony

agency:
Tonic
Communications /
Dubai

05011A

Vincent Raffray
One thing we've learnt in this culturally diverse region is to craft ideas into their simplest form. This has really helped us improve our thought processes when tackling briefs. There's great potential for this region and bringing awards like the One Show to the Middle East will hopefully inspire creatives to produce better work.

Jamie Mietz
It's refreshing to work on products you actually believe in. We visited quite a few electronic stores to do some research. These products had been beautifully crafted by their designers, only to have a shopkeeper slap an ugly price flash on the screen. It was very amusing. We were inspired.

client
Grande Reportagem
Magazine

agency:
Foote Cone and
Belding / Lisbon

05014A

Luis Silva Dias
It was a transition moment for Grande Reportagem (going from a monthly to a weekly magazine), with a new director and a new layout.

But the core was still "hard journalism" and the magazine needed a campaign to say exactly that. So we worked around that, trying to use a "journalistic" way to communicate. From there to the infographics took just one step: We presented the world in hard, cold facts (those who people tend to ignore). In that manner we created a strong and touching feeling around the brand Grande Reportagem. And the size of the response shows that it did the job, and touched people all around the world.

And that's because it's about the world. It's a very open campaign, easy to understand and with great relevance to everybody, no matter where they live.

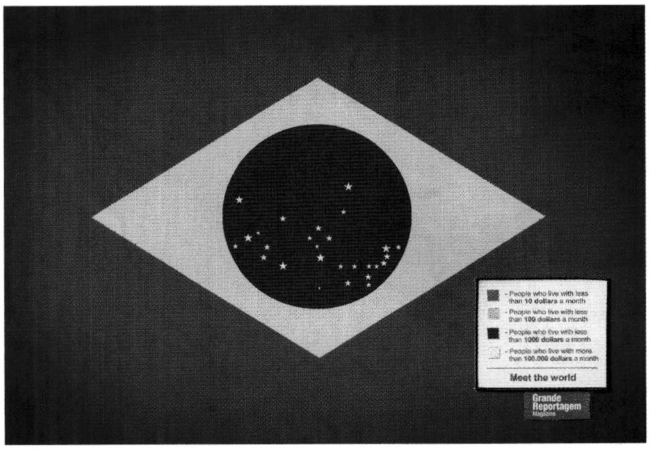

Gold on Gold

client
The Economist

agency:
Abbott Mead Vickers
BBDO / London

05017A

Nigel Roberts
Paul Belford

Twenty years ago, David Abbott started the Economist campaign. And every year since, the brief has come around for the next set of ads and everyone in the AMV creative department has wondered what the hell to do next. Us included. We had some ideas. But we really wanted a big idea. Hmmm, a big idea...a big idea...a big idea...hang on a minute, what if....

client
Smith & Wesson

agency:
Springer & Jacoby /
Hamburg

05020A

Timm Weber

The smaller the target you're aiming at, the better the gun you choose needs to be. So if you want to become the bug shooting champion, you better use a Smith & Wesson. No matter how tiny your target is, with Smith & Wesson precision firearms, you will be always on the spot.

client
Bisley Office Equipment

agency:
Kolle Rebbe / Hamburg

05023A

Andreas Geyer
Ulrich Zünkeler
Ursus Wehrli

Inspired by Bisley's reduced, yet intriguing design and focus on functionality, Kolle Rebbe strived to develop a campaign that was simple, visually appealing, international and with a charming spark — just like its clients products.

Thoroughly immersed in the subject of putting away, tidying up and storing, the same process was adapted to ideas and layouts. Leaving something simple and reduced that reflects Bisley's product philosophy at its best.

client
Y+ Yoga Center

agency:
Leo Burnett / Hong Kong

05026A

Kenny Choo

Bill and Daphne were the two yoga instructors assigned by our client to help us understand this ancient art.

Needing inspiration for the poster, we first got Daphne to do a triangle pose.

That looked way too easy.

Then she tried a Chakrasana or Wheel Pose.

In short, feet spread apart. Inhale. Lift hands over head. Exhale. Bend backwards until palms are flat on the floor, pelvis in the air.

Nice. Very Nice.

Then it was Bill's turn.

"Bill, we just need you to do it once. Great! Thanks."

Then we got Daphne to do it again. And again. And again.

Gold on Gold

client
Weru

agency:
Scholz & Friends /
Berlin

05030A

Jan Leube
Streetfighting dogs, roaring rockers or clumsy dustmen. Thanks to Weru, problems arising from daily noise pollution become insignificant. The visual idea of this campaign had been on our desk for quite some time. But we felt it would be wasted on trivial products like earplugs or hearing aides. So when Germany's leading window manufacturer asked the agency for a campaign to position the brand as a manufacturer of soundproof windows, everything fell into place.

Radio

client
American Legacy Foundation

agency:
Arnold Worldwide / Boston and Crispin Porter + Bogusky / Miami

05001R

Mike Howard
The nicest thing about this spot is that it didn't satisfy any specific brief. There was a brief out there, to be sure. And we made some really great spots that did satisfy the brief. But this wasn't one of them. Instead, we just presented this as another random idea. It was a one-off. It didn't belong anywhere exactly. But our client had a heart for the little wayward radio ad. So they made it, anyhow.

Not many clients are willing to do something like that. Pretty cool.

Thanks guys.

client
National Thoroughbred Racing Association

agency:
DeVito/Verdi /
New York

05005R

Brad Emmett
Lee Seidenberg
We'd like to thank Sal, then God.

WHAT SORT OF MIND DOES IT TAKE TO DISCOVER THE LAW OF GRAVITY?
A TOTALLY DERANGED ONE.

client
Anglican Welfare Council

agency:
Ogilvy & Mather / Singapore

05042A

Tham Khai Meng
Eugene Cheong
"Let us not grow weary while doing good, for in due season we shall reap if we do not lose heart." – St. Paul

Gold on Gold

SHAKING HANDS
SPREADS MORE GERMS
THAN KISSING.

client
Science World

agency:
Rethink / Vancouver

05002T

Rob Sweetman
Rob Tarry
We got to watch girls kiss and won this Pencil.

Thank you, science.

client
Canadian Film
Centreís Worldwide
Short Film Festival

agency:
Taxi / Toronto

05006T

Pete Breton
Dave Douglass
This was the first brief we got at Taxi. It was a daunting task because the agency has always done great work for this client. But after weeks of our creative director riding us like rented mules we shot five spots in one day. Which wasn't too hard because as Ian Heidegger always says: "If you're going to act, act quickly."

client
adidas

agency:
TBWA\Chiat\Day/ San Francisco (180\TBWA)

05008T

Chuck McBride
Tracy McGrady is a scoring machine. He is nearly impossible to stop, even for the NBA's best defenders. "Unstoppable" takes this one step further. The tenacity of T-MAC is shown in a practice setting where he's playing against more than himself, and more than your average defense. As usual, his desire and drive win out, and he defeats an entire army trying to stop him from scoring, which represents all the naysayers and obstacles he's overcome in his career.

client
Honda

agency:
Wieden + Kennedy / London

05009T

W+K Creative Team
The animated "Hate Something, Change Something" ad launched Honda's first-ever diesel engine, by explaining the maverick thinking behind the engine's development, in an equally maverick and unconventional fashion. It promoted a new positive philosophy for life—"Hate Something, Change Something"—which stemmed directly from the way the engine designer used his own hatred of diesel engines to inspire himself to build something better. The whole campaign that followed spanned a wide range of different media platforms, including online gaming, interactive TV, sticker postcards and radio.

client
BC Lions

agency:
Rethink / Vancouver

05015T

Ian Grais
This idea was based on the simple concept of peer pressure. To test the idea we actually went around our office and cheered for people as they performed everyday tasks like stuffing envelopes. We realized that cheering works. Yes we got a lot of strange looks and some counter-aggression, but most of the "cheered" actually tried harder at what they were doing. This commercial along with two others were produced as recreations of this experiment.

client
Ameriquest

agency:
DDB Direct / Los Angeles

05019T

Mark Monteiro
Every campaign seems to have its defining moment. For this campaign, that moment occurred on the day we first presented it to the client. Feh, Pat, Hélène and I had gone in with just a single key frame of a man holding a big, sharp knife in one hand and a bloody cat in the other. As soon as we held up the frame our client started shaking his head furiously and crossing imaginary things out on the paper in front of him. "What were you thinking?" he said. "I can't do that. Are you all crazy?" He had responded exactly as we hoped. Judged too quickly without the facts. When he finally heard the whole commercial, he loved it. The campaign moved forward and here we are today.

client
adidas

agency:
TBWA\Chiat\Day /
San Francisco
(180\TBWA)

05012T

Chuck McBride
adidas has always cut against the grain and celebrated what is truly good about sport. Teamwork, character, honesty and ethics are what this brand admires. Its athletes are cut from a different cloth than Nike, Reebok or And1. Fans will never see Allen Iverson or Dennis Rodman wearing adidas.

The "Impossible Is Nothing" basketball campaign is comprised of the following spots: "Carry," "Unstoppable," and "Made To Perfection." The goal of this campaign was to continue to carve out adidas' perspective in the basketball category, which is to celebrate what's good about the game.

client
VH 1

agency:
la comunidad /
Miami Beach

05023T

Jose Molla
"Siempre nos preguntamos cómo es la verdadera vida de un rockstar. Bueno, así no es."

Translation:
"We always ask ourselves what the real life of a rock star is like. Well, that's not it."

client
Chicago Music Exchange

agency:
Element 79 Partners / Chicago

05026T

Danny Schuman
The owner of the Chicago Music Exchange wanted to separate CME from the Guitar Centers of the world by positioning it as the place for real guitar lovers. So when it came time to shoot, he wanted to make sure the guitar playing was totally awesome and completely legit. No problem since Phil, the guy who plays guitar in this spot, actually works at CME. And while we knew he could play like Hendrix, we didn't know he could act like De Niro.

This spot shows that when you have a group of smart, funny, fearless people infused with boundless passion, you can create work that rocks. Literally.

client
Virgin

agency:
Crispin Porter + Bogusky / Miami

05028T

Andrew Keller
Bill Wright
It started with two simple facts:

1. Virgin Atlantic was launching a new Upper Class Suite featuring the largest fully-flat bed in business class.

2. Aside from the cost of the room, the hotel industry's largest source of revenue comes from selling pay-per-view adult movies.

The first five days "Suite and Innocent" ran on hotel TVs, 46,113 people watched it. (It was the most-viewed title on Lodgenet, beating out "Young Girl Fantasies" by a wide margin)

The average viewing time for "Suite and Innocent" was seven minutes. The average viewing time for all other "Adult Desires" movies? Three minutes.

(A good statistic to have memorized when somebody tells you people don't watch ads anymore.)

client
adidas

agency:
TBWA\Japan / Tokyo (180 TBWA)

05001G

Shintaro Hashimoto
Hirofumi Nakajima
John Merrifield

The client said yes.
The building's management said no.
The building's owners said no.
The police department said no.
The fire department said no.
The public safety authorities said no.
The advertising regulatory body said no.
The ward office said no.
The metropolitan government said no.
The insurance companies said no.
No, no, no, we said.
Impossible is Nothing.

adidas

PLANTS
GROW FASTER
UNDER GLASS
SCIENCE WORLD
Transit shelter filled with living plants

PLANTS
GROW FASTER
UNDER GLASS
SCIENCE WORLD
Week eight

client
Science World

agency:
Rethink / Vancouver

05008G

Rob Sweetman
Rob Tarry
Hylton Mann
Bob Simpson

It's impossible to microwave an ant.

Tigers have striped skin, not just striped fur.

A rat can last without water longer than a camel.

If you tore this page out you couldn't fold it more than seven times.

And, in the time it took you to read this, you lost 15,000 skin cells.

Thanks Science World, you made us nerds.

Gold on Gold

client
Research Surveys

agency
King James RSVP / Cape Town

05001D

Mark Stead
Livio Tronchin
Jenny Ehlers

To celebrate our client Research Surveys' twenty-five years of astounding growth and success, we realized a clever birthday card just would not do. We felt they needed something far more enduring; something that would serve to advertise their company well into the future.

client
Sanyo Shokai

agency
Tugboat / Tokyo

05004D

Seijo Kawaguchi

Our intent was to make Burberry Dots the new icon that would shake up the currently stagnant fashion industry.

While maintaining the DNA of the Burberry Check, we transformed its form and feature into a dot to propel the brand into a more new and challenging arena. Our aim was to develop products where heritage and innovation could be enjoyed simultaneously.

The design concept was invented fairly quickly, but we invested 2 years in the design simulation and product print tests. Such efforts brought us huge success, resulting in successive sellouts from the moment the products hit shelves.

We feel that this award gives us true validation of our work and efforts.

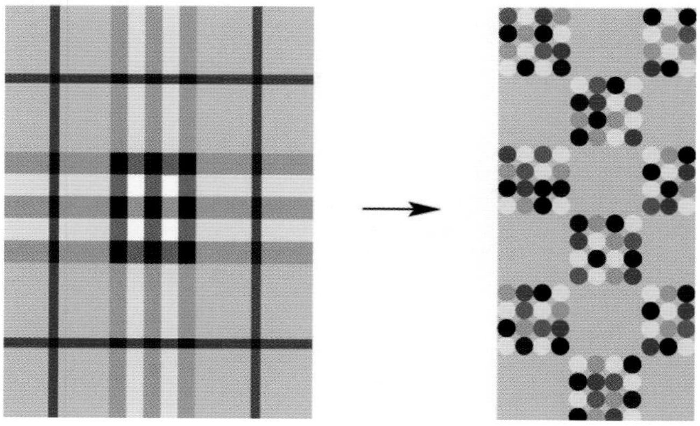

client
Wong CoCo

agency
Kinetic / Singapore

05012D

Roy Poh
Pan Limm

Carolyn (Account Director): Hey guys! We've got a new brief. Here, try this...

Roy (Art Director): Yum! They're juicy and they're shaped like cubes.

Sean (Art Director): Hmm... juicy cubes...let's call it Jubes!

Pann (Art Director): Fantastic! I'll do the logo.

Roy (Art Director): Cool! I'll think of some fun characters.

Alex (Writer): Great! I'll write something good.

Carolyn (Account Director): Ok! That's settled. Let's move on to another brief.

client
French Paper Company

agency
Charles S. Anderson Design / Minneapolis

05016D

Charles S. Anderson

The idea for the French Speckletone and Dur-o-tone posters came about quite naturally. It's actually a pretty obvious solution—vermin and critters with meat, big-eyed girls, and paper dolls. What else?

Jerry French would say, "Those flakey designers at CSA came up with these cute meat-eating critters to promote our butcher paper. I told them, 'How do you explain to your families and friends that you actually sit around and design posters with a giant beaver in work clothes carrying a ham hock, sausage links, and wielding a meat cleaver?' I told them like I always do when they show me a new design idea, 'I don't like it. I don't think it's funny. But go ahead and do it. Damn if all the other flakey designers didn't go crazy for the posters.'"

Roughly 3,000 copies of these posters vanished in the first 15 minutes at the Chicago Annual Report Show, leaving Jerry French with an empty booth and a puzzled look on his face.

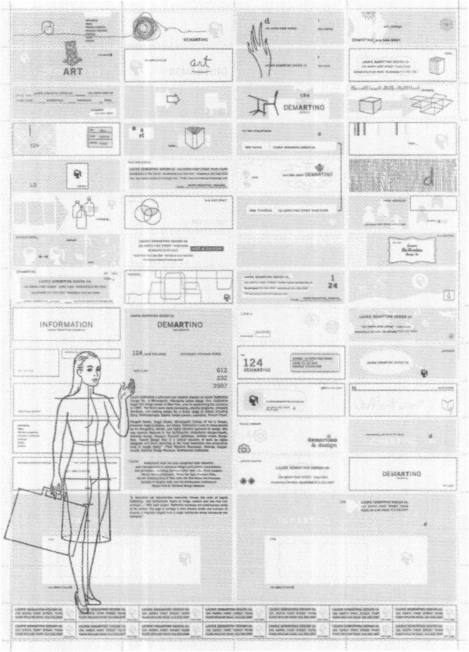

client
Laurie DeMartino Design

agency
Laurie DeMartino Design / Minneapolis

05021D

Laurie DeMartino
A move to a new building created the need for new stationery. The new system centers around the "art" in DeMartino, and these multi-use labels were designed to reinforce this. Sixty-eight gummed labels are used to seal envelopes and packages, to identify presentation boards, as mailing labels, etc.

They were combined and printed as one large sheet, in order to also form this poster which was used as the moving announcement. Letterpress printed, 18"x 24".

client
Vier Pfoten e.V. Foundation for Animal Welfare

agency
Springer & Jacoby / Hamburg

05024D

Tom Hilverkus
A suitcase leads a happy life. It gets to travel around, sees the world and only occasionally has to spend a couple of hours in a locker. A chicken's life isn't that exciting. It is cramped into a cage with no opportunity of ever getting out of there. We want to change that.

At train stations, surprised travellers were confronted with an unusual comparison. Posters on lockers pointed out clearly: any suitcase is better off than 35 million hens.

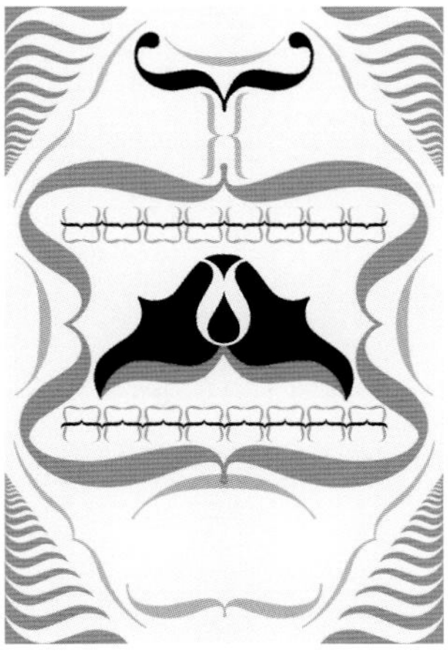

client
Neenah Paper

agency
And Partners / New York

05027D

David Schimmel
"Punc't: Putting Punctuation in its Place," a set of 24 limited-edition serigraphs, began when I invited a host of celebrated, iconoclastic designers each to turn a given punctuation mark into a creative statement for a worthy cause. Tom Wright, Director of Strategic Advertising for Neenah Paper, got behind the project as a distinctive paper promotion. Books for Kids, a New York based children's literacy charity, became the beneficiary. In building a bridge between the visual and the verbal, the ridiculous and the sublime, these artists elevated "Punc't" to an award-winning lesson in irony, humor and the transformative power of imagination.

client
Rheingold Beer

agency
Powell / New York

05028D

Neil Powell
No one had ever utilized New York's nightshades for anything other than vandalism, and the uniqueness of the project ultimately benefited the agency, our client, our artists, the store owners, and downtown New Yorkers as well. Its freshness as a medium appealed to our traditionally "advertising averse" audience, enhancing the delivery of our "Don't Sleep" campaign message and gathering larger groups of Rheingold fans. Our artists benefited by gaining exposure for their work in the new medium. And the store owners benefited as well, since graffiti taggers who might otherwise vandalize their nightshades would refrain, leaving the new artful shades untouched out of respect for our artists work. Finally, as we convert more and more shades into canvases, we like to think we're changing the downtown landscape and the New Yorker experience by encouraging everyone to find art in unexpected places everyday.

client
School of Visual Arts

agency
School of Visual Arts/Advertising & Graphic Design Dept. / New York

05031D

Richard Wilde
In order to best represent the Graphic Design and Advertising Department at the School of Visual Arts, we created a series of books that function as a compendium of the best senior work for the Class of 2003. The intent was to position the school as a leading creative institution, both nationally and internationally. What is particularly unique about this publication is that two of the books work in tandem, one all words, the other just images. The activity of going from one book to another creates a unique experience that signals the new.

client
Pie Books

agency
Hakuhodo / Tokyo

05033D

Chie Morimoto
Normally, dictionaries (jisho) are supposed to give clear definitions and usages of the listed words.

We had a different idea; In case of onomatopoetic (giongo) and mimetic(gitaigo) words, their subtle indication, nuances and meanings should be much more susceptible to the facts like who is saying these words, when they are heard, and in what mood they are uttered. In this context, why don't we have a new approach in compiling a dictionary?

Based on this thought, we wanted to create a dictionary, "giongo gitaigo jisho," that stimulates you to start having richer, wilder and expanded images of the words, not just that usual, narrowly defined explanation.

Because the resulted volume is compiled with a lot of stunning photos, illustration and short stories inspired by each word, "giongo gitaigo jisho" is a dictionary with a completely new idea and format.

We hope this dictionary will give richer images of each word, as well as help expand the power of your imagination. Starting from what we did here, why don't you create your own images?

BE WORK, B

LET THERE BE WORK, BREAD, WATER AND SALT FOR ALL
WORK
2005
SALT
-NELSON MANDELA-

client
Pro Helvetia (Swiss Arts Council)

agency
Daddy buy me a Pony (a 9November Union Company) / Cape Town

05036D

Peet Pienaar
This mailer is for Pro Helvetia, the Swiss arts council operating in the Southern Africa. The brief was to create a postcard that would communicate the events of the following year in a way that people will keep and display it. We created a postcard that folds open into an urban African poster that has a message from Nelson Mandela flocked in green velvet.

client
Diesel

agency
Lobo / São Paulo

05040D

Loic Dubois
Hanging out after work, three of Lobo's artists started a collective drawing activity. On a single piece of paper they let their minds wander, getting inspiration from one another's drawings and keeping a continuous flow of hand-drawn graphics. They named this collective free-association session "Josh", after their own subconscious reasons.

The odd figure combinations this technique creates resemble hypnagogic images from the intermediate consciousness of some periods of sleep. Hence, it fit perfectly the concept of the Diesel Dreams project, which was all about the dreaming experience.

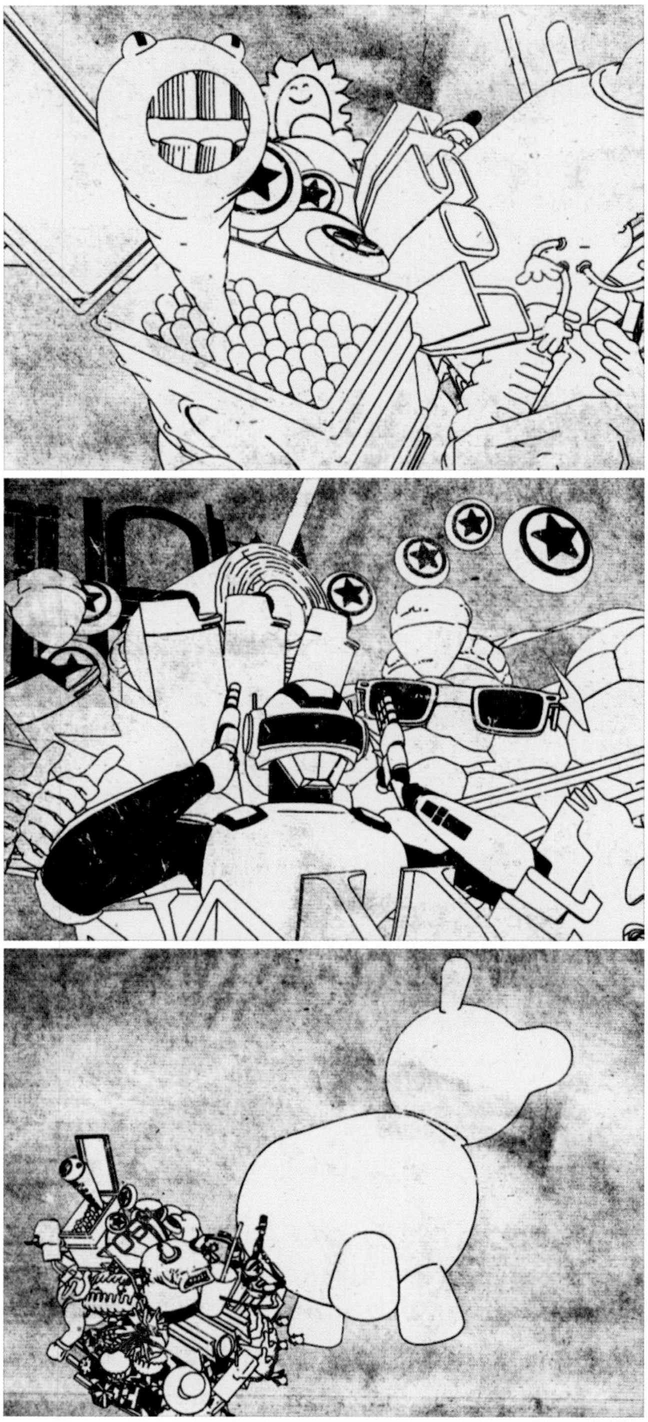

client
MTV Design

agency
MTV Networks / New York

05044D

Jeffrey Keyton
Romy Mann

This character was born on a summer weekend in the countryside when Clay woke up singing and dancing. Lena caught Clay on tape, shooting the first of these spots, which aired on the 2003 Video Music awards. They went on to develop this character into the Intro-guy campaign, which Clay wrote and performed in and Lena directed. In this campaign, "Intro guy" is animated by the joy of living, but otherwise unburdened with the angst of adolescence and content to amuse himself with his hobbies and crafts. His love of music and dancing take priority over every aspect of his life.

1 = black
Help us keep life colourful. Oro Verde. The Rainforest Foundation

client
OroVerde Rainforest Foundation

agency
Ogilvy & Mather / Frankfurt

05048D

Lars Huvart
Helmut Himmler

Sometimes it pays not to have the money for a shoot.

Judge's Choice

Eugene Cheong

Andy Fackrell

Sean Doyle

Kara Goodrich

Eugene Cheong • Ogilvy/Singapore
My favorite was Honda's "Grrr." It had a jingle. It had happy dancing animals. It was "warm and friendly."

It had all the hallmarks of a really awful pre-Bernbach TV commercial, but the Honda film went up to heaven and spat at the stars who made the rules.

Sean Doyle • Campbell Doyle Dye/London
It passes the most important test: it has a look and feel entirely of its own. See a half-second clip of it and you know it's the Honda ad. Hear a half-second snippet and you know it's the Honda ad.

It's uplifting. It changes the way you think about car advertising. It's braver than anything else by a mile because an idea like that could so easily have been naff—a jingle, bright pretty colors, and it's about diesel engines. It shouldn't be good, should it?

There must have been other ideas in the creative department that seemed less risky on paper. I'm glad they remained on paper.

Andy Fackrell • 180 Amsterdam
Honda's "Grrr." There was some cleverly planned, alternative media work that stood out, but in the end I felt this one brilliant TV spot was the most memorable and enjoyable highlight of the week. A jingle with cutesy animation wins it for me.

Kara Goodrich • BBDO/New York
The Burger King "Chicken Fight" work is great. The Virgin Mobile work is great. And, there was a print ad for Nike where France was re-named "Lance." I loved that, too. But, for me in the end, nothing was as inspired as the notion of hating something better.

Porky Hefer • Lowe Bull/Cape Town
Very brave of Honda to move so far from the winning formula of last year with "Cog." No appearance of car advertising's traditional leafy lane and no sheet metal; overall, it gives me a great feeling of anarchy. Animation is fantastic and very original. Soundtrack is very catchy and found myself humming the tune the whole way back on the plane, even before the beers. Big up to all those involved in the origination, production, selling and buying of this little masterpiece. Hopefully Honda can set an example that will be followed by more clients but not sure whether many of them have the balls.

We asked our judges: What rocked this year?

Porky Hefer

Kirk Souder

Joaquin Mollá • la comunidad/Miami Beach
I like the Honda spot. And for me it's even stronger after "Cog" and "Everyday." It's obvious that they are taking the brand to one of "those" places. The difference between shooting spots or writing history.

I also want to mention the Burger King stuff. To choose one: The chicken fight. I spent twelve minutes watching two chickens fighting for no reason and I loved it. I had fun. Something difficult to achieve with two sandwiches in your brief.

It's always inspiring to see big brands investing in great ideas with a great strategy behind them.

Calvin Soh • Fallon/Singapore
My favorite piece of work this year was Honda's "Grrr."

It could have been another shallow ad about having the cleanest diesel engine. But instead, it digs deep into Honda's philosophy and tells us why it's cleaner. It was both a great strategy and a great idea. And the way it was executed is eminently entertaining, deceptively simple and fresh. It was inspirational and at the same time, made us go "Grrr...." Well deserved.

Joaquin Mollá

Monica Taylor

Kirk Souder • Granite Pass / Topanga
My favorite was the Honda "Grrr" spot.

I tried to think about what I could write to explain why, but it's the kind of work that explanations just don't cut it for.

It's my favorite because it makes me feel the way the desert bloom in the Mojave makes me feel.

There. That's the best I can do.

Monica Taylor • Wieden+Kennedy/Portland
My choice would be Honda's "Grrr".

Diesels are ugly and they sound bad. Car advertising is formulaic. Honda was unloved by the public. "Grrr" changed all of that. And it had the nerve to do it while being spot-on for the brand. It's fun and playful, but rooted in crisp smarts. It's crazy good in idea and execution. Sometimes after a bad meeting, I watch it. It cheers me up about advertising. And there are bunnies in it. I fear I may hate them, for jealousy.

Calvin Soh

Oliver Voss

Oliver Voss • Jung von Matt/Berlin
Even if it's boring, because it was voted "Best of Show," I am in love with the Honda ad. Here is why:

1. When I first saw it on the SHOTS reel it immediately blew me away. I was working on some car commercials for MINI on the moment and I had to admit—this stuff is so much better than the stuff I am doing right now.
2. The tender tone, the soft not-selling attitude, the courage to sing a song (man, you can do it so wrong), it's love for the detail and the strategy. Just a perfect mix.
3. I especially love it, because Honda did it. We all know how hard it is to do something brilliant this year and face a new brief in the year after. What the creatives did here is not to follow the successful road of "Cog" and the "collage"—they started from scratch. Everything is different. But still it works amazingly well for the brand. (I hope I don't sound too much like an account guy.) It's the Wieden+Kennedy way at it's best: Never give them what they expect.
4. I predict it will not only be Best of Show at the Clios, but also the Grand Prix in Cannes. And in Ghana and Estonia—if they enter it there.

Judge's Choice

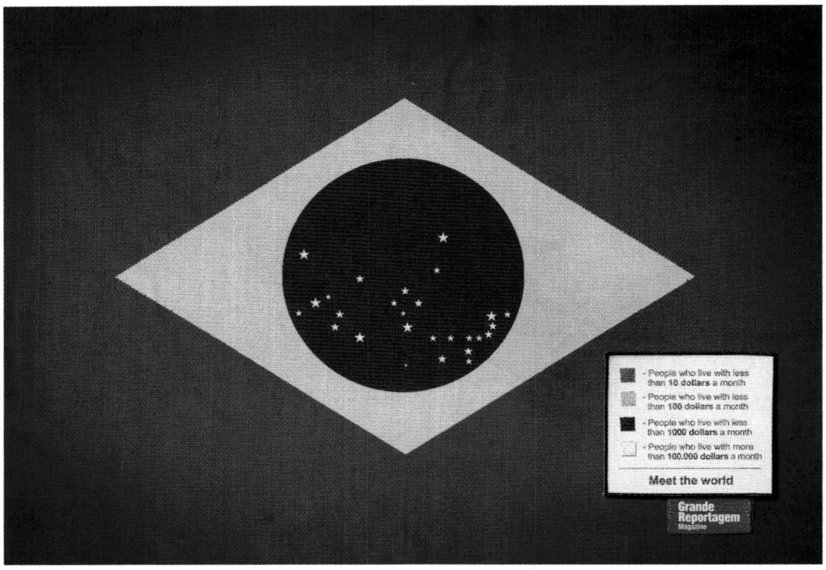

Ian Grais

David Crawford

David Crawford • GSD&M / Austin
The Grande Reportagem magazine campaign featuring flags from around the world. These ads were a real highlight for me. A simple, striking and innovative idea that was produced well and beautifully done. I thought it was an extremely powerful way to make a point. Very memorable. I was envious.

Ian Grais • Rethink/Vancouver
It's hard to stand out from 14,000 ads. This campaign for Grande Reportagem stopped me in my tracks and actually caused me to look around to see if any of the other judges were as impressed as I was. Maybe it was the naturally bold flag graphics, or the beautifully textural photographs, or the interesting color legends. Or maybe it was the surprising copy and shocking statistics, or possibly the smart positioning line. Or how all these details were ingeniously combined to make a beautifully quick, smart, powerful and thought-provoking campaign that we haven't seen the last of I'm sure. Damn, I wish I'd done that.

Marcos Madeiras

Marcos Madeiras • DDB/Sao Paulo
Grande Reportagem. In my opinion it is the best at One Show.

In a nutshell it's smart, well executed and simple, besides that it was competing within a very tough category.

Ann Hayden

Ann Hayden • Saatchi & Saatchi/New York
Ultimately my favorite is the Soken dvd work out of Thailand. It's one of those ideas that feels so simple, you can't believe you hadn't done it yourself. But you hadn't. I hadn't, anyway. And the spots are really well executed. No heavy hand. Perfect timing. It's work like this that makes me want to go d-d-d-d-d-d-d-d-d-d-dancing.

Margaret Johnson

Margaret Johnson • Goodby Silverstein and Partners/San Francisco
My favorite campaign from this year's One Show is the work from Fallon NY for Virgin Mobile. It's a retail campaign and it's good...really good. I have to imagine that when you get the assignment for advertising free music ringtones, you're not jumping up and down for joy, and yet these guys made it truly memorable.

Taking the everyday, mundane conversations that people have on cell phones and singing them is hilarious – stupid-funny – and like nothing else on the air. I love that the cell phone owners are an awkward distance apart and facing camera rather than facing one another. It helps the viewer visualize them on the phone together. I also like that the spots are locked off and shot in one take. Finally, the line "For the love of music." ties up the idea perfectly.

John Jay • Wieden+Kennedy/Tokyo
For any contemporary person, the debate and navel gazing concerning "above the line vs. below the line" creativity or what constitutes advertising is no longer a relevant question. I looked forward to the One Show for insights on the advancement of the concept that any great idea can be "advertising". From 2-D to 3-D to virtual, from analog to digital to bricks and mortar, we have never enjoyed so many creative opportunities to excel.

Yet, what inspired me at this year's One Show was television...especially when executed through an insightful idea with craftsmanship (remember that concept?) but with very little money. The Chicago Music Exchange campaign, winner in the "under $50,000" category, reminded us all that being passionate about your client's business—in this case music—is more powerful than any production value.

John Jay

Judge's Choice

Olivier Altmann

Olivier Altmann • Publicis/Paris

Personally, my favorite ad at the One Show was not an ad but an idea. For Virgin Atlantic and created by CP+B, the ad was in itself good; however, the idea was great. With the aim of selling Virgin's Business Class to businessmen, the agency scrapped the idea of using the traditional business newspapers or TV channels and opted for something different entirely. The agency decided to think outside the box in terms of media, choosing to advertise in the private pay per view TV channels in hotels. Specifically speaking, in the porn section. But why on Earth would a businessman pay to see a Virgin Atlantic commercial? Well, quite simply, he wouldn't. They presented the advertisement not as an ad, but as a free erotic program! So every man (or woman) would have the opportunity to watch it without being charged. What the audience discovered was a funny parody of a porn movie, with the standard actress with the big breasts, presenting all the benefits of Virgin Airways. Every plus proposed by the company, from the chauffeur who picks you up in the luxury sedan to the wide business chair, was included in the erotic story in a clever and funny way. What better contact can you have with a brand and what's more, if it succeeded to "give you pleasure" whilst watching it!

Tay Guan-Hin • JWT/Malaysia

Popcorn has always been associated with watching movies in the cinemas but pizza has always been associated with watching videos at home. So how come nobody has ever thought of putting these two things together until now?

I really wish I'd done this campaign.

Its simplicity stood out in the multitude of the other ads. Since it's flawlessly retouched I could hardly pick a bone with the art direction. The look was kept to such a minimum that even the product shot was seamlessly integrated into the idea. The team was smart in picking an era of movies that brought out the nostalgia of black & white. My favorite, the "Psycho" execution, is particularly funny as it fits in quite nicely with home delivery. Well done to the team! I'm sure it'll do brilliantly elsewhere.

Tay Guan-Hin

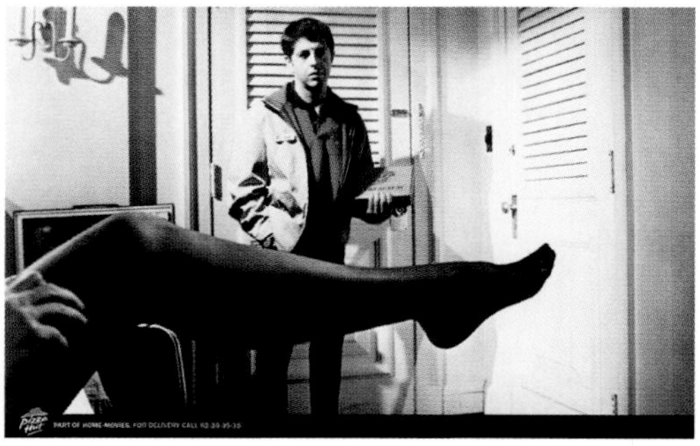

Mike Hughes • The Martin Agency/Richmond
It didn't win any Pencils, but the Hewlett-Packard Picture Book campaign from Goodby, Silverstein & Partners was, in America at least, the campaign of the year for 2004. It was charming, it rewarded repeat viewings like few campaigns in the history of the business, and it made HP seem like a leader in digital photography. I have no idea why my fellow judges don't share my enthusiasm. I suspect that industry people merely like the campaign, but that "real" people love it.

Mike Hughes

Harry Cocciolo

Harry Cocciolo • Tool/Santa Monica
I really like last year's work for the new Sprint calling plan. The one where kids are asked how long they plan to play with a soccer ball, or told that they went over on their "macaroni minutes." The ridiculous premise of each scene calls into question the ridiculous complexity of most calling plans. This work makes me think Sprint might know a better way and I like the company for having a sense of humor. And just think about the brief. This is no small task. This is not sexy stuff. It's a complicated, painfully dry subject. Yet the work is simple, human, even fun. In certain Olympic competitions, athletes are judged not only on their performance, but on the difficulty of the elements they perform. In our business, this subject, despite being well conceived and executed, doesn't even get in the book.

Judge's Choice

Laura Fegley • Cliff Freeman and Partners/New York

Here's how I imagine this could have gone:

- There's this great idea that would capture people's imaginations and make the philosophy of the brand literally come to life.
- Everyone agrees this is a very cool idea.
- Unfortunately, it involves dangling people off the side of a building, 50 stories up.
- Everyone agrees that, of course, this would be cool, but you can't really do that.
- Everyone moves on to the print ideas.
- Impossible is nothing.

Laura Fegley

Allison Williams
J. Philip Williams

Allison Williams and J. Philip Williams • Design MW/New York
We choose Tugboat's Burberry because of the wonderful breadth of skills it showcased. From the abstract reconfiguration of the signature pattern, to the compelling design artifact oversized brochure, this project was well thought out and nicely detailed. The brochure was especially interesting in its translation of the British language of Burberry to a Japanese market.

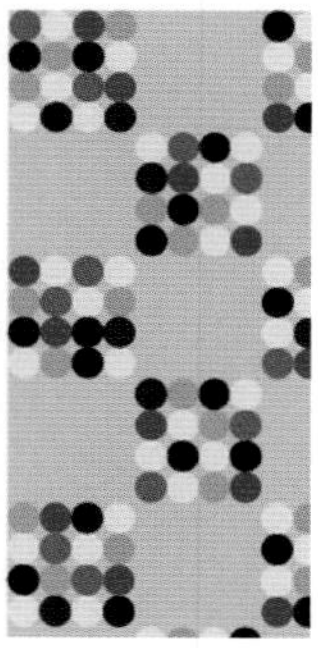

Charles S. Anderson • Charles S. Anderson Design/Minneapolis

On one hand, it may seem a bit self-serving to select Laurie DeMartino's identity system as my judge's choice. And I admit that I may be a little biased due to the fact that she's my wife. But on the other hand, by not selecting this incredible identity, I would be guilty of reverse discrimination. The excruciatingly high level of craft, the tweaky finessed typography, the appropriate appropriation of the postage stamp aesthetic, the design and functionality of the pieces both individually and as a whole, the pure and flawless expression of Laurie's personal aesthetic, and the tactile impression of letterpress printing make this a warm and very human identity system that stands out in stark contrast to the trendy faux modernist style that is already turning generic, growing cold, and fading out just like it did the first time around.

Charles S. Anderson

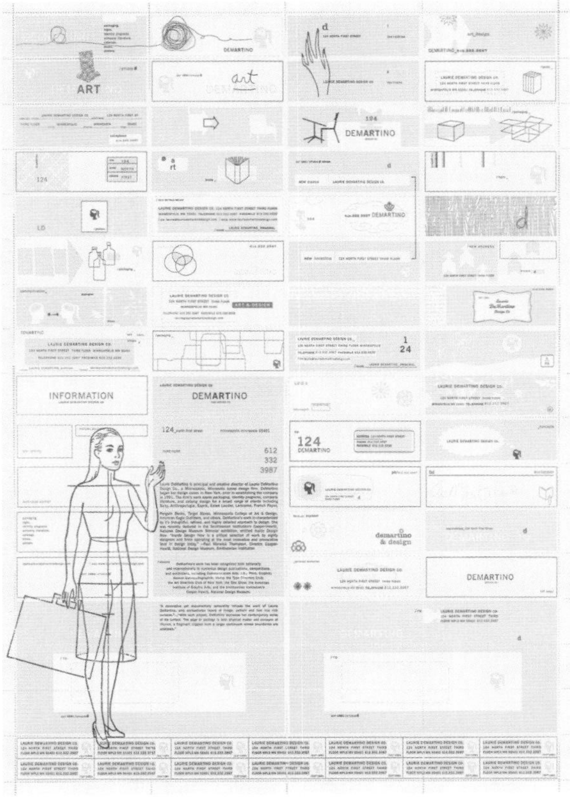

Judge's Choice

Judge's Choice

Kit Hinrichs

Kit Hinrichs • Pentagram/San Francisco

Maybe it was my reading of "Eats, Shoots and Leaves" by Lynne Truss, that focused my attention on "Punc't" by And Partners NY for Neenah Paper Company.

No fussy, typographic nuance, no hot photographers or illustrators, no cool new paper or print technique—just the simple clarity of a good idea, appropriate to the audience and executed to perfection.

The elegance of elevating the lowly period, the misunderstood semicolon, the overused comma, and all their friends in a two color poster series is challenge enough, but taking on the cat herding aspect of asking 20 designers to each complete a poster by a deadline goes over the top.

It's my judge's choice for this year.

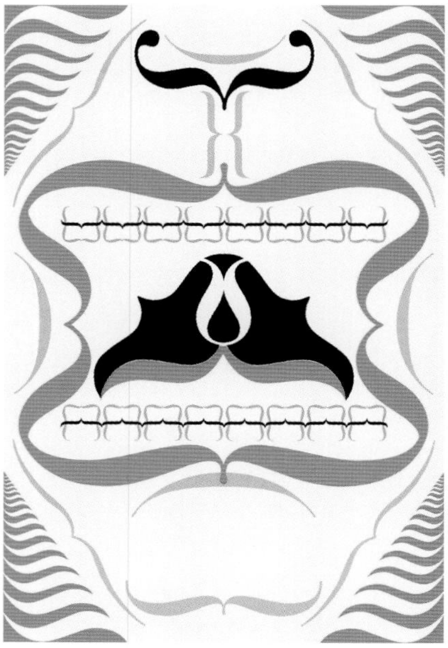

Laurie DeMartino • Laurie DeMartino Design/Minneapolis
I always learn something from the shows that I judge. Sometimes from the entries themselves, and many times from the jurors who each have their own opinions and views. This year's entries reflected an extraordinary collection of work from all corners of the world. Two outstanding international entries that come to mind are Hakuhodo's book entitled "Giongo Gitaigo Jisho," a thoughtfully illustrated dictionary, tastefully executed on each and every page; and Tugboat's progressive rebranding campaign for Burberry, with its striking photographs and dramatic oversized brochure.

Laurie DeMartino

two Dimensions
of Evil
Print Merit

art directors
Daryl Corps
Paul Young

writer
Ben Kay

creative directors
Paul Belford
Nigel Roberts

client
The Economist

agency
Abbott Mead Vickers
BBDO / London

05047A

art directors
Alex Lim Thye Aun
Ali Shabaz

writers
Ali Shabaz
Alex Lim Thye Aun

photographers
Anuchai (Remix Studio)
Teo (Teo Studio)

illustrators
Sin Eng Lee
Procolor

creative director
Francis Wee

client
Pfizer

agency
BBDO / Singapore

05048A

art director
Todd Mackie

writer
Denise Rossetto

photographer
Patrick Nichols

creative directors
William Hammond
Andrew Simon

client
Energizer

agency
DDB / Toronto

05049A

Also Awarded:
merit
P.O.P and In-Store:
Single

art directors
Björn Löper
Arnaud Loix van Hooff

writers
Lina Jachmann
Björn Bremer

photographer
Cecil Arp

creative directors
Alexander Weber-Grün
Bastian Kuhn

client
Volkswagen

agency
DDB / Berlin

05052A

Merit

CONSUMER NEWSPAPER : OVER 600 LINES — SINGLE

CONSUMER NEWSPAPER : OVER 600 LINES — SINGLE

art director
Björn Löper

writer
Lina Jachmann

photographer
Cecil Arp

creative director
Alexander Weber-Grün
Bastian Kuhn

client
Volkswagen

agency
DDB / Berlin

05051A

Kids need space. Sharan.

art directors
Mikko Timonen
Johan Eghammer
Anders Eklind

writer
Jacob Nelson

designer
Jerry Wass

photographer
Jäger Arén

client
Volvo

agency
Forsman & Bodenfors / Gothenburg

05053A

THE NEW VOLVO S60 WITH PARKING ASSISTANCE.
VOLVO
for life

art directors
Rodrigo Campos
Saulo Arruda

writer
Luiz Haruo

photographer
Andre Faccioli

creative directors
Atila Francucci
Alexandre Soares
Fernando Nobre
Joao Linneu

client
Pfizer

agency
J. Walter Thompson / São Paulo

05054A

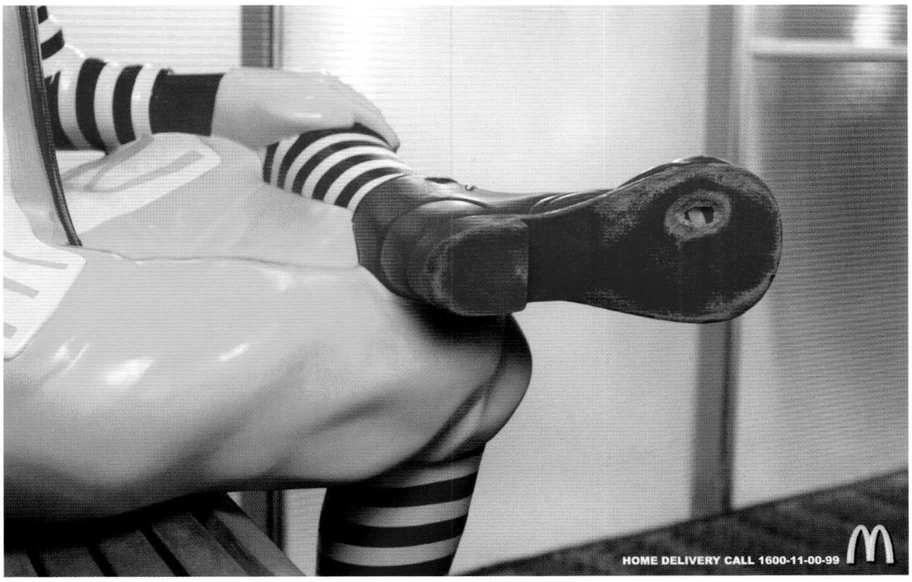

art director
Santosh Padhi

writer
Santosh Padhi

photographer
Sanjeev Angne

illustrator
Bhushan Patil

creative directors
K.V. Sridhar
Agnello Dias
Santosh Padhi

client
McDonald's

agency
Leo Burnett / Mumbai

05056A

CONSUMER NEWSPAPER : OVER 600 LINES — SINGLE

art director
Adam Livesey

writer
Matthew Brink

photographers
Janyon & Camera

creative directors
Rob McLennan
Stuart Walsh

client
Unilever - Axe

agency
Lowe Bull / Bryanston

05057A

art director
Mariana O'Kelly

writer
Gary Du Toit

creative director
Mike Schalit

client
The Economist

agency
Net#Work BBDO /
Hyde Park

05058A

RENAULT
Modus. The only compact car with 5 stars on the Euro NCAP crashtests.

art director
Pascale Gayraud

writer
Fabrice Dubois

photographer
Herv Plumet

creative directors
Olivier Altmann
Herv Plumet

client
Renault

agency
Publicis Conseil / Paris

05059A

Improves memory.

art directors
Ong Shi Ping
Gavin Simpson

writers
Ong Shi Ping
Gavin Simpson

photographer
Mak Kah Heng /
Untold Images

creative director
Gavin Simpson

client
Cerebos

agency
Young & Rubicam /
Kuala Lumpur

05065A

Also Awarded:
merit
P.O.P. and In-Store:
Single

art director
Paul Brazier

writer
Paul Brazier

photographer
Robin Broadbent

illustrator
Mark Elwood

creative director
Paul Brazier

client
Guinness

agency
Abbott Mead Vickers
BBDO / London

050666A

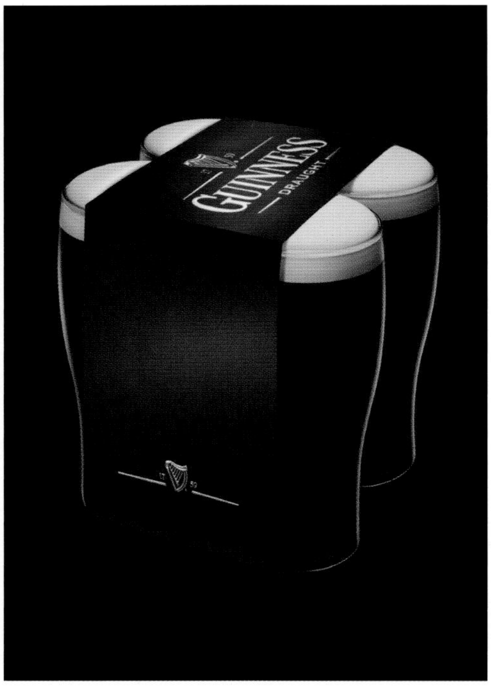

art director
Andreas Böhm

writer
Andreas Böhm

photographer
Pack Shot Boys

creative directors
Mathias Stiller
Wolfgang Schneider

client
Henkel

agency
DDB / Berlin

05067A

Also Awarded:
merit
Consumer Newspaper
Over 600 Lines: Single

< Merit >

For boys who were always men.
The new Golf GTI.

< Merit >

For boys who were always men.
The new Golf GTI.

art directors
Sandra Schilling
Andreas Böhm
Michael Janke

writers
Ulrich Lützenkirchen
Ilja Schmuschkowitsch

photographer
F.A. Cesar

illustrator
Djamila Rabenstein

creative directors
Amir Kassaei
Wolfgang Schneider
Mathias Stiller

client
Volkswagen

agency
DDB / Berlin

05068A

Also Awarded:
merit
Consumer Magazine
Color: Full Page: Single

merit
Consumer Magazine
Color: Full Page:
Campaign

For boys who were always men.
The new Golf GTI.

For boys who were always men.
The new Golf GTI.

One Show

CONSUMER NEWSPAPER : OVER 600 LINES — CAMPAIGN

art directors
Justin Tindall
(Camouflage, Lipstick)
Lovisa Almgren
(Winter Garden)

writers
Adam Tucker
(Camouflage, Lipstick)
Matt Lee (Camouflage)
Ben Wade
(Winter Garden)

photographers
Colin Campbell
(Lipstick)
Me Company
(Winter Garden)

illustrator
Peter Mould
(Camouflage)

creative director
Andrew Fraser

client
The Guardian

agency
DDB / London

05069A

THE UGLY SIDE OF
BEAUTY PRODUCTS
'Chemical World' a three part investigation
into the hidden dangers of modern living
Starts next Saturday
The Guardian

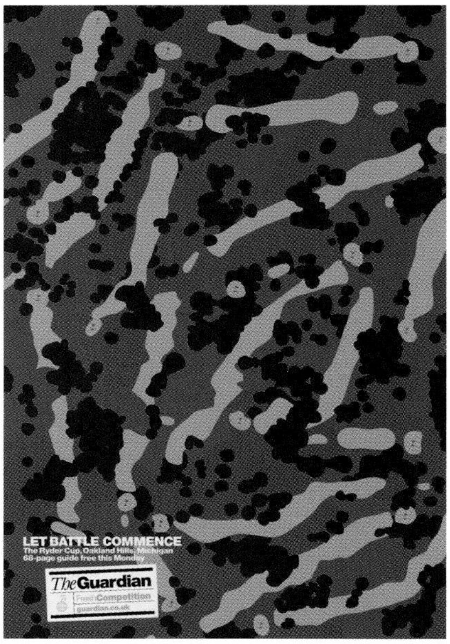
LET BATTLE COMMENCE
The Ryder Cup, Oakland Hills, Michigan
68-page guide free this Monday
The Guardian
Competition
guardian.co.uk

WINTER GARDENING
Tips and advice every Saturday
in Weekend
The Guardian
Look
guardian.co.uk

art director
Kris Ng

writer
Priscilla Swee

illustrator
Tan Keng Wee

creative director
Robert Gaxiola

client
Samsung

agency
Foote Cone & Belding / Singapore

05070A

Merit

CONSUMER NEWSPAPER : OVER 600 LINES — CAMPAIGN

CONSUMER NEWSPAPER : OVER 600 LINES — CAMPAIGN

art director
Mikkel Jangaard

writer
Niels Thomsen

photographer
Mikkel Jangaard

client
Metro

agency
Grey / Copenhagen

05071A

Metro
Rush through town without stress

Metro
Rush through town without stress

Metro

< Merit >

< Merit (2) >

art directors
Tan Chee Keong
Brian Capel

writer
Donevan Chew

photographer
Allen Dang
(Wizard Photography)

illustrator
Simon Ong

creative directors
Chan Lee Shon
Alex Lim

client
PetsUnite

agency
Leo Burnett /
Kuala Lumpur

05072A

Also Awarded:

merit
Collateral
Posters: Single

merit
Collateral
Posters: Single

merit
Consumer Newspaper:
Over 600 Lines: Single

Merit

One Show

CONSUMER NEWSPAPER : OVER 600 LINES — CAMPAIGN

art director
Gareth Lessing

writer
Xander Smith

creative director
Rob McLennan

client
Pentel

agency
Lowe Bull / Bryanston

05073A

The built the pyramids.
You'll never know

is the truth about Roswell.
You'll never know

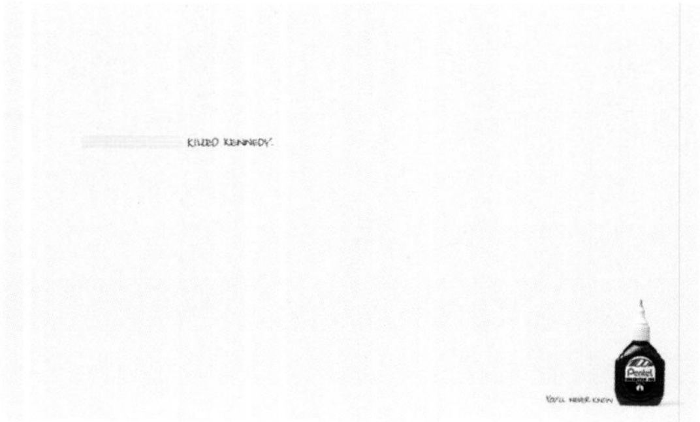
KILLED KENNEDY.

THE WERE FIRST TO LAND ON THE MOON.

< Merit >

< Merit >

art directors
Szymon Rose
Jonathan Schupp

illustrator
Szymon Rose

creative directors
Toygar Bazarkaya
Stefan Meske

client
Mercedes-Benz

agency
Springer & Jacoby /
Hamburg

05074A

Also Awarded:

merit
Consumer Newspaper
Over 600 Lines: Single

merit
Consumer Newspaper
Over 600 Lines: Single

Merit

CONSUMER NEWSPAPER : OVER 600 LINES — CAMPAIGN

One Show

CONSUMER NEWSPAPER : OVER 600 LINES — CAMPAIGN

art director
Mark Bamfield

writer
Jasun Vare

photographers
Groovy Studio
Getty Images

creative directors
Mark Bamfield
Jasun Vare

client
Sphere

agency
TBWA \ Singapore

05075A

SPHERE 1/6th ACTION FIGURES.
AS REAL AS IT GETS.

SPHERE 1/6th ACTION FIGURES.
AS REAL AS IT GETS.

ER
SPHERE 1/6th ACTION FIGURES.
AS REAL AS IT GETS.
WWW.SPHEREMARKETING.NET

art director
Brent Singer

photographer
Rob Frew

creative director
Paul Warner

client
Masterfoods/Pedigree

agency
TBWA\Hunt\Lascaris / Sandton

05076A

Merit

CONSUMER NEWSPAPER : OVER 600 LINES — CAMPAIGN

art director
Vidi Sibilla

writer
Rodrigo Ruiz

illustrator
Hugo Horita

creative directors
Guillermo Vega
Pablo Capara
Sebastián Olivieri

client
Visa Argentina

agency
Y&R / Buenos Aires

05077A

Also Awarded:
merit
Consumer Newspaper:
600 Lines or Less: Single

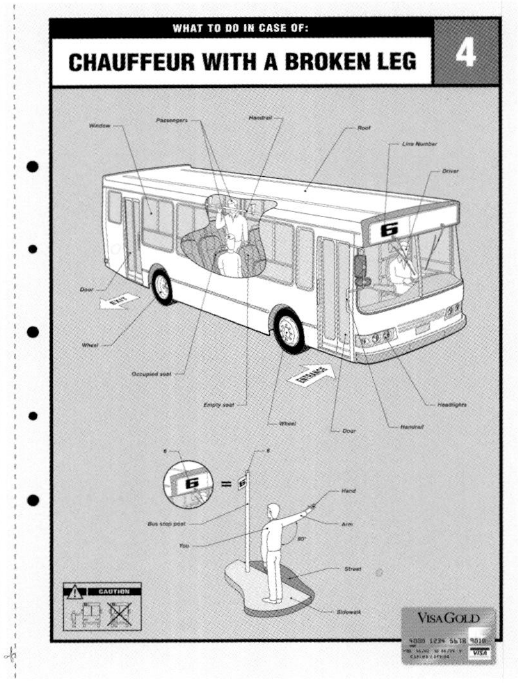

< Merit >

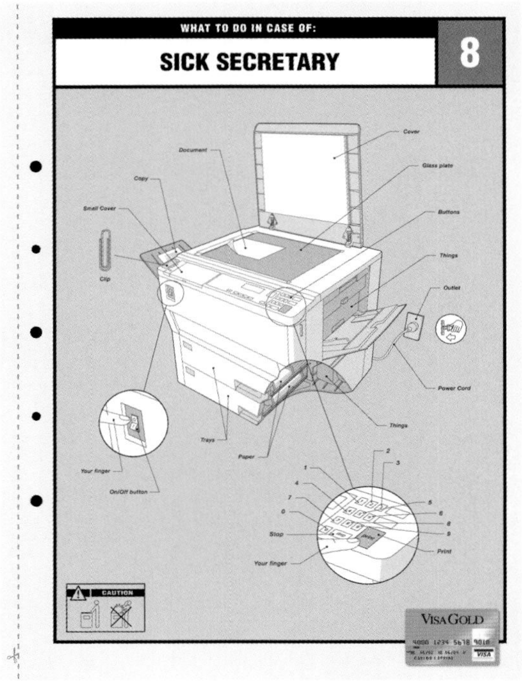

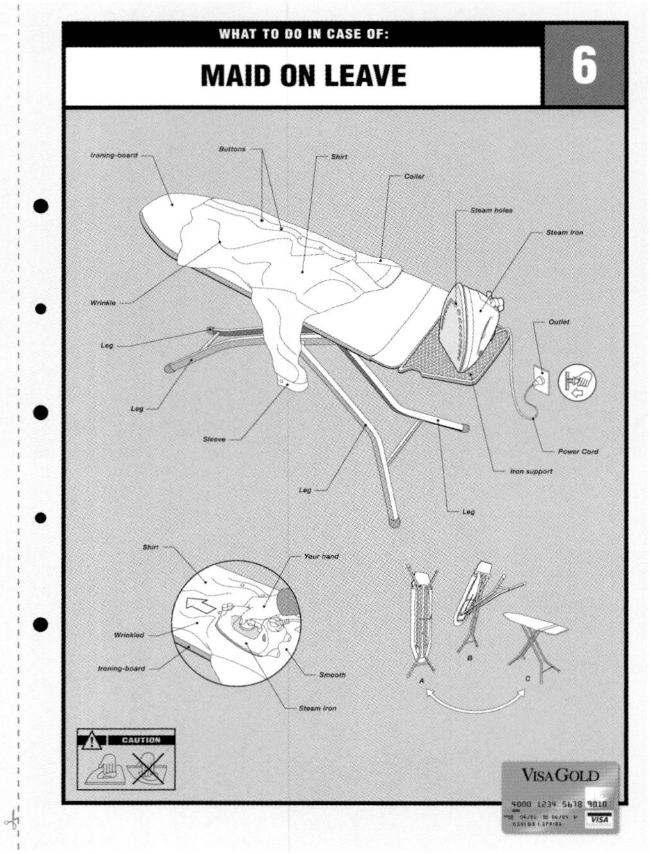

IT ALL STARTS WITH A GOOD GUITAR
Dan's Chelsea Guitars inc.
220 W 23 NYC NY 10011 • CHELSEAGUITARS.COM

art director
David Cuccinello

writer
Bob Cohen

photographer
Emily Wilson

creative director
Kevin Roddy

client
Chelsea Guitars

agency
Euro RSCG / New York

05078A

Also Awarded:
merit
P.O.P. and In-Store: Single

art director
Alan Vladusic

writer
Clay Weiner

photographer
Simon Harsent

creative directors
Duncan Marshall
Howard Willmott

client
Allied Domecq

agency
Publicis / New York

05081A

Merit

CONSUMER NEWSPAPER : 600 LINES OR LESS — SINGLE

One Show

CONSUMER NEWSPAPER : 600 LINES OR LESS — SINGLE

art director
Alan Vladusic

writer
Clay Weiner

photographer
Simon Harsent

creative directors
Duncan Marshall
Howard Willmott

client
Allied Domecq

agency
Publicis / New York

05080A

art director
Michael Bond

writer
Bernard Hunter

photographer
Simon Harsent

creative director
David Corr

client
Procter & Gamble - Pepto

agency
Publicis / New York

05082A

art director
Vinayak Gaikwad

writer
Vinayak Gaikwad

creative directors
Elsie Nanji
Pushpinder Singh

client
Western Union Money Transfer

agency
Ambience Publicis / Mumbai

05084A

art director
Jason Musante

writer
Jon Wagner

creative director
David Baldwin

client
Classic Tattoo

agency
McKinney / Durham

05085A

CONSUMER NEWSPAPER : 600 LINES OR LESS — CAMPAIGN

art directors
Lou Flores
John Parker

writers
Mike Lear
Adam Moroze
Keith Greenstein
Rob Katzenstein

creative director
Mike Lear

client
The Onion

agency
The Martin Agency / Richmond

05086A

Also Awarded:
merit
Consumer Newspaper
600 Lines or Less: Single

ALWAYS POLITICALLY CORRECT.
EXCEPT FOR THE STORIES ON RETARDS.
the ONION
SUBSCRIBE
A full year (52 issues) of the award-winning Onion is only $49.95 (US), $110 (Canada) $200 (Europe). Please call for information on other rates. VISA, MasterCard, AMEX, check or money order accepted. Please no cash. Mail coupon with payment to: Onion Subscriptions, 544 East Ogden Ave., Suite 700-388, Milwaukee, WI 53202. Visit us at www.theonion.com to order with your VISA, MasterCard or AMEX. GIFT SUBSCRIPTIONS: fill out this form with the recipient's name and address, but also include your name and phone number. Or just call us toll-free at 1.800.695.4376.
Please send a gift card ( )YES ( )NO from prior to the first issue.
Name
Address
City State Zip
Daytime Phone
VISA or MC # Exp:
Signature

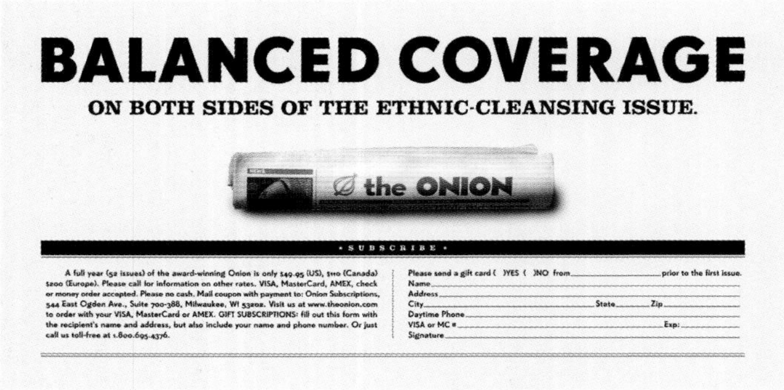
BALANCED COVERAGE
ON BOTH SIDES OF THE ETHNIC-CLEANSING ISSUE.
the ONION
SUBSCRIBE

WE FIRED OUR FACT-CHECKERS
AND PASSED THE SAVINGS ON TO YOU.
the ONION
SUBSCRIBE

IT'S JUST A NEWSPAPER.
YEAH, AND GANDHI WAS JUST A MEXICAN.
the ONION
SUBSCRIBE

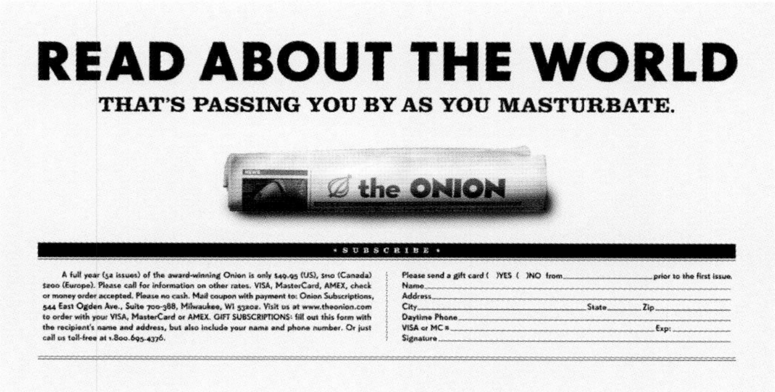
READ ABOUT THE WORLD
THAT'S PASSING YOU BY AS YOU MASTURBATE.
the ONION
SUBSCRIBE

< Merit >

21,873 STITCHES IN EVERY SUIT.
ENOUGH TO DRIVE ANY TAILOR INSANE.
HERRINGBONE

art director
Graham Johnson

writer
Oliver Devaris

photographer
Michael Corridore

creative director
Ben Welsh

client
Herringbone

agency
M&C Saatchi / Sydney

05088A

Merit

CONSUMER MAGAZINE : BLACK AND WHITE : FULL PAGE OR SPREAD — CAMPAIGN

One Show

CONSUMER MAGAZINE : COLOR : FULL PAGE OR SPREAD — SINGLE

art directors
Justin Harris
Rick Bryson

writers
Clarence Bradley
John Spalding

photographer
Ken Gehle

creative directors
Dave Stanton
Jeff Nixon
Bill Pauls

client
Cingular

agency
BBDO / Atlanta

05093A

Also Awarded:
merit
Posters: Single

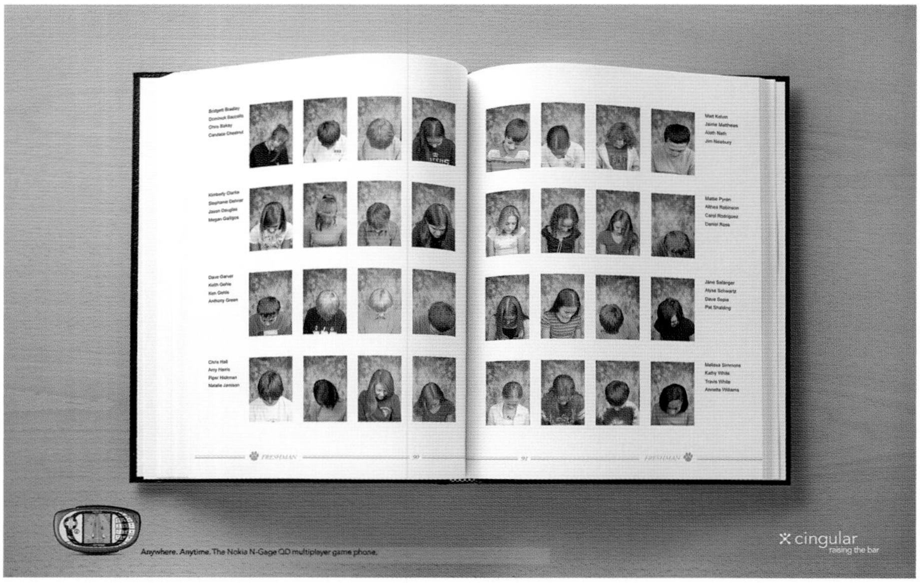
Anywhere. Anytime. The Nokia N-Gage QD multiplayer game phone.
cingular
raising the bar

art directors
Ariyawat Juntaratip
Korakot Konkaew
Winna Kiao-on

writers
Subun Khow
Chanatthapol Tiensri
Parinya Sarasung
Suthisak Sucharittanonta

photographer
Remix Studio

creative directors
Suthisak Sucharittanonta
Subun Khow

client
Indosport (Thailand)

agency
BBDO / Bankok

05094A

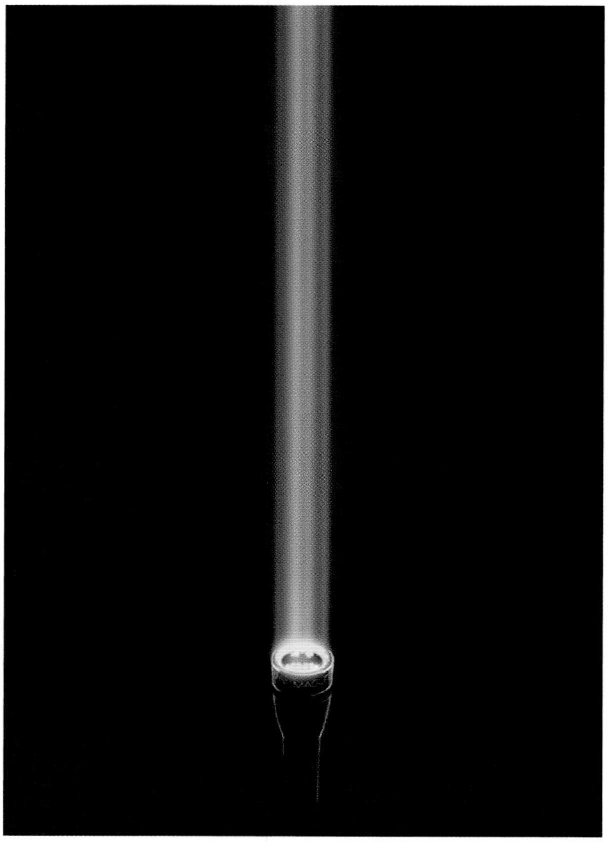

New
Orbit
White
whitens teeth

art director
Frank Dattalo

writer
Dave Schiff

photographer
Nadav Kander

creative director
Marty Orzio

client
Wm. Wrigley Jr. Company-
Orbit White

agency
BBDO / Chicago

05095A

Lift away your dead skin cells with every wash.

art director
Carl Urgino

writer
Carol Ong

photographer
Xander Angeles

illustrator
Vilma Magsino

creative directors
David Guerrero
Raoul Panes
Dave Ferrer

client
Splash

agency
BBDO Guerrero Ortega /
Makati City

05096A

One Show

CONSUMER MAGAZINE : COLOR : FULL PAGE OR SPREAD — SINGLE

art director
Ivan Johnson

writer
Kyle Cockeran

photographer
Pete Maltby

creative director
Ivan Johnson

client
Subaru

agency
Berry Bush BBDO /
Cape Town

05097A

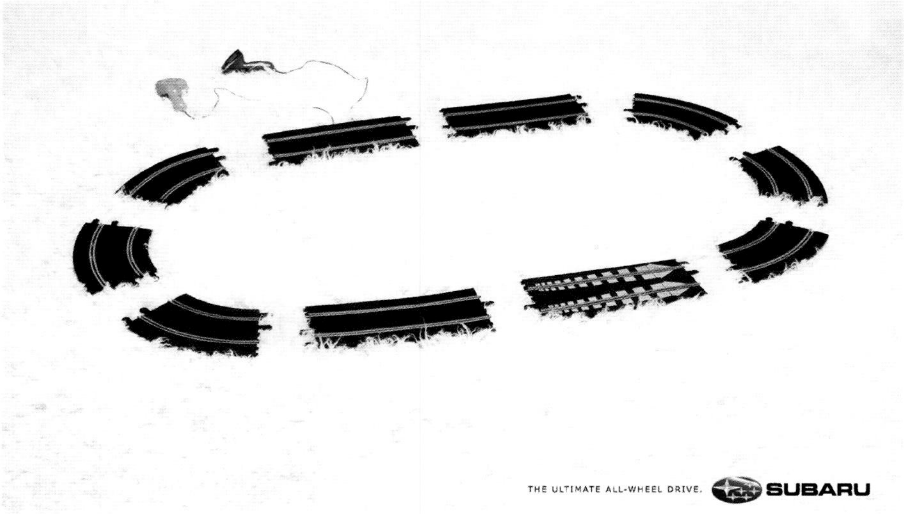

THE ULTIMATE ALL-WHEEL DRIVE.
SUBARU

art directors
Hans Hansen
Jeff Terwilliger

writer
Eric Sorensen

photographer
Georg Fischer

creative director
Jud Smith

client
Porsche

agency
Carmichael Lynch /
Minneapolis

05098A

It's every bit the sports car you've heard it is. It's more attainable than you might think.
$42,600 secures you a mid-mounted flat-six engine, timeless Porsche lines, and the kind
of balance and control you simply cannot put a price on. Porsche. There is no substitute.
A dollar a mile for the first 42,600 miles.
Free after that.
PORSCHE

art director
Steve Cochran

writer
Karl Fleet

photographer
Paul Ashley

illustrator
Jacko van Deventer

creative directors
Toby Talbot
Rich Maddocks

client
Lion Breweries

agency
Colenso BBDO /
Auckland

05099A

art directors
Tim Huse
Guy Rooke

writers
Guy Rooke
Tim Huse

photographer
Fraser Clements

illustrator
Ben Lockwood

creative directors
Rich Maddocks
Toby Talbot

client
Monaco

agency
Colenso BBDO /
Auckland

05100A

CONSUMER MAGAZINE : COLOR : FULL PAGE OR SPREAD — SINGLE

art directors
Carla Romeu
Lorena Mart

writer
Sara Piñana

creative directors
Antonio Montero
Toms Oliva

client
Mercedes Benz

agency
Contrapunto / Madrid

05101A

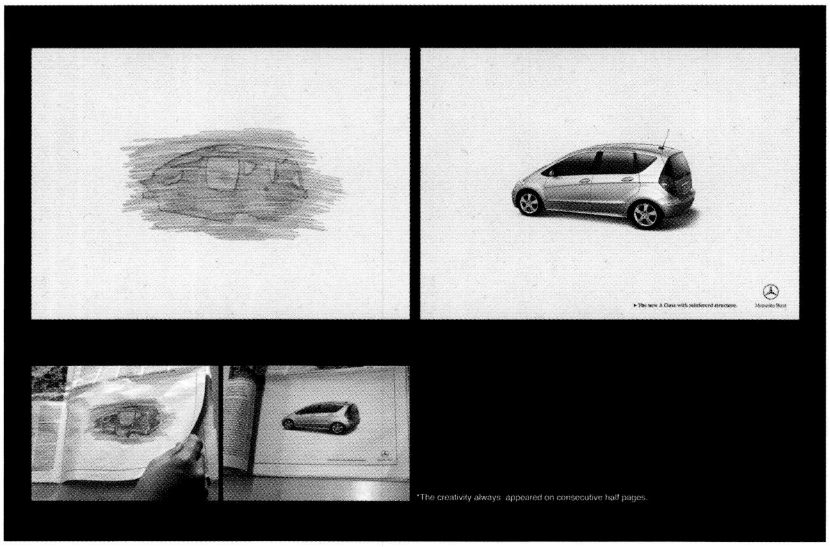
*The creativity always appeared on consecutive half pages.

art director
Tiffany Kosel

writer
Scott Linnen

producers
Sebastian Gray
Julieana Stechschulte

illustrator
Timmy Kucynda

creative directors
Alex Bogusky
Andrew Keller

client
MINI

agency
Crispin Porter + Bogusky / Miami

05106A

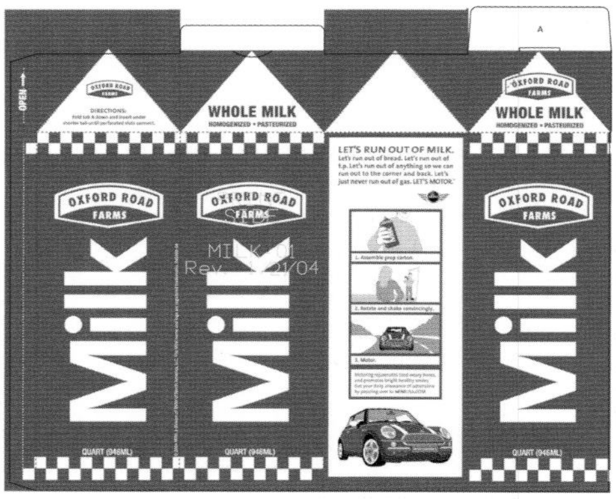
WHOLE MILK
HOMOGENIZED • PASTEURIZED
OXFORD ROAD FARMS
Milk
QUART (946ML)
LET'S RUN OUT OF MILK.
Let's run out of bread. Let's run out of t.p. Let's run out of anything so we can run out to the corner and back. Let's just never run out of gas. LET'S MOTOR.

WHOLE MILK
HOMOGENIZED • PASTEURIZED
OXFORD ROAD FARMS
Milk
QUART (946ML)

BAR FIGHTS
WHERE TO BUY
WHOLE MILK
HOMOGENIZED • PASTEURIZED
OXFORD ROAD FARMS
Milk
QUART (946ML)
LET'S RUN OUT OF MILK.
Let's run out of bread. Let's run out of t.p. Let's run out of anything so we can run out to the corner and back. Let's just never run out of gas. LET'S MOTOR.

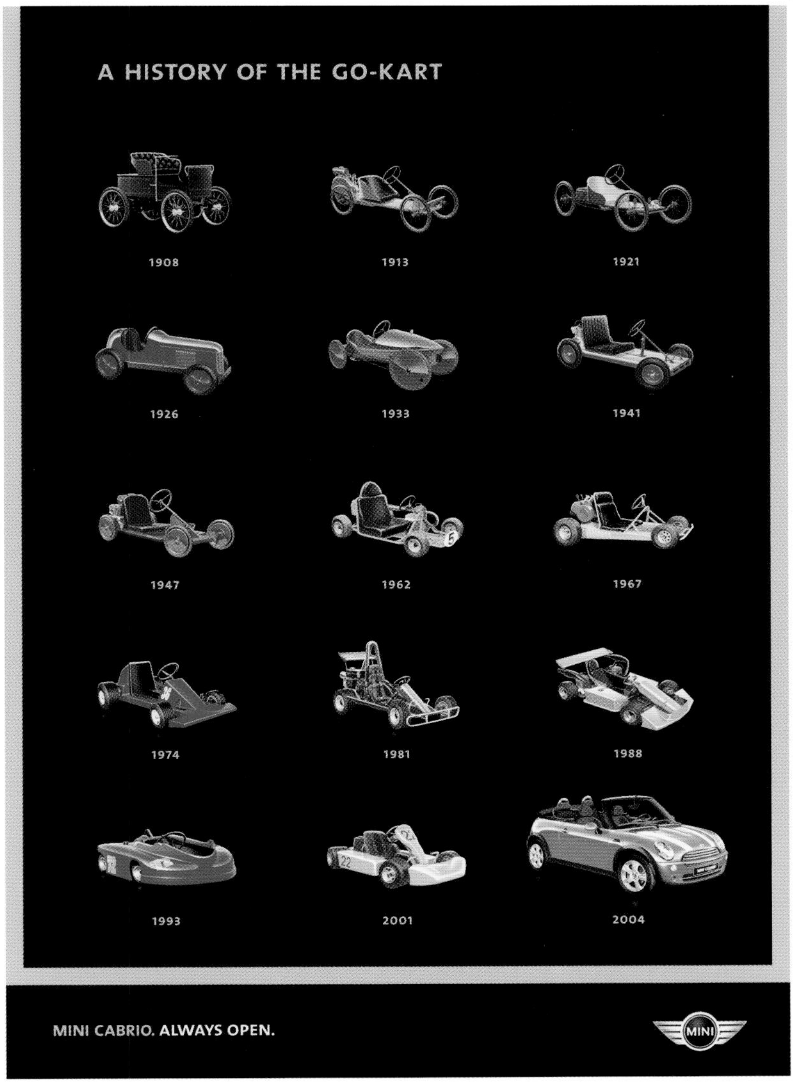

art directors
Geordie Stephens
Tiffany Kosel

writer
Rob Reilly

producers
Sebastian Gray
Julieana Stechschulte

illustrator
Harry Whiver

creative directors
Alex Bogusky
Andrew Keller

client
MINI

agency
Crispin Porter + Bogusky / Miami

05104A

One Show

CONSUMER MAGAZINE : COLOR : FULL PAGE OR SPREAD — SINGLE

art directors
Tony Calcao
Jason Ambrose

writers
Rob Strasberg
Steve O'Connell

producers
Sebastian Gray
Julieana Stechschulte

illustrators
Harry Whitver
Matt Moody
Rebecca Perry

creative directors
Alex Bogusky
Andrew Keller
Steve O'Connell

client
MINI

agency
Crispin Porter + Bogusky / Miami

05102A

ENCYCLOPEDIA OF OPEN MOTORING
ANSWERS TO COMMON QUESTIONS INCLUDING:
• WHAT HAPPENS IN THE COLD?
• HOW DO YOU GET IN?
• WHAT ABOUT HAIR?
CONTINUE YOUR SEARCH FOR KNOWLEDGE AT MINIUSA.COM
37
THE MINI CONVERTIBLE. ALWAYS OPEN.

ENCYCLOPEDIA OF OPEN MOTORING
THE LAW OF THE TOP
THE LAW OF THE TOP

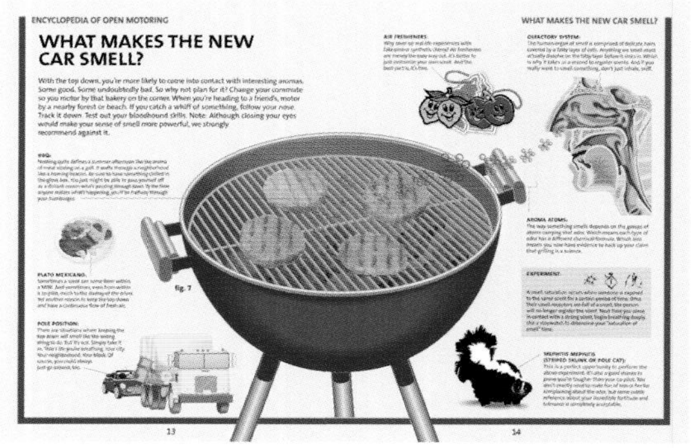
ENCYCLOPEDIA OF OPEN MOTORING
WHAT MAKES THE NEW CAR SMELL?
WHAT MAKES THE NEW CAR SMELL?

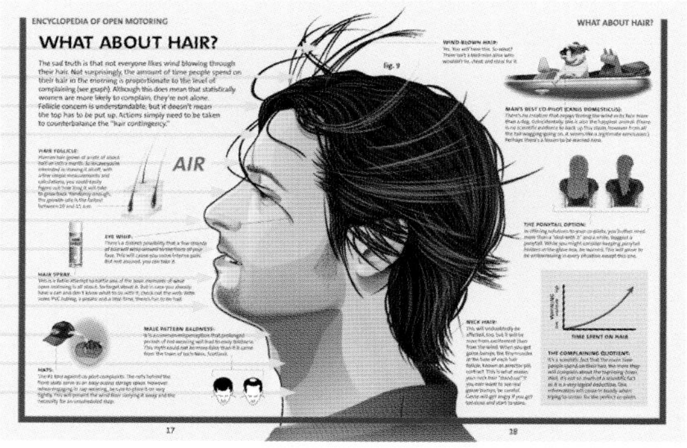
ENCYCLOPEDIA OF OPEN MOTORING
WHAT ABOUT HAIR?
AIR
WHAT ABOUT HAIR?

art directors
Michael Pfeiffer-Belli
Andreas Böhm

writer
Thomas Chudalla

photographer
Marijke de Gruyter

creative directors
Thomas Chudalla
Amir Kassaei

client
Volkswagen

agency
DDB / Berlin

05107A

Also Awarded:
merit
Outdoor: Single

Small but tough. Polo.

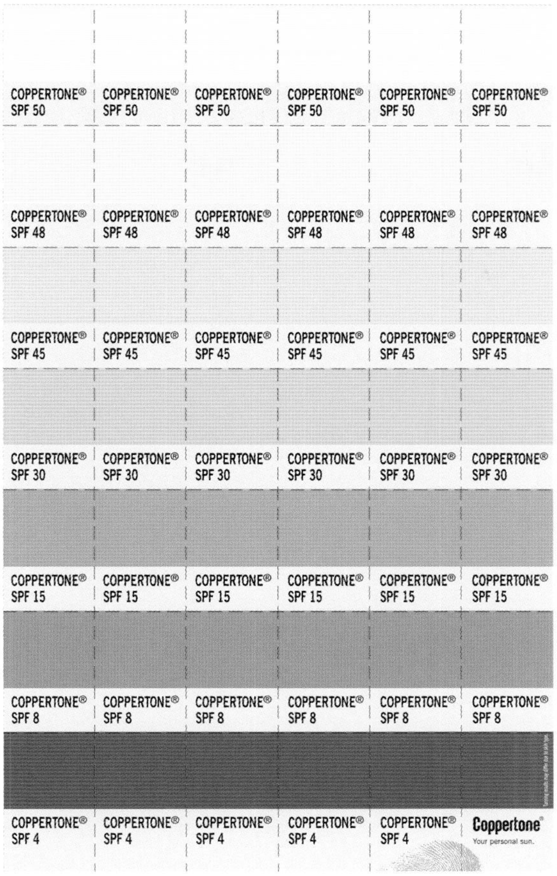

art directors
Edmond Chan
Thomas Law

writers
Derek Wong
Sally Lai

creative directors
CC Tang
Steven Lee
Derek Wong

client
Schering-Plough

agency
DDB / Hong Kong

05110A

art director
Mark Wiggins

writer
Mark Wiggins

photographers
Poon
121 Studios

creative director
Tony Pereira

client
WD40

agency
Dentsu / Singapore

05111A

CONSUMER MAGAZINE : COLOR : FULL PAGE OR SPREAD — SINGLE

art director
Robson Oliveira

writer
Mauricio Machado

photographer
Lucio Cunha

illustrator
Robson Oliveira

creative directors
Jose Zaragoza
Carlos Rocca

client
Lego

agency
DPZ Propaganda / São Paulo

05113A

art director
Carol Chaladus

writer
Elvire Cavaillé

photographer
Vincent Dixon

creative directors
Antoine Barthuel
Daniel Fohr
Lorraine Holl

client
Procter & Gamble

agency
Leo Burnett / Paris

05116A

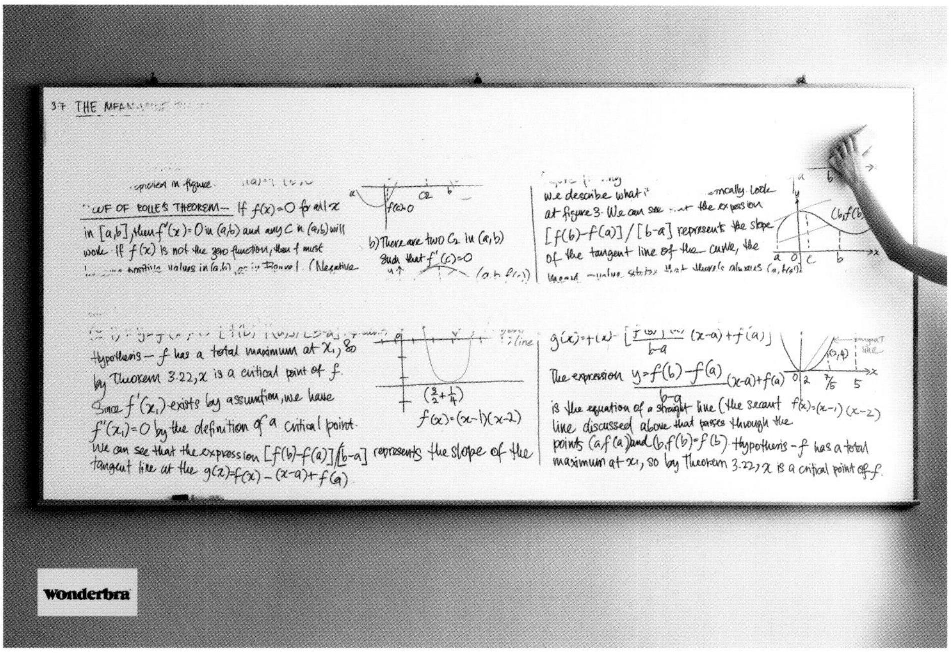
in [a,b], then f'(x) = 0 in (a,b) and any c in (a,b) will
work. If f(x) is not the zero function, then f must
b) There are two C2 in (a,b)
Such that f'(c)=0
at figure 3. We can see
[f(b)-f(a)]/[b-a] represent the slope
of the tangent line of the curve, the
Hypothesis — f has a total maximum at x1, so
by Theorem 3.22, x is a critical point of f.
Since f'(x1) exists by assumption, we have
f'(x1)=0 by the definition of a critical point.
We can see that the expression [f(b)-f(a)]/[b-a] represents the slope of the
tangent line at the g(x)=f(x) - (x-a)+f(a).
f(x)=(x-1)(x-2)
The expression y=f(b)-f(a) / b-a (x-a)+f(a)
is the equation of a straight line (the secant
line discussed above that passes through the
points (a,f(a)) and (b,f(b)=f(b). Hypothesis - f has a total
maximum at x1, so by Theorem 3.22, x is a critical point of f.
Wonderbra

art directors
MUN
Tan Yee Kiang

writer
Kevin Le

photographer
Mark (Untold Images)

illustrator
Ng Lye Yee

creative director
Ted Lim

client
EUT Fashion
(Wonderbra)

agency
Naga DDB / Malaysia

05117A

Also Awarded:
merit
Posters: Single

Merit

CONSUMER MAGAZINE : COLOR : FULL PAGE OR SPREAD — SINGLE

art director
Mike Dietrich

writers
Brian Sheppard (and anonymous contributors)

photographer
Edward Pond

illustrator
Michael Fellini

creative directors
Janet Kestin
Nancy Vonk

client
Unilever - Dove Beauty Bar

agency
Ogilvy & Mather / Toronto

05118A

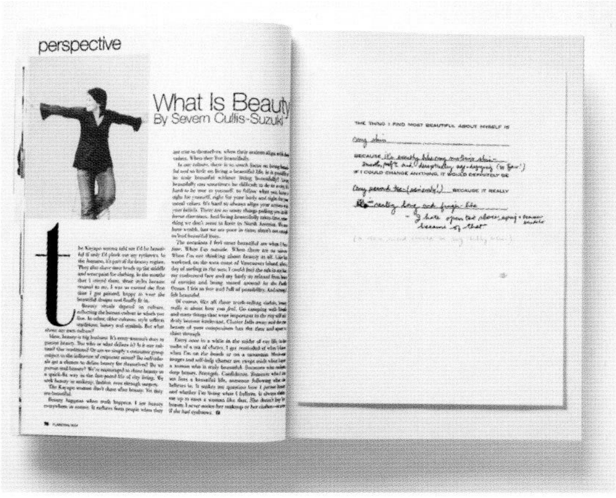

art directors
Alejandro Guadarrama
Iván Carrasco

writer
Alejandro Guadarrama

creative directors
Marco Colín
Miguel Angel Ruiz

client
Land Rover

agency
Ogilvy / Mexico

05121A

Also Awarded:
merit
Collateral
Posters: Single

art director
Tim Forte

writer
Paul Bootlis

creative director
Darren Spiller

client
Nike

agency
Publicis Mojo / Melbourne

05123A

Also Awarded:

merit
Collateral
P.O.P. and In-Store: Single

merit
Collateral
Posters: Single

merit
One Show Design
Collateral Design
Posters: Single

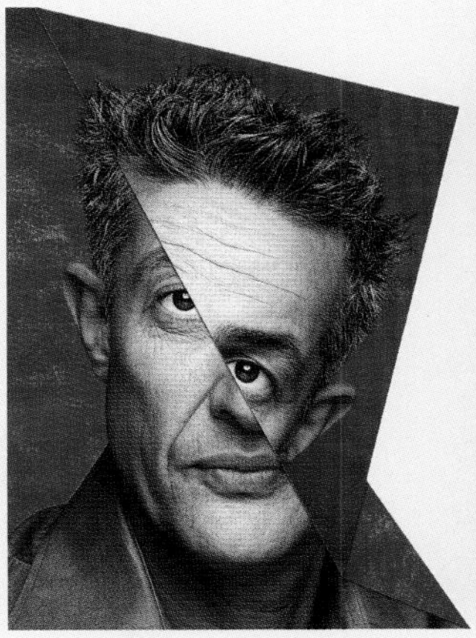

It came folded in the Magazine

When one unfolds, the headline appears

Back

art director
Luciano Santos

writer
Sérgio Franco

photographer
Rodrigo Ribeiro

creative directors
Tio Bernardi
Luciano Santos

client
Bradesco Bank

agency
Publicis Salles Norton / São Paulo

05124A

art directors
Dave Askwith
Kevin Jones

writers
Dave Askwith
Kevin Jones

photographer
David Gill

creative director
Tony Granger

client
Olay

agency
Saatchi & Saatchi /
London

05126A

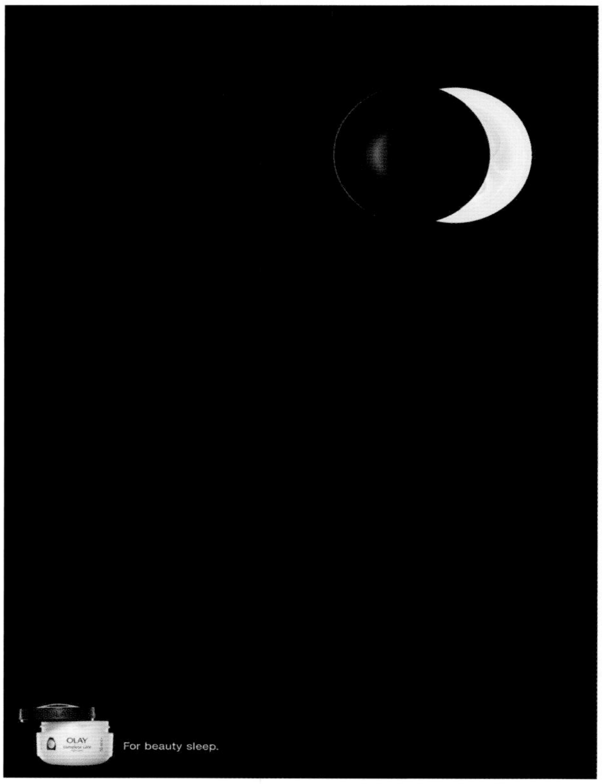

art directors
Carlos Anuncibay
Paloma Acedo
David Valgañón

writers
Carlos Anuncibay
Juan Carlos Monroy
Carmen Pacheco

photographer
Carlos Yebra

creative director
Carlos Anuncibay

client
Queserías Bel España
S.A.

agency
Saatchi & Saatchi /
Madrid

05127A

art director
Din Sumedi

writer
Robert Tsao

photographer
Hon

creative director
Graham Kelly

client
Toyota

agency
Saatchi & Saatchi / Singapore

05128A

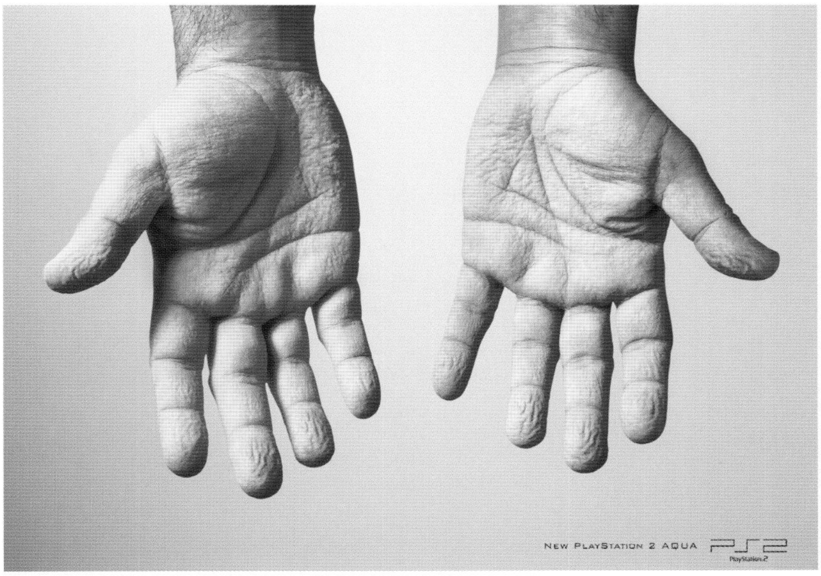

art director
Angel Iglesias

writer
Guillermo Ginés

photographer
Angel Alvarez

creative directors
Agustín Vaquero
Angel Iglesias
Guillermo Ginés

client
Sony

agency
TBWA\ESPAA / Madrid

05130A

One Show

CONSUMER MAGAZINE : COLOR : FULL PAGE OR SPREAD — SINGLE

art director
Pablo Gonzalez de la Peña

writer
César Sastre

photographer
Angel Alvarez

creative directors
Agustín Vaquero
Angel Iglesias
Guillermo Ginés

client
Sony

agency
TBWA\ESPAA / Madrid

05131A

art directors
Nicholas van Renen
Nicole Cohen

writers
Nicholas van Renen
Nicole Cohen

photographers
Beith Digital
Justin Barlow

creative directors
Paul Warner
Camilla Herberstein

client
Shatterprufe Safety Glass

agency
TBWA\Hunt\Lascaris / Sandton

05129A

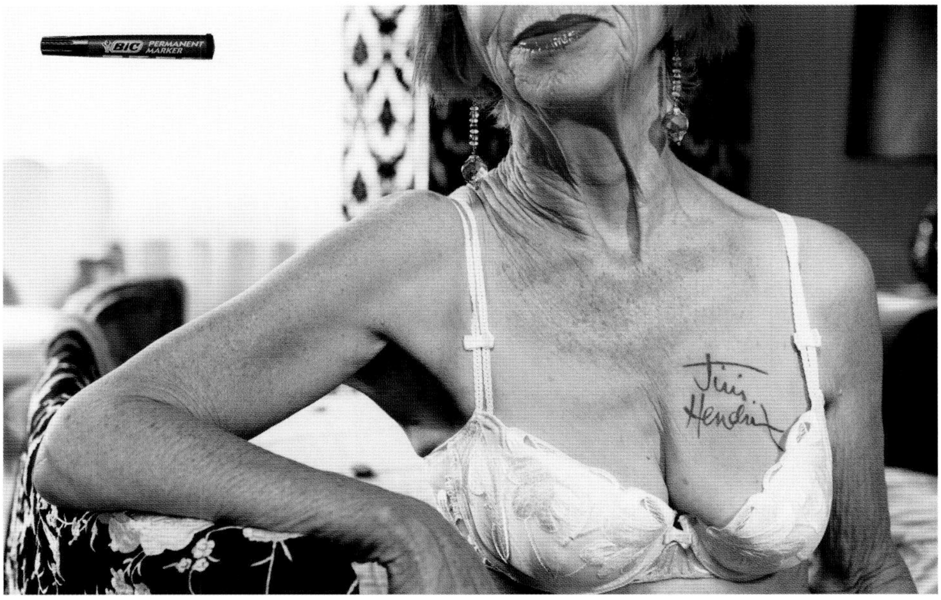

art director
Nick Hine

writers
Nick Hine
Jake Rusznyak

photographer
Garry Simpson

creative director
Erik Vervroegen

client
Bic

agency
TBWA\Paris

05132A

Also Awarded:
merit
P.O.P and In-Store:
Single

art director
Jessica Gérard-Huet

writer
Jean-François Bouchet

photographer
Richard Dobson

creative director
Erik Vervroegen

client
Nissan

agency
TBWA\Paris

05133A

Also Awarded:
merit
Collateral
P.O.P. and In-Store:
Single

CONSUMER MAGAZINE : COLOR : FULL PAGE OR SPREAD — SINGLE

art director
Marianne Fonferrier

writer
Ghislaine De Germon

photographer
Ebo Fraterman

creative director
Erik Vervroegen

client
Nissan

agency
TBWA\Paris

05134A

PICK-UP
THINK BIGGER.
NISSAN

art director
Stephanie Sigg

writer
Bobby Hershfield

creative directors
Todd Waterbury
Ty Montague
Kevin Proudfoot
Paul Renner

client
ESPN

agency
Wieden + Kennedy / New York

05137A

HELLO GOD.
I'M A RED SOX FAN.
NICE TO FINALLY
MEET YOU.
ESPN

SNICKERS
PLEASE
CLEAR AWAY
BODY PARTS
BETWEEN JUMPS

SNICKERS
STAMINA OF A RUNNER
SKILL OF A SHAOLIN
SELF PRESERVATION
OF A LEMMING

SNICKERS
PRACTICE MAKES
COMPOUND FRACTURES
BEFORE IT
MAKES
PERFECT

art directors
Paul Belford
Paul Young

writer
Ben Kay

photographer
Nadav Kander

illustrators
Kev Grey
OTWO (James Carey)
Pete Lewis

creative directors
Paul Belford
Nigel Roberts

client
Snickers

agency
Abbott Mead Vickers
BBDO / London

05138A

Get both sides.
veja
Magazine

< Merit >

Freedom
Get both sides.
veja
Magazine

< Merit >

Get both sides.
veja
Magazine

< Merit >

Get both sides.
veja
Magazine

< Merit >

art director
Roberto Fernandez

writer
Sophie Schoenburg

illustrator
Roberto Fernandez

creative director
Marcello Serpa

client
Editora Abril

agency
AlmapBBDO / São Paulo

05139A

Also Awarded:

merit
Consumer Magazine
Color: Full Page: Single

merit
Consumer Magazine
Color: Full Page: Single

merit
Consumer Magazine
Color: Full Page: Single

merit
Consumer Magazine
Color: Full Page: Single

CONSUMER MAGAZINE : COLOR : FULL PAGE OR SPREAD — CAMPAIGN

art director
Gonzalo Vecino

writer
Pablo Alvarez Travieso

creative director
Papon Ricciarelli

client
Nike

agency
BBDO Argentina /
Buenos Aires

05140A

CONTROL
THE
BALL.
EVERYBODY WANTS
TO STEAL IT FROM YOU.
FOOTBALL

CONTROL
THE
BALL.

CONTROL
THE
BALL.

art director
Jason Smith

writer
Tom Camp

photographer
Dente

creative director
Jim Nelson

client
Harley-Davidson Parts &
Accessories

agency
Carmichael Lynch /
Minneapolis

05141A

THIS COUNTRY WASN'T FOUNDED ON THE DECLARATION OF BLENDING IN.

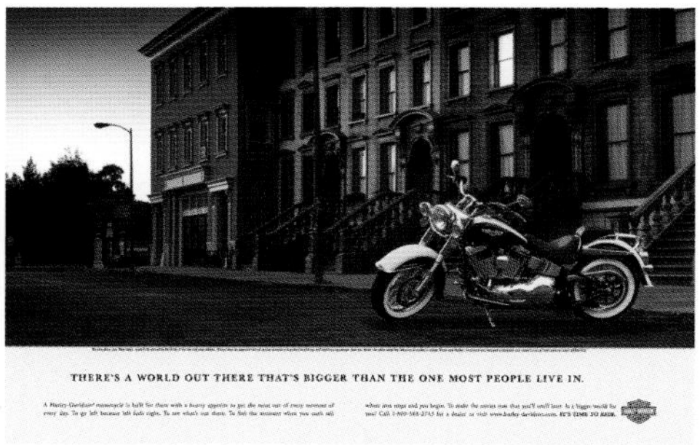
THERE'S A WORLD OUT THERE THAT'S BIGGER THAN THE ONE MOST PEOPLE LIVE IN.

WE'RE ALL CREATED EQUAL. BUT AFTER THAT, IT'S UP TO YOU.
Every single Harley-Davidson® motorcycle is designed to set you apart from the masses. But for the chosen few who want to take the idea yet a step further, meet the V-Rod.® The sculpted aluminum bodywork is pure art. And the high-revving
Revolution® V-Twin engine instantly puts a little distance between you and the other six billion people on the planet. 1-800-588-2743 for a dealer or visit www.harley-davidson.com. IT'S TIME TO RIDE.

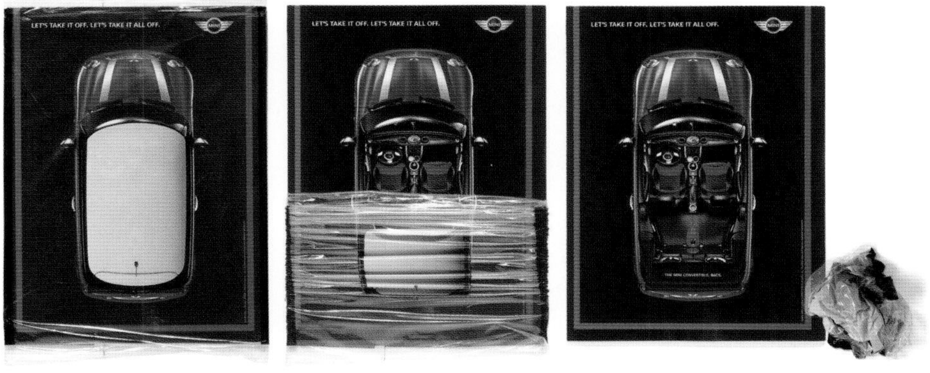
LET'S TAKE IT OFF. LET'S TAKE IT ALL OFF.
LET'S TAKE IT OFF. LET'S TAKE IT ALL OFF.
LET'S TAKE IT OFF. LET'S TAKE IT ALL OFF.

HIDDEN SPREAD
By purposefully creating an ad that most people would miss, we rewarded people who found it with an exclusive invitation.

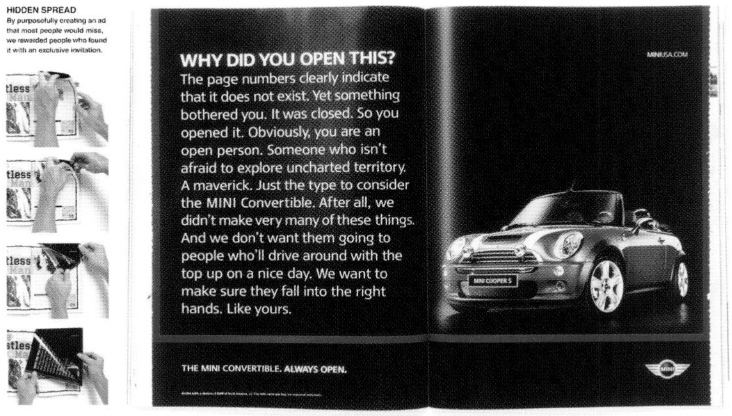
WHY DID YOU OPEN THIS?
The page numbers clearly indicate that it does not exist. Yet something bothered you. It was closed. So you opened it. Obviously, you are an open person. Someone who isn't afraid to explore uncharted territory. A maverick. Just the type to consider the MINI Convertible. After all, we didn't make very many of these things. And we don't want them going to people who'll drive around with the top up on a nice day. We want to make sure they fall into the right hands. Like yours.
MINIUSA.COM
MINI COOPER S
THE MINI CONVERTIBLE. ALWAYS OPEN.

< Merit >

art directors
Alex Burnard
Mike del Marmol
Paul Stechschulte
Geordie Stephens
Tiffany Kosel

writers
Dave Schiff
Tom Adams
Rob Reilly

photographers
Peter Hetzmannseder

producers
Sebastian Gray
Julieana Stechschulte
Barrie Bamberg

illustrators
Charlie Caldarin
Doink Design

creative directors
Alex Bogusky
Andrew Keller

client
MINI

agency
Crispin Porter + Bogusky / Miami

05143A

Also Awarded:
merit
Consumer Magazine
Color: Full Page: Single

art director
Valdir Bianchi

writer
Fernando Campos

photographer
Edu Rodrigues

creative directors
Fernando Campos
Valdir Bianchi

client
Fenda Seguros

agency
Giovanni, FCB / Sao Paulo

05155A

Merit

One Show

CONSUMER MAGAZINE : COLOR : FULL PAGE OR SPREAD — CAMPAIGN

art director
Tiffany Kosel

writer
Scott Linnen

photographers
Jim Gallop
Richard Hamilton Smith
Daniel Hartz

producers
Julieana Stechschulte
Sebastian Gray

creative directors
Alex Bogusky
Andrew Keller

client
MINI

agency
Crispin Porter + Bogusky / Miami

05142A

Kawasaki
You're not sure if you need a boat launch or a torpedo tube.
THE LEADING EDGE OF / POWER / PERFORMANCE / EXHILARATION /
Kawasaki

MINI COOPER
THE MINI CONVERTIBLE. ALWAYS OPEN.

THE RIDE WILL TAKE AWAY WHATEVER LITTLE BREATH YOU HAVE LEFT.
ARCTIC CAT

MINI COOPER S
THE MINI CONVERTIBLE. ALWAYS OPEN.

MINI COOPER S
THE MINI CONVERTIBLE. ALWAYS OPEN.

THOROUGHBRE TIMES
Every day. Every week. Every year. The leader in racing coverage.

TIME TO GO. ALWAYS OPEN.

MAN AND MACHINE. ALWAYS OPEN.

LAST MINUTE PLANS. ALWAYS OPEN.
MINI COOPER

art director
Paul Keister

writers
Bill Wright
Bob Cianfrone

photographer
Zach Gold

producers
Sebastian Gray
Julieana Stechschulte

creative directors
Alex Bogusky
Andrew Keller

client
MINI

agency
Crispin Porter + Bogusky / Miami

05144A

XTREME
ASPIRING GROOM
IS SHE THE ONE?
MOLSON TWIN COVER TECHNOLOGY
COMMITMENT HAS NEVER BEEN SO EASY

ACTUAL COVER IMPROVED MOLSON BACK COVER INSIDE MOLSON BACK COVER

ANNA
TRUSTFUND
PRIVATE JET UPHOLSTERY
MOLSON TWIN COVER TECHNOLOGY
A WHOPPING $90,000 INVESTMENT IN YOU

ACTUAL COVER IMPROVED MOLSON BACK COVER INSIDE MOLSON BACK COVER

XTREME
ANIMAL RESCUER
WILD PONIES of Assateague Island
MOLSON TWIN COVER TECHNOLOGY
BECAUSE WOMEN LOVE GUYS WHO LOVE ANIMALS

ACTUAL COVER IMPROVED MOLSON BACK COVER INSIDE MOLSON BACK COVER

art directors
Alex Burnard
Mike del Marmol
Tony Calcao

writers
Dave Schiff
Rob Strasberg
Rob Reilly

photographer
Harry DeZeitter

producers
Jessica Hoffman
Brian McMillen

creative directors
Alex Bogusky
Bill Wright

client
Molson

agency
Crispin Porter + Bogusky / Miami

05146A

Merit

One Show

CONSUMER MAGAZINE : COLOR : FULL PAGE OR SPREAD — CAMPAIGN

art directors
Jason Ambrose
Tony Calcao
Paul Stechschulte

writers
Dustin Ballard
Rob Strasberg
Franklin Tipton

producers
Jessica Hoffman
Barry Bamberg

illustrator
Timmy Kucynda

creative directors
Alex Bogusky
Bill Wright
Andrew Keller

client
Virgin

agency
Crispin Porter + Bogusky / Miami

05147A

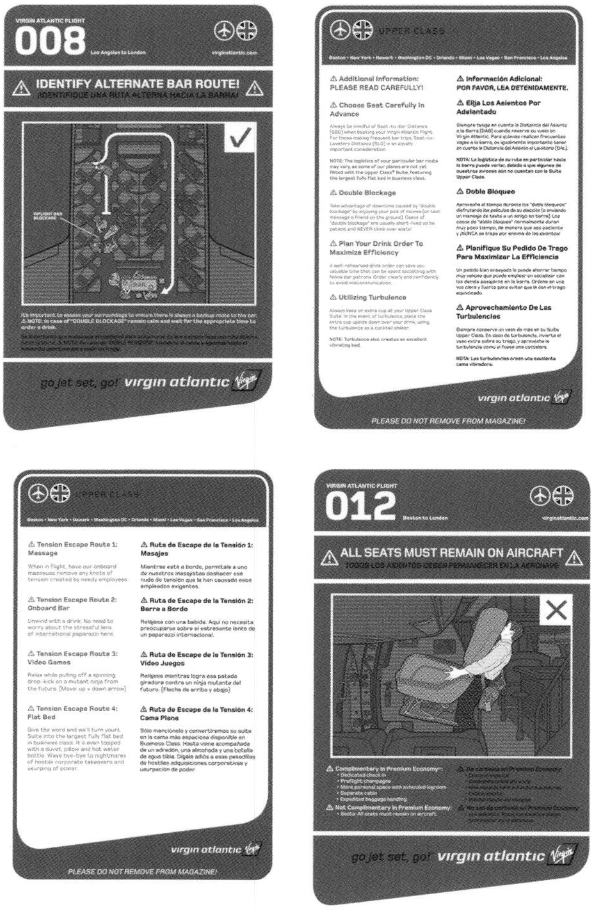

VIRGIN ATLANTIC FLIGHT
008
Los Angeles to London
virginatlantic.com
IDENTIFY ALTERNATE BAR ROUTE!
¡IDENTIFIQUE UNA RUTA ALTERNA HACIA LA BARRA!
go jet set, go! virgin atlantic
UPPER CLASS
Additional Information: PLEASE READ CAREFULLY!
Información Adicional: POR FAVOR, LEA DETENIDAMENTE.
Double Blockage
Doble Bloqueo
Utilizing Turbulence
virgin atlantic
PLEASE DO NOT REMOVE FROM MAGAZINE!
UPPER CLASS
virgin atlantic
PLEASE DO NOT REMOVE FROM MAGAZINE!
VIRGIN ATLANTIC FLIGHT
012
Boston to London
virginatlantic.com
ALL SEATS MUST REMAIN ON AIRCRAFT
TODOS LOS ASIENTOS DEBEN PERMANECER EN LA AERONAVE
go jet set, go! virgin atlantic

art director
Marcos Medeiros

writer
Flavio Casarotti

illustrator
Marcos Medeiros

creative directors
Pedro Cappelletti
Sergio Valente

client
Philips

agency
DDB / São Paulo

05148A

Push play.
PHILIPS
Push play.
PHILIPS
Push play.
PHILIPS
Push play.
PHILIPS

art director
Jean-Yves Lemoigne

writers
Jérôme Langlade
Marie-Eve Schoettle

photographer
Jean-Yves Lemoigne

creative directors
Sylvain Thirache
Alexandre Herve

client
Le Barran

agency
DDB / Paris

05150A

"The price of sharing Family Plan minutes meant that I couldn't have a brother."
Pay As You Go by Virgin mobile Live without a plan.

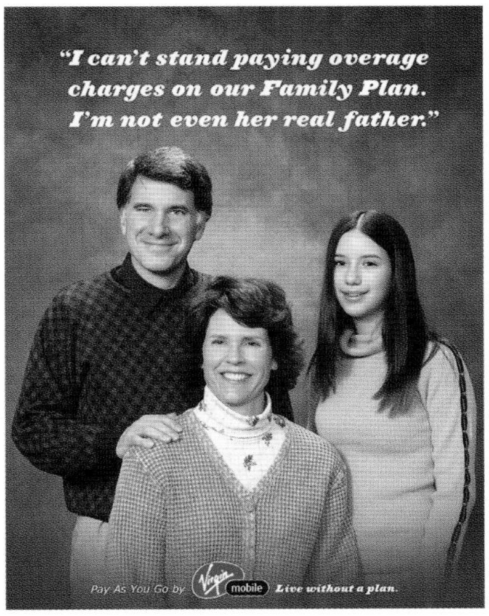
"I can't stand paying overage charges on our Family Plan. I'm not even her real father."
Pay As You Go by Virgin mobile Live without a plan.

"After we heard the high price of Family Plans, Ross and I stopped having sex completely."
Pay As You Go by Virgin mobile Live without a plan.

< Merit >

art director
Molly Sheahan

writer
Marty Senn

photographer
Ken Ahlstrom

creative director
Ari Merkin

client
Virgin Mobile USA

agency
Fallon / New York

05153A

Also Awarded:
merit
Consumer Magazine:
Color: Full Page: Single

Merit

One Show

CONSUMER MAGAZINE : COLOR : FULL PAGE OR SPREAD — CAMPAIGN

art director
Jean-Roux Bezuidenhout

writer
Molefi Thulo

photographer
David Prior

creative directors
Brett Morris
Gerhard Myburgh
Eliot Powell

client
Sonovision Recording Studios

agency
FCB / Johannesburg

05154A

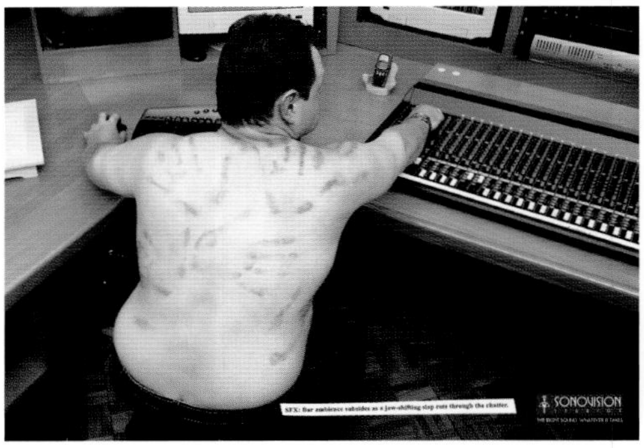

art director
Jeff Lable

writer
Tom O'Connor

photographers
Seth Taras
National Archives

creative director
Court Crandall

client
The History Channel

agency
Ground Zero / Los Angeles

05156A

Also Awarded:
merit
Consumer Magazine
Color: Full Page: Single

art director
Christian Bobst

writers
Jan Harbeck
Daniel Henning

photographer
Mag!c Group

creative directors
Burkhart von Scheven
Stephan Ganser

client
Junge Karriere

agency
Jung von Matt / Berlin

05157A

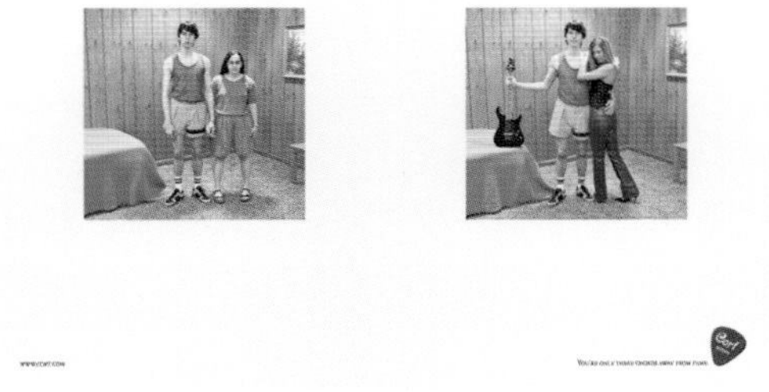

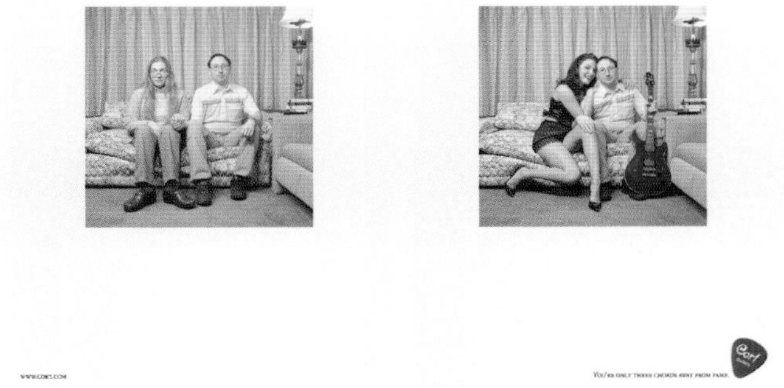

art director
Jim Genell

writers
Josh Denberg
Paul Hirsch
Jim Genell

photographer
Lars Topelman

creative directors
Josh Denberg
Paul Hirsch

client
Cort Guitar

agency
Leo Burnett / Chicago

05158A

art directors
Gumpon Laksanajinda
Voarachai Sooksai

writers
Kulvadee Doksroy
Kris Spindler
Sirilak Chitpanvong

photographer
Paiboon Suwansangroj

illustrator
Gumpon Laksanajinda

creative director
Wisit Lumsiri-charoenchoke

client
Amusement Creation

agency
Ogilvy & Mather / Bangkok

05159A

art director
Marion Cohen

writer
Cassandra Yap

photographer
Stas Jitcky

creative directors
Tony Granger
Jan Jacobs

client
Coco de Mer

agency
Saatchi & Saatchi / London

05160A

Also awarded:
merit
Consumer Magazine
Color: Full Page: Single

< Merit >

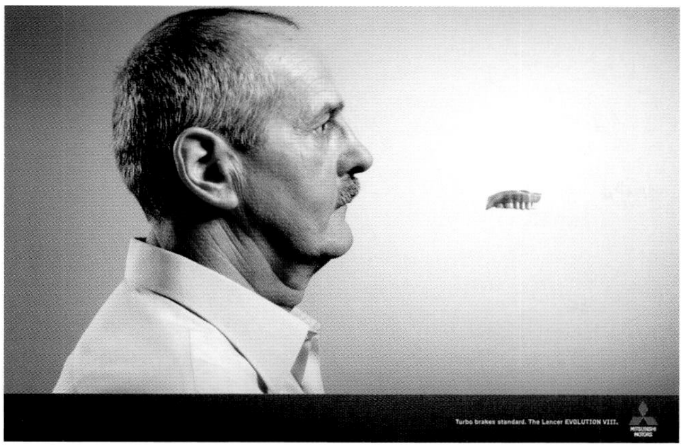
Turbo brakes standard. The Lancer EVOLUTION VIII.

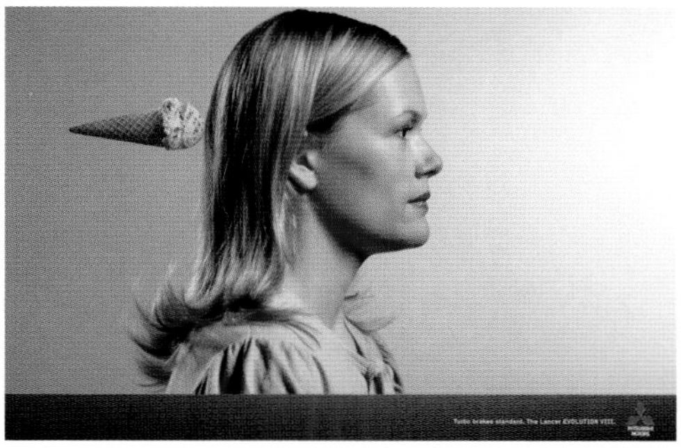

art director
Gregory French

writer
Peter Quester

photographer
Piet Truhlar

creative director
Matthias Schmidt

client
Mitsubishi Motors

agency
Scholz & Friends / Berlin

05151A

Also Awarded:
merit
Collateral
Posters: Campaign

Tom Grammerstorf believes in Polaroid

Polaroid

Polaroid

art director
Mareike Ledeboer

writer
Christian Vosshagen

photographers
Anatol Kotte
Kai-Uwe Gundlach
Tom Grammerstorf

creative director
Richard Jung

client
Polaroid

agency
Scholz & Friends / Hamburg

05161A

CONSUMER MAGAZINE : COLOR : FULL PAGE OR SPREAD — CAMPAIGN

art directors
Adam Regan
Antoine Minczeles
Curt Detweiler

writer
Curt Detweiler

illustrators
Albertus Seba
Jean Larcher

creative director
Curt Detweiler

client
Nissan

agency
TBWA\G1\Champs Elysees / Paris

05162A

IT TAKES A
BRAVE MAN
TO VENTURE DEEP INTO
THE JUNGLE.
IT TAKES A
SPECIAL KIND OF IDIOT
TO OPEN THE SUNROOF.
FORTUNATELY, YOUR NEW PATROL COMES EQUIPPED WITH CLIMATE CONTROL, NOT TO MENTION 3,500 KILOGRAMS OF TOWING CAPABILITY, FOUR WHEEL DRIVE & IT CAN WADE TO A DEPTH OF 700 MM BECAUSE WE KNOW IN BORNEO, AIR TEMPERATURES SOAR TO OVER 100°, ROADS RISE TO INCLINES OF 39° & THE SPIDERS ARE BIGGER THAN YOUR FIST.
WELCOME TO THE JUNGLE.
SHIFT_adventure

IF YOU SEE
BIRD SHIT
ON A PATROL,
CHANCES ARE IT DIDN'T COME
FROM A PIGEON.

TO CATCH DINNER
IN IRYAN JAYA
YOU DON'T NEED A SPEAR,
A GUN OR A FISHING ROD.
YOU NEED
MULTI-PARABOLA
HEADLIGHTS.

art director
Storm Tharp

writer
Derek Barnes

photographer
Melodie McDaniel

illustrator
Patrick Long

creative directors
Todd Waterbury
Mike Byrne
Hal Curtis

client
Nike

agency
Wieden + Kennedy / Portland

05163A

THE ARROGANT YET STOIC MUSK OX
THEY STAY WARM IN THE COLD.
THANK YOU MUSK OX.
MAKE YOUR BODY WORK BETTER

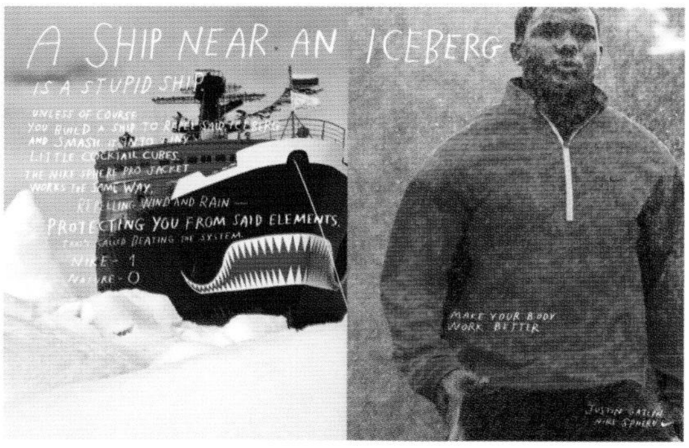

A SHIP NEAR AN ICEBERG
IS A STUPID SHIP
PROTECTING YOU FROM SAID ELEMENTS.
NIKE - 1
NATURE - 0
MAKE YOUR BODY WORK BETTER

IT'S WEIRD THE ANCIENT GREEKS
NIKE SPHERE DRY SHIRTS
KEEP YOU COOL AND DRY
PISS OFF THE GOD OF SWEATING?
MAKE YOUR BODY WORK BETTER

WITHOUT SPORTS, HOW WOULD WE KNOW WHAT WE'RE MADE OF?
ESPN

WITHOUT SPORTS, WHAT WOULD WE DO OVER THE HOLIDAYS?
ESPN

WITHOUT SPORTS, WHERE WOULD WE WRITE HISTORY?
ESPN

art directors
Alan Buchanan
Paul Renner
Stephanie Sigg

writers
Greg Kalleres
Charles Hall
Andy Carrigan

photographers
Melodie McDaniel
Ron Haviv
Bettmann/Corbis

creative directors
Todd Waterbury
Ty Montague

client
ESPN

agency
Wieden + Kennedy / New York

05164A

WORLD POKER TOUR
Travel

WINNER TAKES ALL.
WORLD POKER TOUR
Travel

WINNER TAKES ALL.
WORLD POKER TOUR
Travel

art director
Denison Kusano

writers
Tohru Oyasu
Dave Loew

creative directors
Mark Figliulo
Dave Loew

client
Travel Channel

agency
Y&R / Chicago

05166A

Merit

One Show

CONSUMER MAGAZINE : LESS THAN A PAGE : BLACK AND WHITE OR COLOR — CAMPAIGN

art director
Brock Davis

writer
Eric Sorensen

photographer
Madison Ford

creative director
Hans Hansen

client
Harley-Davidson Parts & Accessories

agency
Carmichael Lynch / Minneapolis

05167A

GENUINE
MOTOR ACCESSORIES
IT SIMULTANEOUSLY SAYS "LOOK AT ME" AND "WHAT ARE YOU LOOKING AT?"
Go for custom impact where it'll get noticed first. This chrome front end kit with flamed upper-fork slider covers is one of hundreds of ways Harley-Davidson® Genuine Motor Accessories let you be your own styling guru. Pick up a catalog at your Harley™ dealer. 1-800-588-2743.
©2004 H-D

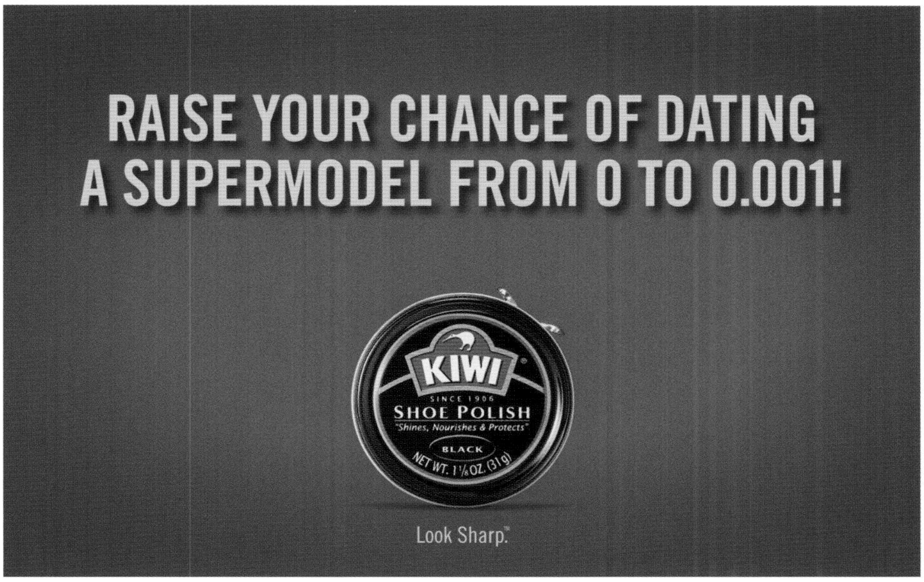
RAISE YOUR CHANCE OF DATING
A SUPERMODEL FROM 0 TO 0.001!
KIWI
SHOE POLISH
Look Sharp.

< Merit >

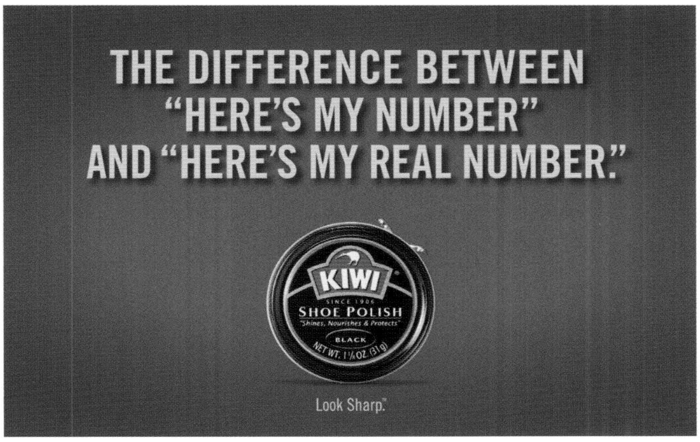
THE DIFFERENCE BETWEEN
"HERE'S MY NUMBER"
AND "HERE'S MY REAL NUMBER."
KIWI
SHOE POLISH
Look Sharp.

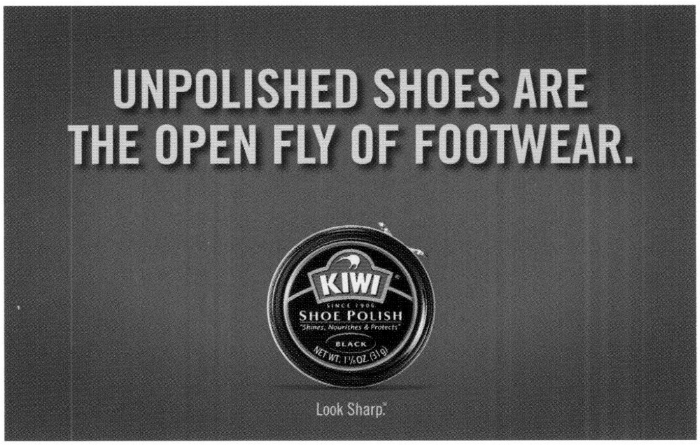
UNPOLISHED SHOES ARE
THE OPEN FLY OF FOOTWEAR.
KIWI
SHOE POLISH
Look Sharp.

art director
Peter Everitt

writer
David Canright

photographer
Mark Bumgarner

creative director
Glenn Dady

client
KIWI

agency
The Richards Group /
Dallas

05169A

Also Awarded:
merit
Consumer Magazine: Less than a Page: Black and White or Color: Single

Merit

CONSUMER MAGAZINE : LESS THAN A PAGE : BLACK AND WHITE OR COLOR — CAMPAIGN

art directors
Jayson Atienza
Frank Anselmo
Chris Maiorino

writers
Chris Maiorino
Frank Anselmo
Jayson Atienza

creative directors
David Lubars
Don Schneider

client
HBO/Soprano's

agency
BBDO / New York

05170A

art directors
Ashutosh Karkhanis
Niranjan Kaushik

writers
Niranjan Kaushik
Ashutosh Karkhanis

designer
Ashutosh Karkhanis

photographer
Ashutosh Karkhanis

creative directors
Raj Nair
Ashutosh Karkhanis
Niranjan Kaushik

client
Fame Adlabs

agency
Contract Advertising / Mumbai

05171A

art director
Tiffany Kosel

writer
Scott Linnen

photographers
Igor Panitz

producer
Julieana Stechschulte

creative directors
Alex Bogusky
Andrew Keller

client
MINI

agency
Crispin Porter + Bogusky / Miami

05172A

(front view)

(side view)

This outdoor is lenticular. No matter the way you look, the camera looks back at you.

art director
Pedro Bexiga

writer
Marcelo Lourenço

photographer
Francisco Prata

creative director
Jorge Teixeira

client
TVI

agency
Euro RSCG / Lisbon

05176A

One Show

OUTDOOR : SINGLE

art director
Molly Sheahan

writer
Marty Senn

creative director
Ari Merkin

client
TIME Magazine

agency
Fallon / New York

05177A

What more can we do
to keep our buildings safe?

art director
Eric Yeo

writer
Robert Gaxiola

illustrators
Tan Keng Wee
May Chew

creative director
Robert Gaxiola

client
SC Johnson & Son

agency
Foote Cone & Belding / Singapore

05178A

Also Awarded:
merit
Collateral
P.O.P. and In-Store: Single

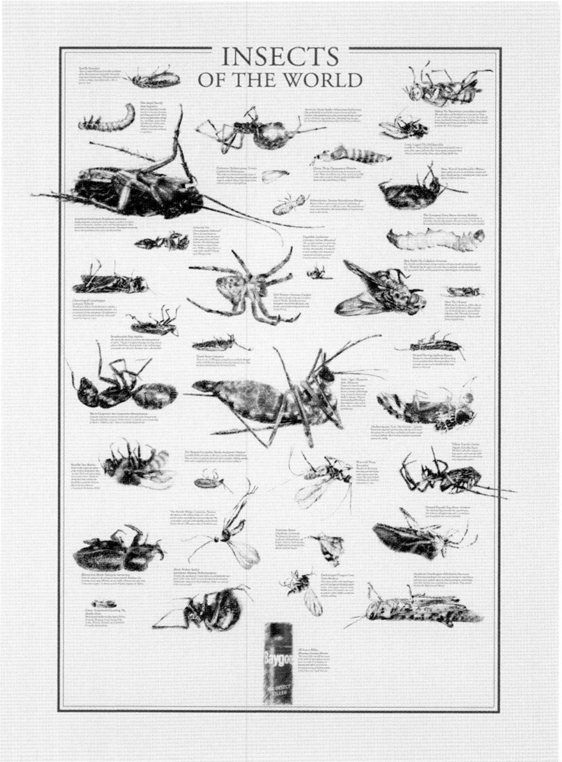
INSECTS
OF THE WORLD

The Touareg with 58 cm wading depth.
The Touareg with 58 cm wading depth.

art director
Tomas Tulinius

writer
Martien Delfgaauw

photographer
Nico Weymann

creative directors
Ralf Nolting
Patricia Pätzold
Ralf Heuel

client
Volkswagen

agency
Grabarz & Partner /
Hamburg

05179A

Green Curry
Red Curry

Spring

Green Curry
Red Curry

Autumn

art directors
Nils Andersson
Keiichi Sasaki

writers
Keiichi Sasaki
Nils Andersson

designers
Nobuya Mochinaga
Hitoshi Miyamoto
Nanae Sega

photographer
Chihiro Aono

creative director
Mitsuaki Aota

client
House Foods

agency
HAKUHODO\TBWA\
G1 / Tokyo

05190A

Also Awarded:
merit
Exceptional Innovation
in Marketing: Single

merit
One Show Design
Environmental Design:
Single

One Show

OUTDOOR : SINGLE

art director
Brian Shembeda

writer
Avery Gross

photographer
Greg Mohrs

creative directors
Mark Tutssel
John Montgomery

client
McDonald's

agency
Leo Burnett / Chicago

05180A

Also Awarded:
merit
Collateral
P.O.P. and In-Store:
Single

Triple thick milkshakes
i'm lovin' it

art directors
Puneet Kapoor
Satish Sethumadhavan
Rahul Mathew

writers
Rahul Mathew
Puneet Kapoor

photographer
Altaf Khan

creative director
Prasoon Joshi

client
Big Babol Bubble Gum

agency
McCann Erickson /
Mumbai

05182A

NOW EVEN BIGGER

air zoom swift vapor
nikespeed.com

art directors
Lii Chiang
Kit Koh

writers
Giant Kung
Kurt Lu

creative directors
Murphy Chou
Rich Shiue

client
Nike

agency
Ogilvy & Mather / Taipei

05183A

RENAULT
The Renault Modus. Safest small car, awarded five-star rating in Euro NCAP crash tests.

art director
Nico Juenger

writer
Konstantinos Manikas

photographer
Teresa Kinast

illustrator
Robin Preston

creative director
Claudia Willvonseder

client
Renault

agency
Publicis / Frankfurt

05184A

One Show

OUTDOOR : SINGLE

art director
Rob Sweetman

writer
Bryan Collins

creative directors
Ian Grais
Chris Staples

client
3M Trim-Line

agency
Rethink / Vancouver

05186A

art directors
Tadashi Tsujimoto
Hirofumi Nakajima

writer
Katsuhisa Fujita

creative director
John Merrifield

client
adidas

agency
TBWA\Japan / Tokyo
(180\TBWA)

05187A

As part of the launch of *Impossible is Nothing* we painted a number of buses.

But instead of driving them around, we placed them in different locations each morning before dawn.
Then we had people pull them along the road. We even invited members of the public to have a go.

Naturally this captured all sorts of attention and free publicity. But more than this, it allowed us to demonstrate the spirit of *Impossible is Nothing*, not just talk about it.

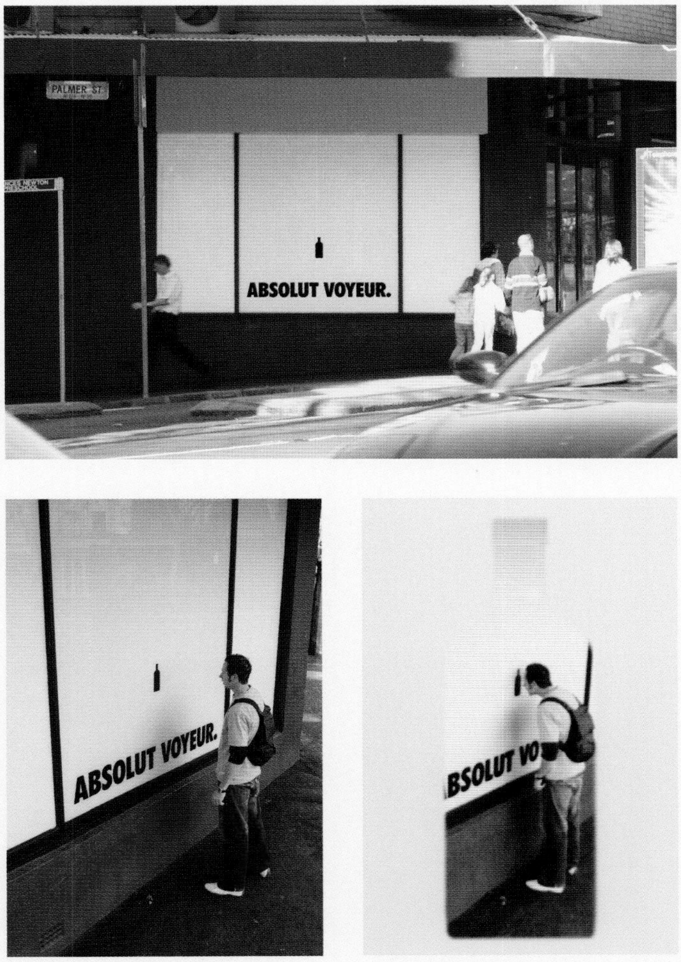

Passers-by tempted to look through the peephole were amused to see themselves on a closed circuit television; essentially caught spying on themselves.

art director
Gary Godkin

writer
Stuart Clark

creative director
Stuart Clark

client
Absolut Vodka

agency
Whybin TBWA / Pyrmont

05191A

art director
Dave Dye

writer
Sean Doyle

illustrators
Rene Milot
Mark Summers
Mark Denton
Marc Burkhard
George Underwood

creative director
Dave Dye

client
Merrydown

agency
Campbell Doyle Dye /
London

05192A

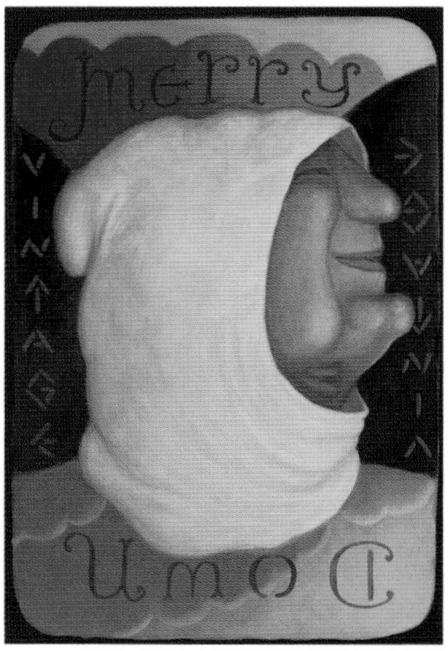

art directors
David Sin
Ian Lee

writers
Adrian Miller
Christie Herman
James Yap

photographers
Wizard Photography
Character Studio

creative director
Adrian Miller

client
Land Rover Owners Club

agency
Lowe & Partners /
Selangor

05195A

art director
Raphael Puettmann

writer
Stephan Deisenhofer

designers
Miriam Bloching
Lorenz Clormann

photographer
Piet Truhlar

creative directors
Stefan Leick
Mario Gamper

client
Yamaha

agency
Scholz & Friends / Berlin

05194A

Also Awarded:
merit
Consumer Magazine
Color: Full Page:
Campaign

< Merit >

< Merit >

art directors
Steven Chung
David Chu
Leo Wan
Tif Wu
Eddie Wong

writer
King Zhang

illustrators
Zhang Wen Yao
Amoeba Digital Imaging

creative directors
Eddie Wong
Tif Wu
John Merrifield

client
adidas China

agency
TBWA\Shanghai
(180\TBWA)

05196A

Also Awarded:
merit
Outdoor: Single

merit
Outdoor: Single

OUTDOOR : CAMPAIGN

art director
Amy Rakowski

writer
Amy Rakowski

client
Gotham Comedy Club

agency
Tractenberg Advertising / New York

05197A

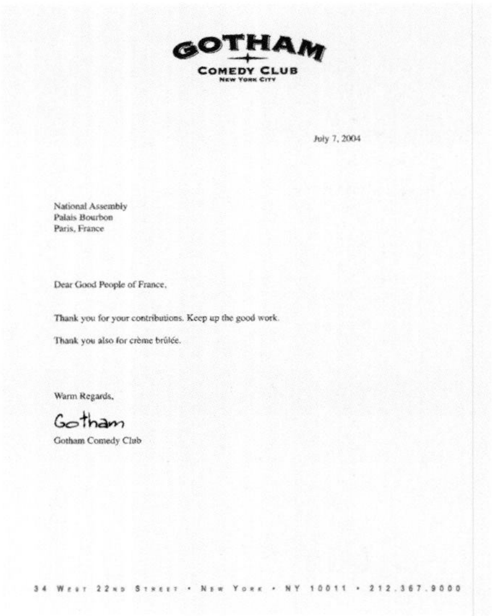

GOTHAM
COMEDY CLUB
NEW YORK CITY

July 7, 2004

National Assembly
Palais Bourbon
Paris, France

Dear Good People of France,

Thank you for your contributions. Keep up the good work.

Thank you also for crème brûlée.

Warm Regards,
Gotham
Gotham Comedy Club

34 WEST 22ND STREET • NEW YORK • NY 10011 • 212.367.9000

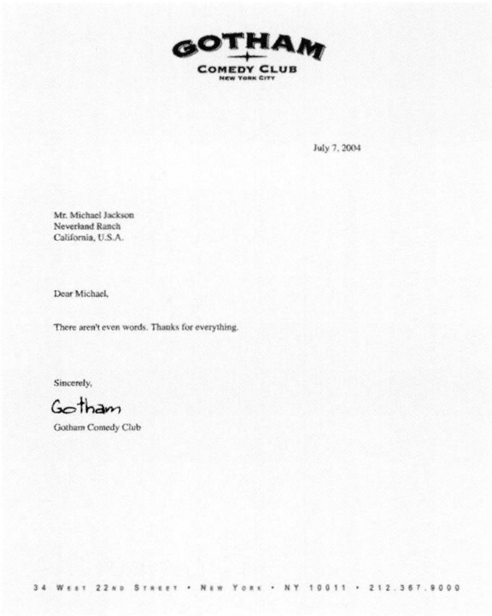

GOTHAM
COMEDY CLUB
NEW YORK CITY

July 7, 2004

Mr. Michael Jackson
Neverland Ranch
California, U.S.A.

Dear Michael,

There aren't even words. Thanks for everything.

Sincerely,
Gotham
Gotham Comedy Club

34 WEST 22ND STREET • NEW YORK • NY 10011 • 212.367.9000

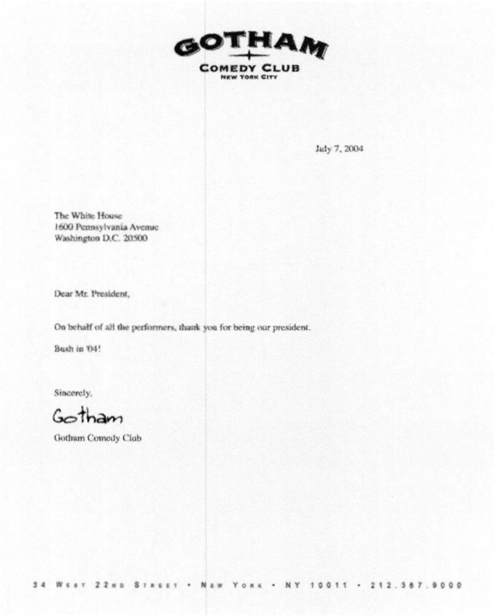

GOTHAM
COMEDY CLUB
NEW YORK CITY

July 7, 2004

The White House
1600 Pennsylvania Avenue
Washington D.C. 20500

Dear Mr. President,

On behalf of all the performers, thank you for being our president.

Bush in '04!

Sincerely,
Gotham
Gotham Comedy Club

34 WEST 22ND STREET • NEW YORK • NY 10011 • 212.367.9000

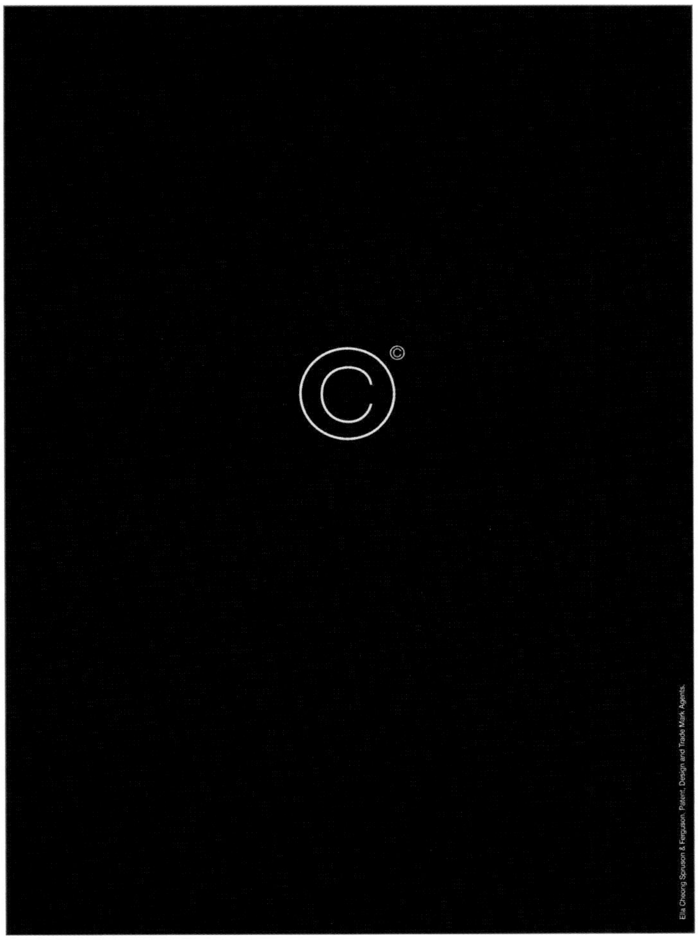

art director
Goh Wee Kim

writer
Andrew McKechnie

creative director
Francis Wee

client
Ella Cheong Spruson & Ferguson

agency
BBDO / Singapore

05198A

A

Merit

One Show

TRADE : COLOR : FULL PAGE OR SPREAD — SINGLE

art director
Frank Haggerty

writer
Brian Tierney

creative director
Jim Nelson

client
Rapala

agency
Carmichael Lynch /
Minneapolis

05199A

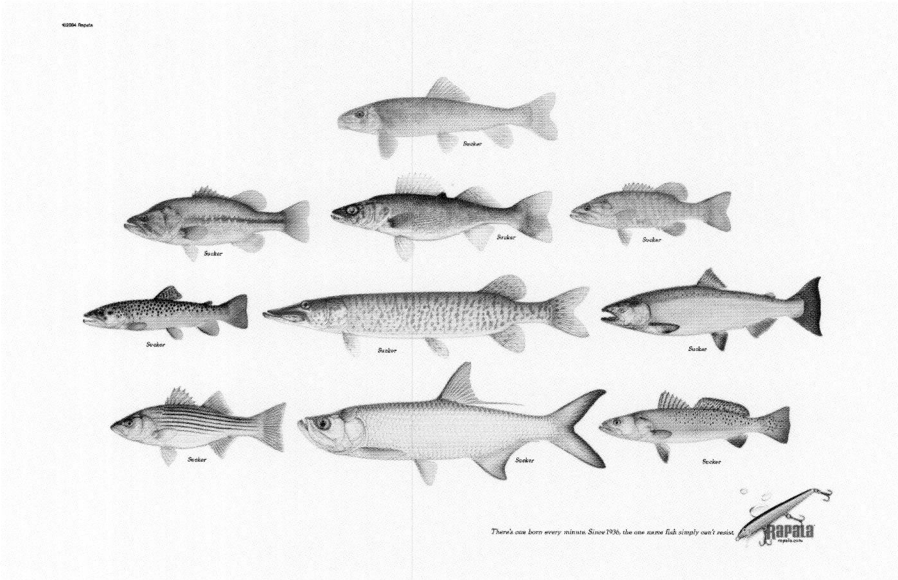

art director
Dean Lee

writer
James Lee

photographer
CWS

creative director
Alan Russell

client
DDB Canada

agency
DDB / Vancouver

05200A

"THE STORE ROOM? IT'S THE SECOND ROW, FIFTH SWITCH FROM LEFT."
BEEN THERE TOO LONG?
AQUENT
Staffing | Executive Search | Outsourcing
WWW.AQUENT.COM

art director
Goh Wee Kim

writer
Priti Kapur

photographer
Rick Tang
Shutterbug

creative directors
Steve Straw
Linda Locke
Tay Guan Hin

client
Aquent

agency
Leo Burnett / Far East Square

05202A

"THE BUTTON FOR TEA DISPENSES HORLICKS. THE BUTTON FOR SOUP DISPENSES TEA."
Coffee
Tea
Chocolate
Soup
Whitener
Sugar
Power
Serve
Cancel
Water
Steam
Cuppa Corner
BEEN THERE TOO LONG?
AQUENT
Staffing | Executive Search | Outsourcing
WWW.AQUENT.COM

art director
Goh Wee Kim

writer
Priti Kapur

photographer
Rick Tang
Shutterbug

creative directors
Steve Straw
Linda Locke
Tay Guan Hin

client
Aquent

agency
Leo Burnett / Far East Square

05201A

One Show

TRADE : COLOR : FULL PAGE OR SPREAD — SINGLE

art directors
Reed Collins
Mark McGinnis

writers
Reed Collins
Kash Sree

illustrator
Mark McGinnis

client
Young Guns

agency
Reed Collins / Chicago

05203A

Aa Atomic
Bb Blow
Cc Camel toe
Dd Drive-by
Ee Embryo
Ff F.B.I.
Gg Gimp
Hh Homos
Ii Instant noodles
Jj Jah
Kk Knocked up
Ll Lobotomy
Mm Merkin
Nn No. 2
Oo Orthodox
Pp Peyote
Qq Q-tip
Rr Road kill
Ss Subliminal
Tt Third nipple
Uu Euthanasia
Vv Vegan
Ww W.A.S.P.
Xx Xanax
Yy Y-fronts
Zz Zits
YOUNG GUNS
CALL FOR ENTRIES
FOR THE KIDS

art director
Jeff Hopfer

writer
Mike Renfro

creative directors
Jeff Hopfer
Mike Renfro

client
Jackson Walker Law Firm

agency
The Richards Group / Dallas

05204A

Ever NOTICE how most advertisements have a bunch of mouse type written across the bottom of the page that nobody ever looks at because it's written by lawyers? Nobody really even pays attention to it anymore because it's so incomprehensible—which begs the question. Why is it there? Is it just to give certain lawyers something to do? Rather than indulge such lawyers, maybe you should look at Jackson Walker. After all, if they can make you read this stuff, they must be very different lawyers indeed. www.jw.com

High powered blower. STIHL

art director
Martin Darfeuille

writer
Edouard Perarnaud

photographer
Corbis

creative directors
Sylvain Thirache
Alexandre Herve

client
STIHL

agency
DDB / Paris

05205A

Cut your brush. STIHL

Cut your brush. STIHL

art director
Martin Darfeuille

writer
Edouard Perarnaud

photographer
David Harriman

creative directors
Sylvain Thirache
Alexandre Herve

client
STIHL

agency
DDB / Paris

05206A

One Show

TRADE : COLOR : FULL PAGE OR SPREAD — CAMPAIGN

art director
Poh Hwee Beng

writers
Eliza Yick
Danny Chan

photographers
Eliza Yick
Poh Hwee Beng

illustrator
Lee Pui Ho

creative director
Poh Hwee Beng

client
McDonald's

agency
Foote Cone & Belding / Shanghai

05209A

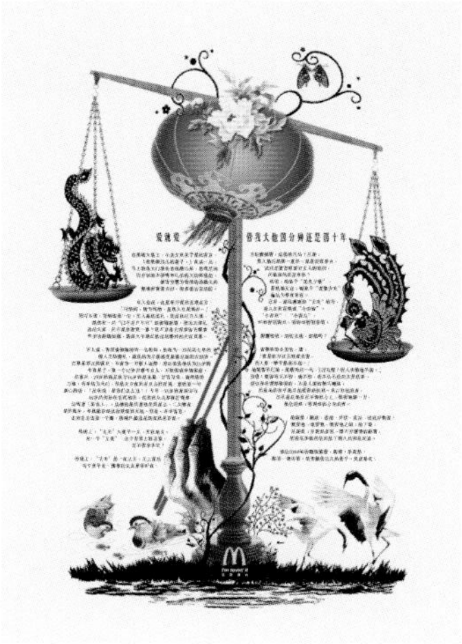

art director
Phil Clarke

writer
Joel Bradley

photographer
Donald Milne

creative director
Tony Granger

client
Manfrotto

agency
Saatchi & Saatchi / London

05210A

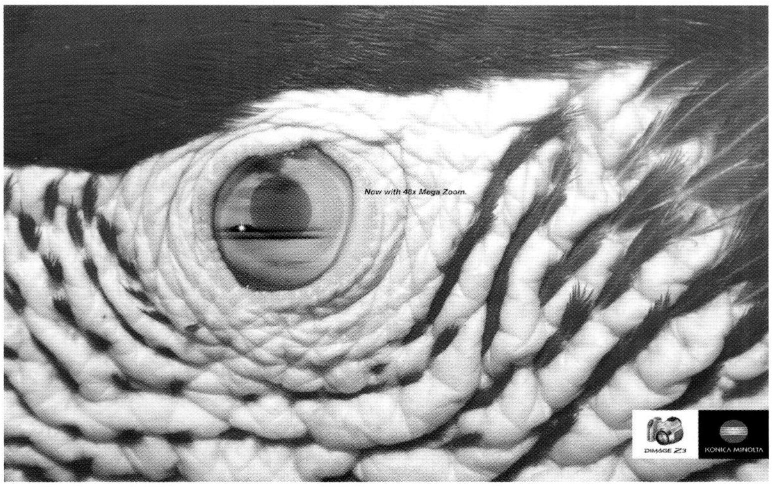
Now with 40x Mega Zoom.
DiMAGE Z3
KONICA MINOLTA

art director
Volkmar Weiss

writer
Stephan Deisenhofer

photographers
Zefa
Corbis
Image Bank

creative directors
Stefan Leick
Mario Gamper

client
Konica Minolta

agency
Scholz & Friends / Berlin

05207A

Also Awarded:
merit
Collateral
P.O.P. and In-Store: Campaign

Modern Digital. We're so awesome, we don't need advertising! Call us:
(206) 623-3444 or visit www.moderndigital.com

Could Modern Digital get even more Modern?
Do you have a nose, noseface?
Let's battle!
Use of the double logo.
Well, sue us for living.

At Modern Digital, our post facilities are so amazing we don't even need advertising!
It's time you realize there is no better high tech post equipment. It is so like NASA that we don't even have to show pictures of it.
And our graphic artist Deborah Ristic is so recognized for her greatness we don't even have to show her picture. She needs no introduction, snap out of it.
So this isn't even her!
It's someone almost no one recognizes, Wendy Flanagan Combs, who doesn't even know Deb but would totally recognize her. Deb is too busy using her Phantom xk9 subdivider right now anyhow! We thought we made that up, but she really works on the Phantom xk9!
Or something totally new like that and the best, so pinch yourself it's true. We know we didn't have to tell you about that so we almost didn't.
Even if she was available she wouldn't even need to be. Whatever! Try this on, we don't even need to tell you about our new kitchen remodel, give us a break, of course it'll be awesome and totally sweetness and done by a real architect with the best degrees of all time. He's too good even for the Sistine Chapel or Monticello or the White House so they don't even call him. MD is so awesome we don't even have to say our whole name
anymore, Modern Digital. You'll know us as MD and our editorial wizard Kevin Adams is so awesome, I mean shut up, this frame didn't even make sense
until he cut it and now you can't even tell how much better it is than when he started but that's what awesomeness is about, it's totally seamless! For the most part you already knew all this of course because MD doesn't even need to advertise but grow up buttercup maybe you scratch our back and we'll scratch yours with a paw from a Cannes Lion or whatever else you totally care about in your business.
moderndigital
Modern Digital. We're so awesome, we don't need advertising! Call us:
(206) 623-3444 or visit www.moderndigital.com

Stop looking for it.
We're so awesome we don't even need to use our full page!
Because when you've got the DUMB-SILLY-BEST motion graphic designers in the entire Milky Way, or whatever planet you're living on, then you don't even need it.
But you know that, so let's talk about raccoons. They are pretty cool with those sa-weeet masks! But you know that, too. That's why we like each other. See ya.
Modern Digital. We're so awesome we don't even need a full page!
Call us: (206) 623-3444 or visit www.moderndigital.com.

art directors
Maari Thrall
Josh Combs
Cal McAllister

writers
Cal McAllister
Ian Cohen

photographer
Nicole Schofield

illustrator
Craig Styles

creative directors
Cal McAllister
Ian Cohen

client
Modern Digital

agency
Wexley School for Girls / Seattle

05211A

Merit

art director
Nadine Prada

writer
Sally Smallwood

illustrator
Stephen Bowes

creative directors
Tim Kavander
Bill Newbery

client
Volkswagen

agency
Arnold Worldwide / Toronto

05212A

Happy Holidays.
Drivers wanted.

art director
James Clunie

writer
Tom Christmann

designer
James Clunie

creative director
David Lubars

client
In Touch Magazine

agency
BBDO / New York

05214A

The war in Iraq.
What does Ashton think?
IN TOUCH
HUNK!
Get InTouch!

THE TOPLESS MINI IS HERE
MINI

art directors
Alex Lim Thye Aun
Ali Shabaz

writer
Ali Shabaz
Alex Lim Thye Aun
Raoul Panes

designers
Alex Lim Thye Aun
Ali Shabaz

illustrator
Tang Kee Hong

creative directors
Francis Wee
David Guerrero
Suthisak Sucharittanonta
Mike Schalit
Ronald Ng

client
BMW

agency
BBDO / Singapore

05215A

LOVE YOUR LAWN.
ACE
THE PLACE FOR LAWNCARE.

art director
Scot Crooker

writer
Chris Dutton

photographer
Jeff Von Hoene

creative director
Joe Paprocki

client
Intown Ace Hardware

agency
Huey/Paprocki / Atlanta

05219A

One Show

COLLATERAL ADVERTISING : P.O.P. AND IN-STORE — SINGLE

art directors
Kevin Lee
Robin Wu

writers
Cecilia Zhu
Roy Yeo

photographer
Benny of
One-Twenty-One

creative directors
Sheung Yan Lo
Kevin Lee

client
Nike

agency
JWT / Shanghai

05220A

art director
Vancelee Teng

writer
Panusard
Tanashindawong

designer
Saovapa Toesangaun

photographer
Studio De Nagara

illustrator
Studio De Nagara

creative director
Jeffrey Curtis

client
Axe / Unilever Thai
Holdings

agency
Lowe / Bangkok

05222A

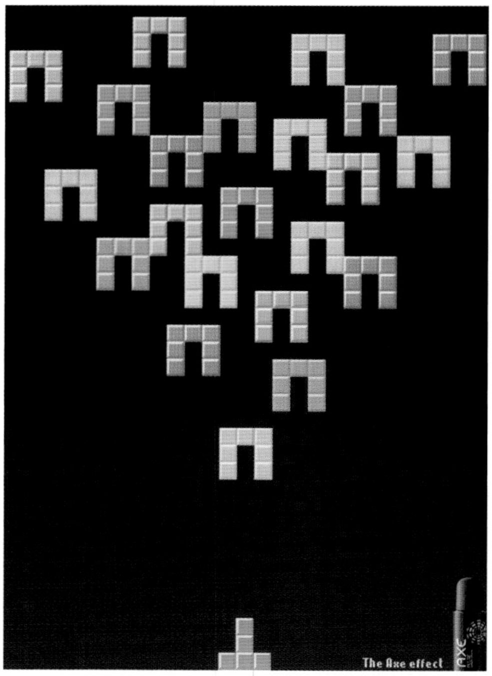

Tide
with a touch of
Downy
New softer Tide with a touch of Downy. Works wonders.

art director
Fern Cohen

writer
Margot Owett

designer
Hamish McArthur

creative directors
Sarah Barclay
Tod Seisser
Tony Granger

client
Procter & Gamble/Tide

agency
Saatchi & Saatchi /
New York

05225A

Hansaplast
Banana flavoured condoms.

art director
Jessica Gérard-Huet

writer
Jean-Francois Bouchet

photographer
Philippe Gueguen

creative director
Erik Vervroegen

client
Hansaplast

agency
TBWA\Paris

05229A

One Show

COLLATERAL ADVERTISING : P.O.P. AND IN-STORE — SINGLE

art directors
Karen Wong
Gavin Simpson

writers
Karen Wong
Edward Ong

creative director
Gavin Simpson

client
Campbell Soup

agency
Young & Rubicam /
Kuala Lumpur

05231A

New bigger cans
SAME OLD LABELS
Campbell's
CREAM OF CHICKEN
KRIM AYAM
To highlight the fact that Campbell's Soup is now available in a larger 420g can, we put their usual 290g label on the new can. These limited-edition cans were displayed at participating supermarkets during the launch period. They were also sold to members of the public at a ...well, smaller price.

art director
Bernie Hogya

writer
Brian Ahern

photographer
Bernie Hogya

creative directors
Tony Granger
Jan Jacobs

client
Adorama Camera

agency
Bozell / New York

05234A

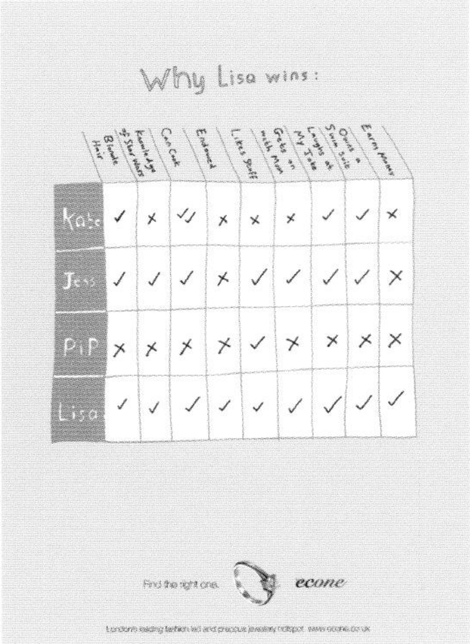

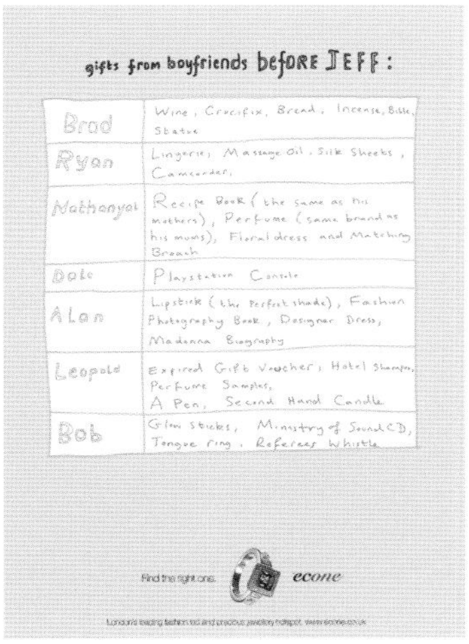

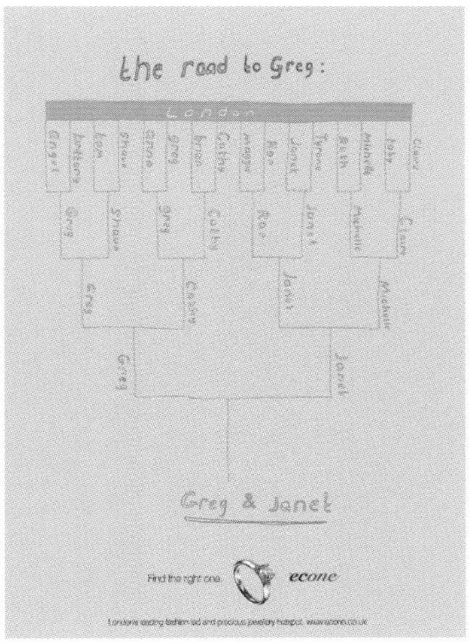

art directors
Matt Keon
Oliver Green

writers
Matt Keon
Oliver Green

illustrator
Fuzzy

creative directors
Al Young
Matt Keon
Oliver Green

client
JOS

agency
FCB / London

05236A

One Show

COLLATERAL ADVERTISING : P.O.P. AND IN-STORE — CAMPAIGN

art directors
Pann Lim
Roy Poh

writers
Pann Lim
Roy Poh
Alex Goh

designers
Pann Lim
Roy Poh

photographer
Roy Poh

illustrators
Pann Lim
Roy Poh

creative director
Kinetic

client
Noble Education

agency
Kinetic / Singapore

05237A

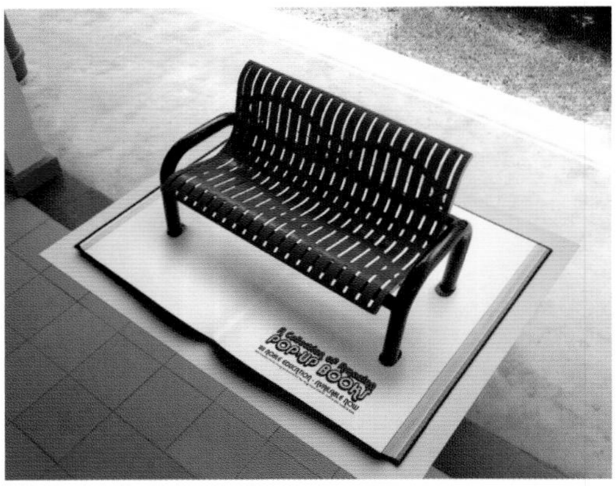

art director
Kai Fang

writer
Al Jackson

photographers
Getty Images
Bill Curtsinger
Tim Laman
John Dunn

creative director
Bill Pauls

client
Polartec / High Country

agency
BBDO / Atlanta

05233A

< Merit >

art director
Eddie Wong Yew Heng

writer
Farrokh Madon

photographer
Hon (Shutterbug)

illustrator
Lay Leng (Procolor)

creative directors
Terrence Tan
Farrokh Madon

client
Toykar

agency
M&C Saatchi / Singapore

05238A

Also Awarded:
merit
P.O.P and In-Store: Single

art director
Deepak Dogra

writer
Deepak Dogra

photographer
Deepak Dogra

creative director
N. Ramesh

client
Gillette

agency
Ogilvy & Mather / New Delhi

05239A

Merit

One Show

COLLATERAL ADVERTISING : P.O.P. AND IN-STORE — CAMPAIGN

art director
John Stapleton

writer
Ryan Stafford

creative director
Scott Sheinberg

client
Twin Palms Publishing

agency
WestWayne / Tampa

05241A

A powerful reminder of
SOME THINGS
we'd like to forget.
LYNCHING PHOTOGRAPHY IN AMERICA

A NEGATIVE.
LYNCHING PHOTOGRAPHY IN AMERICA

A THOUSAND WORDS.

art directors
Vasan Wangpaitoon
Aniruth Assawanapanon

writers
Juntiga Nasunee
Wirat Charoenwiwatchai
Suthisak Sucharittanonta
Nikrom Kulkosa

illustrator
Remix Studio

creative directors
Suthisak Sucharittanonta
Nikrom Kulkosa
Vasan Wangpaitoon

client
Daimler Chrysler

agency
BBDO / Bankok

05243A

art directors
Jayson Atienza
Frank Anselmo

writers
Frank Anselmo
Jayson Atienza

photographer
Mike Wilson

creative directors
Gerry Graf
David Lubars

client
Guinness

agency
BBDO / New York

05244A

art director
David Smail

writers
David Smail
Ngo Xuan Hien

designers
Pham Tuan Minh
Loc Nguyen

creative directors
Tim Green
David Smail

client
Nike

agency
JWT / Ho Chi Minh City

05246A

GIAI VIET DA NU TOAN THANH 1984
the spirit was here before the shoes.

art directors
Khoo Choo Kian
MUN

writers
Lim Shu-Lin
Mindy Teh

photographer
Studio ROM

creative directors
Ted Lim
Alvin Teoh

client
Nikon

agency
Naga DDB / Malaysia

05251A

The widest lens in its class.
Nikon

Comfort

art director
Santaya Saralak

writer
Sirilak Chitpanvong

photographer
Anuchai Sricharoenputong

illustrator
Remix Studio

creative director
Wisit Lumsiricharoenchoke
Karanee Areekul

client
Unilever Thai Holding

agency
Ogilvy & Mather / Bangkok

05252A

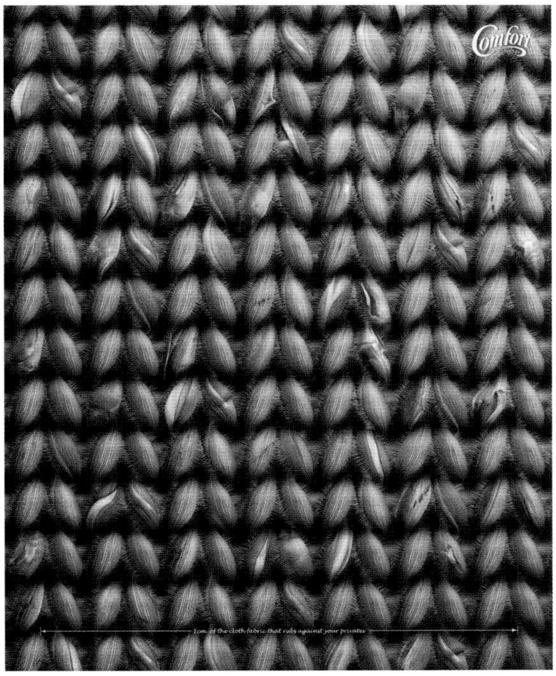
Comfort
1cm. of the cloth fabric that rubs against your privates

art director
Santaya Saralak

writer
Sirilak Chitpanvong

photographer
Anuchai Sricharoenputong

illustrator
Remix Studio

creative directors
Wisit Lumsiricharoenchoke
Karanee Areekul

client
Unilever Thai Holding

agency
Ogilvy & Mather / Bangkok

05253A

art director
Tan Chee Keong

writer
Donevan Chew

photographer
K.H. Mak of
Untold Images

creative directors
Sonal Dabral
Peter Chan

client
Pizza Hut Restaurants

agency
Ogilvy & Mather /
Kuala Lumpur

05254A

Introducing Pizza Hut Hot Pouch. For oven-hot pizzas, call 1-300-88-2525.
Pizza Hut

art director
Bryan Courtney

writer
Nick Gordon

photographer
Shahn Rowe

creative director
Rajesh Ranchod

client
Osram Long Life Bulbs

agency
Saatchi & Saatchi /
Johannesburg

05258A

Long life bulbs.
OSRAM

The new A-Class with
Side-Impact Protection.

Gelb
GelbeSei

The new A-Class with
Side-Impact Protection.
Gelb

art directors
Myles Lord
Bill Yom

writer
Michael Benzinger

designer
Stefan Schabenberger

creative directors
Dirk Haeusermann
Matthias Harbeck
Arno Lindemann
Stefan Meske

client
Mercedes Benz

agency
Springer & Jacoby /
Hamburg

05259A

One Show

COLLATERAL ADVERTISING : POSTERS — CAMPAIGN

art director
Jon Loke

writer
Victor Ng

photographers
Hon
Stock

illustrator
Lay Leng

creative director
Steve Straw

client
Victorinox

agency
Leo Burnett /
Far East Square

05263A

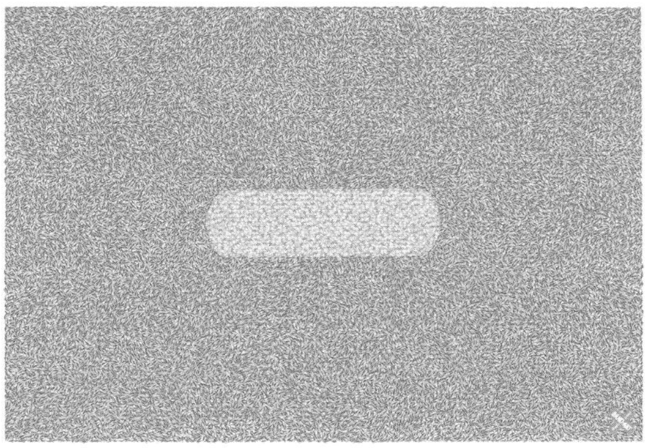

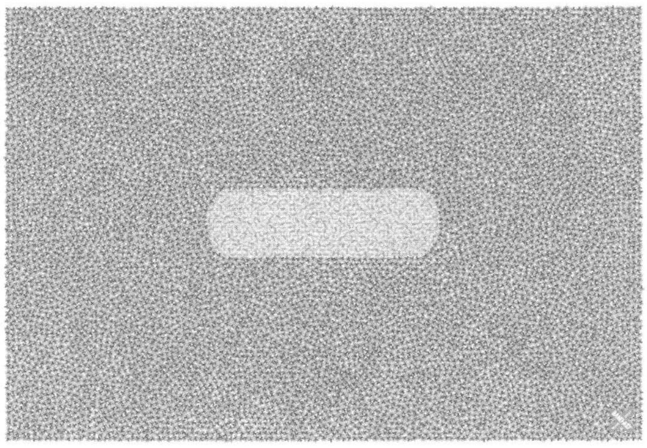

art directors
Manish Bhatt
Raghu Bhat
Manasi Kotian
Renu Karwa

writers
Raghu Bhat
Manish Bhatt

illustrators
Manish Bhatt
Manasi Kotian
Renu Karwa

creative director
Prasoon Joshi

client
Band Aid Washproof

agency
McCann Erickson / Mumbai

05264A

< Merit >

art director
Ivan Hady Wibowo

writer
Craig Rosenthal

photographer
Charles Chua
Groovy Studio

illustrator
Christopher Ng
Procolor

creative director
Ng Tian It

client
Microsoft

agency
McCann Erickson / Singapore

05265A

Also Awarded:
merit
Collateral
Posters: Single

One Show

COLLATERAL ADVERTISING : POSTERS — CAMPAIGN

art director
Michael Lees-Rolfe

writer
Jake Bester

photographer
Guy Neveling

creative directors
Greg Burke
Mark Fisher
Ryan Reed
Chris Gotz

client
Parmalat - Everfresh

agency
Ogilvy South Africa / Cape Town

05266A

Also awarded:
merit
Consumer Newspaper
600 Lines or Less: Single

< Merit >

art directors
Chow Kok Keong
Eric Chow

writer
Steve Clay

illustrators
Chow Kok Keong
Eric Chow
Loo Kok Seng
Akiyoshi Kitaoka

creative directors
Steve Clay
Ted Royer

client
GP Battery

agency
Publicis / Kuala Lumpur

05267A

Also Awarded:
merit
Consumer Magazine
Color: Full Page: Single

merit
One Show Design
Posters: Campaign

< Merit >

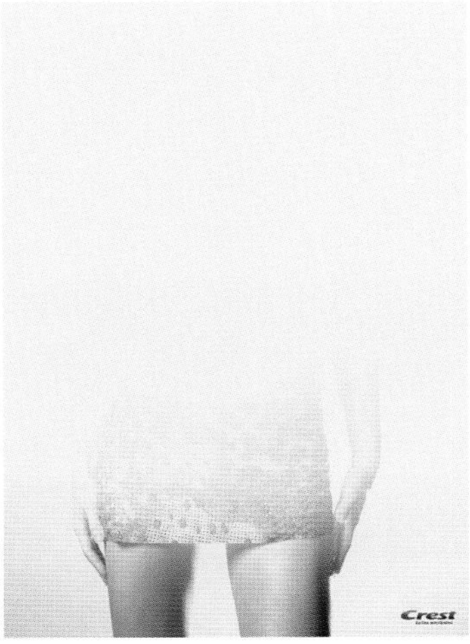

art director
Phil Clarke

writer
Joel Bradley

photographer
Morten Laursen

creative director
Tony Granger

client
Crest

agency
Saatchi & Saatchi /
London

05268A

One Show

COLLATERAL ADVERTISING : POSTERS — CAMPAIGN

art directors
Kelvin Leong
Henry Yap

writer
Ronald Ng

photographer
Raymond Sih

creative director
Edmund Choe

client
EUT Marketing

agency
Saatchi & Saatchi /
Petaling Jaya

05269A

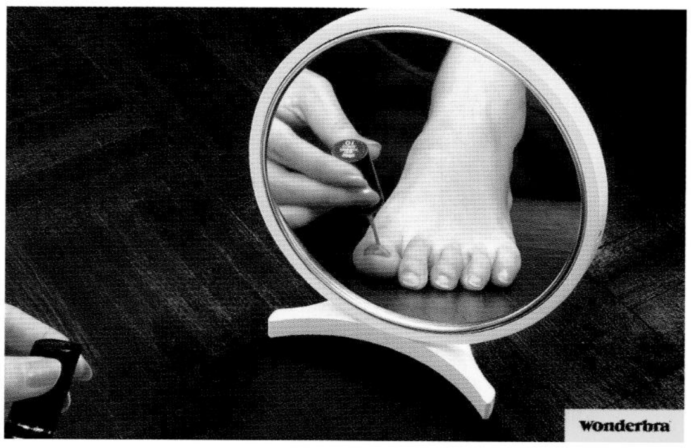

I WAS YOUR EX-BOYFRIEND
AND NOW I'M A TOAD.
TRUST ME
I GET THE IRONY!
BUT BETH, THIS IS JUST ANOTHER EXAMPLE OF WHY "WE" DON'T WORK. YOU GET INTO SOMETHING, LIKE MAGIC, AND SUDDENLY, YOU'RE CONSUMED BY IT. THEN, I MAKE AN INNOCENT REMARK ABOUT HOW MAGIC IS FOR GEEKS AND—POOF! I'M A FLYLICKER. BETH, IF YOU'RE READING THIS, YOU HAVE TO LET THE PAST BE THE PAST AND CHANGE ME BACK. OKAY, I'LL BE WAITING IN THE DRAINAGE DITCH ON YOUR LEFT. (P.S. I'M THE ONE WEARING A BOTTLE CAP FOR A HAT.)
SEATTLE MAGIC • 106 1ST AVENUE • YOU WILL BELIEVE

MY WIFE IS ASKING
FOR A
DIVORCE
IN MY CURRENT STATE
RALPH, I APOLOGIZE FOR MAKING FUN OF YOUR MAGIC TRICKS. OKAY? SORRY. BUT I HARDLY THINK THE PUNISHMENT FITS THE CRIME WHEN YOU TURN A MAN INTO A CHICKEN FOR MAKING A WISECRACK. NO MAN SHOULD HAVE TO TELL HIS WIFE HE CAN'T MOW THE LAWN BECAUSE HE'S GOT WINGS. WINGS, RALPH! DO YOU KNOW HOW HUMILIATING THAT IS?! DAMN HUMILIATING YOU SICK SON-OF-A...SORRY. I'M GETTING EMOTIONAL. LISTEN, LETS DO LUNCH AT THE PETTING ZOO. I NEED TO BE HUMAN AGAIN ASAP.
SEATTLE MAGIC • 106 1ST AVENUE • YOU WILL BELIEVE

art director
Jason Wood

writer
Mike Roe

photographer
Stock

client
Seattle Magic

agency
Spearhead / Seattle

05270A

BEING A GOAT
FOR THREE DAYS
HAS TAUGHT ME A LOT ABOUT MYSELF
SPECIFICALLY, I'VE LEARNED THAT I'M ARROGANT, CONDESCENDING, AND INSENSITIVE TOWARD THE PEOPLE AROUND ME. AND TO ROB, I WANTED TO SAY THAT I AM VERY SORRY FOR HAVING EVER CALLED YOUR MAGIC TRICKS "GOOFY" AND TELLING YOU WHERE TO STICK THAT MAGIC WAND OF YOURS. IT WAS WRONG AND I APOLOGIZE. NOW PLEASE, FOR THE LOVE OF CHRIST, CHANGE ME BACK!! I PROMISE TO BE A BETTER SUPERVISOR FROM HERE ON OUT.
SEATTLE MAGIC • 106 1ST AVENUE • YOU WILL BELIEVE

art directors
Michael Ashley
Diana Tung

writers
Dinesh Kapoor
Michael Ashley

designer
Michael Ashley

creative director
Michael Ashley

client
Arnika

agency
Arnika / Richmond

05271A

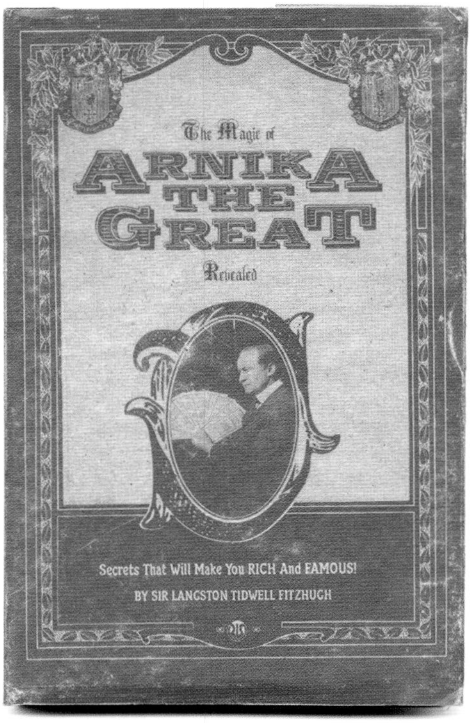
The Magic of
ARNIKA THE GREAT
Revealed
Secrets That Will Make You RICH And FAMOUS!
BY SIR LANGSTON TIDWELL FITZHUGH

art director
Mark Braddock

writers
Ned McNeilage
Linda Knight

designer
Mark Braddock

illustrators
Ned McNeilage
Linda Knight
Mark Braddock

creative directors
Ned McNeilage
Linda Knight
Mark Braddock
Tanya Sim

clients
Ned McNeilage
Linda Knight

agency
Block / Leederville

05273A

HOW THE HELL DID I BECOME A
COWBOY?
The Tale of a Suburban
I GREW UP IN AUSTRALIA
LINDA
Once upon a time
there was a sassy little art director named Linda
The two young ad wankers started their career at

art director
Dean Lee

writer
James Lee

photographer
CWS

creative director
Alan Russell

client
DDB Canada

agency
DDB / Vancouver

05272A

Merit

timowuerz.com

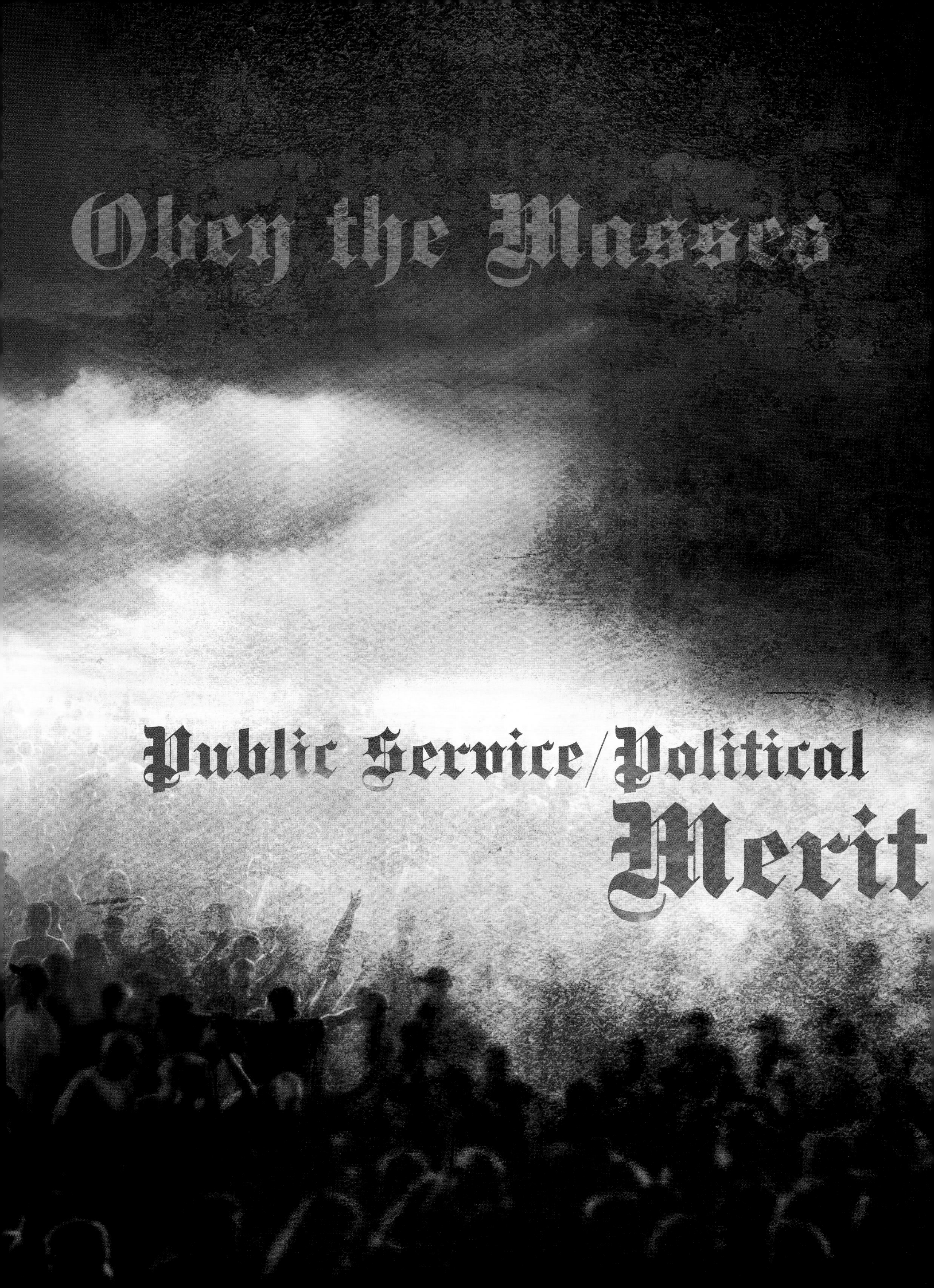
Obey the Masses
Public Service/Political
Merit

PUBLIC SERVICE / POLITICAL — PRINT : NEWSPAPER OR MAGAZINE — SINGLE

art director
Cosmo Campbell

writer
Joseph Bonnici

photographer
Cosmo Campbell

creative director
Alan Russell

client
First United Mission

agency
DDB / Vancouver

05275A

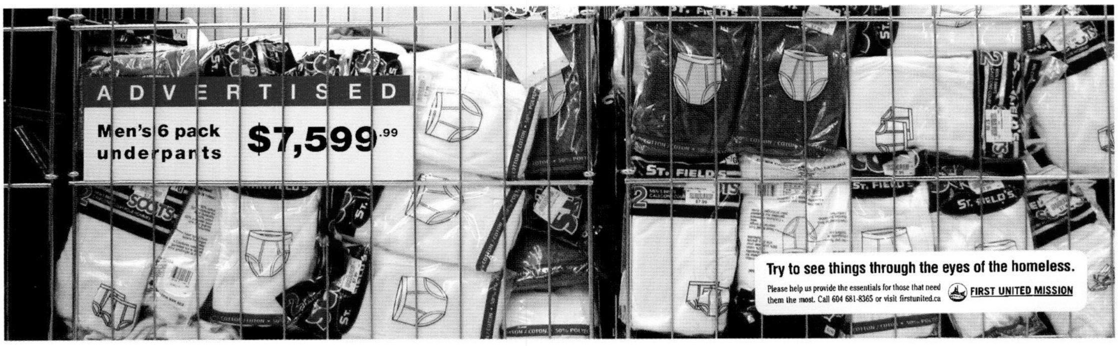
ADVERTISED
Men's 6 pack underparts
$7,599.99
Try to see things through the eyes of the homeless.
Please help us provide the essentials for those that need them the most. Call 604 681-8365 or visit firstunited.ca
FIRST UNITED MISSION

art director
Cosmo Campbell

writer
Joseph Bonnici

photographer
Cosmo Campbell

creative director
Alan Russell

client
First United Mission

agency
DDB/ Vancouver

05274A

Bright's
Anti-Bacterial Flouride Toothpaste
MANAGERS SPECIAL
BRIGHT'S T/PASTE - MINT
$2,799.99
Try to see things through the eyes of the homeless.
Please help us provide the essentials for those that need them the most. Call 604 681-8365 or visit firstunited.ca
FIRST UNITED MISSION

BUENOS AIRES
ZOO
115 YEARS

art directors
Daniel Fierro
Pablo Tajer

writers
Hernán Rebaldería
Pablo Gil

creative director
Chavo Demilio

client
Buenos Aires Zoo

agency
Del Campo Nazca Saatchi & Saatchi / Martinez

05276A

Also Awarded:
merit
Outdoor and Posters: Single

MATCHES. BE CAREFUL WHERE YOU THROW THEM.

art director
Luciano Lincoln

writer
Eduardo Lima

photographer
Chema Madoz

creative directors
Fábio Fernandes
Eduardo Lima

client
Fundação SOS Mata Atlântica

agency
F/Nazca Saatchi & Saatchi / São Paulo

05277A

art director
Vanessa Castelau

writer
Marco Figueiredo

photographer
Filipe Rebelo

creative director
João Espírito Santo

client
Salvation Army

agency
J. Walter Thompson / Lisbon

05279A

EXÉRCITO DE SALVAÇÃO
WITHOUT YOUR HELP THE HOMELESS WILL NEVER LEAVE THE STREETS. CHRISTMAS DONATIONS CAMPAIGN, DECEMBER 13 - 24.
SERVING OUR NEIGHBOUR

art director
Terrence Tan

writer
Farrokh Madon

photographer
Eric Seow

illustrator
Yau Digital Imaging

creative directors
Terrence Tan
Farrokh Madon

client
Think Centre

agency
M&C Saatchi / Singapore

05280A

Ever wondered why Cambodia is ranked 178 in world soccer?
Over 40,000 Cambodians have lost their legs to landmines. 6 million mines still remain. Please send your contributions to Jesuit Refugee Service: Cambodia Landmine Campaign in Phnom Penh. For details, contact Denise Coghlan. Tel: 855 23 880 455. E-mail: jrscam@forum.org.kh
DESTROY LANDMINES BEFORE THEY DESTROY LIVES.
THINK CENTRE is a public service organization committed to raising awareness of landmine victims.

WORDS SAVE LIVES
AMNESTY INTERNATIONAL
www.amnesty.org.nz

art director
Josh Moore

writer
Seymour Pope

illustrator
Department of Motion Graphics

creative director
Nick Worthington

client
Amnesty International

agency
Publicis Mojo / Auckland

05283A

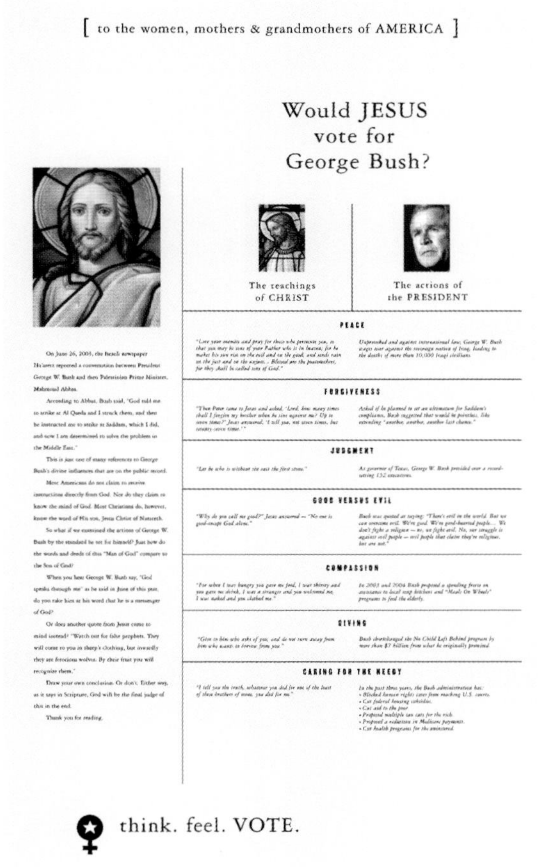
[to the women, mothers & grandmothers of AMERICA]
Would JESUS vote for George Bush?
The teachings of CHRIST
The actions of the PRESIDENT
think. feel. VOTE.

art director
Tracy Wong

writer
John Schofield

illustrators
Tracy Wong
Stock

creative directors
Tracy Wong
John Schofield

client
Think
Feel
Vote

agency
Shong! / Seattle

05284A

PUBLIC SERVICE / POLITICAL — PRINT : NEWSPAPER OR MAGAZINE — SINGLE

art directors
Minna Lavola
Jyri Konttinen

writers
Tommy Makinen
Markku Ronkko
Eeva Kekalainen

photographer
Reetta Pasanen

client
Amnesty International

agency
TBWA\PHS Helsinki

05287A

Every day one out of three women runs into a door.
Stop violence against women. www.amnesty.fi

ICKEN
THE MORE YOU SAVE, THE MORE THE CHICKEN PAYS.
RSPCA
48
PORTIONS
● Instead of saving money, you could save suffering. ● Just a little more money means chickens have more room to move, helping to prevent deformed bones and infected joints due to lack of exercise. ● A little more money means birds are more likely to avoid searing ammonia burns and blisters caused by standing in built-up excrement. ● A little more money might not make much difference to you, but it can reduce suffering for the chicken. ● Look out for the Free Range, Organic and Freedom Food labels. ● Or for more information visit us at www.rspca.org/chickens

If chickens have more room to exercise when they're reared, they're less likely to suffer deformed bones and infected joints. They're less likely to suffer blisters and ammonia burns from standing in built-up excrement. If only you were more likely to buy them. Look for the free range, organic or freedom food labels. For more information visit www.rspca.org.uk/chickens
RSPCA
x1
GRILLED/
FRIED/
ROASTED/
HOWEVER IT'S COOKED, SOME CHICKEN WILL ALWAYS LEAVE A BAD TASTE IN THE MOUTH.

RSPCA
■ How do you like your chicken? With pasta? Maybe a salad would be nice. ■ But how about with a little extra room to live? ■ Just a little more space to exercise helps prevent deformed bones and infected joints that can result from being so tightly packed. ■ It also means they're less likely to endure a life of searing ammonia burns and blisters caused by standing in built-up excrement. ■ It's good to look after yourself, but can't we also be kinder to chickens? ■ Look for the Free Range, Organic and Freedom Food labels. ■ For more information visit www.rspca.org.uk/chickens
Chicken
IS ALL ABOUT A HEALTHIER LIFESTYLE. UNLESS OF COURSE YOU'RE THE CHICKEN.

art director
Paul Belford

writers
Mark Fairbanks
Markham Smith

illustrators
Paul Belford
John Tisdall

creative directors
Paul Belford
Nigel Roberts

client
RSPCA

agency
Abbott Mead Vickers
BBDO / London

05288A

PUBLIC SERVICE / POLITICAL — PRINT : NEWSPAPER OR MAGAZINE — CAMPAIGN

art director
Paul Keister

writer
Bob Cianfrone

photographers
Jim Knight
Sebastian Gray

producers
Sandy DeMouy
Barry Bamberg

creative directors
Ron Lawner
Alex Bogusky
Pete Favat
Tom Adams
Roger Baldacci

client
American Legacy
Foundation

agency
Arnold Worldwide /
Boston and Crispin
Porter + Bogusky / Miami

05289A

connect
truth

Every year, 95% of people who try to stop smoking are not successful.
Marlboro
6.80
Pack
In as little as two weeks, nicotine changes the brain's chemistry and addiction can begin.
Tobacco companies make billions a year feeding an addiction they help create.
The impact of nicotine is jacked up because tobacco companies add ammonia. The same stuff you clean with.
connect
truth

GOVERNMENT WARNING:
NEW LOWER PRICE!
5.50
Pleasure to Burn
connect
6.85
connect-truth.com keyword: cha-ching
NO SMOKING
1985
On Sale Here
NEWS
Tobacco companies make $1.8 billion from sales to under-age people every year.
A tobacco company has called teenagers "tomorrow's potential customers."
Newport
SAVE $1.00
Tobacco signage is often placed at a child's eye level.

Doctors in Japan's Togo Unit didn't
observe the Geneva Convention.
Or for that matter, the Hippocratic Oath.
二战日本东乡部队医生

As a wounded POW at
Ping Fan, being denied
medical treatment
could just save your life.
身为平房战俘，受伤不送院，
也许更能保命。

< Merit (2) >

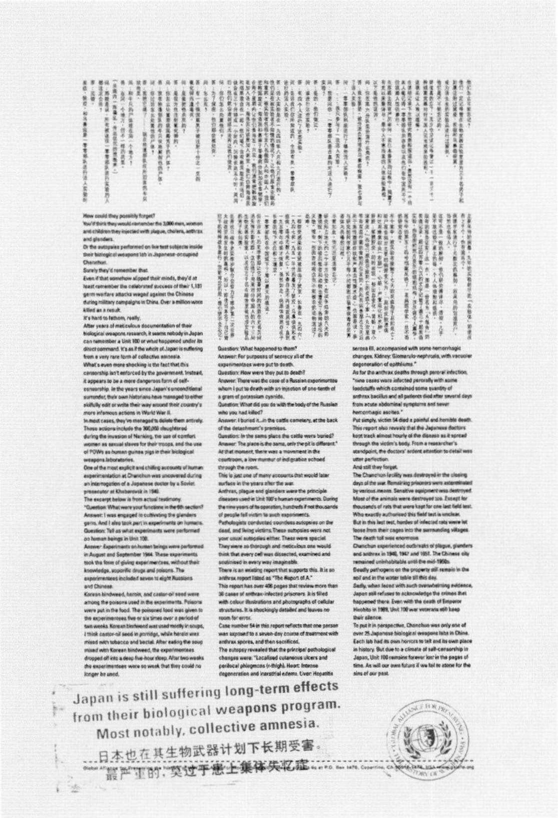
Japan is still suffering long-term effects
from their biological weapons program.
Most notably, collective amnesia.
日本也在其生物武器计划下长期受害。
最严重的，莫过于患上集体失忆症

< Merit >

art director
Eric Yeo

writers
Robert Gaxiola
Mandy Siow
Chen Ting
Calvin Loo

illustrator
Judy Low

creative director
Robert Gaxiola

client
Global Alliance

agency
Foote Cone & Belding / Singapore

05290A

Also Awarded:

merit
Public Service: Newspaper or Magazine: Single

merit
Outdoor and Posters: Single

merit
Outdoor and Posters: Single

Merit

PUBLIC SERVICE / POLITICAL — PRINT : NEWSPAPER OR MAGAZINE — CAMPAIGN

art director
Michael Martin

writer
Michael Yee

photographers
Goran Tacevski
Nikola Tacevski

creative director
Basil Mina

client
Association of Librarians
of the Czech Republic

agency
Leo Burnett / Prague

05291A

Also Awarded:
merit
Outdoor and Posters:
Campaign

FYODOR DOSTOEVSKY
CRIME AND PUNISHMENT
READ IT BEFORE HOLLYWOOD DOES
ASSOCIATION OF LIBRARIANS OF THE CZECH REPUBLIC

CHARLOTTE BRONTE
jane eyre
READ IT BEFORE HOLLYWOOD DOES
ASSOCIATION OF LIBRARIANS OF THE CZECH REPUBLIC

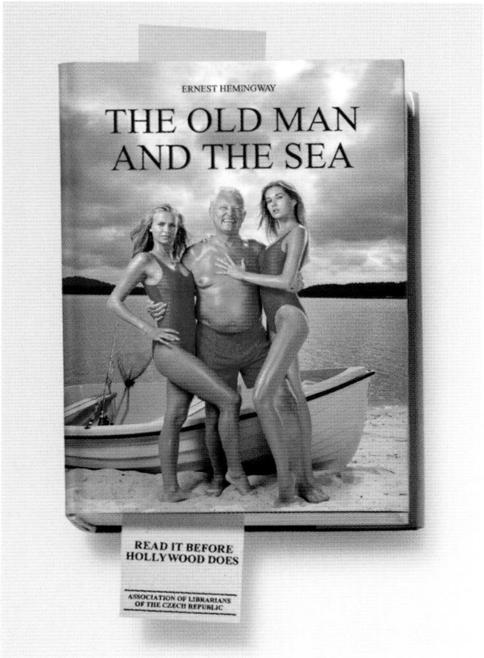
ERNEST HEMINGWAY
THE OLD MAN AND THE SEA
READ IT BEFORE HOLLYWOOD DOES
ASSOCIATION OF LIBRARIANS OF THE CZECH REPUBLIC

art director
Noah Regan

writer
Jason Mendes

photographer
Tommy Morris

creative director
David Nobay

client
UNIFEM

agency
Saatchi & Saatchi / Sydney

05292A

This page The galley-style kitchen gleams in stainless steel. Keith dragged his girlfriend, by her hair, across the original, polished floorboards. His favourite place to belittle her in front of guests is on the 2-meter Muebles dining table. **23% of Australian women suffer abuse during a relationship. We need some serious home improvement.** Wear a white ribbon on the 25th of November and help end the violence. www.ribbons@unifem.org.au

One Show

PUBLIC SERVICE / POLITICAL — PRINT : NEWSPAPER OR MAGAZINE — CAMPAIGN

art directors
Victor Aguilar
Pablo Gonzalez De La Peña

writers
Nacho Guillo
Cesar Sastre

creative director
Juan Nonzioli

client
Save the Children

agency
Shackleton / Madrid

05293A

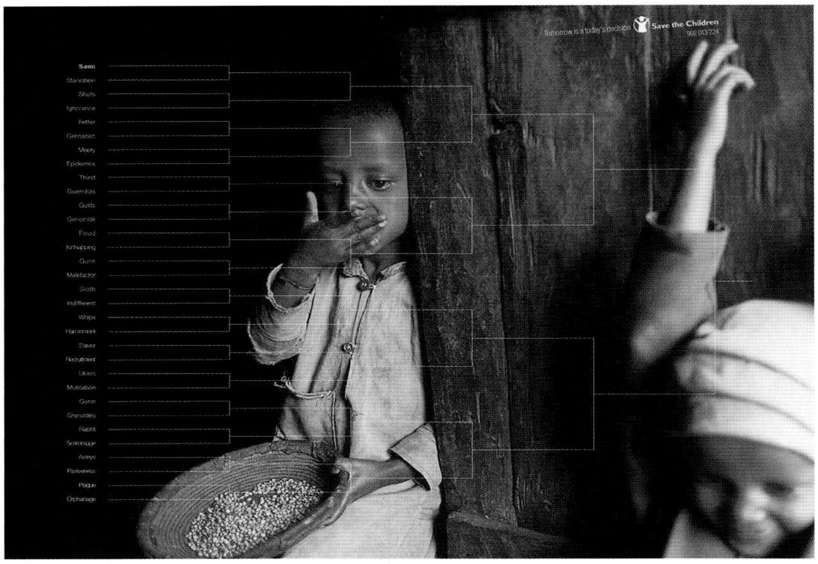

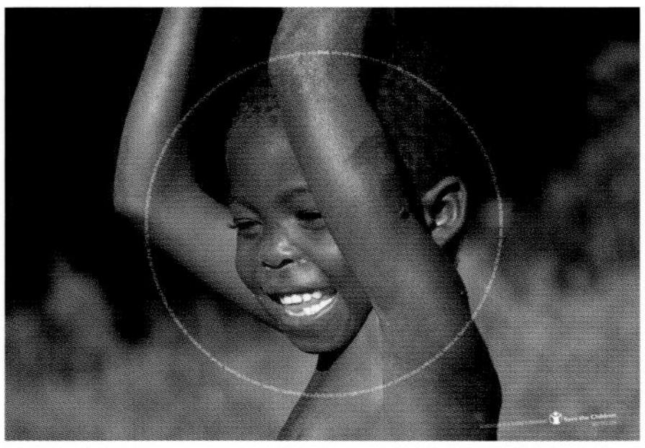

HAVE YOU SEEN THIS MAN?
Eric
Last seen driving away in a big car
If you see him please tell him that
I want to come home.
And I promise never to chew his magazines
or pee on the carpet again.
I feel so lost without him.

LOST
HWEE LING

Missing
Jamal
Last seen jumping into a taxi on a stormy night. If you see him, tell him I miss taking long naps with his shoes. Tell him I miss his gentle rubs under my chin. Tell him I miss him. If you have any information, call Mimi at 6287 5135.
www.spca.org.sg Over 1,000 pet owners abandon their pets every month. Don't be one of them.

art director
Patrick Low

writers
Rashid Sidek
Mark Tan

photographer
Patrick Low

illustrator
Procolor

creative directors
Patrick Low
Neil French

client
SPCA

agency
Y&R / Singapore

05294A

Merit

PUBLIC SERVICE / POLITICAL — PRINT : OUTDOOR AND POSTERS — SINGLE

art directors
Mike Fetrow
James Clunie

writer
Brian Tierney

illustrators
Mike Fetrow
James Clunie

client
Cub Scouts (Viking Indianhead Council BSA)

agency
Carmichael Lynch / Minneapolis

05295A

SLOWLY STEP AWAY FROM THE JOYSTICK.
JOINCUBS.COM

art directors
Mark Sorensen
Jim Landry

writer
Troy Longie

creative director
Jac Coverdale

client
MNCASA

agency
Clarity Coverdale Fury / Minneapolis

05296A

DON'T READ THIS.
Stop it. Seriously, stop it right now. All right, that's it. Not one more word. You're still reading, aren't you? How would you like it if nobody listened when you asked them to stop? Sadly, it happens to an estimated 13,000 date rape victims in Minnesota every year.

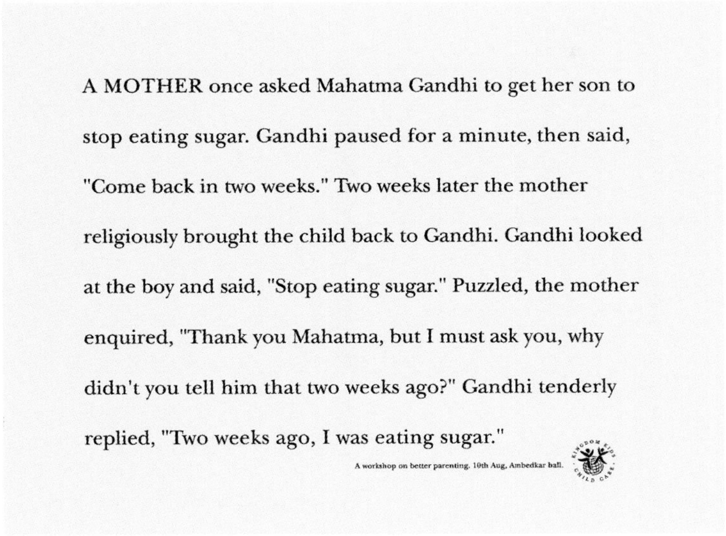
A MOTHER once asked Mahatma Gandhi to get her son to stop eating sugar. Gandhi paused for a minute, then said, "Come back in two weeks." Two weeks later the mother religiously brought the child back to Gandhi. Gandhi looked at the boy and said, "Stop eating sugar." Puzzled, the mother enquired, "Thank you Mahatma, but I must ask you, why didn't you tell him that two weeks ago?" Gandhi tenderly replied, "Two weeks ago, I was eating sugar."
A workshop on better parenting. 10th Aug, Ambedkar hall.
KINGDOM KIDS CHILD CARE

art directors
Ramprasad Dasari
Prabhu Kumar

writer
Ramprasad Dasari

creative director
Ramprasad Dasari

client
Kingdom Kids

agency
Emphasis Media / Bangalore

05299A

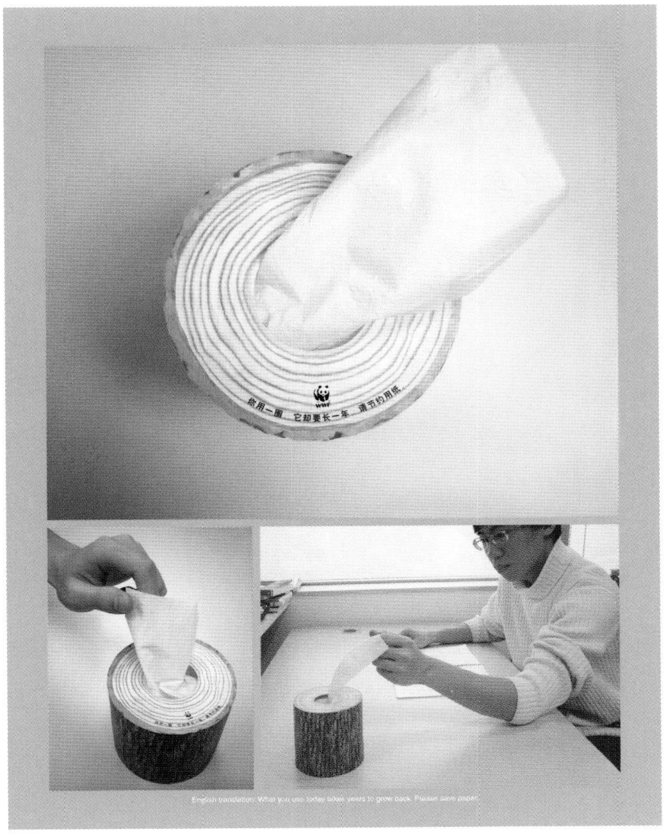
你用一圈 它却要长一年 请节约用纸
WWF

art director
Maggie Yuan

writer
Billy Deng

photographers
Guo Xiaowen
Zhang Zhiwen

creative directors
Poh Hwee Beng
Danny Chan

client
WWF

agency
Foote Cone & Belding / Shanghai

05300A

PUBLIC SERVICE / POLITICAL — PRINT : OUTDOOR AND POSTERS — SINGLE

art director
Ralph Watson

writer
David Parson

creative directors
Ralph Watson
David Parson

client
Truthout.org

agency
GSD&M / Austin

05303A

OVER HALF THE PEOPLE IN CONGRESS
are
MILLIONAIRES.
Affordable PRESCRIPTION DRUGS TO THEM
MAY NOT BE AFFORDABLE PRESCRIPTION DRUGS TO YOU.
TRUTHOUT.ORG
They may not be LIKE YOU, but they do REPRESENT YOU. Make sure they do, VOTE.

art directors
Teboho Mosothoane
Ryan Reed

writer
Gordon Ray

photographer
Guy Neveling

creative director
Greg Burke

client
City Mission

agency
Ogilvy South Africa / Cape Town

05305A

SOME EAT OUT EVERY DAY
Help us feed the homeless. (021) 691 9547
city mission

SOME EAT OUT EVERY DAY
city mission

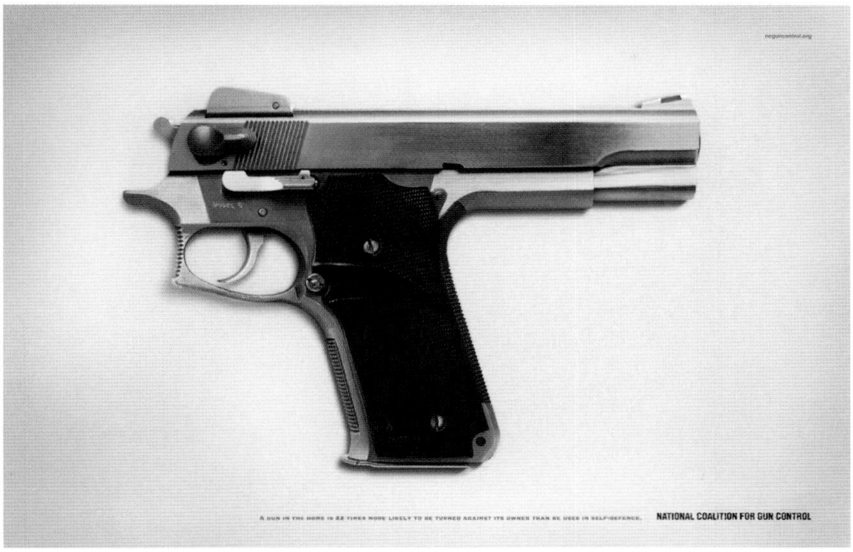

art directors
Jay Benjamin
Andy DiLallo

writers
Andy DiLallo
Jay Benjamin

creative director
David Nobay

client
National Coalition for Gun Control

agency
Saatchi & Saatchi / Sydney

05306A

art director
Gregory French

writer
Peter Quester

creative directors
Martin Pross
Julia Schmidt
Matthias Schmidt

client
Graffiti Exhibition

agency
Scholz & Friends / Berlin

05298A

One Show

PUBLIC SERVICE / POLITICAL — PRINT : NEWSPAPER OR MAGAZINE — SINGLE

art directors
Minna Lavola
Jyri Konttinen

writers
Tommy Makinen
Markku Ronkko
Eeva Kekalainen

client
Amnesty International

agency
TBWA\PHS Helsinki

05310A

Kaivopuisto 0436
Kaivopuisto Brunnsparken 0436
Every day
one out of three women
runs into a pole or
bumps into a corner.
Stop violence against women.
www.amnesty.fi
Karhupuisto 0256

Kaivopuisto 0436
Kaivopuisto Brunnsparken 0436
Every day
one out of three women
runs into a pole or
bumps into a corner.
Stop violence against women.
www.amnesty.fi

Keep Reading.

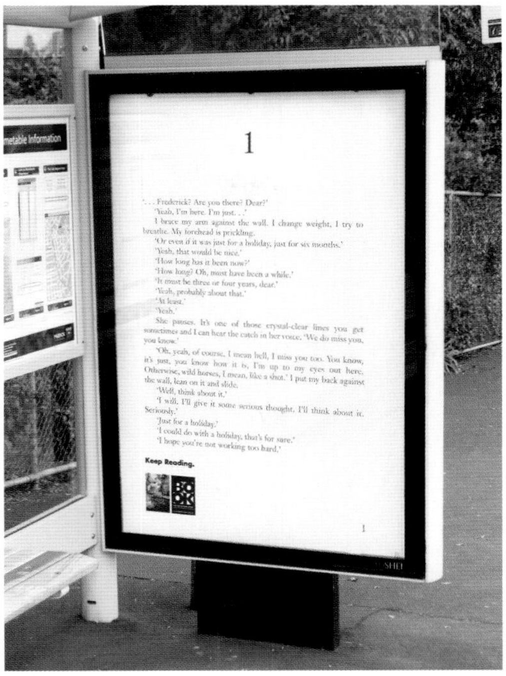
1
Keep Reading.

art directors
Tim Huse
Guy Rooke

writers
Guy Rooke
Tim Huse

designer
Maria Lishman

creative directors
Rich Maddocks
Toby Talbot

client
New Zealand Book Council

agency
Colenso BBDO / Auckland

05312A

SEE THE ALL-SENSATIONAL, UNFAIR, DYNAMITE EXPLODE. NON TELEVISED.
IN THEIR OWN HOME
WEEKLY
ALL YEAR LONG
A UNIQUE EVENT - 1 ROUND
JOSE "THE DRUNK"
ALVARADO
VS
JOSE
ALVARADO JR.
STOP WATCHING FROM THE SIDELINES
DENOUNCE CHILD ABUSE - 239 47 47
NATIONAL CORPORATION AGAINST CHILD ABUSE

IN THEIR SAME HOUSE
MON-SUN.
ALL YEAR LONG
1 FIGHT - 1 ROUND
HERNANDEZ
VS.
HERNANDEZ
STOP WATCHING FROM THE SIDELINES
DENOUNCE CHILD ABUSE - 239 47 47
NATIONAL CORPORATION AGAINST CHILD ABUSE

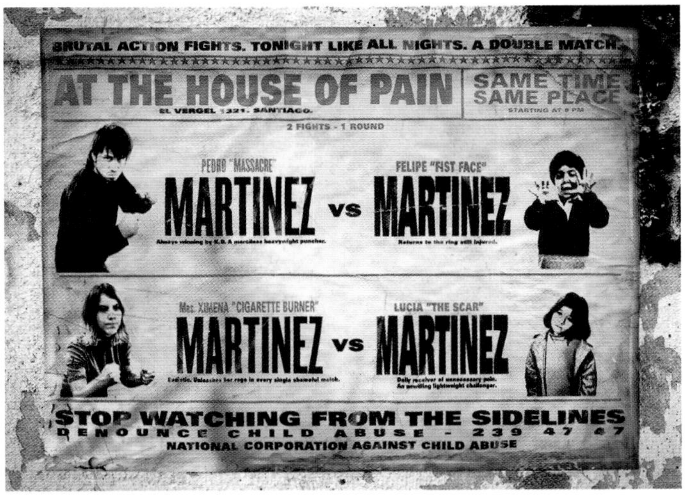
BRUTAL ACTION FIGHTS. TONIGHT LIKE ALL NIGHTS. A DOUBLE MATCH.
AT THE HOUSE OF PAIN
SAME TIME
SAME PLACE
2 FIGHTS - 1 ROUND
PEDRO "MASSACRE"
MARTINEZ vs MARTINEZ
FELIPE "FIST FACE"
Mrs. XIMENA "CIGARETTE BURNER"
MARTINEZ vs MARTINEZ
LUCIA "THE SCAR"
STOP WATCHING FROM THE SIDELINES
DENOUNCE CHILD ABUSE - 239 47 47
NATIONAL CORPORATION AGAINST CHILD ABUSE

art director
Sebastian Alvarado

writers
Felipe Manalich
Nicolas Lopez

photographers
Sergio Vera
Carlos Ruiz Tagle

illustrator
Sebastian Alvarado

creative director
Cesar Agost - Carreno

client
National Corporation Against Child Abuse

agency
Ogilvy & Mather / Santiago

05314A

One Show

PUBLIC SERVICE / POLITICAL — PRINT : NEWSPAPER OR MAGAZINE — CAMPAIGN

art director
Derrick Kim

writer
Karl Fleet

photographer
Mark Lever

illustrator
Len Cheeseman

creative director
Nick Worthington

client
New Zealand Blood Service

agency
Publicis Mojo / Auckland

05315A

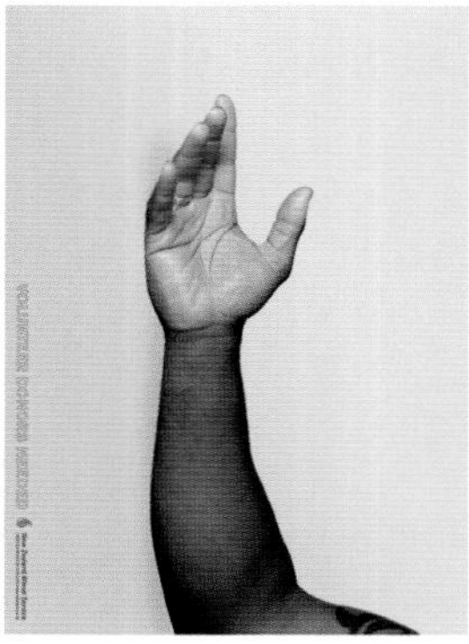

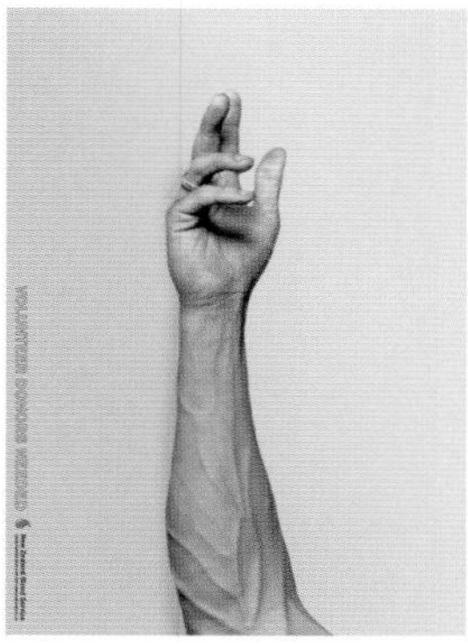

STOP THE WILDLIFE TRADE.
IFAW
1 18909202990817

STOP THE WILDLIFE TRADE.
IFAW
1 18109202989027

< Merit (2) >

STOP THE WILDLIFE TRADE.
DONATIONS: ACCOUNT NO. 84263-00, SOZIALBANK, SORTCODE 251 205 10
IFAW
INTERNATIONAL FUND FOR ANIMAL WELFARE
WWW.IFAW.ORG
1 18909202990817

< Merit >

STOP THE WILDLIFE TRADE.
IFAW

< Merit (2) >

art director
Birigit Hogrefe

writer
Christiane Rein

designer
Simone Grün

photographers
Nadav Kander
Till Leeser

creative directors
Dirk Haeusermann
Matthias Harbeck

client
IFAW

agency
Springer & Jacoby / Hamburg

05316A

Also Awarded:

merit
Public Service/Political: Newspaper or Magazine: Single

merit
Public Service/Political: Newspaper or Magazine: Single

merit
Public Service/Political: Outdoor and Posters: Single

merit
Public Service/Political: Outdoor and Posters: Single

merit
Public Service/Political: Outdoor and Posters: Single

Merit

PUBLIC SERVICE / POLITICAL — PRINT : COLLATERAL (BROCHURES / DIRECT MAIL) — SINGLE

art director
Ang Sheng Jin

writer
Clarence Chiew

photographer
Jimmy Fok

creative director
Lim Sau Hoong

client
Singapore Environment Council

agency
10AM Communications / Singapore

05317A

2005
THE PROBLEM GETS WORSE EVERY DAY.
The Ozone layer is disappearing at a rate of 4,000 square kilometers per day. To find out how you can help, log on to www.sec.org.sg
SINGAPORE ENVIRONMENT COUNCIL

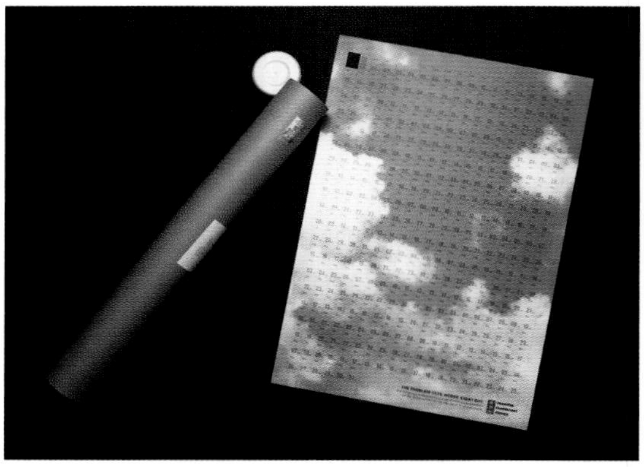

2005

Detect breast cancer before it strikes.
To find out how, insert and play.

art director
Chow Kok Keong

writers
Herbie Phoon
Steve Clay

photographers
Alex Tow
IFL Studio

creative directors
Steve Clay
Ted Royer

client
Radiology Malaysia

agency
Publicis / Kuala Lumpur

05318A

Some children will have nothing to look forward to this Christmas.
24 Milk Chocolate Figurines
Net Wt.
75 g. (2.6 oz.)

art director
Leighton Dyer

writer
Leighton Dyer

creative director
Nick Worthington

client
Auckland City Mission

agency
Publicis Mojo / Auckland

05319A

Merit

PUBLIC SERVICE / POLITICAL — PRINT : COLLATERAL (BROCHURES / DIRECT MAIL) — SINGLE

art director
Kirk Gainsford

writer
Avital Pinchevsky

creative director
Sandra de Witt

client
South African National Blood Service

agency
TBWA\Hunt\Lascaris / Sandton

05320A

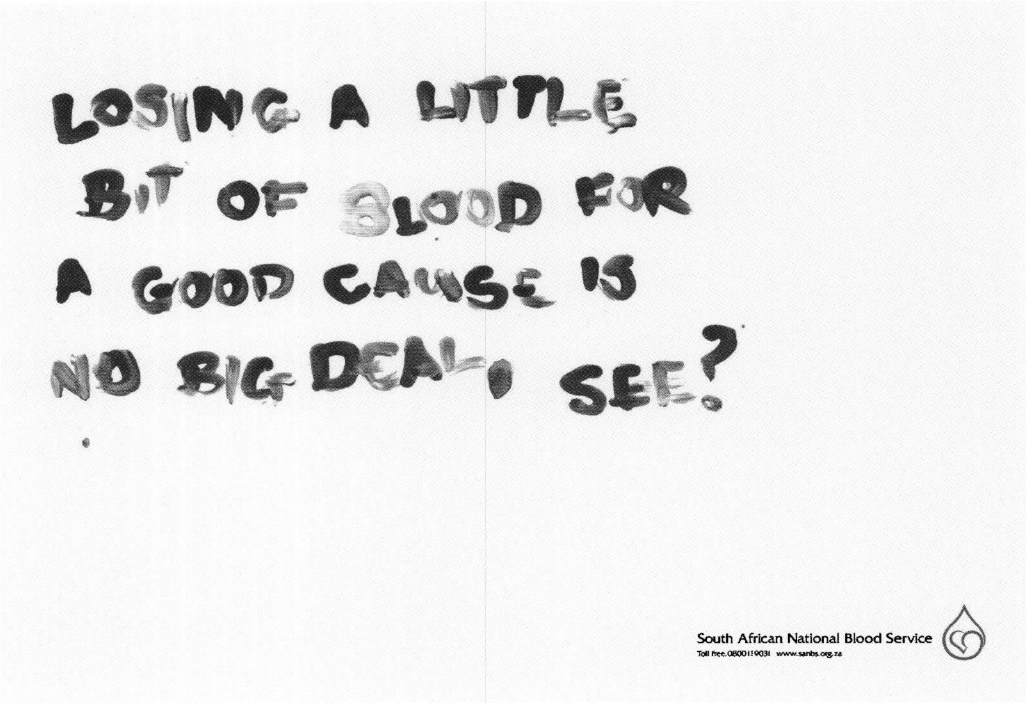
LOSING A LITTLE BIT OF BLOOD FOR A GOOD CAUSE IS NO BIG DEAL, SEE?
South African National Blood Service
Toll free.0800119031 www.sanbs.org.za

(We see a business executive in a suit standing in front of a conveyor belt. He is wearing a hair net and protective eyewear. He walks and speaks to the camera. As he does so, we see various aspects of the assembly line. We see shards of glass being dumped into the popsicle molds, purple liquid pumped into the molds, workers on the conveyor belt line, a large first-aid station in the background, etc.)

MAN: At Shards O Glass Freeze Pops, we want you to know where we stand on important glass pop issues. For example, we now agree there is no such thing as a safe glass freeze pop. They are addictive and can cause serious health issues. In fact, one third of people who enjoy our product will eventually die from shards-related ailments. The only proven way to reduce health risks from our freeze pops is to not eat them. For more, including information and links on how to help quit our freeze pops, visit our website.

(We see close-up of computer url address "shardsoglass.com")

MAN: And remember, Shards O Glass Freeze Pops are for adults only!

SUPER: Imagine if all companies sold products like tobacco.

(We cut to exterior shot of the manufacturing plant with the Crazyworld sign flickering in front in the foreground.). Truth logo.

art director
Pete Favat

writer
Roger Baldacci

agency producer
Amy Favat

production company
Biscuit Filmworks

director
Tim Godsall

creative directors
Ron Lawner
Pete Favat
Alex Bogusky
Roger Baldacci
Tom Adams

client
American Legacy Foundation

agency
Arnold Worldwide / Boston and Crispin Porter + Bogusky / Miami

05032T

PUBLIC SERVICE / POLITICAL — TELEVISION : SINGLE

art director
Andrew Ostrom

writer
Andrew Petch

agency producer
Mandy Payne

production company
Caravan Pictures

director
Ben Lawrence

creative director
Warren Brown

client
Australian Red Cross
Blood Service

agency
BMF Advertising /
Pyrmont

05033T

(We see people donating blood at the Australian Red Cross Blood Service donor centre. We see the director of this commercial giving blood.)

SUPER: The director of this commercial.

(We then see the cinematographer giving blood. And then others.)

SUPER: Cinematographer

SUPER: Ad Agency Creative
Sound recordist
Producer
Assistant director
Runner
Camera Assistant
Gaffer
Caterer
Editor
Colour grader
Voice Over Artist

(Being the voice over artist, he turns and speaks to camera.)

VOICE OVER: The Australian Red Cross Blood Service needs blood, so we gave blood to make this ad. Now we're asking you to. Because Australia needs 20,000 donations every week.

SUPER: Don't ignore the need for blood. To give call 13 14 95 or visit donateblood.com.au

The Assistant Director

The Voice Over Artist

DON'T IGNORE
THE NEED FOR BLOOD
To give call 13 14 95
or visit donateblood.com.au
Australian Red Cross
BLOOD SERVICE

VOICE OVER: (In French) Since he's been working in this company, Marc has smoked 145,430 cigarettes in his office, 64,720 at the coffee machine area, 82,860 in the meeting room, 6,380 in the elevator, 16,410 in the copy machine room...In total Marc has smoked 315,800 cigarettes. That's a lot, especially for a non-smoker.

When you smoke, non-smokers smoke, too.

art director
Jean-Michel Alirol

writer
Dominique Marchand

agency producer
Suzanne Hormain

production company
@radical. media

director
Les Elvis

creative director
Thomas Stern

client
Inpes Passive Smoking

agency
FCB / Paris

05036T

art director
Bryan Michurski

writer
Linda Birkenstock

agency producer
Deb Lustig

production company
Hungry Man

director
Scott Vincent

creative director
Thomas Moudry

client
Mediawise

agency
Martin Williams / Minneapolis

05037T

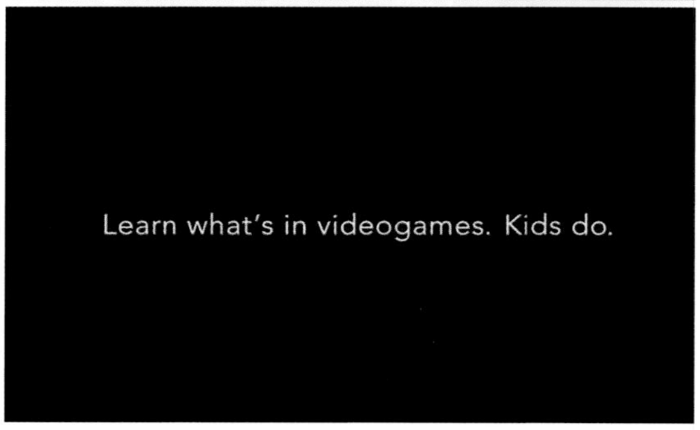
Learn what's in videogames. Kids do.

(Open on a young boy sitting on the arm of the couch in his living room.)

BOY: There's this club down the street that's fun so I go in and shoot this woman in the head, and people are screaming and running all over and there's blood everywhere.

There's this cop next to me who sees what I did. He's got body armor on, so I can't shoot him, so I throw gasoline on him and light it and he screams and runs around and he died.

SUPER: Learn what's in video games. Kids do. Go to mediawise.org

BOY: There's this prostitute and they're super hard to kill, so I grab a machete and cut her head off.

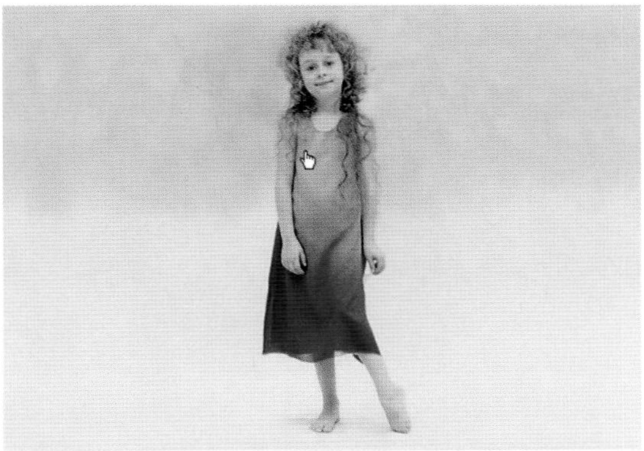

The next time you witness child abuse,
don't keep quiet about it.
www.prayas.org

(The film opens on the photograph of a little girl. A cursor appears on the screen and begins to move all over her body. When the cursor reaches her crotch, the film fades to black.)

SUPER: Thankfully, she did not feel a thing. But millions of children are not as fortunate. The next time you witness child abuse, don't keep quiet about it.
www.prayas.org

art director
Mohammed Soaeb

writer
Ritu Sharda

production company
Neelratan

directors
Mohammed Soaeb
Ritu Sharda

creative director
Prasoon Joshi

client
www.prayas.org

agency
McCann Erickson / New Delhi

05038T

Merit

art director
Clay Weiner

writers
Clay Weiner
Alan Vladusic

agency producer
Sally-Ann Dale

production company
Food Chain Films

director
Vince Malone

creative directors
Duncan Marshall
Howard Willmott

client
MTV

agency
Publicis / New York

05039T

(We see a nervous young man in a suit adjusting his tie. He approaches a house and a man answers the door.)

YOUNG MAN: Hello sir. I'd like to ask for Meghan's hand in marriage.

DAD: Alright, son.

YOUNG MAN: Thanks, sir.

(We then see him walk next door and a woman answers the door.)

YOUNG MAN: Hi, I'd like to ask for Meghan's hand in marriage.

WOMAN: OK.

YOUNG MAN: Thank you.

(We then see him knock on different houses' doors, then buildings, then apartments asking the same question. He then walks up to a man on a farm.)

YOUNG MAN: Excuse me, but I'd like to ask for Meghan's hand in marriage.

SUPER: How would you feel if you had to ask 260 million people for the right to marry?

MTV logo. Vote on gay marriage.

How would you feel if you had to ask
260 million people for the right to marry?

(We see the inside of a sparsely furnished classroom. A blackboard with "Short film actor's workshop - Establishing a character" written on it is in the background. A group of students sit cross-legged on the floor, their backs to us - watching the scene. The teacher is standing before the group with two students. After a moment, one of the students begins the scene.)

STUDENT 1: Flavious, you have angered the Gods.

STUDENT 2: And what of the senate, Minimus?

(The teacher immediately stops the students.)

TEACHER: What?? I don't get it? Who's who?

(The teacher points to one of the students.)

TEACHER: Okay, sit down. When establishing your character in a short film, it's got to be quick. Like this. Go again.

(The student again begins the scene.)

STUDENT 1: Flavious...you

(The teacher reaches out and twists the student's nipple.)

STUDENT 1: Ouch!

(The teacher steps back and points to the student and them himself as he speaks to the class while tapping his watch. The student nurses his nipple.)

TEACHER: See that, good guy...bad guy. Two seconds.

SUPER: Worldwide Short Film Festival logo.

art director
Dave Douglass

writer
Pete Breton

agency producer
Sam Benson

production company
untitled

director
Tim Godsall

creative director
Zak Mroueh

client
Canadian Film Centrés Worldwide Short Film Festival

agency
TAXI / Toronto

05040T

PUBLIC SERVICE / POLITICAL — TELEVISION : CAMPAIGN

art directors
Phil Covitz
Brandon Sides
Tricia Ting

writers
John Kearse
Marc Einhorn
Jackie Hathiramani

agency producer
Carron Pedonti

production company
Redtree Productions

director
Christian Hoagland

creative directors
Ron Lawner
Pete Favat
Alex Bogusky
John Kearse
Tom Adams

client
American Legacy Foundation

agency
Arnold Worldwide / Boston and Crispin Porter + Bogusky / Miami

05042T

Also Awarded:
merit
Public Service/Political Television: Single

Outside a major tobacco company

Q:

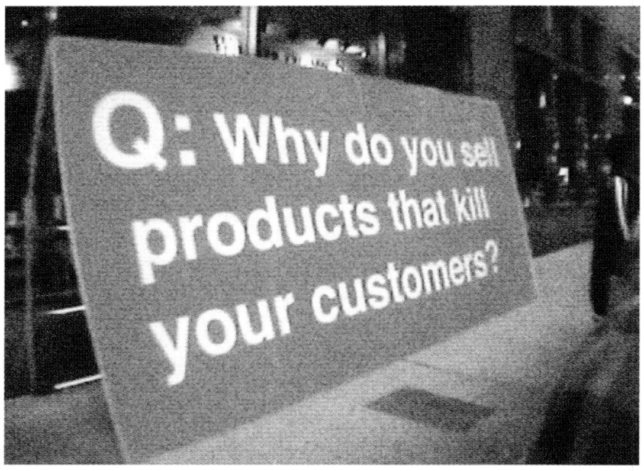
Q: Why do you sell products that kill your customers?

(We see the back of a moving truck.)

TEEN: Let's go! Let's go!

(Then we see quick shots of several truth teens unloading two podiums and a p.a. system in front of a tobacco company in NYC. People on the street stop and look to see what's going on.)

TEEN: Get the platform!

(The teens set up one podium with an "A:" sign on it in front of the tobacco office building. On the other side of the street facing the tobacco company they set up another podium with a "Q:" sign on it. Behind the podium a giant Virginia Slims ad hangs with the tagline, "Find your voice.")

TEEN: Tobacco companies have been targeting women for the past 70 years, asking us to find our own voice. Today, my friend Grace has a question for you guys...

(A woman named Grace approaches the microphone. We realize she's a throat cancer patient, who's had a tracheostomy/larengectomy. She speaks through an electronic voice box.)

GRACE: (Looking up to building) Is this the voice you expected me to find?

(Cut to the "A:" podium in front of the tobacco company. No one comes out from the building or approaches the podium. It remains vacant.)

SUPER: Ask questions. Seek truth.

(We see a business meeting in progress.
A woman employee walks in late.)

WOMAN: Good morning.

(The boss stands up, interrupts the conversation and punches the woman in the face.)

BOSS: (Yelling) You're late.
You think you can just stroll in here like that?
Well, you can't. What am I supposed to do with you?
How am I supposed to work this way? Do you understand me? What's the matter with you?

SUPER: You wouldn't take it from him.
Why should you from a partner?

MY SISTERS' PLACE

Call 1-800-799-SAFE

art director
Desirré Jones

writer
Molly Schachner

agency producers
Dominic Ferro
Erin Gaboriau

production company
Partizan

director
Dominic Murphy

creative directors
Gary Goldsmith
Dean Hacohen
Sally Overheu

client
My Sisters' Place

agency
Lowe / New York

05044T

Television/Radio
Merit
the Sounds of War

CONSUMER TELEVISION : OVER :30 — SINGLE

art directors
So & Sau

writers
So & Sau

agency producer
Fabrice Brovelli

production companies
Capitaine Plouf
Wizz/Quad Productions

directors
So & Sau

creative directors
Rémi Babinet
Fabrice Brovelli

client
Evian

agency
BETC Euro RSCG / Paris

05045T

(Waterboy, a little character made of water, goes through various situations symbolizing the element of water. He is singing to Queen's "We Will Rock You." He runs through different objects and divides into several smaller characters only to rejoin into one large one. On his adventures, he meets a gorgeous girlfriend who is also made of water. Together, they start a family and walk off into the sunset.)

SUPER: Evian logo. Live young.

(We see what looks like home movies from the seventies where boys behave like real men: chasing after girls, playing soccer and fouling their dad, reading hot rod magazines – for these boys, who already acted manly when they were little, the legend Golf GTI has returned.)

SUPER: For boys who were always men.

(We see a Golf GTI driving towards us.)

SUPER: The new Golf GTI. Volkswagen logo.

art director
Sandra Schilling

writer
Ulrich Lützenkirchen

agency producer
Marion Lange

production company
@radical.media

director
Steve Miller

creative directors
Amir Kassaei
Wolfgang Schneider
Mathias Stiller

client
Volkswagen

agency
DDB / Berlin

05116T

Also Awarded:
merit
Consumer Television
Non-Broadcast: Single

Merit

CONSUMER TELEVISION : OVER :30 — SINGLE — MAX. :90

art director
Rob Baird

writer
Allon Tatarka

agency producer
John Cline

production company
Biscuit Filmworks

director
Noam Murro

creative directors
David Lubars
Ari Merkin

client
North American Coffee Partnership

agency
Fallon / New York

05046T

(We see a young guy pull a can of Starbucks Doubleshot out of the fridge. We hear the opening of the song "Eye of the Tiger" and see Survivor playing in his living room.)

SURVIVOR: Glen! Glen, Glen, Glen...
Glen, Glen, Glennn!

(He is shaving and we see the band in the bathroom with him. Then we see him walking with the band behind him still playing. They follow him everywhere he goes.)

SURVIVOR: Glen's the Man, going to work...
got his tie, got ambition.
Middle management is right in his grasp,
It's a dream he will never let die. Glen's the man of the hour, he's the king of his cube. Status call reports have finally met their rival. Burnin' the...candle at both ends on his way to the top. He knows one day he just could become...supervisor.

(We see the elevator doors open and Glen strides out.)

VOICE OVER: Starbucks Doubleshot Espresso Drink. Bring on the day.

(Another guy walks by the elevator drinking a Doubleshot. The band then follows him instead.)

SURVIVOR: Roy! Roy, Roy, Roy!

art directors
Wayne Best
Marcus Woolcott

writer
Adam Alshin

agency producer
Zarina Mak

production company
Morton Jankel Zander

directors
Tom Kuntz
Mike Maguire

creative directors
Ari Merkin
Wayne Best

client
Virgin Mobile USA

agency
Fallon / New York

05047T

(We see a winter wonderland-type soundstage. It is populated by numerous characters representing various belief systems, ethnicities, holidays, and cross-pollinations. A druid sits near a naked girl holding an oversized phone prop, a caveman, and a sweet little Tiny Tim-esque crippled kid. In the center of the stage is a Nat King Cole-esque lead singer.)

SINGER: It's ok if you're a muslim, a christian, or a jew...

HASIDIC TWINS: It's OK if you're agnostic, and you don't know what to do...

SINGER: An all-inclusive celebration,

NAKED GIRL: No contractual obligations.

EVERYBODY: Happy Chrismahanukwanzakah to you.

DRUID: And pagans too!

CAVEMAN: In some ways we're all monkeys, well maybe just a smidgen.

NAKED GIRL: I'm a scientologist!

SINGER: That's kind of a religion.

SINGER AND ELF: Whose faith is the right one, it's anybody's guess.

SANTA: What matters most is camera phones for $20 less.

SINGER: And there's never any hidden fees, oh what a joyous day

ELF: No commitments means I'm proud to go both ways.

(The caveman blows the elf a kiss.)

EVERYBODY: Happy Chrismahanukwanzakah to you

(The crippled kid hobbles into frame as if he's going to deliver an optimistic holiday cliché. He coughs, and dies.)

SUPER: Virgin mobile logo.

VOICE OVER: $20 off and no contract. It's a holiday for all of us.

art director
Rob Palmer

writer
Jamie Barrett

agency producers
Cindy Fluitt
Mary Jane Otto

production company
Biscuit Filmworks

director
Noam Murro

creative directors
Jeffrey Goodby
Jamie Barrett
Rob Palmer

client
eBay

agency
Goodby Silverstein & Partners / San Francisco

05048T

(We see a take-a-penny container, often found near a cash register. It has pennies in it. Then we see a lost dog poster on a tree trunk, then an urban street and a woman sweeping in front of her house. We see recycling bins, a businessman tossing a basketball over a fence to someone else, a welcome mat on a doorstep of a suburban home, an urban deck with some sunflowers and a guy waving, a nurse in uniform, a man delivering food, a man holding the elevator for someone else, a boy scout uniform on a door, a handmade sign on a lightpost that says "smile," a coffee cup in a diner with a $10 tip, a man trying to grab some papers that he's dropped with other people helping him grab it. Then we see a note on a windshield that says "Sorry I hit your car" and a phone number, and various other scenes of good will.)

SUPER: We began with the belief that people are good. You proved it.
eBay logo. The power of all of us.

art director
John Norman

writer
Steve Simpson

agency producers
Josh Reynolds
Brian Coate

production company
Paranoid Pictures:
TOOL of North America

director
Francois Vogel

creative directors
Rich Silverstein
John Norman
Steve Simpson

client
Hewlett Packard

agency
Goodby Silverstein & Partners / San Francisco

05049T

(We hear the song "Picture Book" by the Kinks. We see people in a line in the middle of a square posing for a picture, except they're all holding white empty frames around their faces. They start to switch the frames and their faces switch as well. Then a woman's hand comes from out of the frame and pulls a snapshot of a woman jumping in the air while the woman falls back down. We then see a young girl running across a village street to a wall with a hole in it, where a 8-1/2 x 11 frame is being passed through to her. She smiles as she puts the frame with the new scene up to the lens. Then we see a man in his home office and he picks up a blank white frame and holds it before his face, where the frame takes the picture. He sets the print down and holds up another printed one to his face where it becomes a live shot, then he puts the blank frame around his head to hang around his neck.)

SUPER: (While scenes are playing) + hp
You find pictures everywhere
YOU
You play with pictures
YOU
You capture every color
YOU
You think all the world's a photo album

- Kids, these gentlemen say that in the
tin box you have... a plane...

agency producer
Screenplay

production company
Compañía
Cinematografica

director
Javier Blanco

creative directors
Leandro Raposo
Pablo Stricker
Santiago Lucero
Pablo Colonnese

client
Aerolineas Argentinas

agency
J. Walter Thompson /
Buenos Aires

05050T

(We see a young boy and girl playing and watching planes go by overhead on a rooftop. They follow the shadow of each of them as they fly by but then it goes past the edge. The next day at the same time, they are back on the rooftop except the boy brings a box and manages to catch one of the shadows of the plane. They run back home.)

MOTHER: What's in there??

BOY: A plane, Mom. A giant plane!

MOTHER: Oh, a plane.

(We see them at the dinner table.)

MAN: What's that?

MOTHER: They say they have a plane.

(Next we see the boy in a bath.)

GIRL: And can you fly anywhere with the plane?

BOY: Yes, everywhere in the world.

GIRL: Papua, too?

BOY: What's Papua?

GIRL: An island.

BOY: Yes...I guess it can.

(The next day at class, several people from an airline appear.)

TEACHER: Kids, these gentlemen say that in the tin box you have a plane.

PILOT: Matias, that plane has to be in Rome tomorrow at 10:35. Lots of people need to travel and lots are waiting for the plane. Everyone needs that plane to arrive.

(In the schoolyard, as everyone watches, the boy releases the plane from the box and they watch it fly off.)

VOICE OVER: And if this time, those who believe are more right than those who don't? In Aerolineas Argentinas we believed we could make a different airline. And we did it. We're making the most important trip from the Argentina we were to the one we dream to be.

SUPER: Aerolineas Argentinas

CONSUMER TELEVISION : OVER :30 — SINGLE — MAX. :90

art director
David Horowitz

writer
David Horowitz

agency producer
Betsy Blakemore

production company
MTV In-House

director
David Horowitz

creative director
Kevin Mackall

client
MTV On-Air Promos

agency
MTV Networks / New York

05053T

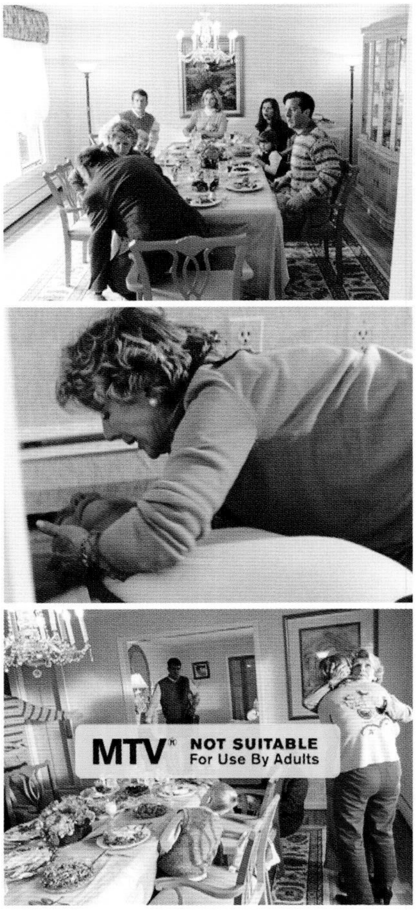
MTV NOT SUITABLE
For Use By Adults

(We see a small Thanksgiving/family dinner. There's Grandma and Grandpa, their adult kids with their spouses, and their small kids. They are having a nice family discussion, laughing about something. Suddenly, the grandfather clutches his chest and lets out a wail.)

DAUGHTER: Dad, dad are you okay!

GRANDPA: I. . . can't breathe!

SON: Dad!

DAUGHTER: Omigod, Steve, call an ambulance!

(Daughter's husband runs to the phone)

SON: Julie do you have any. . .what does he take mom?

GRANDMA: Aspirin!

DAUGHTER: In the kitchen!

(One of the kids is upset, starts to cry. The daughter in law (the son's wife) comforts her.)

DAUGHTER-IN-LAW: Shhh..it's ok, baby.

GRANDMA: Harold, Harold can you hear me. . .

GRANDPA: I can't. . I love you.

GRANDMA: Oh, please God, no. Julie, water!

(Then, suddenly, he starts laughing. Everyone is confused for a second.)

GRANDMA: Harold why, why are you laughing?

GRANDPA: I punked you! I punked you all!

DAUGHTER: What?

GRANDPA: I'm fine. You've all been punked!

(He's still laughing. There is an awkward silence. Son-in-law hangs up phone.)

GRANDPA: You shoulda seen the looks on your faces!

DAUGHTER: (Crying) Dad, how could you do that!

SON: Really nice, Dad. I think we're gonna go. C'mon, honey.

GRANDPA: What?

SUPER: MTV. Not suitable for use by adults

(We see a full synagogue. The rabbi stands at the podium, next to an old couple.)

CONGREGATION: Amen.

RABBI: And now Sophie will read from the Torah for the first time.

(From the front row of the audience, a 13 yr old Sophie, who sits with her parents and two brothers, stands and walks to the platform. She kisses her Grandma and Grandpa, who then sit in chairs on the platform. She looks nervous.)

RABBI: (Whispering) Whenever you're ready. . .

(She launches into the Hebrew prayer, but instead of the traditional melody, she sings it in an R&B style that sounds like Mariah Carey meets Christina Aguilera meets Kelly Clarkson. She moves her hand and closes her eyes dramatically while she sings.)

SOPHIE: Bar chu et adonai hamvora!

(Everyone is stunned. There is an awkward pause. Then, a smattering of the dumbfounded audience murmurs the next verse in response.)

CROWD: Bar uch adonai hamvora lay—oh—lum vawhed

(Our girl continues, assaulting the song like a star search contestant. Grandma is not pleased.)

SUPER: Blame MTV

art director
David Horowitz

writer
David Horowitz

agency producer
Jerelyn Orlandi

production company
MTV In-House

director
David Horowitz

creative director
Kevin Mackall

client
MTV On-Air Promos

agency
MTV Networks / New York

05052T

CONSUMER TELEVISION : OVER :30 — SINGLE — MAX. :90

art director
Jason Levine

writer
Eric Quennoy

agency producer
Colin Pearsall

production company
Hungry Man

director
Jim Jenkins

creative directors
Duncan Marshall
Howard Willmott

client
TimeWarner/TBS

agency
Publicis / New York

05054T

(We see a giant control room with operators in a TBS building. One of them answers a call.)

OPERATOR: 1-800-TBS-FUNNY?

CALLER: I just saw a man sit on one of my buffalo wings. Is this funny?

OPERATOR: Were those wings fried or saucy?

CALLER: Real saucy, you're talking to the wing king right here...

OPERATOR: Describe the stain, sir.

CALLER: It looks like a Rorschach test. I'm seeing two dogs kissing.

OPERATOR: Can you place the stain for me, sir? Right buttock or left buttock?

CALLER: Hey, I'm not getting into all that...

OPERATOR: Is he with people?

CALLER: He's with four Japanese men.

OPERATOR: Can you move the phone closer?

(Caller walks closer to table and lets operator hear conversation. She translates.)

OPERATOR: This man is an idiot...let us go fly fishing...how's his demeanor?

CALLER: Well, he thinks he's the man.

OPERATOR: OK, let's review this then. Saucy wings, cocksure, goodbye contract...we're going to go ahead and give you a pretty funny on this one.

CALLER: Really?

OPERATOR: Wait...you're calling from Buffalo. That added irony, so that bumps it up to pretty darn funny.

CALLER: Pretty darn funny! (Points with coworker to table and starts laughing).

MAN: ...last play is coming up...hey, here, I'm over here...so I get the ball and throw it to myself...

SUPER: TBS logo. Very funny.

IMPOSSIBLE IS NOTHING

(We see a boy looking up towards the sky. Then we see a pink plastic bag blowing around in the sky. The boy retrieves it from the air, stepping on it he picks it up and places it in his pocket. Then we see him walking along the street where he puts another bag in his pocket. A chain link fence is in the foreground. He climbs the fence and carefully picks a bag out of the barbed wire. He jumps down and walks on his way. We then see him jumping up and leaning over into a city garbage bin. The shopkeeper comes out and bids him to leave. The boy walks away with a bag in his hand. He then comes across a man sleeping. The boy watches the man sleep, and then we see him carefully pull a plastic bag from the man's shopping cart; he quickly walks away. The boy keeps collecting bags. Finally, we see him in a yard sitting with the bags, which he begins to tie up. The boy gets up with his plastic ball; the city lies in the background. He does a back kick sending the ball into the air and bounces it from knee to knee.)

Logo: Impossible is Nothing

Logo: adidas

art director
Chuck McBride

writers
Chuck McBride
John Hunt

agency producers
Jennifer Golub
Andrea Bustabade

production company
Smuggler

director
David Frankham

creative director
Chuck McBride

client
adidas

agency
TBWA\Chiat\Day / San Francisco (180\TBWA)

05055T

(We see an amusement park ride, "The Michael Vick Experience." Kids are getting into MVE harnesses. We see a boy getting strapped in and carried foreward.)

FEMALE ANNOUNCER (on loudspeaker): Welcome to the Michael Vick Experience. Please go to the next available chair.

EMPLOYEE: Enjoy the ride.

(The boy cheers and raises his hand in excitement. Then he is taken inside a tunnel, where holograms of Michael Vick giving instructions materialize throughout. As the boy leaves the tunnel, we then see him being lowered in darkness and stopping. Suddenly, stadium lights flip on. The kid is in a real football game. NFL defensive players are preparing to blitz. We see the ball snapped and he catches it by surprise; he is yanked backwards and his harness carries him through the game as if he were Vick. The boy yells in fear as he is charged by the players. He narrowly misses a series of tacklers. As he crosses the end zone, he flips over a defender and scores. We then see a photo of the boy on the ride.)

SUPER: Just Do It
nikegridiron.com

art director
Ryan O'Rourke

writer
Derek Barnes

agency producer
Vic Palumbo

production company
Smith and Jones

director
Ulf Johansson

creative directors
Mike Byrne
Hal Curtis

client
Nike

agency
Wieden + Kennedy / Portland

05059T

art director
James Selman

writer
Mike Byrne

agency producer
Vic Palumbo

production company
RSA

director
Jake Scott

creative directors
Mike Byrne
Hal Curtis

client
Nike

agency
Wieden + Kennedy / Portland

05058T

(We zoom in over the coast to a lone biker riding his bicycle along the road. It is Lance Armstrong. He is being followed by the shadows of geese and along a train. Then we see him riding with motorcycle riders. Children in a hospital run toward the window and watch him ride by. He pumps his fist. He rides through the plains, through the rain. He rides through the city and is joined by hundreds of other cyclists. A young boy pursues him on a small bike and rides behind him.)

SUPER: Just do it. Nike logo.

art director
Bill Karow

writer
Alberto Ponte

agency producer
Andrew Loevenguth

production company
Gorgeous

director
Chris Palmer

creative directors
Mike Byrne
Hal Curtis

client
Nike

agency
Wieden + Kennedy / Portland

05060T

(We see a bunch of young girls primping themselves in front of the mirror in a locker room. The tennis instructor arrives, a long-haired attractive man. The girls are screaming in delight. They all smile and stare at him. He then walks along the court and we see a young girl serving. Suddenly, she transforms into Serena Williams. He keeps watching different girls as they turn into Serena making several shots. He gets hit by a ball and they all rush over. All he sees is many Serena Williams. They change back to the young girls.)

SUPER: You're faster than you think.
Nikespeed.com
Nike logo.

(We see a white Saturn Ion parked in a residential neighborhood. A football enters the frame and hits the car. The car doesn't dent. From this moment on, we cut to a rapid series of cuts of different objects bouncing off various dent-resistant side panels of parked Saturns. Each Saturn is set in a different location. The various thuds we hear become a rhythm track.)

SUPER: Saturn logo.
People first.

art directors
Dave Laden
Stefan Copiz
Stephen Goldblatt

writers
Jamie Barrett
Albert Kelly
Chris Ford

agency producers
James Horner
Tod Puckett
Todd Porter
Ashley Sferro

production companies
Anonymous Content
MJZ
Omaha Pictures

directors
Mark Romanek
Craig Gillespie
Rupert Sanders

creative directors
Jamie Barrett
Mark Wenneker
Dave Laden

client
Saturn

agency
Goodby, Silverstein & Partners / San Francisco

05061T

creative directors
Alex Bogusky
Paul Keister

writer
Bob Cianfrone

agency producer
David Rolfe

production company
Smuggler
NY

director
Happy

client
IKEA

agency
Crispin Porter + Bogusky / Miami

05062T

(We see an apartment door and a pile of mail on the floor. More envelopes slide through the mail slot and fall onto the pile. Then we see dust bunnies on the floor. As a breeze blows through the window, it blows one dust bunny on top of another dust bunny. The action of the wind makes it look like they are in an embrace. Then we see a spoon and a fork lying in a sink full of dirty dishes. The fork falls on top of the spoon. Then we see two trashbags in the kitchen. They nestle against each other. Two remote controls on a couch, and one slides on top of the other. Then two socks become intertwined, rolling around on the floor, in the same way that snakes mate. We then see the mail again, and one envelope slides up on another.)

SUPER: Mess breeds more mess.
Get organized.

SUPER: IKEA
Help yourself to unböring.

mess breeds more mess

art directors
Peter Ogden
Michael Faudet

writers
Peter Ogden
Michael Faudet

agency producers
Justine Carey
Lynne Bishop

production company
Plaza Films

director
Paul Middleditch

creative directors
Garry Horner
Michael Faudet

client
Volkswagen

agency
DDB / Sydney

05064T

(We see a CEO's office: black leather, a huge desk and an awesome chair facing the door. The CEO is sitting in the chair. Opposite him is a man in his early thirties: he's smart, switched-on and a professional businessman.)

CEO: You know Stephen, you've only been with the company for a short time but I feel you are going to be integral to our success. You've got the respect of your peers. You're smart.

(He nods in silent agreements. The CEO stands and walks towards the large windows. He beckons him over.)

CEO: It has taken seventy years to build this company.

(We see a prosperous factory and industrial complex outside the windows.)

CEO: ...and all this could be yours. In fact, I can't think of what's stopping you from one day sitting in this very seat.

(He smiles, then pushes him out of the window. He looks down to the car park below and smiles to himself. He's not looking in the direction his CEO has fallen, instead he's looking at his Volkswagen Bora.)

SUPER: People in a hurry love Volkswagen Bora
VW Bora and AUS Liebe Zum Automobil
www.volkswagen.com.au

(We see the lab of the Bud Light Institute. The CEO, Keith Geurtz, walks through. There's all sorts of crazy experiments going on behind him.)

KEITH: Here at the Bud Light Institute, we're committed to finding innovative ways of getting guys out with their friends and maybe having a Bud Light.

(He stops in front of a wooden office desk. There's a steaming cup of coffee. A Bud Light scientist is standing there holding a clipboard.)

KEITH: Like the "Fake Cup of Coffee 3000."

(We then see a typical business office. A "boss" type guy walks by one office with another man. No one's sitting there, but the steaming cup of coffee is on the desk. He looks at his watch. It says 8AM. He's impressed.)

BOSS: Well, looks as though Johnson's in early.

(We then see Johnson snoring in his bed with a hot young lady beside him. He's smiling and his alarm clock reads 8AM. We then see his office again, and the time reads 2:30 pm. Two young office workers walk by the desk.)

GIRL: Where's Johnson?

(The guy points at the steaming cup of coffee.)

GUY: I don't know, but there's a steaming cup of coffee.

(Johnson is now sitting in the stands at a ball game. He's having a great time and even catches a foul ball. We then see the office in the evening. The clock on the wall reads 9PM. We see the same boss going home. He passes by Johnson's office and sees the steaming cup of coffee. He shakes his head. He's impressed.)

BOSS: Johnson.

(Then we see Johnson with his buddies and some ladies in a bar laughing and having Bud Lights. At the institute, Keith Geurtz is holding the steaming cup of coffee and looks impressed.)

KEITH: Science. Working so you don't have to.

(We see the Bud Light bottle cap.)

KEITH: This calls for a Bud Light.

art director
Carlos Moreno

writer
Peter Ignazi

agency producer
Sharon Kosokowsky

production company
Avion Films

director
Martin Granger

creative director
Dan Pawych

client
Labatt Breweries - Bud Light

agency
Downtown Partners / Toronto

05065T

art director
Steve Driggs

writer
Ryan Peck

agency producers
Rob van de Weteringe Buys
Sofia Akinyele-Trokey

production company
Thomas Thomas Films

director
Kevin Thomas

creative directors
David Lubars
Steve Driggs
John Matejczyk

client
Citibank

agency
Fallon / Minneapolis

05066T

(We see a woman sitting in a dentist's office. She is looking at the camera, telling us a story. When she opens her mouth to speak, it is actually a Leslie Nielson-like man's voice lip-synched to hers. The voice is lounge lizard-like. The woman is a prim, proper, asian lady, perhaps a dental assistant/ technician.)

WOMAN: I used her credit card to treat myself to a little chunk of heaven, baby. That singles weekend in Tijuana. Freaky-deaky. But first, I needed to power-up my babe magnet. Self-tanning cream, fresh hair plugs and a complete wax job on the old chassis. Ouch...uh...slow down, ladies...there's enough Larry for everyone. (Laughs)

SUPER: Helen D. Identity theft victim

VOICE OVER: Fraud early warning. If someone's using your card, we'll alert you and stop it. Citi identity theft solutions. That's using your card wisely.

SUPER: Fraud early warning.
Citi logo. Live richly.
1-800-246-citi
Citicards.com

art director
Marcus Woolcott

writer
Adam Alshin

agency producers
Erika Best
Tammy Auel

production company
Morton Jankel Zander

directors
Tom Kuntz
Mike Maguire

creative director
Ari Merkin

client
Virgin Mobile USA

agency
Fallon / New York

05070T

(We see a young woman and man, awkwardly standing side by side on a gritty urban street. They face straight ahead, and belt out a phone conversation a cappella.)

MAN: Hello?

WOMAN: Yo Mike, whatchoo doin?

MAN: I just stepped out the shower.

WOMAN: Are you naked?

MAN: No, I'm not. I got my terry-cloth robe on.

WOMAN: Oooh. Terry-cloth is my favorite thing in the world.

MAN: I'll call you back, girl.

SUPER: For the love of music (Virgin mobile logo)
Get free real music ringtones on the Vox 8610
Now $20 off

(We see a mother and two girls shopping. They are at the cash register.)

GIRL 1: Mom, I really like this.

MOM: Cute.

GIRL 1: What's it made of?

SALESGIRL: Wool.

GIRL 1: From a cow?

SALESGIRL: Uh-huh.

GIRL 2: Duh Ashley, all wool comes from a cow.

MOM: Does cashmere come from a cow too?

SALESGIRL: Uh-huh.

MOM: The boy cow or the girl cow?

VOICE OVER: If there's any place that could really use a county fair, it's L.A.

SALESGIRL: The boy cow...

MOM: Oh, okay.

GIRL 1: Oh, you mean the one with the...

SALESGIRL: Tusks?...Uh-huh.

VOICE OVER: The L.A. County Fair. Kinder. Simpler. Funner.

art director
Dino Santilli

writer
Cary Sacks

agency producer
Janine Carlson

production company
RSA

director
Chris Nelson

creative director
Dino Santilli

client
Los Angeles County Fair

agency
Ideaology / Marina del Rey

05071T

(We see a man entering another mans' cubicle area.)

BOSS: Hi, Johnson. Yeah, listen. We've decided we're going to have to let you go.

(Johnson looks up while eating his Raisin Bran Crunch. We hear crunching and see the boss talking but can't hear anything.)

BOSS: You're taking this well. You'll go far with that attitude. Only not here. Cause you're fired.

SUPER: Kellogg Raisin Bran Crunch. Sounds good.

art director
Adrien Bindi

writer
Nick Cade

agency producer
Frank Brooks

production company
Moxie Pictures

director
Frank Tadaro

creative director
John Condon

client
Kellogg Raisin Bran Crunch

agency
Leo Burnett / Chicago

05072T

art director
Aaron Stoller

writer
Randy Krallman

agency producer
Keif Matera

production company
MTV In-House

directors
Aaron Stoller
Randy Krallman

creative director
Kevin Mackall

client
MTV On-Air Promos

agency
MTV Networks / New York

05073T

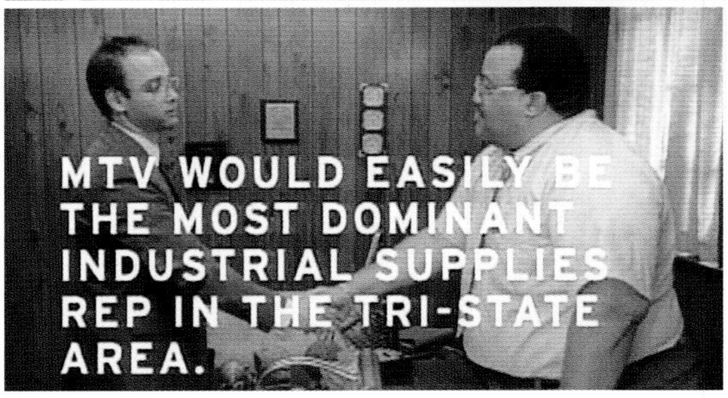
MTV WOULD EASILY BE THE MOST DOMINANT INDUSTRIAL SUPPLIES REP IN THE TRI-STATE AREA.

(We see a Chrysler K car pulling into a parking spot in one of those low-rent, aging, windowless office parks.)

VOICE OVER: If MTV were a regional sales rep for an industrial supplies company, he would easily garner the highest sales in the Tri-State area, even though it was just his first year doing it and he didn't have the good accounts yet...

(We see a balding Greg Gumble-looking guy gathering catalogs in his car. He looks in the rearview mirror, straightens his tie and gets out of the car to enter the offices of some client.)

VOICE OVER: ...because he would roll up to his clients with confidence, and treat the receptionists and others with respect even though he doesn't have to be nice to them because they don't make the purchasing decisions. And then when he meets the people who do make the purchasing decisions he'd present the products to them but he wouldn't sweat them, he'd just lay back in the cut like "That's what's up, take it or leave it"...

VOICE OVER: ...the people who order stuff would be like "What is it about this dude? He's not sweating me..."

VOICE OVER: ...and then they would order stuff from him because he doesn't stunt, he just reps quality supplies backed up by quality service.

(We see the balding client signing several pages of purchase orders.)

VOICE OVER: MTV would easily be the most dominant industrial supplies rep in the Tri-State area. If it were an industrial supplies rep.

(We see our guy walking out. He hands the receptionist a business card. She smiles and seems smitten with him. On the card, his name and title are: MTV. #1 in Sales (Tri-State Region))

art director
Scott Vitrone

writer
Ian Reichenthal

agency producer
Nathy Aviram

production company
Hungry Man

director
Jim Jenkins

creative director
Gerry Graf

client
Nextel

agency
TBWA\Chiat\Day / New York

05074T

(We see three coworkers in an office and music is playing. Two of them are dancing while one is sitting on a filing cabinet with a boombox. The boss walks in the door.)

BOSS: What's going on? We don't know how many converters we have in stock. We don't know where our trucks are, no one knows where Mackler is...

(Music stops. One of the men takes out his cell phone and looks at the screen)

MAN: We have 6000 converters. Trucks are at 4 exit 9. Mackler, where are you?

MACKLER: (Over speaker cell phone) In the airport.

(Man closes his phone, the boombox is turned on again and they go back to dancing.)

SUPER: Inventory management. GPS service. Coast-to-coast walkie-talki. Nextel. Done.

(We see someone's hand setting up a table for dinner. A man sits down at table and begins to prepare himself a plate of food. Right before he is about to eat he gets up a grabs himself Miller High Life Light beer.)

VOICE OVER: A lot of Johnnys' come lately are getting rich peddling of food regiment you've long enjoyed with food rich in essential fats and proteins these experts also recommend a reduction in carbohydrates, okay, so throw in a miller high life light, look at you right on the frontier of gastronomic science and that's the light way to live the "high life"

SUPER: Miller High Life Light logo.

art director
Jeff Williams

writer
Jeff Kling

agency producer
Jeff Selis

production company
@radical.media

director
Errol Morris

creative directors
Susan Hoffman
Roger Camp

client
Miller High Life

agency
Wieden + Kennedy / Portland

05075T

STUART SCOTT: Ever since the show went to High Definition technology, we've had to hire a much more... sophisticated staff.

(We see the breakroom and Chewbacca banging a coffee pot against the counter as a Storm Trooper reads the paper next to C-3PO and a Sportscenter anchor.)

CHEWBACCA: Arrrghhhh!

(We then see the tape room, where Darth Vader brandishes his lightsaber toward Lennox Lewis, who happens to be walking by.)

LENNOX LEWIS: Excuse me.

(We see Andy Roddick trying to give C-3PO tennis lessons. C-3PO accidentally drops the racket.)

ANDY RODDICK: Just... no... why you gotta throw my racket?

STUART SCOTT: Once they start to grasp sports, the possibilities are endless.

(Cut to Sportscenter set where Scott Van Pelt sits at the anchor desk with R2-D2.)

SCOTT VAN PELT: So, is there a quarterback controversy in New York? That's...

R2-D2: Help me Obi-Wan Kenobi. You're my only hope. Help me Obi-Wan Kenobi...

SUPER: THIS IS SPORTSCENTER

art director
Jesse Coulter

writer
Greg Kalleres

agency producer
Temma Shoaf

production company
Hungry Man

director
David Shane

creative directors
Todd Waterbury
Kevin Proudfoot
Paul Renner

client
ESPN Sportscenter

agency
Wieden+Kennedy / New York

05076T

Also Awarded:
merit
Consumer Television: Commercials of Var. Length: Campaign

One Show

CONSUMER TELEVISION : :30/:25 — CAMPAIGN

art directors
Brad Emmett
Lee Seidenberg

writers
Lee Seidenberg
Brad Emmett

agency producers
Clair Grupp
Greg Tharp

production companies
Independent Media
Smuggler

director
Chris Smith

creative directors
Cliff Freeman
Arthur Bijur
Dan Morales

client
Cadbury Schweppes - Snapple

agency
Cliff Freeman and Partners / New York

05077T

WENDY: Presenting Natalie, Snapple fan and animal rescuer.

NATALIE: My favorite flavor is Diet Snapple Lemonade Tea. It's so refreshing, it tastes great, you can't tell it's a diet drink.

WENDY: Natalie, you've said some nice things about us, so to return the favor, here are some nice things about you.

JANET: Natalie can talk to the animals. She knows when they're frightened. She knows when they're hungry, scared, or hurt, and because of this gift...

(Dog groans.)

WENDY: Snapple, the best flavors on Earth made for the best people on Earth.

WENDY: Presenting Brian, devoted Snapple fan.

BRIAN: I like Go Bananas because I like lots of bananas and banana bread and just regular bananas because they're really good.

WENDY: Brian, you just said some nice things about us, so to return the favor, here's some nice things about you.

DENTIST: These are Brian's teeth. He does have some crowding but they're very nicely shaped teeth.

SUPER: Snapple, the best flavors on Earth, made for the best people on Earth.

art directors
Brad Emmett
Lee Seidenberg

writers
Lee Seidenberg
Brad Emmett

agency producer
Clair Grupp

production companies
Independent Media

director
Chris Smith

creative directors
Cliff Freeman
Arthur Bijur
Dan Morales

client
Cadbury Schweppes - Snapple

agency
Cliff Freeman and Partners / New York

05078T

CONSUMER TELEVISION : :30/:25 — CAMPAIGN

art director
Tony Calcao

writers
Rob Strasberg
Tom Adams

agency producers
Rupert Samuel
David Rolfe

production company
Moxie Pictures

director
Martin Granger

creative directors
Alex Bogusky
Andrew Keller
Rob Reilly

client
Burger King

agency
Crispin Porter +
Bogusky / Miami

05079T

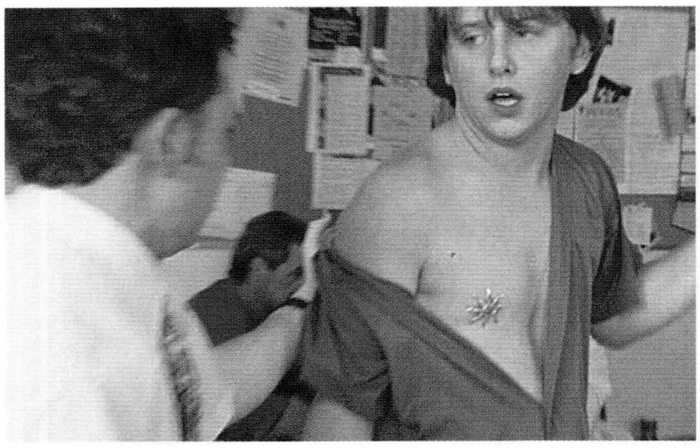

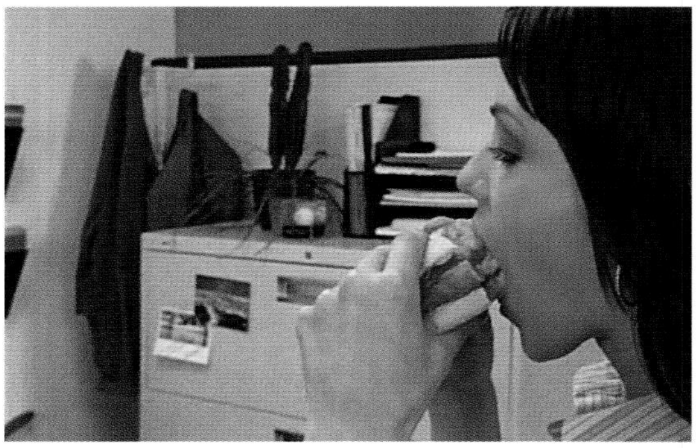

(We open in the office lunch room. Everyone is eating a Spicy Tendercrisp and having a good time, and then Hank walks in.)

HANK: Is that the new Spicy Tendercrisp?

(No one answers. Hank points to a sandwich on the table.)

HANK: You went and got it without me?

(Upset he was left out, Hank grabs for the Spicy Tendercrisp on the table. Gabe tries to stop him. They have an awkward, wimpy tussle until Hank's shirt is ripped. It's revealed that Hank has a starburst nipple covering. Everyone laughs.)

(Hank tries not to be embarrassed.)

HANK: Get a good look. Everybody, check it out.

VOICE OVER: It's here. The new Spicy Tendercrisp Chicken Sandwich. Get ready for a mouth whupping.

SUPER: Logo. Have it your way.

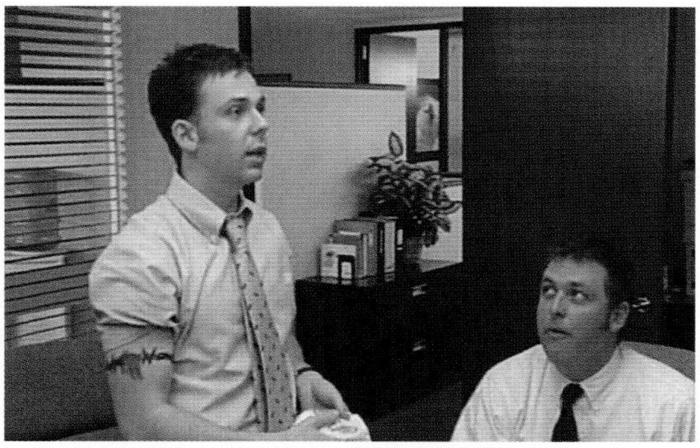

(We open on everyone in an office getting their Burger King orders.)

JOEL: Angus, straight up. No toppings.

(Gabe reaches for it. Joel pulls it away.)

JOEL: Sure you're man enough for that?

(Gabe reaches for it again.)

JOEL: Whoa...Is that a tattoo?

(We see a barbed wire tattoo around his arm.)

MICHELLE: That's tough.

(Michelle grabs it to look closer and the tattoo rubs off on her hand.)

GABE: It's a placeholder. It'll be cool and then we'll see who's laughing.

JOEL: I'll be laughing. Who else?

(Joel raises his hand and looks around the room. Everyone else raises their hand and laughs in agreement.)

VOICE OVER: Step up to the new Angus. A steak burger made with 100% Angus beef. Can you handle it?

SUPER: Logo. Have It Your Way.

art director
Tony Calcao

writers
Rob Strasberg
Tom Adams

agency producers
David Rolfe
Rupert Samuel
Terry Stavoe
Cheri Anderson
Letitia Jacobs

production company
Moxie Pictures

director
Martin Granger

creative directors
Alex Bogusky
Andrew Keller
Rob Reilly

client
Burger King

agency
Crispin Porter + Bogusky / Miami

05081T

CONSUMER TELEVISION : :30/:25 — CAMPAIGN

art director
Tony Calcao

writers
Rob Strasberg
Tom Adams

agency producers
David Rolfe
Rupert Samuel
Terry Stavoe
Jen Denise

production company
Moxie Pictures

director
Martin Granger

creative directors
Alex Bogusky
Andrew Keller
Rob Reilly

client
Burger King

agency
Crispin Porter +
Bogusky / Miami

05080T

(Open in a meeting room, five employees are receiving their Burger King lunch orders from a co-worker. She hands each employee their order as she reads them out.)

FEMALE CO-WORKER: A Whopper, no onions?

CO-WORKER 1: Uh, that's me.

FEMALE CO-WORKER: A Whopper, no lettuce, double tomato, double bacon.

(Co-workers 2 (shorter) and 3 (taller) both raise there hands to claim their Whopper.)

CO-WORKER 3: (Asks co-worker 2) You copied my Whopper?

(Co-worker 3 is staring at co-worker 2 in disbelief as he waits for the answer.)

CO-WORKER 2: (Uncomfortably responds) Yes.

SUPER: Logo. Have it your way.

CLIENTS ARE EXPECTED
FOR PROFESSIONAL SERV

(We see a small veterinary practice. The veterinarian is having a phone conversation with a city clerk.)

CLERK: You've reached the county clerk. For a business license, please press 1 now.

(The veterinarian opens his mouth and interrupts the clerk. Instead of saying words, he speaks in "touch-tones.")

VETERINARIAN: Boop.

CLERK: ...For a fishing license, press 2 now.

VETERINARIAN: Beep.

CLERK: For a fishing license, press 2 now.

VETERINARIAN: Beep?

CLERK: For a fishing license, press—

VETERINARIAN: beep.

CLERK: For a fishing license, press 2 now.

VETERINARIAN: No. Boop?

CLERK: Please hold. (singing) --ing with the queen of hearts, knowing it ain't really smart the joker ain't the only fool who'll do anything for you...

SUPER: Sometimes a small business owner needs to talk to a real person. Citibusiness®

VOICE OVER: The citibusiness card.

SUPER: Small business specialists

VOICE OVER: With real, live, small business specialists on the phone. That's a card you can count on.

SUPER: Citi. Live richly.

art director
Chris Toland

writer
Mike Smith

agency producers
Rob van de Weteringe Buys
Kate Hildebrant

production company
Thomas Thomas Films

director
Kevin Thomas

creative directors
Bruce Bildsten
Steve Driggs
John Matejczyk

client
Citibank

agency
Fallon / Minneapolis

05082T

Also Awarded:
merit
Consumer Television
:30/:25: Single

Merit

One Show

CONSUMER TELEVISION : :30/:25 — CAMPAIGN

writers
Brendan Gibbon
Brooklyn Brothers

production company
Hungry Man

director
Brendan Gibbons

creative directors
Brendan Gibbons
Brooklyn Brothers

client
CNN.com

agency
Hungry Man / New York

05083T

(We open on Anderson Cooper and a young man in his office.)

COOPER: You want the headlines?

MAN: Just the weather.

COOPER: Partly sunny, high of 60.

MAN: How about Detroit?

COOPER: Oregon or Michigan?

MAN: Both.

COOPER: Overcast, rain later...
and fair, feels like 64.

MAN: What's the largest democracy in the world?

COOPER: India.

MAN: Abalone is what?

COOPER: Sea mollusk.

MAN: Knicks, Lakers?

COOPER: Knicks.

MAN: What's the speed of light?

COOPER: One hundred eighty-six thousand miles per second.

MAN: How do hurricanes get their names?

COOPER: There's a list.

MAN: Can I get on the list?

COOPER: What's your name?

MAN: Scooter.

COOPER: (pause) Doubt it.

MAN: You seem to have all the answers.

COOPER: I'm a reporter. That's my job.

SUPER: cnn.com
the power of CNN under your command

COOPER: You want the headlines now?

MAN: No, just the weather.

302

(We see a man carrying several unwieldy suitcases on a long trip from his car's trunk into the house. He deposits the heavy bags in a room and rewards himself with a beer.)

VOICE OVER: Now that's how you do that. The day a man wheels a suitcase is the day he ought to pack his pride inside and throw away the key.

The manner in which a man carries his family's luggage reflects how he carries himself. It's backbone both moral and load bearing, that earns him his share of

.... The High Life

SUPER: Miller High Life logo.

art director
Jeff Williams

writers
Ginger Robinson
Derek Barnes

agency producer
Jeff Selis

production company
@radical.media

director
Errol Morris

client
Miller High Life

agency
Wieden + Kennedy / Portland

05084T

Merit

CONSUMER TELEVISION : :30/:25 — CAMPAIGN

One Show

CONSUMER TELEVISION : :30/:25 — CAMPAIGN

art director
Mishy Cass

writer
Forrest Healy

agency producer
Jane Jacobsen

production company
MJZ

director
Craig Gillespie

creative director
Steve Johnston

client
Washington Mutual

agency
Sedgwick Rd / Seattle

05086T

(Jenn, a young public defender, is in court disputing evidence.)

JENN: (scoffs) Is DNA really "evidence?"

VOICE OVER: For Jenn, truth was relative.

(We see Jenn at a Washington Mutual financial Center. An employee offers a simple demonstration of how free checking has no hidden fees.)

VOICE OVER: Then she got Washington Mutual Free Checking. She liked the no hidden fees and they inspired Jenn to be more truthful.

(Then we see Jenn in court offering a plea that surprises her client.)

JENN: Your Honor, my client pleads guilty.

CLIENT: I wha..?

JENN: Well, you are.

(Two bicycle policemen giving a car a ticket.)

JENN: Hi, I just changed lanes without signaling. Oh, and my plates are expired.

(We see Jenn and her Husband showing their house. Jenn pats one of the deck supports and the deck immediately collapses.)

BUYER: Nice deck.

JENN: Not really. We built it ourselves.

VOICE OVER: Way to go, Jenn. We appreciate your bold honesty.

SUPER: Washington Mutual logo.
Home Loans. More Human Interest

(We see Jim and Karen at a movie theater concessions stand. The clerk is about to hand them a bag of popcorn. Jim and Karen look addled.)

CLERK: Ya want butter with that?

VOICE OVER: The home loan process made Jim and Karen indecisive.

(Jim and Karen are in a Washington Mutual Home loans center with a loan consultant. Jim and Karen become emboldened by their new knowledge.)

VOICE OVER: Fortunately, Washington Mutual cut through the confusion and got them their loan. Now Jim and Karen always know what to do.

(Jim and Karen are at a shoe store. A salesman asks Karen to decide between a high-heeled shoe and a flat. Just as he asks the question, a woman trying on high heels in the background trips and falls.)

SALESMAN: Would you like the stiletto or the flat?

KAREN: Flat.

JIM: Yeah.

(Jim and Karen are at a casual restaurant as the waitress takes their order. Suddenly, behind the waitress, a large, sweaty man sneezes all over the salad bar.)

WAITRESS: ...you want soup or salad?

JIM AND KAREN: Soup

(We see Jim and Karen with their 4-year-old son at a bike shop talking with a salesman. Their son is throwing a tantrum.)

SON: I want a scooter!

(Across the Bike shop, another salesman is demonstrating the scooter. He fires it up and it takes off, launching him through a plate-glass window. Then we see Jim and Karen as they turn to the salesman. The kid has stopped yelling and is staring at the wreckage.)

JIM AND KAREN: We'll take the bike.

KAREN: Bike's good.

VOICE OVER: Sharp thinking, Jim and Karen. That's why you're homeowners.

SUPER: Washington Mutual logo.
Home Loans
More Human Interest

art director
Mishy Cass

writer
Forrest Healy

agency producer
Margaret Overley

production company
MJZ

director
Craig Gillespie

creative director
Steve Johnston

client
Washington Mutual

agency
Sedgwick Rd / Seattle

05085T

One Show

CONSUMER TELEVISION : :30/:25 — CAMPAIGN

art director
Susan Alinsangan

agency producers
Cheryl Childers
Serena Auroux

production company
@radical.media

director
Dave Meyers

creative directors
Lee Clow
Duncan Milner
Eric Grunbaum

client
Apple

agency
TBWA\Chiat\Day / Los Angeles

05087T

(We see U2 as silhouettes playing "Vertigo.")

SUPER: Vertigo by U2. iPod + iTunes. Apple logo.

(We see two boys on a city rooftop, getting ready to try out a gun by shooting at a sculpture set up on roof of building.)

BOY: All right, were here to try out the Lava gun from Ratchet & Clank up your arsenal.

(Shooter misses sculpture and hits a car at street level. The car catches fire and explodes.)

BOY: Oh, nice shot dude.

(We hear sirens in the background. One boy runs to hide.)

VOICE OVER: Lava gun, yet another weapon not for this world.

SUPER: Ratchet and Clank. Up Your Arsenal
Live in your world. Play in ours.
Playstation 2 logo.

art director
Becca Morton

writer
Raymond Hwang

agency producers
Elizabeth Giersbrook
Nancy Hwang

production company
@radical.media

director
Peter Darley Miller

creative director
Jerry Gentile

client
PlayStation

agency
TBWA\Chiat\Day /
Los Angeles

05088T

CONSUMER TELEVISION : :30/:25 — CAMPAIGN

art director
Brian Lee Hughes

writer
Crockett Jeffers

agency producers
Rob Sondik
Andrea Bustabade

production company
Smuggler

director
David Frankham

creative director
Chuck McBride

client
Fox Sports Net

agency
TBWA\Chiat\Day / San Francisco

05089T

(We see a man putting pieces of lumber on a shelf. Two of his coworkers walk up to him.)

COWORKER 1: Hey, Pete.

PETE: Hey guys, what's up?

COWORKER 1: We're thinking of catching the Giants game at Daryls.

PETE: Baseball? I'm not all that into baseball, you guys go ahead.

COWORKER 1: You sure?

PETE: Yeah, I've got a lot to do.

COWORKER 2: OK.

[As they walk off, Pete gets a splinter. A whole pile of lumber then falls on his head.]

SUPER: You really should follow the Giants. FSN logo. Fox Sports Net.

You really should follow the Giants

(In moody black and white, the surfers from the original Guinness ad run off screen towards the sea.)

VOICE OVER: Tick followed tock followed tick followed tock...

(As they reach the water we hear them scream and run back. From their reactions the water is obviously freezing.)

SUPER: Guinness. But extra cold.

art director
Mark Fairbanks

writers
Mark Fairbanks
Markham Smith

agency producer
Anita Sasdy

production company
Exposure Films

director
JJ Keith

creative directors
Nigel Roberts
Paul Belford

client
Guinness Extra Cold

agency
Abbott Mead Vickers
BBDO / London

05090T

(We see inside a house on a hot day. A plump, shirtless father notices that his baby is crying in the cot. He takes the baby in his arms and starts to comfort him. To everyone's surprise, the baby tries to suck on his father's breast. The father finds the baby's reaction strange.)

SUPER: Get in shape.
Companhia Athletica logo.
Heath and Wellness
www.ciaathletica.com.br

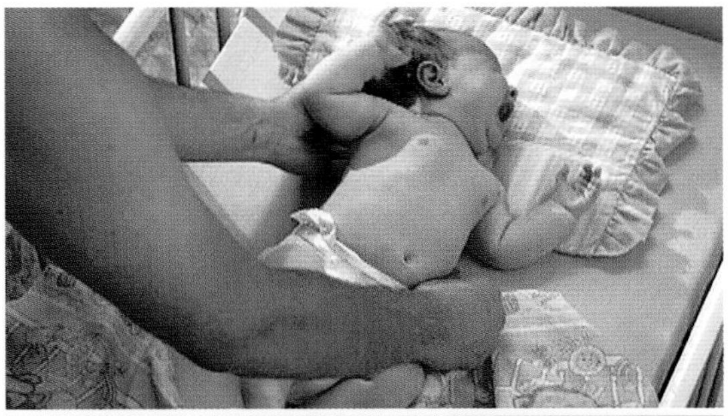

art director
Felipe Cama

writer
Ricardo Chester

agency producers
Luiz Filipe Fratino
Jaqueline Couto

production company
Jodaf

director
Joao Daniel Tikhomiroff

creative directors
Sergio Valente
Pedro Cappeletti

client
Companhia Athletica
(Gym)

agency
DDB / São Paulo

05091T

art director
Jon Soto

writer
Mike McCommon

agency producers
Michael Damiani
Alex Lind

production company
Partizan

director
Jim Hosking

creative directors
Jeffrey Goodby
Jon Soto

client
Diamond of California

agency
Goodby, Silverstein & Partners / San Francisco

05092T

(Open on tight shot of a Norwegian archery coach in Norwegian athletic wear. He's standing by the target eating Emerald Nuts, hollering words of encouragement to his athlete.

COACH: Goood job. Niice aiim...

(We see the coach, target, and some precariously close arrows. One flies into frame and hits his leg and he winces but recovers.)

COACH: "Aahhhhhh!...Dat's okay! Try agin!"

(We then see the Norwegian coach eating his nuts.)

SUPER: Encouraging Norwegians. Emerald Nuts.

VOICE OVER: Encouraging Norwegians love Emerald Nuts.

SUPER: Emerald of California logo.

(We hear choir singing and bell sound.)

EMERALD
NUTS

art director
Jeff Spillane

writer
Heather Gorman

agency producer
Susan Crimley

production company
MJZ

director
Craig Gillespie

creative directors
Brent Ladd
Steve Miller

client
Southwest Airlines

agency
GSD&M / Austin

05093T

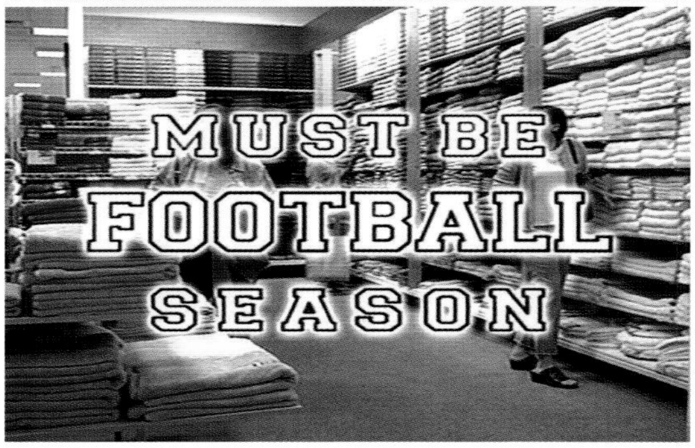
MUST BE
FOOTBALL
SEASON

(We see the inside of a department store in the towel and linen section. We see a woman looking at the towels. She picks one up and is checking it out. Another woman enters behind her. As the other woman is bending over, looking at towels, she suddenly pops her with the towel. She then pumps her fist.)

WOMAN (POPPER): Yeah!

(The woman who was popped by the towel rubs her thigh and looks at her as if she's crazy.)

SUPER: Must be football season. Southwest logo. Proud Sponsor of the NFL

(We see an apartment room with a stereo system and lamp in corner of the room.)

NEIGHBORS: Have some respect! We're trying to sleep! Don't you people ever sleep or what?

(The music is still blaring and the light is still on.)

NEIGHBORS: Shut it off!

(A man walks over to stereo and lamp. He turns off the lamp and leaves stereo on.)

NEIGHBORS: Thanks!

SUPER: Extra bright. Sylvania Spiral logo.

art directors
Thana Rittirajcomporn
Tawatchai Suknipitapong

writer
Wiparat Nantananontchai

agency producer
Natee Wangtrakoon

production company
Matching Studio Public Co.

director
Suthon Petchsuwan

creative director
Jureeporn Thaidumrong

client
Sylvania

agency
Saatchi & Saatchi / Bangkok

05095T

One Show

CONSUMER TELEVISION : :20 AND UNDER – CAMPAIGN

art director
Frank Aldorf

writers
Daniel Frericks
Eskil Puhl

agency producer
Mark Rota

production companies
Cobblestone
Deli Pictures
Postproduction

director
Kai Sehr

creative directors
Constantin Kaloff
Ove Gley

client
K-fee

agency
Jung von Matt / Hamburg

05096T

(We see two people on the beach standing several feet away looking at each other shyly. The sun is setting and it's a very romantic scene. Suddenly, a screaming monster appears.)

SUPER: Ever been so wide awake?
K-fee. Canned caffeine with coffee.

(We see a dormitory-style room at night. Two women are fast asleep. Both are in twin beds and both are lying in identical positions. When one woman rolls over, the other does the exact same roll at the exact same time. When one woman tosses her arm above her head, the other reflexively does the same. In unison, both women flip their legs up and do a complex scissor kick before finally coming to rest in the same position.)

SUPER: Sealy logo.
Official supplier of the U.S. Olympic team.

art director
Bill Starkey

writer
Richard Parubrub

agency producer
Keith Rose

production company
JGF Films

director
Jeff Gorman

creative director
John Brockenbrough

client
Sealy

agency
Mullen Advertising / Winston-Salem

05097T

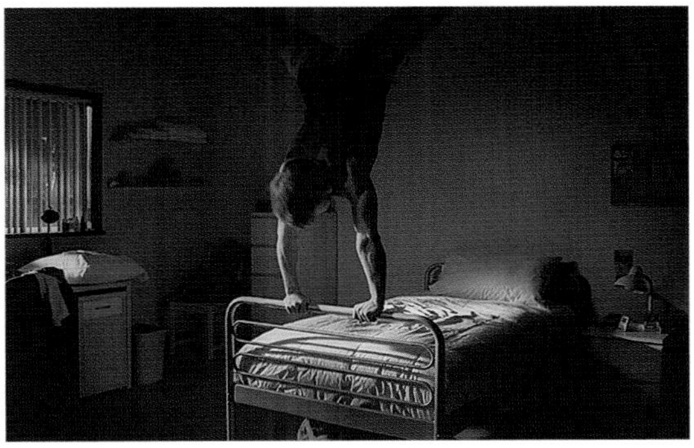

art directors
Gianfranco Arena
John Hobbs
Thomas Hayo

writers
Peter Kain
Peter Rosch
Thomas Hayo

agency producer
Liz Graves

production companies
MJZ
Traktor/Partizan

directors
Dante Ariola
Traktor

creative director
Thomas Hayo

client
Levi Strauss & Co.

agency
Bartle Bogle Hegarty / New York

05098T

(A girl exits a house. A ferocious dog lunges after her starting a mad chase. Eventually it catches her pant-leg. Her only chance is to take off the jeans. The dog runs back to the house and delivers them to her boyfriend, who puts them on, as she returns half naked.)

SUPER: Levis.

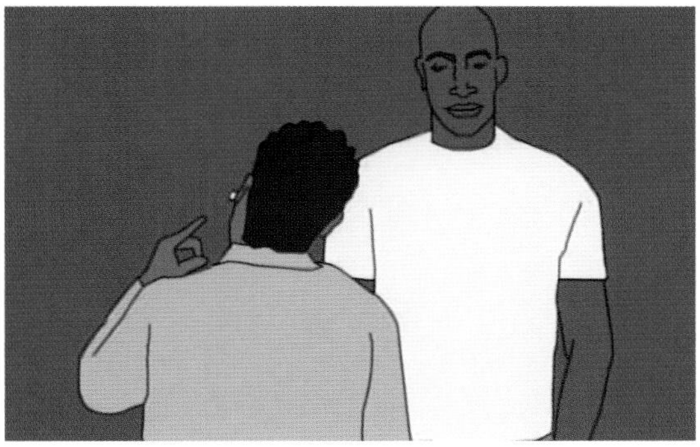

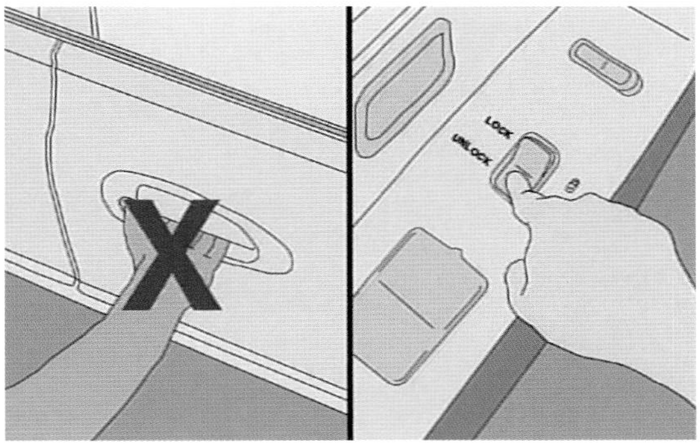

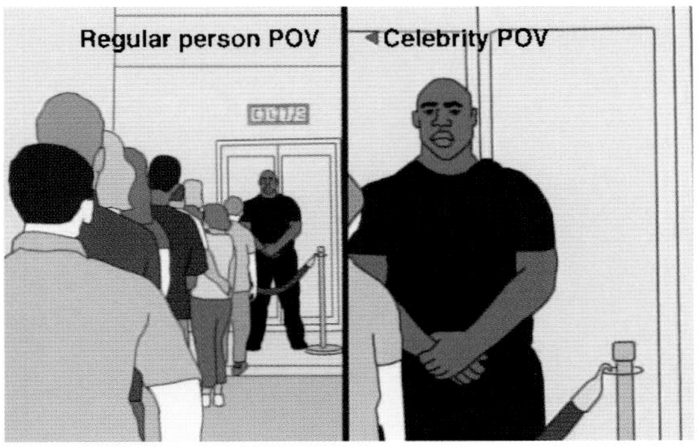

(We see a rap concert. The two rappers are holding and pointing to large jewelry on their bodies.)

GROUP: (Singing): Bling bling. Bling bling.

(We see a close up of one man at the concert listening. He walks up to a friend and points to his diamond earring.)

MAN: Bling bling.

(Then we see that man's friend being interviewed by a sports reporter. We realize that he is a pro basketball player. He points to the championship ring on his finger.)

BASKETBALL PLAYER: Bling bling.

(Then we see the interview playing on a tv where a teenage boy is watching. Then we see that same boy at school at his locker. He points to the chain around his neck.)

KID: Bling bling.

(Another kid next to them overhears the teenage boy saying "bling bling" to his friend, and then we see her with her friend, and she points to her bracelet.)

Girl: Bling bling.

(A teacher nearby has over heard the girl saying bling bling. Cut to that teacher at home with his wife. He gives her some jewelry.)

TEACHER: Bling bling.

(Then we see his wife with her mother. She shows her mother the jewelry.)

WIFE: Bling bling.

SUPER: Bling, bling. 1997-2003.
MTV logo. Watch and learn.

art director
Matthew Vescovo

writer
Matthew Vescovo

agency producer
Michael Bellino

production company
Fad New York

director
Matthew Vescovo

creative directors
Matthew Vescovo
Kevin Mackall

client
MTV

agency
Matthew Vescovo / Brooklyn

05099T

Also Awarded:
merit
Consumer Television
Under $50,000 Budget:
Campaign

writers
Sam Mazur
Mike Rovner

agency producer
Andrew Lippman

production company
Big Look Productions

director
Tom Jones

creative directors
Sam Mazur
Mike Rovner

client
Fatty Golf Open

agency
Agency212 / New York

05101T

(A fat man, dressed like Tiger Woods on Sunday, tosses and catches a hamburger with his spatula. Over and over, he continues to flip the burger, all without dropping the meat. Finally he takes the patty and tosses it down the fairway.)

SUPER: The 7th Annual Fatty Golf Open. June 21st. Register at www.fattygolf.com. Sponsored by Liberty Mortgage Group, LLC

art director
Scott Sugiuchi

writer
Jonathan Helfman

agency producer
Sean Hobbs

production company
Backyard

director
Steve Burrows

creative director
Eric Hartsock

client
Bob & Ronna
Real Estate Team

agency
Underground / Baltimore

05102T

(It is the middle of the night and a husband and wife are in bed. The man gets up and quickly shuffles off to the bathroom without closing the door or turning on the light. As we hear the sound of him urinating, something is a bit off – enough to wake the wife. She leans over and turns on the light, revealing that the man is actually going to the bathroom in the closet. Confused, the man stops, looks around, then jogs awkwardly to another room. He turns on the light to the bathroom, lifts the seat, and finishes his business.)

VOICE OVER: Getting adjusted to your new home is about the only thing the Bob and Ronna Real Estate Team can't help you with. Visit Bob and Ronna at www.bobandronna.com

SUPER: Bob and Ronna Real Estate Team.

(We see The Rick sitting on the edge of the bed in his room.)

SUPER: The ESPY Awards hosted by Jamie Foxx Sunday, July 18th 9pm ET ESPN

THE RICK: Hi, my name is Rick, but everybody calls me "The Rick." And I've noticed, ah, a lot of people nominated for the ESPY Awards have nicknames, like Tracy McGrady is T-Mac and Kevin Garnett is K.G. So I've been thinking about changing my name to "T-Rick." And hopefully that'll get me some more playing time on my softball team. It's not my softball team, it's a city league team for guys over, ah, thirty...five.

VOICE OVER: The ESPY Awards. Sunday July 18th at 9PM on ESPN.

art directors
Pat Harris
Steve O'Brien

writer
Steve O'Brien

agency producer
Anne Katherine Friis

production company
Go Film

director
Christopher Guest

creative director
Court Crandall

client
ESPN

agency
Ground Zero / Los Angeles

05106T

Merit

CONSUMER TELEVISION : UNDER $50K BUDGET — CAMPAIGN

art director
Jeff Lable

writer
Tom O'Connor

agency producer
Monique Veillette

production company
A52

director
Patrick Murphy

creative director
Court Crandall

client
The History Channel

agency
Ground Zero /
Los Angeles

05107T

(We're on a beach in Normandy. A young mother and her daughter are playing in the surf. It's a quiet, peaceful moment. Then, black-and-white footage begins to fade up around them. It's footage of the WWII allied beach invasions, which took place in this exact spot. The mother and daughter keep playing, and take no notice of what's going on around them. The footage fades in and out, in bits and pieces: soliders rush onto the beach... armored ships appear on the water... The war footage fades away. We're left with just the mother and her daughter.)

SUPER: Know where you stand.
The History Channel

(We see a girl in the distinctly designed kids section of Borders (we see store signage in background) reading aloud.

GIRL: It was a dark and stormy night...

(Then we see a 60-ish woman reading a book jacket aloud to her husband in the bestseller fiction aisle inside Borders.)

WOMAN: ... using whatever means necessary, Jack Ryan confronts a new breed of...

(We see people gathered on a balcony at a party.)

GUY: Zombies... zombies...

(We see a group of teen boys telling stories in a tent.)

TEEN BOY: They're stumble around goin'....

(We see a teacher reading a Shakespeare passage out of a book to her class.)

TEACHER: How now, my love! Why is your cheek so pale?

(Then we see a book club meeting.)

WOMAN: Because her face actually contained...

BOOK CLUB WOMAN: Part of the code and the main character...

(We see boys playing basketball.)

BOY: ...comes running out of the cave and there's cobwebs all over him and the music is goin'..

(The narrative continues with a guy at his computer humming "in a gadda da vida," a comedian, a businessman reading aloud "Who Moved My Cheese," a dad reading to his son "Green Eggs and Ham," and a forklift operator telling a story to his buddies. Then we see the book club woman, comedian, a guy listening to music and three buddies all screaming "Ahh!" at the same time. The narrative continues with intermingled passages and sentences from various people. We then see it's Christmas morning. A dad regales his 3 kids with presents while re-enacting a classic film. He shouts out a line as he hands each kid a gift.

DAD: Merrrrrry Christmas, Mr. Potterrrrr!

DAD: (To 2nd child) Merrrrrry Christmas, you old building and loan!

(He hands out more gifts)

SUPER: Books Music Movies Connect

THIRD CHILD: Bedford falls.

DAD: Bedford falls!

SUPER: Borders

art director
Dave Swartz

writer
Tim Roper

agency producers
David Rolfe
Rupert Samuel
Terry Stavoe

production company
Moxie Pictures

director
Jim Sheridan

creative directors
Alex Bogusky
Tim Roper

client
Borders

agency
Crispin Porter + Bogusky / Miami / Los Angeles

05109T

One Show

NON-BROADCAST : SINGLE

art director
Thomas Chudalla

writer
Thomas Chudalla

agency producer
Marion Lange

production company
@radical.media

director
Steve Miller

creative directors
Amir Kassaei
Wolfgang Schneider
Mathias Stiller

client
Volkswagen

agency
DDB / Berlin

05118T

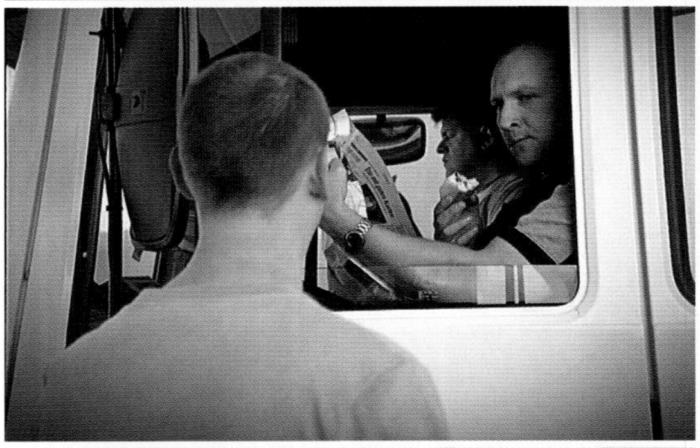

(A young man backs into a parking space in his Polo, slightly touching the truck behind him. The guy is extremely worried about the truck driver's condition, because his Polo is small but tough.)

SUPER: Polo. Small but Tough. Volkswagen logo.

art director
Mathias Stiller

writer
Wolfgang Schneider

agency producer
Marion Lange

production company
Cobblestone Hamburg
Filmproduktion

director
Sebastian Strasser

creative directors
Amir Kassaei
Wolfgang Schneider
Mathias Stiller

client
Volkswagen

agency
DDB / Berlin

05120T

(After winding up a small toy Golf, a boy gets pulled – by the car - out of the house into the garden. Even a VW toy car with FSI- or TDI-technology is extremely powerful.)

SUPER: More power. Less consumption.
With FSI – and TDI – Technology.
Volkswagen logo.

art director
Katrien Bottez

writer
Peter Ampe

agency producer
Andreas Hasle

production company
Czar.be

director
Lionel Goldstein

creative director
Jens Mortier

client
Axion-Youth Banking

agency
Duval Guillaume /
Brussels

05110T

(A very spotty boy finds out that the spots on his face spell beautiful stories in braille. He sells the stories and makes a fortune.)

SUPER: Axion-Youth banking.

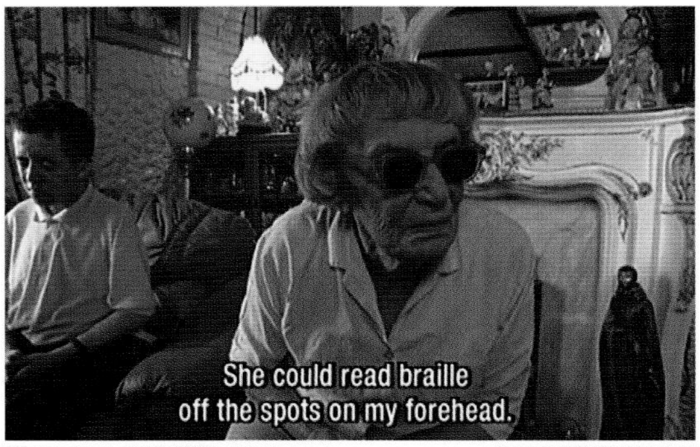

She could read braille
off the spots on my forehead.

This is a reading mask they can use,
like that there.

(We open inside a supermarket. It's empty. Except for an attractive young woman, an older lady and a young guy who's manning the checkout line. It's 3am. The young woman pushes her basket through his checkout station. The clerk gets to work. He picks up a box of strawberries.)

CLERK: Wild Strawberries?

(She ignores him. The clerk now picks up a papaya.)

CLERK: The Scent of Green Papaya.

(Undaunted, the clerk tries again.)

CLERK: Chocolate?

WOMAN: (In dead sexy French accent) Chocolate!

CLERK: Big Night?

WOMAN: Insomnia.

(He picks up a bottle of wine. He looks at her.)

CLERK: Identity?

(She is amused as she hands over her license. He reads it. He's interested.)

CLERK: Single ...White Female.

(She snatches the license out of his hands.)

WOMAN: Indecent proposal!

CLERK: Wild At Heart.

CLERK: Harold... and...

WOMAN: Maude.

CLERK: Anything else?

(She stops looks at him and pulls out a key and dangles it front of him.)

WOMAN: Guess Who's Coming to Dinner?

(The young woman turns and leaves. We catch his reaction as the older woman is now standing at the checkout, she looks at the checkout guy slyly.)

OLDER WOMAN: Midnight Cowboy...
Y tu mama tambien.

SUPER: Only in LA...

Ten days. 60 films.

LA Film Festival

writers
Shyam Madiraju
Bob Strickland

agency producer
Vidya Shenoi

production company
Untitled

director
Shyam Madiraju

creative director
Shyam Madiraju

client
Los Angeles Film Festival (IFP)

agency
Germ / Santa Monica

05111T

Merit

NON-BROADCAST : SINGLE

art directors
Justus v. Engelhardt
Tobias Gradert-Hinzpeter

writers
Florian Kähler
Florian Pagel

production company
Sehsucht

directors
Ole Peters
Timo Schädel

creative directors
Till Hohmann
Axel Thomsen

client
Mercedes-Benz

agency
Springer & Jacoby / Hamburg

05112T

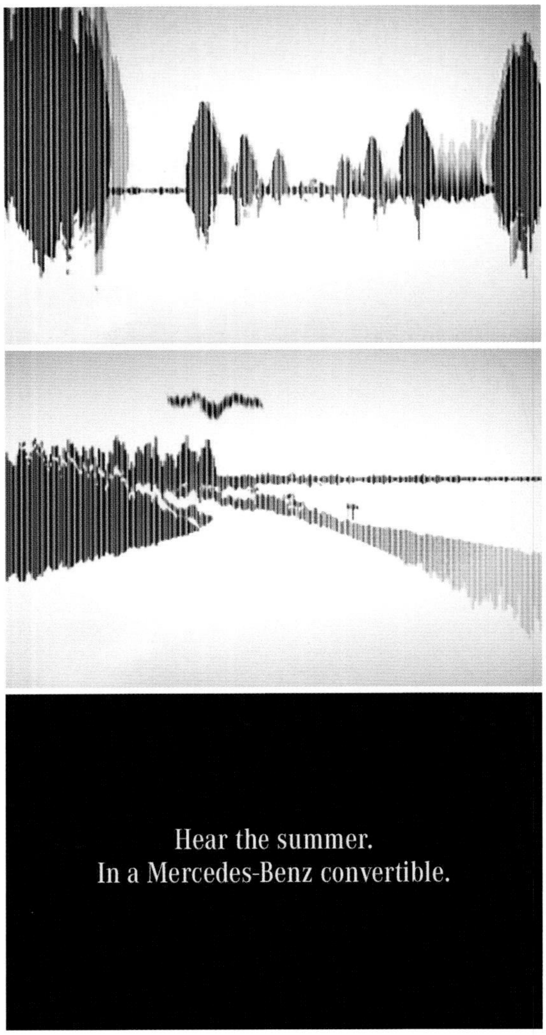
Hear the summer.
In a Mercedes-Benz convertible.

(We hear a car start and see sound waves. These transform into trees and various landscapes. Birds fly by, then we see mountains and bridges.)

SUPER: Hear the summer. In a Mercedes-Benz convertible. Mercedes-Benz logo.

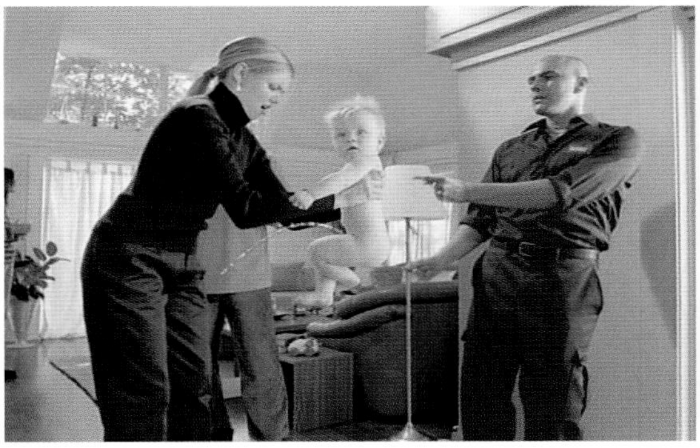

>> TO UNSCRAMBLE
CALL 1-800-565-MOVIES

art director
Guybrush Taylor

writer
Zak Mroueh

agency producer
Sam Benson

production company
Creative Post

creative director
Zak Mroueh

client
TAXI

agency
TAXI / Toronto

05113T

(The video showcases TAXI's most well known campaigns. Juxtaposed over the images are the voices of some irate consumers. We see video clips from TAXI's Viagra campaign.)

NURSE: Hello there. I'm a nurse working in a nursing home. I feel it totally inappropriate to advertise the product Viagra. Do you not realize the problems these ads cause for the gentlemen in our homes who are sexually inactive through no fault of their own?

OLD MAN: It seems that you suggest that all the people in our society are sex-starved and need to have this Viagra to live. Well, I'm very disgusted.

NURSE: I really feel your company should be a lot more socially responsible.

(We then see scenes and stills from MINI commercials, one of which features a "threesome" to illustrate the car's spaciousness.)

FATHER: I just want to comment about how promiscuous our society has become when you're creating ads encouraging our young people to be promiscuous in cars...

HUSBAND: My buddy and I tried to have a threesome in the backseat and my wife was not comfortable at all.

FATHER: And I think it's very ridiculous and I think you are all heathens.

(Scenes and stills from pro-bono Covenant House commercials, which parody reality-based shows. The fictional show is called "Street Kid Survivor".)

WOMAN: I've just been...umm...interrupted by your commercial for Covenant House while... umm... watching my show...and I...it comes on and it's so offensive.

YOUNG GUY: Do you not see the reality shows that are out there? Are you kidding me? Sleeping in a cardboard box, who would do that?

LAWYER: The network is currently looking into legal action in regards to copyright infringement.

YOUNG GUY: (mumbling)... Homeless people, they're suffering and they eat pizza crusts...I don't want to see that.

(Scenes and stills from "The Movie Network" campaign featuring scrambled images from famous movies. The idea was that you could see what you were missing if you subscribed to the Movie Network. Obviously, the traffic co-coordinator from the TV station didn't understand the concept.)

PRODUCER: Hi, this is Arlita calling from CFTO. It's looks like the tapes TAXI sent over for the Movie Network weren't dubbed properly on your end. This happens from time to time. Usually adjusting the tracking will help. Kindly give me a call when I should expect them.

(Scenes and stills from "Mark's Work Warehouse" commercial featuring the peeing baby.)

MOTHER: I'm calling to complain about the latest Mark's Work Warehouse ad that TAXI has put on the air with the Mom holding the little baby that's peeing everywhere. My kids thought it was hilarious and they've gone around the house and they're peeing everywhere... umm... I'm disgusted by the ad.

WOMAN: It's kind of offensive.

NURSE: Inappropriate.

OLD MAN: Irresponsible.

MOTHER: I just want you to know I won't be shopping at Mark's Work Warehouse anymore.

SUPER: TAXI logo.

FATHER: Grow up guys. All right. Just grow up.

PUBLIC SERVICE/ POLITICAL-RADIO: SINGLE

writer
Rob Tarry
agency producer
Christine Pacheco
production company
Wave Productions
directors
Rob Tarry, Colin Weinmaster
creative directors
Ian Grais, Chris Staples
client
Science World
agency
Rethink / Vancouver

05008R

✦

writer
Markus Ruf
agency producer
Markus Ruf
production company
Studio Bellerive
director
Martin A. Fueter
creative directors
Markus Ruf, Danielle Lanz
client
Muehlehalde Home of the Blind Zurich
agency
Ruf Lanz / Zurich

05009R

✦

writers
Slade Gill, Conn Bertish
agency producer
Julie Gardiner
production company
B&S Studios
directors
Slade Gill, Conn Bertish
creative director
Conn Bertish
client
Engen - Arrive Alive
agency
Saatchi & Saatchi / Cape Town

05010R

✦

writer
Neil Gardiner
agency producer
Phillipa Bresler
production company
B&S Studios
creative directors
Graham Lang, PJ Kensley, Ahmed Tilly
client
POWA
agency
The Jupiter Drawing Room (South Africa) / Cape Town

05011R

✦

writer
Matt McCain
agency producer
Dax Estorninos
production company
Clatter & Din
creative director
Tracy Wong
client
Fare Start
agency
WONGDOODY / Seattle

05012R

✦

writer
John Schofield
agency producer
Dax Estorninos
production company
Clatter & Din
creative director
Tracy Wong
client
Museum of Flight
agency
WONGDOODY / Seattle

05013R

✦

PUBLIC SERVICE/ POLITICAL-RADIO: CAMPAIGN

writers
Cesar Sastre, Nacho Guillo, Pablo Gonzalez De La Peña, Victor Aguilar
agency producer
Manuela Zamora
production company
Rafa Arnau, Jingle Box
creative director
Juan Nonzioli
client
Save the Children
agency
Shackleton / Madrid

05014R

✦

CONSUMER RADIO: SINGLE

writer
Gaëtan Namouric
agency producer
Normand Vaillancourt
production company
Audio Z
creative director
Gaëtan Namouric
client
CHUM
agency
Bleu Blanc Rouge / Montreal

05015R

✦

writer
Wayne Winfield
agency producer
Barbara Michelson
production company
McHale Barone
creative director
Sal DeVito
client
Mount Sinai Medical Center
agency
DeVito/Verdi / New York

05019R

✦

writer
Brett Morris
agency producer
Karin Keylock
production company
Sonovision Studios
director
Brett Morris
creative director
Brett Morris
client
Toyota
agency
FCB / Johannesburg

05024R

✦

writers
Stephan Ganser, Jan Harbeck, Mirko Stolz
production company
Studio Funk
creative directors
Burkhart von Scheven, Stephan Ganser
client
Berliner Morgenpost
agency
Jung von Matt / Berlin

05025R

✦

writer
Götz Ulmer, Paul Fleig
production company
Hastings
creative directors
Götz Ulmer, Oliver Voss
client
BMW Motors/Mini Cooper One
agency
Jung von Matt / Stuttgart

05026R

✦

writers
Matthew Brink, Adam Livesey
agency producer
Mthuli Bam
production company
Sterling Sound
director
Matthew Brink
creative directors
Rob McLennan, Stuart Walsh
client
Unilever SA
agency
Lowe Bull / Bryanston

05027R

✦

writer
Trevor Sacks
agency producer
Tracey Ashman
production company
Sterling Sound
director
Lorens Persson
creative directors
Gerry Human, Fran Luckin
client
M Net
agency
Ogilvy South Africa / Johannesburg

05028R

✦

writers
Pablo Videla, Howard Green
agency producer
Louise McKeown
production company
Shell Like
creative director
Tony Granger
client
Toyota
agency
Saatchi & Saatchi / London

05029R

✦

writer
Aaron Starkman
agency producer
Amanda Loughran
production company
Rosnick Mackinon Webster
creative directors
Elspeth Lynn, Lorraine Tao
client
IKEA
agency
ZiG / Toronto

05031R

◆

CONSUMER RADIO: CAMPAIGN

writers
John Immesoete, Chuck Rachford
agency producer
Marianne Newton
production company
Chicago Recording Company
director
Dave Gerbosi
creative directors
John Immesoete, Mark Gross
client
Anheuser-Busch
agency
DDB / Chicago

05034R

Also awarded:
{Merit}
Consumer Radio: Single

◆

writers
John Immesoete, Chuck Rachford
agency producer
Marianne Newton
production company
Chicago Recording Company
director
Dave Gerbosi
creative directors
John Immesoete, Mark Gross
client
Anheuser-Busch
agency
DDB / Chicago

05032R

Also awarded:
{Merit}
Consumer Radio: Single

◆

writers
Bob Winter, Chris Roe, Chuck Rachford
agency producer
Marianne Newton
production company
Chicago Recording Company
director
Dave Gerbosi
creative directors
John Immesoete, Mark Gross
client
Anheuser-Busch
agency
DDB / Chicago

05033R

Also awarded:
{Merit}
Consumer Radio: Single

◆

writer
Marty Senn
agency producer
Shannon Barnes
production company
Kamen Entertainment Group
creative directors
Ari Merkin, Wayne Best
client
Virgin Mobile USA
agency
Fallon / New York

05035R

Also awarded:
{Merit}
Consumer Radio: Single
{Merit}
Consumer Radio: Single

◆

writers
Daniel Frericks, Eskil Puhl, Jana Liebig
agency producer
Daniel Frericks
production companies
Hastings, Doublehead
director
Frank Aldorf
creative director
Constantin Kaloff, Ove Gley
client
K-fee
agency
Jung von Matt / Hamburg

05036R

◆

writer
Donna McCarthy
agency producer
Richard Nelson
production company
Pirate Radio
director
Terry O'Reilly
creative directors
Tom Murphy, Donna McCarthy
client
Irving Oil Limited
agency
Target Marketing / St. John's

05037R

◆

writers
Tohru Oyasu, Dave Loew, Ian Reichenthal, Scott Vitrone
agency producer
Monica Wilkins
production companies
CRC, Another Country, Kamen Entertainment
creative directors
Mark Figliulo, Dave Loew, Jon Wyville
client
Miller Brewing Company
agency
Y&R / Chicago

05038R

Also awarded:
{Merit}
Consumer Radio: Single

◆

DEATH IS THE ANSWER

performed by
Early Man
courtesy of
Matador Records
www.matadorrecords.com
www.earlymanarmy.com

Innövative/Integrated

Merit

Visions of Destruction

One Show

EXCEPTIONAL INNOVATION IN MARKETING : SINGLE

art director
Tom Millar

writer
Marc Guttesman

agency producers
Marc Guttesman
Tom Millar

content strategist
Marc Guttesman

director
Joe Leih

creative directors
Tom Millar
Marc Guttesman

client
marcandtom.com

agency
marcandtom.com / Ossining

05012G

art director
Joel Davis

writer
Kevin Botfeld

designer
Nate Anderson

creative directors
Rich Wakefield
Scott Sheinberg

client
Ad Council

agency
WestWayne / Atlanta

05016G

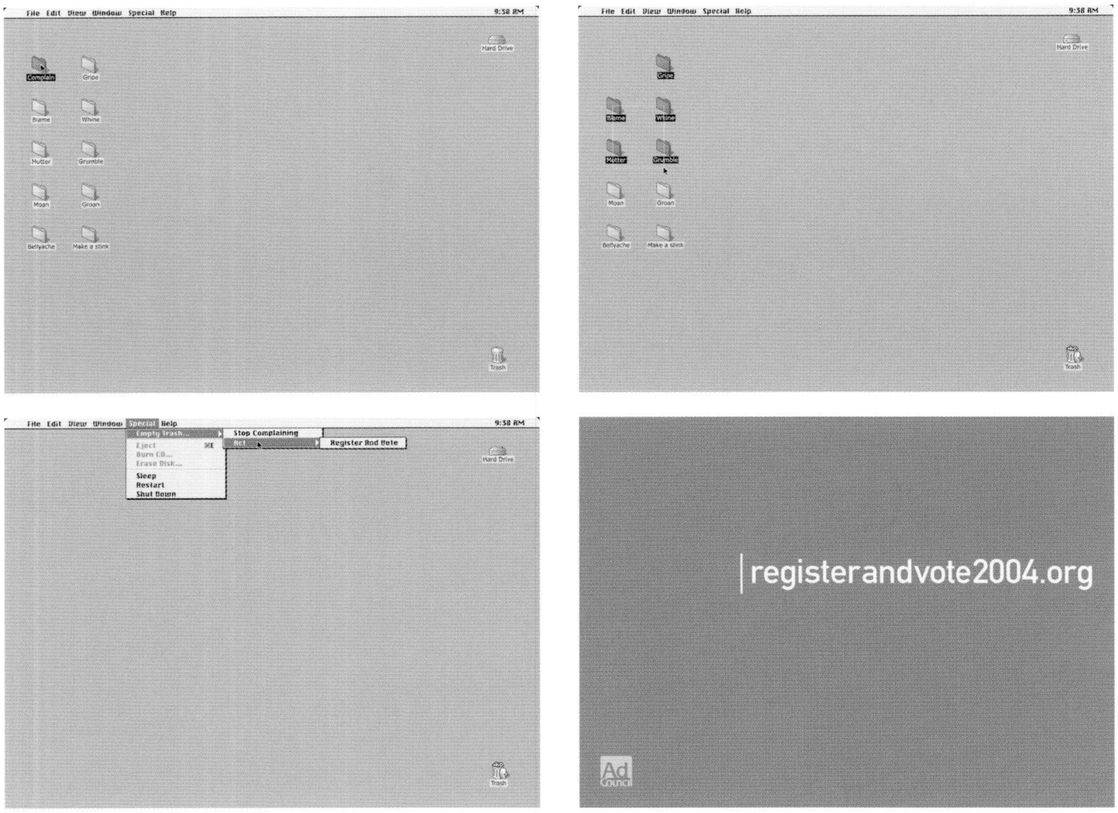

MARK DUNNE
LIVED HERE

ORLA HEALY
HOMELESS PERSON
LIVED HERE
DECEMBER 2003

SINEAD KELLY
LIVED HERE

PAUL KEOGH
LIVED HERE

art director
Dave Milligan-Croft

writer
Ted Barry

creative director
Mike Garner

client
Focus Ireland

agency
Chemistry / Dublin 6

05017G

NOTHING CAN REPLACE A TREE.

NOTHING CAN REPLACE A TREE.

NOTHING CAN REPLACE A TREE.

art directors
Rebecca Johnson-Pond
Steve Back

writer
Kimberley Ragan
Toby Talbot

designer
Maria Lishman

illustrators
Maria Lishman
Jae Morrison

agency producer
Jo McMillan

production company
Colenso BBDO

creative directors
Rich Maddocks
Toby Talbot

client
Auckland Regional Council

agency
Colenso BBDO / Auckland

05018G

Also Awarded:
merit
Outdoor and Posters: Campaign

One Show

EXCEPTIONAL INNOVATION IN MARKETING : CAMPAIGN

art director
Mark Taylor

writer
Bob Cianfrone

illustrator
Pres Rodriguez

agency producers
David Rolfe
Terry Stavoe

production companies
MJZ
Barbarian Group

director
Rocky Morton

creative directors
Alex Bogusky
Andrew Keller
Jeff Benjamin
Rob Reilly

client
Burger King

agency
Crispin Porter + Bogusky / Miami

05020G

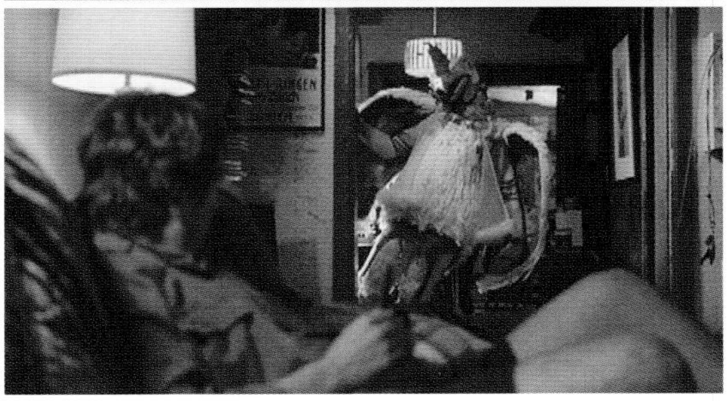

Sample pages from book.

130-page, hard-cover book created to launch The Angus Steakburger from Burger King. *Eating the Angus Diet* by "Dr. Angus" was featured in direct-response television spots and a 30-minute infomercial. It was also available for purchase or pdf-download on www.angusdiet.com

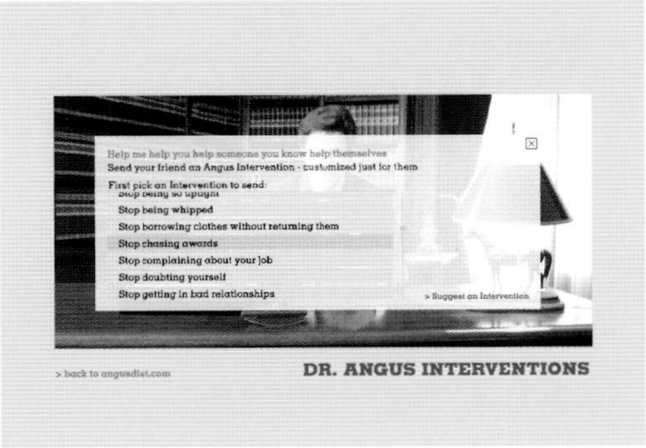

art directors
John Parker
Kevin Koller
Rahul Panchal

writers
Evan Fry
Ryan Kutscher

photographers
John Parker
stock

producers
Eva Dimick
David Niblick
Sandy DeMouy

illustrators
Dwight Allott
Lin Wilson

digital artist/multimedia
Loyalkaspar

programmer
Barbarian / Oddcast

agency producer
Rupert Samuel

production company
ASD

director
Harry Enfield

creative directors
Alex Bogusky
Andrew Keller
Jeff Benjamin
Rob Reilly

client
Burger King

agency
Crispin Porter + Bogusky / Miami

05019G

One Show

EXCEPTIONAL INNOVATION IN MARKETING : CAMPAIGN

art director
Thomas Yang

writer
Farrokh Madon

photographer
Stock

digital artist/multimedia
Procolor

creative directors
Terrence Tan
Farrokh Madon

client
Jeep

agency
M&C Saatchi / Singapore

05021G

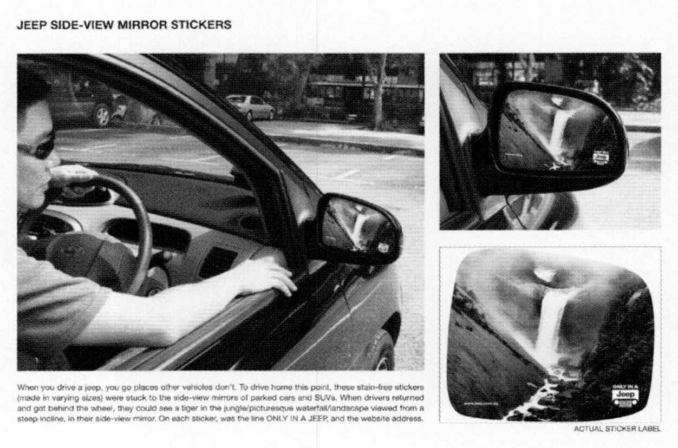

art directors
Gunther Schreiber
Björn Rühmann

designers
Bertrand Kirschenhofer
Nicole Fiebig

writers
Ingmar Bartels
Christoph Bielefeldt
Philipp Dörner

content strategist
Mathias Müller-Using

production company
Silbersee Film

director
Marc Malze

creative director
Lars Rühmann

client
Renault Germany

agency
Nordpol / Hamburg

05022G

One Show

EXCEPTIONAL INNOVATION IN MARKETING : CAMPAIGN

art director
Rohit Devgun

writer
Amit Nandwani

illustrator
Rishi Chanana

creative director
Josy Paul

client
WWF - India

agency
RMG David / New Delhi

05023G

Also Awarded:
merit
One Show Design
Public Service/Non-Profit/Educational
Collateral: Campaign

You never kill just the tree.

You never kill just the tree.

You never kill just the tree.
Travellers Cheques

art director
Din Sumedi

writer
Robert Tsao

photographer
Teo Studio

creative director
Graham Kelly

client
AXN

agency
Saatchi & Saatchi /
Singapore

05024G

One Show

EXCEPTIONAL INNOVATION IN MARKETING : CAMPAIGN

art directors
Anne Max Bostad
Miguel de María

writers
Francisco Cassis
Juan Carlos Martínez

agency producer
Rodrigo Roco

creative directors
Rafa Antón
Javier Álvarez
Fernando Martín

client
Sitges Sci-fi and Fantasy Film Festival

agency
Vitruvio Leo Burnett / Madrid

05025G

art directors
Phil Covitz
Meghan Siegal

designers
Max Pfennighaus
Jason Warne
Meghan Siegal
Cindy Moon

writers
John Kearse
Mike Howard
Marc Einhorn

programmers
Ebbey Mathew
Adam Buhler

agency producers
Amy Favat
Carron Pedonti
Barry Frechette

production companies
Harvest Films
Bartradio

information architect
Melissa Goldstein

directors
Baker Smith
Bart Smith

creative directors
Ron Lawner
Pete Favat
Alex Bogusky
Roger Baldacci
Tom Adams

client
American Legacy Foundation

agency
Arnold Worldwide / Boston and Crispin Porter + Bogusky / Miami

05026G

One Show

INTEGRATED BRANDING : CAMPAIGN

art directors
John Parker
Dave Swartz

designers
Curtis C. Chen
Wei-Hwa Huang

writers
Evan Fry
Mike Lear
Bill Wright

photographer
Rick Whittey

illustrator
Robert Finkbeiner

programmer
Curtis C. Chen

agency producers
Barrie Bamberg
Curtis C. Chen
Sebastian Gray

creative directors
Alex Bogusky
Bill Wright

client
Google

agency
Crispin Porter + Bogusky / Miami

05027G

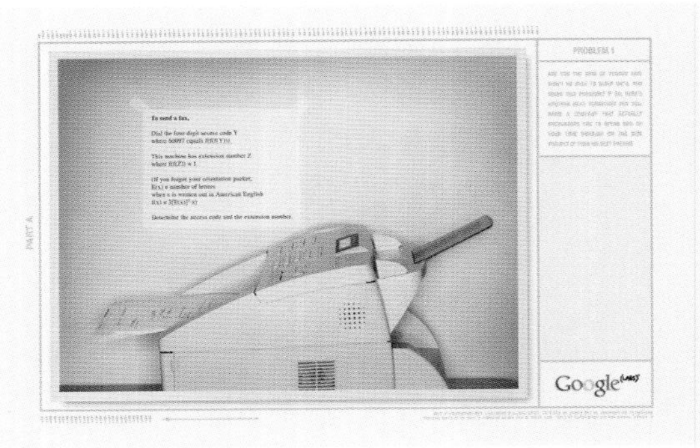

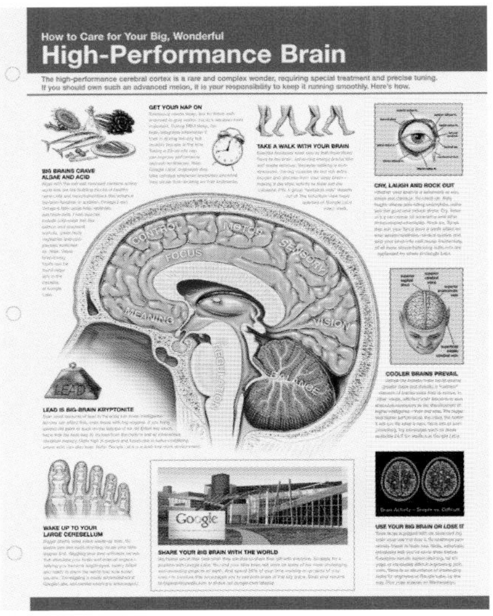

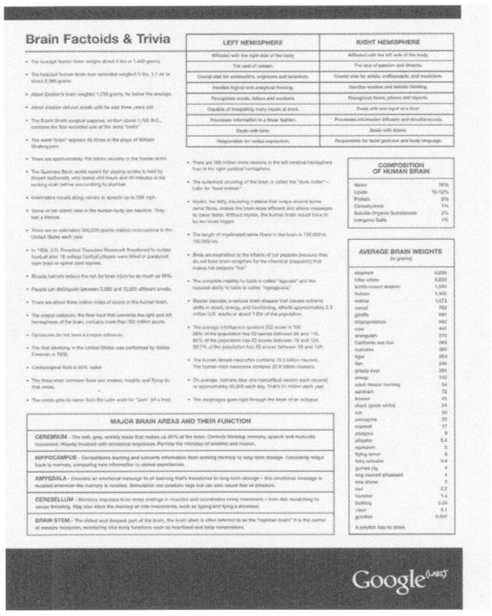

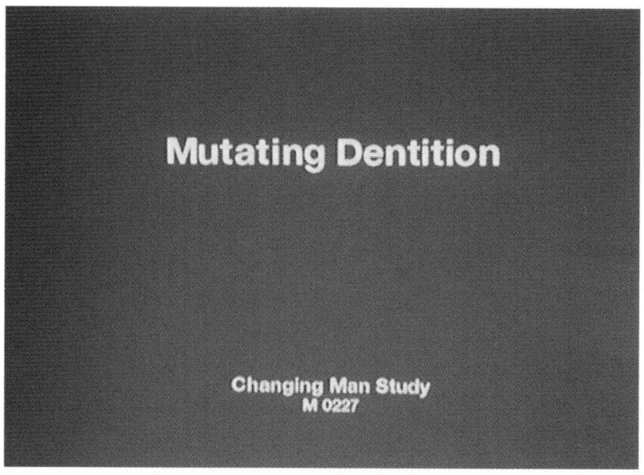
Mutating Dentition
Changing Man Study
M 0227

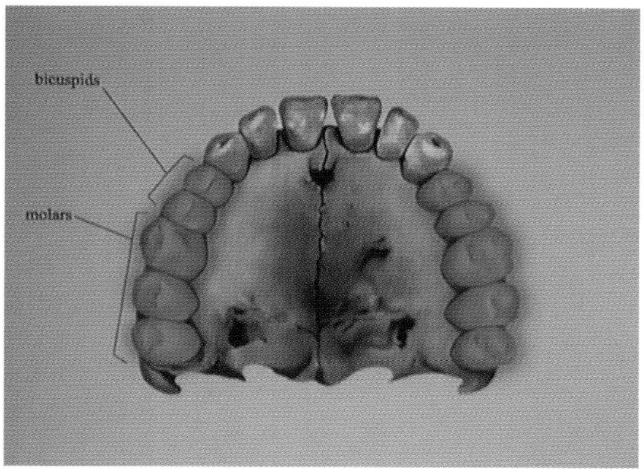
bicuspids
molars

ARE YOU DYING INSIDE?
Mantropy Disease

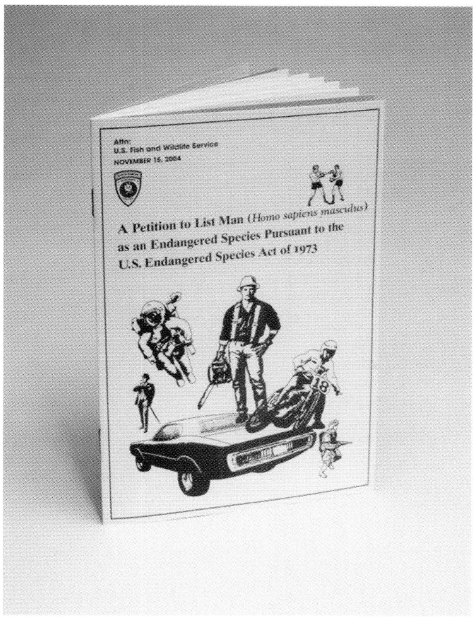
Attn:
U.S. Fish and Wildlife Service
NOVEMBER 15, 2004
A Petition to List Man (Homo sapiens masculus) as an Endangered Species Pursuant to the U.S. Endangered Species Act of 1973

art directors
Alex Burnard
Mike del Marmol
Geordie Stephens

designers
Alex Burnard
Rahul Panchal
Oscar Rivas

writer
David Schiff

illustrator
Mike del Marmol

programmer
Andrew Reale

agency producers
Paul Sutton
Pam Sturchio
Sheri Radel
Cindy Prez

creative directors
Alex Bogusky
Dave Schiff
Alex Burnard

client
Maxim

agency
Crispin Porter + Bogusky / Miami

05028G

Don't Feed Tofu to the Man
When you feed the man cubes of organic bean curd, you are actually doing more harm than good. Though delicious to some, they can actually kill the part of the man that makes him a man. If left in peace, the man will hunt down a more indigenous meal — beef nachos or half a barbequed chicken or something.
MAXIM
MAN'S NATURAL HABITAT
©2004

Don't Manicure the Man
Attempting to improve the man by clipping his cuticles or blow-drying his hair may actually destroy him. The "rough edges" you are so carefully removing are part of his natural defense system. Without them, his masculinity is severely depleted, leaving him poorly equipped to compete for food or a mate.
MAXIM
MAN'S NATURAL HABITAT
©2004

Don't Speed Bump the Man
Slowing the man down may seem like a good way to ensure his safety. Unfortunately this will only hasten his demise. Man's natural tendency is to go fast. When his habitat is curtailed with "safety measures," he becomes listless and depressed — easy prey for stronger faster rivals.
MAXIM
MAN'S NATURAL HABITAT
©2004

One Show

INTEGRATED BRANDING : CAMPAIGN

art director
Sandra Schilling

writers
Ulrich Lützenkirchen
Ilja Schmuschkowitsch

designers
Andreas Böhm
Michael Janke

photographer
F.A. Cesar

illustrator
Djamila Rabenstein

agency producer
Marion Lange

content stragtegists
Jason Lusty
Wiebke Dreyer
Phillip Schilling

production company
@radical.media

director
Steve Miller

creative directors
Amir Kassaei
Wolfgang Schneider
Mathias Stiller

client
Volkswagen

agency
DDB / Berlin

05033G

For boys who were always men.

WOB G 8200
The new Golf GTI®.

For boys who were always men.

The new Golf GTI®.

For boys who were always men.
The new Golf GTI®.

There are
thousands
who love
the things
you love.
How
will you
find them?
People are good.
eBay
The power of all of us.

eBay home | Invite a friend
TV Spots
People are Good
Enter to Win
Move In
Store
Privacy policy
eBay
The power of all of us.

How else
could
something
you loved
back then
return
to become
something
she loves
now?
People are good.
eBay
The power of all of us.

eBay home | Invite a friend
TV Spots
People are Good
Enter to Win
Move In
Store
Back
Sign up, and we'll contact you on Move-in Day.
email address
Send
Privacy policy
eBay
The power of all of us.

art directors
Rob Palmer
Steve Mapp
John Nussbaum

writers
Jamie Barrett
Toria Emery

photographers
Jake Chessum
Sol Neelman
Kelly Jordan

programmer
WDDG Production House

agency producers
Cindy Fluitt
MJ Otto
Jenny Taich
Mike Geiger

production company
Biscuit Filmworks

director
Noam Murro

creative directors
Jeff Goodby
Jamie Barrett
Rob Palmer

client
eBay

agency
Goodby Silverstein & Partners / San Francisco

05029G

One Show

INTEGRATED BRANDING : CAMPAIGN

art director
Tom Richards

writer
Pete Armstrong

agency producer
Annelise Smith

production company
Godman

director
Lab Ky Mo

creative director
Andy Cheetham

client
Scruffs

agency
JWT Cheethambell / Manchester

05030G

Extra grip for when the earth moves

HARDCORE
A DIRTY MOVIE
scruffs
HARDWEAR
IT'S GONNA GET DIRTY

Always wear protection
Sample from pack containing 30 different cards.

ALWAYS WEAR PROTECTION, IN CASE YOU SPILL YOUR LOAD.
scruffs
HARDWEAR
IT'S GONNA GET DIRTY
For all your on the job needs visit www.scruffs.com

DESIGNED FOR SCREWING, BANGING AND DRILLING.
scruffs
HARDWEAR
IT'S GONNA GET DIRTY
For all your on the job needs visit www.scruffs.com

RE-INFORCED KNEES, IDEAL FOR LAYING SLABS, TILES AND LONELY HOUSEWIVES.
scruffs
HARDWEAR
IT'S GONNA GET DIRTY
For all your on the job needs visit www.scruffs.com

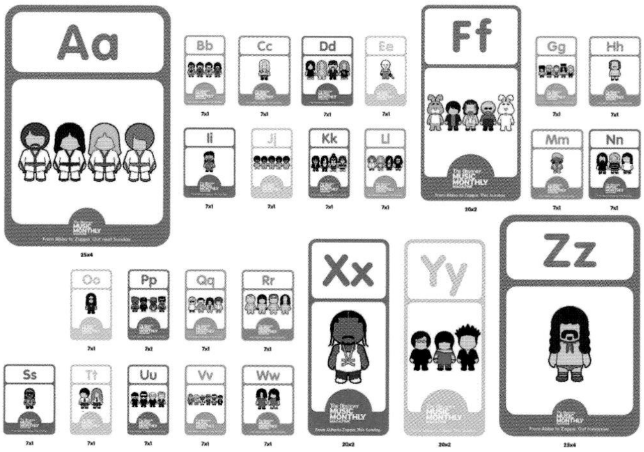

art directors
Ben Middleton
Stuart Outhwaite

writers
Ben Middlton
Stuart Outhwaite

designer
Emil Lanne

illustrator
Craig Robinson

agency producer
Emma Starzacher

production company
Nexus

directors
Adam Foulkes
Adam Smith

creative directors
Robert Saville
Mark Waites
Nicholas Roope

client
The Observer

agency
Mother / London

05031G

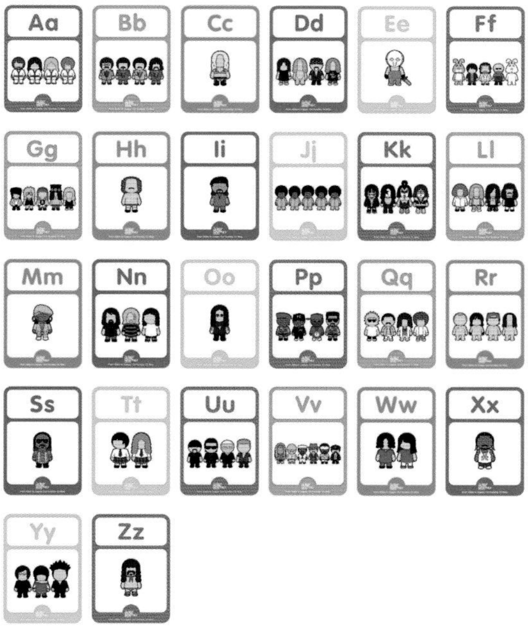

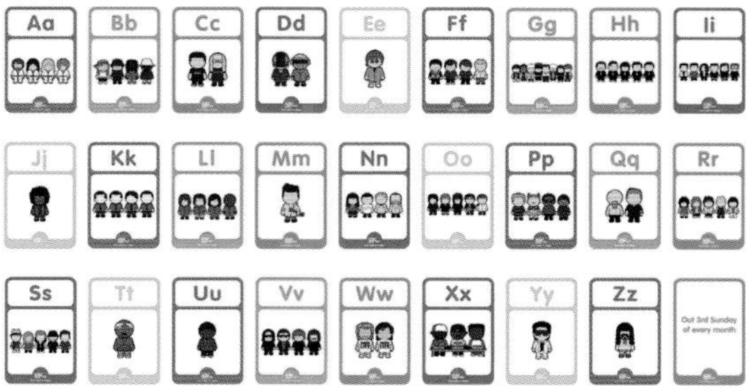

Merit

INTEGRATED BRANDING : CAMPAIGN

One Show

INTEGRATED BRANDING : CAMPAIGN

art director
Ian Grais

writer
Andy Linardatos

photographer
Hans Sipma

illustrator
Stephen Dittberner

agency producer
Christine Pacheco

production company
Spy Films

director
Trevor Cornish

creative directors
Ian Grais
Chris Staples

client
BC Lions

agency
Rethink / Vancouver

05032G

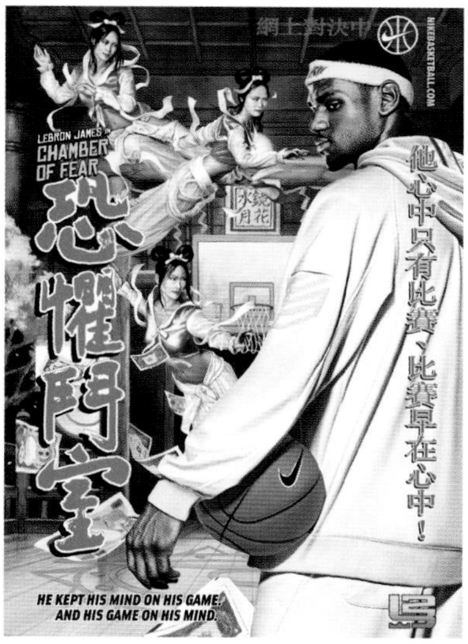
網上對決中
NIKEBASKETBALL.COM
LEBRON JAMES IN CHAMBER OF FEAR
恐懼鬥室
他心中只有比賽、比賽早在心中！
HE KEPT HIS MIND ON HIS GAME. AND HIS GAME ON HIS MIND.

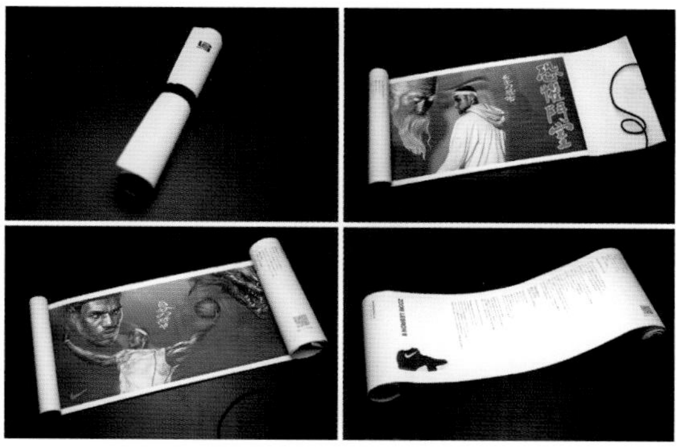

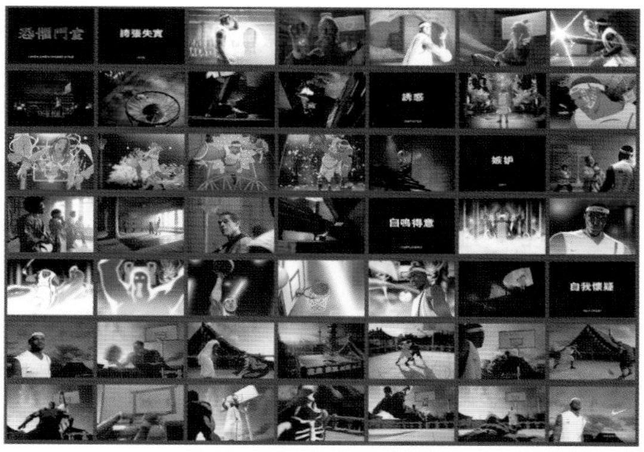

LEBRON JAMES IN CHAMBER OF FEAR
恐懼鬥室
Their breath was worse than their bite.
網上對決中

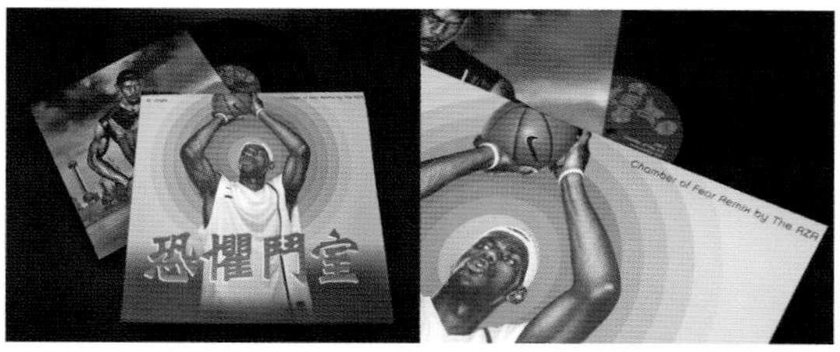
恐懼鬥室
Chamber of Fear Remix by The RZA

art directors
John Jay
Jayanta Jenkins

writer
Jimmy Smith

photographer
Thierry des Fontaines

illustrator
Boris + Julie

agency producer
Tieneke Pavesic

production company
@radical.media

director
Dave Meyers

creative directors
John Jay
Sumiko Sato
Jimmy Smith

client
Nike

agency
Wieden + Kennedy / Tokyo

05034G

敵人不守門規，更仇視球員！
恐懼鬥室
LEBRON JAMES IN CHAMBER OF FEAR
NIKEBASKETBALL.COM

他進攻，瞄準，再迎頭痛擊！
LEBRON JAMES IN CHAMBER OF FEAR
恐懼鬥室
HE CAME. HE SAW. HE BANGED ON SOME HEADS.
網上對決中
NIKEBASKETBALL.COM

網上對決中
知己不知彼，如何取勝？
HOW DO YOU DEFEAT AN OPPONENT WHO KNOWS YOUR EVERY MOVE?
恐懼鬥室
LEBRON JAMES IN CHAMBER OF FEAR

www.monozelle.de

Design Merit
Hell Bent
on Style

One Show Design

BRAND AND CORPORATE IDENTITY DESIGN: ANNUAL REPORT

designer
Barry Quinn

art director
Barry Quinn

writer
Irfan Khan

photographer
Edward Lynds

creative director
Barry Quinn

client
Distress Centres of Toronto

agency
GJP _ Gee Jeffery & Partners / Toronto

05052D

THERE'S A LIFE ON THE LINE.
2003 ANNUAL REPORT
DISTRESS CENTRES

HOUSE TODAY. THERE'S FOR ME OUT
MATTER.
WE ANSWERED HER CALL AT 2:45
SHE WENT FOR A WALK AT 4:00

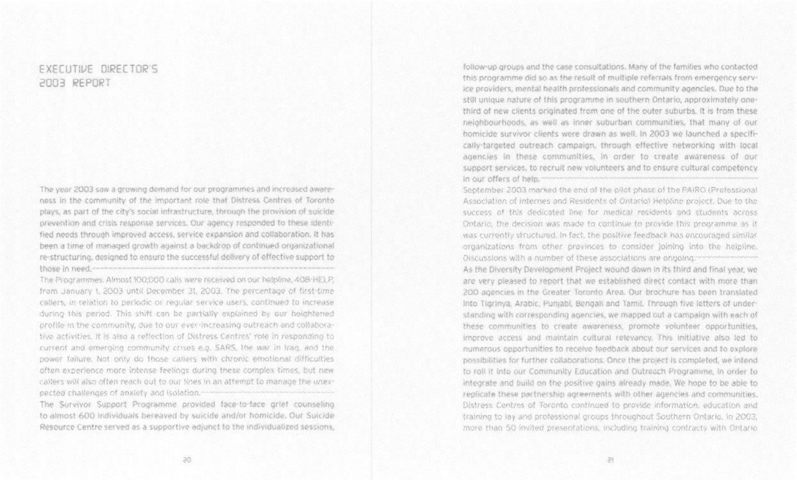

EXECUTIVE DIRECTOR'S
2003 REPORT

The year 2003 saw a growing demand for our programmes and increased awareness in the community of the important role that Distress Centres of Toronto plays, as part of the city's social infrastructure, through the provision of suicide prevention and crisis response services. Our agency responded to these identified needs through improved access, service expansion and collaboration. It has been a time of managed growth against a backdrop of continued organizational re-structuring, designed to ensure the successful delivery of effective support to those in need.

The Programmes. Almost 100,000 calls were received on our helpline, 408-HELP, from January 1, 2003 until December 31, 2003. The percentage of first-time callers, in relation to periodic or regular service users, continued to increase during this period. This shift can be partially explained by our heightened profile in the community, due to our ever-increasing outreach and collaborative activities. It is also a reflection of Distress Centres' role in responding to current and emerging community crises e.g. SARS, the war in Iraq, and the power failure. Not only do those callers with chronic emotional difficulties often experience more intense feelings during these complex times, but new callers will also often reach out to our lines in an attempt to manage the unexpected challenges of anxiety and isolation.

The Survivor Support Programme provided face-to-face grief counseling to almost 600 individuals bereaved by suicide and/or homicide. Our Suicide Resource Centre served as a supportive adjunct to the individualized sessions,

20

follow-up groups and the case consultations. Many of the families who contacted this programme did so as the result of multiple referrals from emergency service providers, mental health professionals and community agencies. Due to the still unique nature of this programme in southern Ontario, approximately one-third of new clients originated from one of the outer suburbs. It is from these neighbourhoods, as well as inner suburban communities, that many of our homicide survivor clients were drawn as well. In 2003 we launched a specifically targeted outreach campaign, through effective networking with local agencies in these communities, in order to create awareness of our support services, to recruit new volunteers and to ensure cultural competency in our offers of help.

September 2003 marked the end of the pilot phase of the PAIRO (Professional Association of Internes and Residents of Ontario) Helpline project. Due to the success of this dedicated line for medical residents and students across Ontario, the decision was made to continue to provide this programme as it was currently structured. In fact, the positive feedback has encouraged similar organizations from other provinces to consider joining into the helpline. Discussions with a number of these associations are ongoing.

As the Diversity Development Project wound down in its third and final year, we are very pleased to report that we established direct contact with more than 200 agencies in the Greater Toronto Area. Our brochure has been translated into Tigrinya, Arabic, Punjabi, Bengali and Tamil. Through five letters of understanding with corresponding agencies, we mapped out a campaign with each of these communities to create awareness, promote volunteer opportunities, improve access and maintain cultural relevancy. This initiative also led to numerous opportunities to receive feedback about our services and to explore possibilities for further collaborations. Once the project is completed, we intend to roll it into our Community Education and Outreach Programme, in order to integrate and build on the positive gains already made. We hope to be able to replicate these partnership agreements with other agencies and communities. Distress Centres of Toronto continued to provide information, education and training to lay and professional groups throughout Southern Ontario. In 2003, more than 50 invited presentations, including training contracts with Ontario

21

designer
Andrew Dull

writer
Clark Malcolm

photographer
Jim Powell

creative director
Steve Frykholm

client
Herman Miller

agency
Herman Miller / Zeeland

05053D

BRAND AND CORPORATE IDENTITY DESIGN: BOOKLET BROCHURE

designers
Marie-Élaine Benoit
Jonathan Nicol

writer
Jonathan Rosman

photographer
Jean-François Bouchard

illustrators
Luc Normandin
Jonathan Nicol
Marie-Élaine Benoit

creative directors
Héléne Godin
Philippe Meunier

client
Guru Bicycle

agency
Diesel / Montreal

05054D

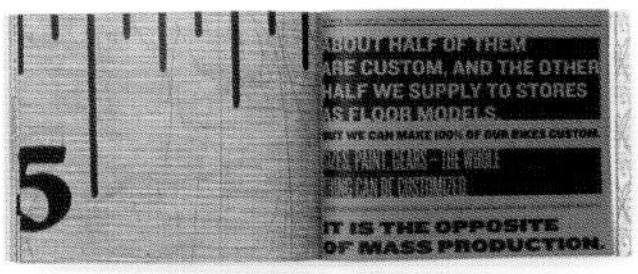
5
ABOUT HALF OF THEM ARE CUSTOM, AND THE OTHER HALF WE SUPPLY TO STORES AS FLOOR MODELS.
IT IS THE OPPOSITE OF MASS PRODUCTION.

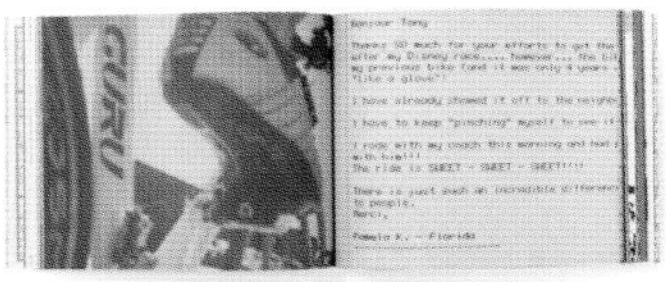
GURU

GURU
1735 4TH AVE

designers
Urs Frick
Uschi Henkes
Jenny Nerman

art directors
Urs Frick
Uschi Henkes
Jenny Nerman

creative directors
Uschi Henkes
Urs Frick
Manolo Moreno.

client
Buenavista

agency
Grupo Zapping / Madrid

05056D

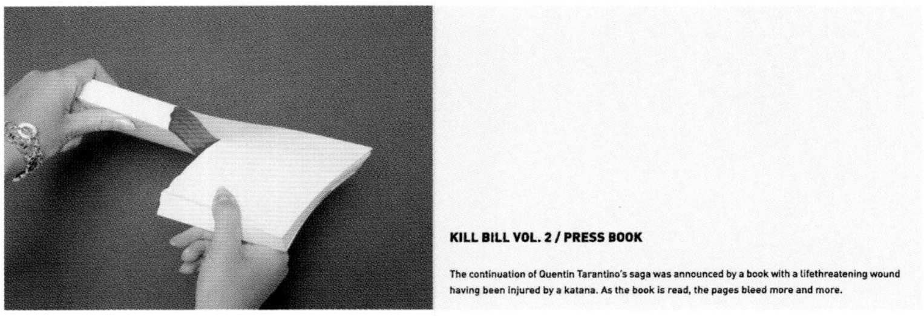
KILL BILL VOL. 2 / PRESS BOOK
The continuation of Quentin Tarantino's saga was announced by a book with a lifethreatening wound having been injured by a katana. As the book is read, the pages bleed more and more.

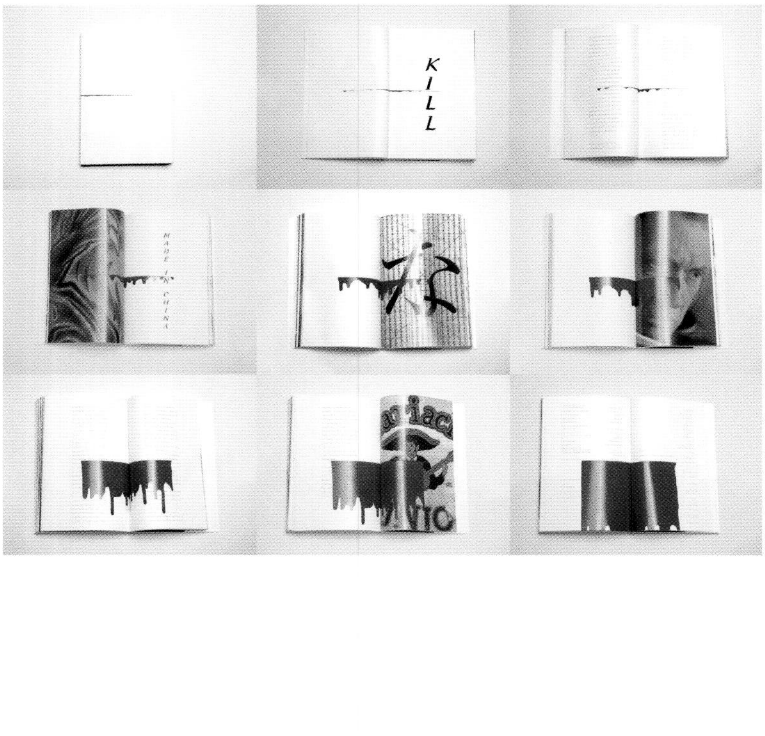
KILL
MADE IN CHINA

art director
Jörg Bauer

writer
Oliver Flohrs

photographer
Jörg Schieferecke

illustrator
Thilo Rothacker

creative director
Achim Jäger

client
The Neckar Valley
Green Space Foundation

agency
Jung von Matt / Stuttgart

05057D

Also Awarded:
merit
Public Service/
Non-Profit/Educational
Collateral: Single

designer
T T Ho

art director
T T Ho

writers
Victoria Low
Ajay Bakhshi

illustrators
Julian Yap
Toh Tee Reei
Victoria Low

creative directors
Ean-Hwa Huang
Szu-Hung Lee

client
McCann Erickson

agency
McCann Erickson /
Kuala Lumpur

05058D

designers
Weston Bingham
Apirat Infahsaeng
Thomas Griffiths

creative directors
Weston Bingham
Brian Collins

client
Crystal Group

agency
Ogilvy & Mather /
New York

05059D

designers
Sally Morrow
Starlee Matz
Shanin Andrew

art director
Sally Morrow

writer
Mark Waggoner

photographers
David Emmite
Various

creative director
Sally Morrow

client
Converse

agency
Sandstrom Design /
Portland

05060D

354

designers
James Parker
Kristin Anderson

art director
James Parker

photographer
Dave Bradley

creative director
Steve Sandstrom

client
Converse

agency
Sandstrom Design / Portland

05061D

designers
Cathrin Ciuraj
Claudia Locherer
Sebastian Richter

art director
Tim Stockmar

writer
Torsten Lindner

photographers
Heribert Schindler
Ralph Baiker
Katrin Denkewitz

creative directors
Matthias Spaetgens
Jan Leube

client
Frankfurter Allgemeine Zeitung

agency
Scholz & Friends / Berlin

05055D

Also Awarded:
merit
Direct Mail: Single

What do you get from F.A.Z.-sized ads?
Frankfurter Allgemeine
Adverts in the F.A.Z.
www.faz.net/anzeigen

More power.

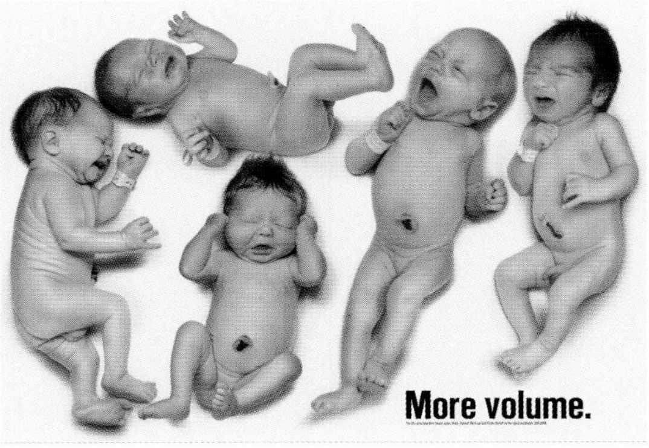
More volume.

Faust
More substance.

More punch.

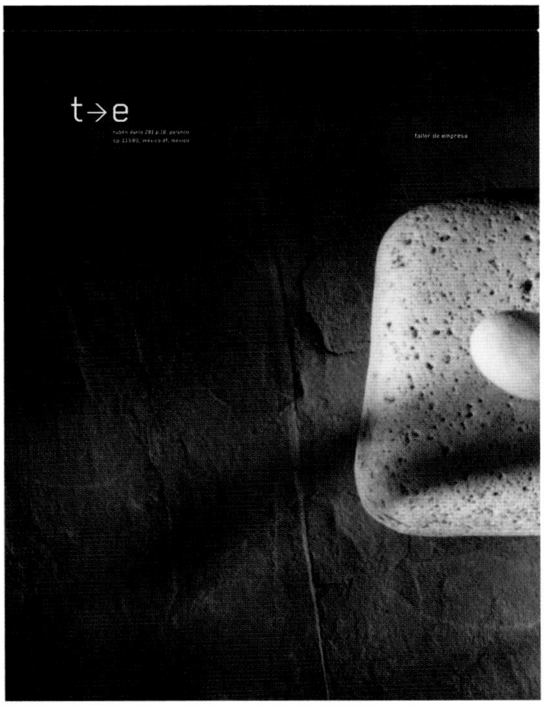

designers
Vanessa Eckstein
Vanessa Enriquez

art director
Vanessa Eckstein

photographer
Fernando Cordero

creative director
Vanessa Eckstein

client
Taller de Empresa

agency
Blok Design / Mexico

05062D

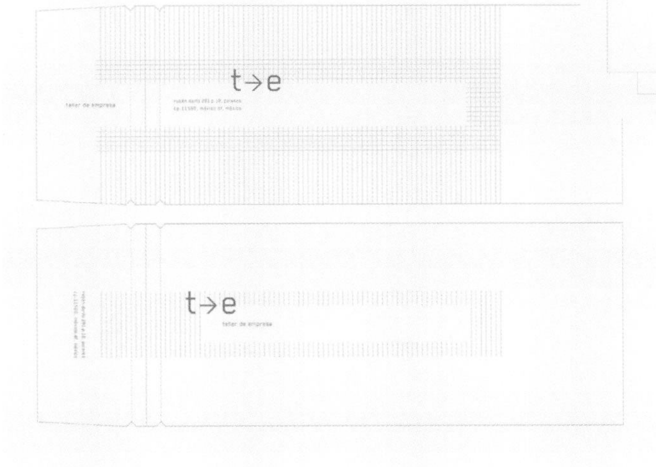

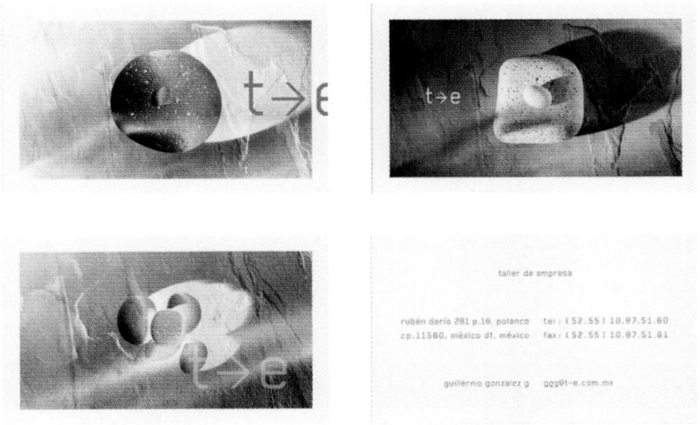

designer
Priti Rodricks

art director
Priti Rodricks

photographer
Ashish Vaidya

creative directors
Devesh Desai
Raj Nair

client
Dr. Pradumna S. Mamtora

agency
Contract Advertising / Mumbai

05063D

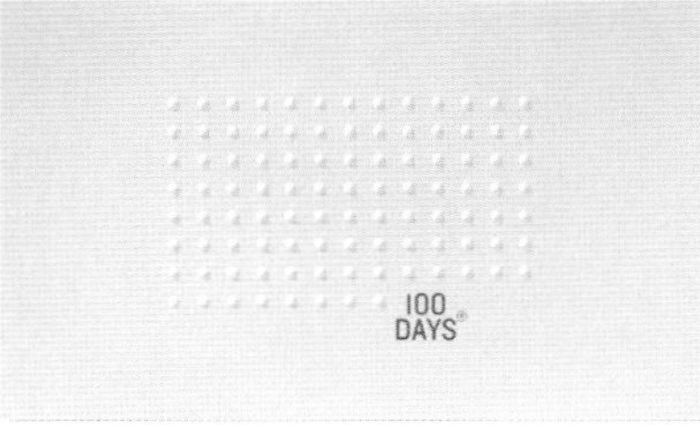

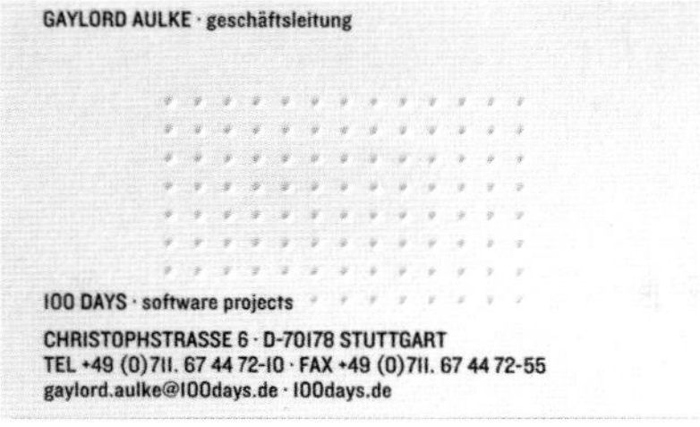

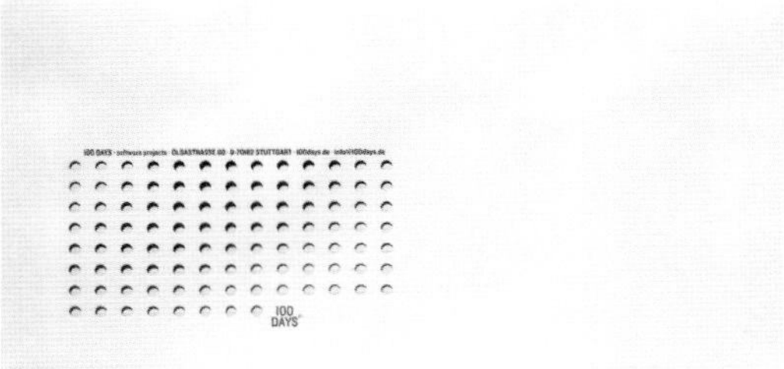

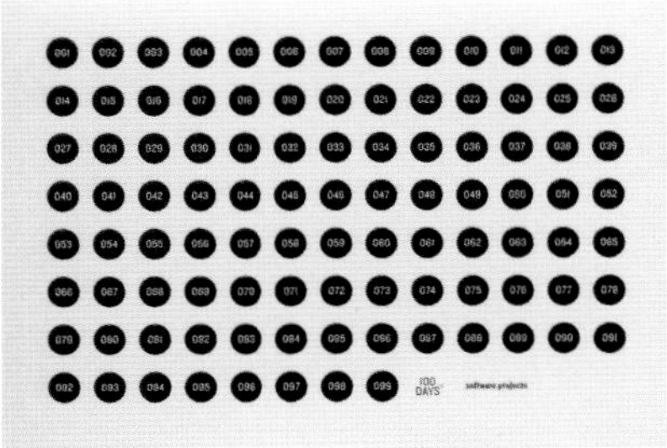

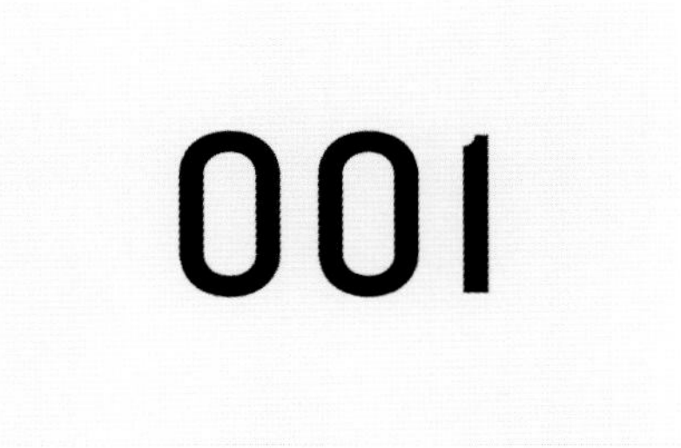

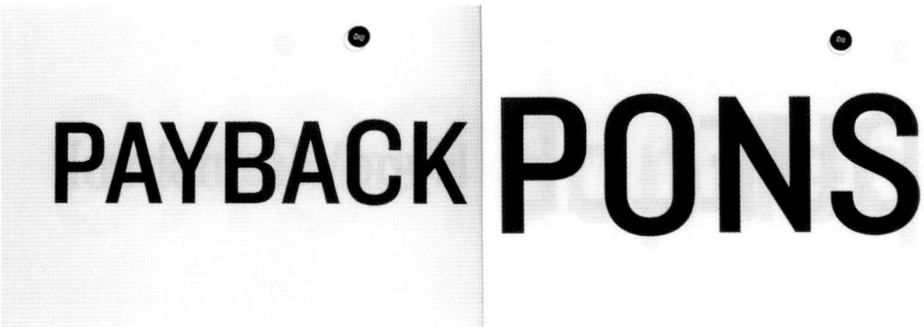

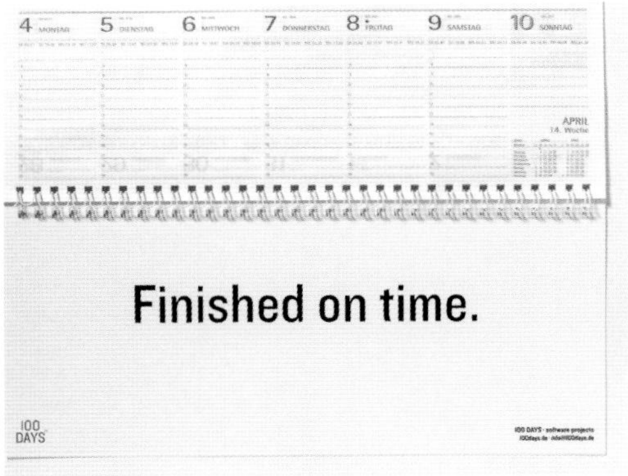

art director
Jörg Bauer

creative directors
Jörg Bauer
Christian Schwarm

client
100 Days

agency
Dorten / Stuttgart

05064D

BRAND AND CORPORATE IDENTITY DESIGN : CORPORATE IDENTITY

designer
Brenton Bubb

art director
Brenton Bubb

writer
Dylan Kidson

photographer
Anthony de Klerk

creative director
Francois de Villiers

client
Justine Drake

agency
FCB South Africa / Cape Town

05065D

art director
Lisa Careborg

photographer
The Archive of the Museum

creative director
Anders Kornestedt

client
The Swedish Museum of Architecture

agency
Happy Forsman & Bodenfors / Gothenburg

05066D

Also Awarded:
merit
One Show Design
Public Service/Non-Profit/Educational
Collateral: Single

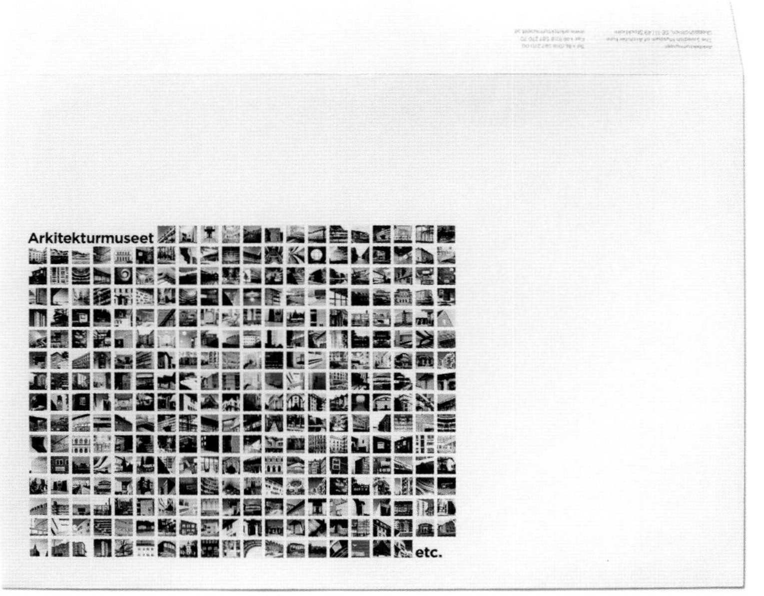

designers
Jonathan Yuen
Pann Lim
Roy Poh

art directors
Pann Lim
Roy Poh
Jonathan Yuen

writers
Pann Lim
Roy Poh

illustrator
Jonathan Yuen

creative director
Kinetic

client
Miracle Creations

agency
Kinetic / Singapore

05067D

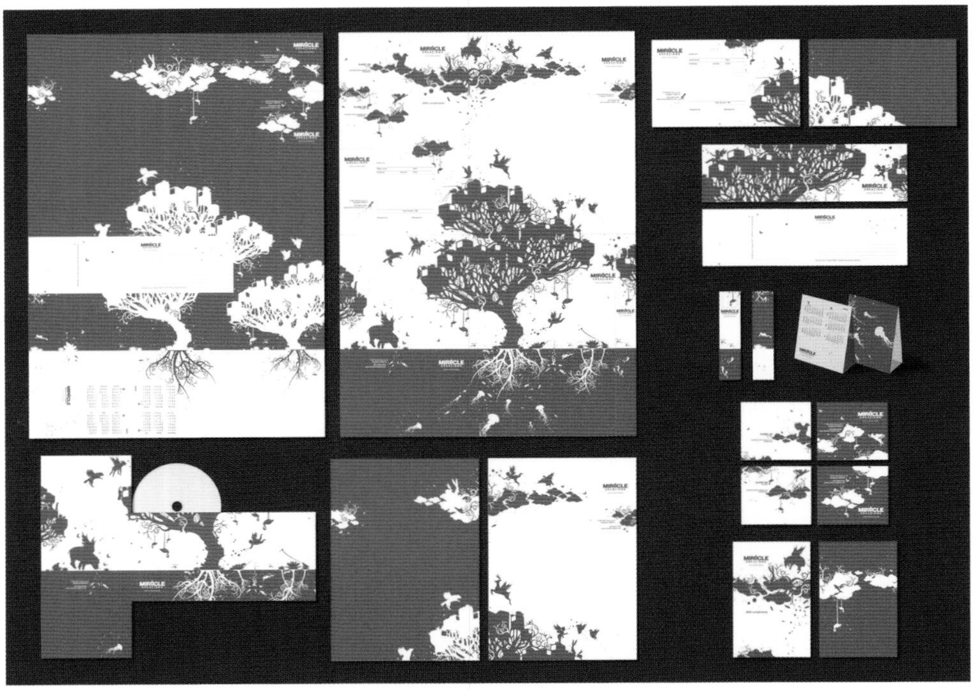

designer
Mangesh Rane

art director
Mangesh Rane

writer
Malobi Dasgupta

photographer
Ashok Salian

illustrators
Santosh Bane
Prashant Pedneker

creative director
Ravi Deshpande

client
Culture Curry

agency
Lemon / Mumbai

05068D

designers
Kim Gehrig
Luke Williamson

art directors
Kim Gehrig
Luke Williamson

creative directors
Robert Saville
Mark Waites

client
Mother

agency
Mother / London

05070D

designer
Niket Parekh

art director
Niket Parekh

writer
Niket Parekh

illustrator
Niket Parekh

client
Ashutosh Parikh

agency
Niket Parekh / Mumbai

05071D

art directors
Doug Pedersen

writer
Lee Remias

photographer
Sarah Peter

client
Steele Technologies

agency
No Luggage / Charlotte

05072D

THIS PERIPHERAL NOT DESIGNED FOR USE AS A PROJECTILE
Call Steele Technologies to resolve hardware issues 704-905-0862 steele-tech.net
DANGER!
KICKING SERVER MAY RESULT IN BROKEN FOOT
Notify steele technologies of problems. 704-905-0862 steele-tech.net
PELIGRO!
NEVER USE MALFUNCTIONING PRINTERS FOR TARGET PRACTICE
Report faulty equipment to steele technologies 704-905-0862 steele-tech.net
TEMPER TANTRUMS WILL NOT RESOLVE SOFTWARE CONFLICTS
Steele Technologies steele-tech.net 704-905-0862
HITTING MONITOR WILL NOT RECALIBRATE SCREEN
CALL STEELE TECHNOLOGIES 704-905-0862 STEELE-TECH.NET

THROWING LAPTOP ACROSS OFFICE MAY RESULT IN PERMANENT DATA LOSS
Contact Steele Technologies first 704-905-0862 steele-tech.net
WARNING!
INTERNET PORN COLLECTION MUST NOT EXCEED MAXIMUM HARD DRIVE STORAGE CAPACITY
Steele Technologies 704-905-0862 steele-tech.net
SLAMMING MOUSE INTO DESK WILL NOT UNFREEZE APPLICATION
Steele Technologies 704-905-0862 steele-tech.net
STEELE-TECH.NET
DO NOT DROP KICK CPU
704-905-0862
704-905-0862
EMPLOY DEEP BREATHING TECHNIQUES TO DEAL WITH SYSTEM CRASHES
Then contact Steele Technologies 704-905-0862 steele-tech.net

PROPER HARDWARE MAINTENANCE INVOLVES MORE THAN DUSTING CRUMBS FROM KEYBOARD
Steele Technologies 704-905-0862 steele-tech.net
BEFORE THROWING MONITOR TO FLOOR IN ANGER CALL STEELE TECHNOLOGIES
704-905-0862 STEELE-TECH.NET
NEVER TROUBLESHOOT EXTERNAL HARD DRIVE WITH BASEBALL BAT
Steele Technologies 704-905-0862 steele-tech.net
PRINTER WILL NOT RESPOND TO BEGGING, CURSING, OR THREATS. MALFUNCTIONING UNITS SHOULD BE REPORTED TO STEELE TECHNOLOGIES 704-905-0862 STEELE-TECH.NET
CAUTION
KEYBOARD NOT DESIGNED TO WITHSTAND IMPACT WITH WALL
Call Steele Technologies with tech problems 704-905-0862 steele-tech.net

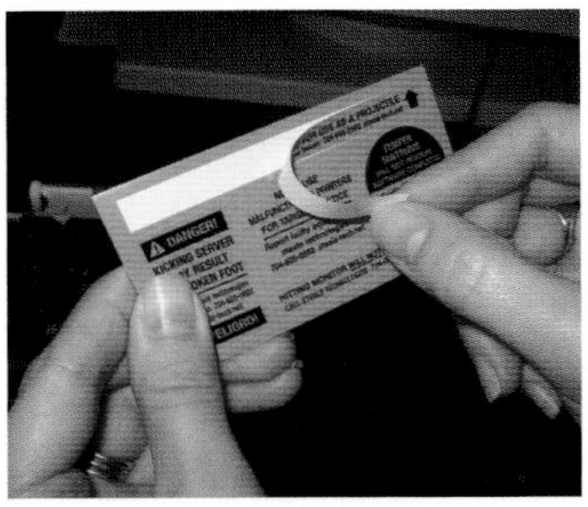

CAUTION
KEYBOARD NOT DESIGNED TO WITHSTAND IMPACT WITH WALL

WARNING!
INTERNET PORN COLLECTION MUST NOT EXCEED MAXIMUM HARD DRIVE STORAGE CAPACITY

NEVER TROUBLESHOOT EXTERNAL HARD DRIVE WITH BASEBALL BAT
Steele Technologies
704-905-0862 steele-tech.net

designer
Maytinee Jaranphairee

art director
Maytinee Jaranphairee

illustrator
Prasit Chanitrapirak

creative director
Nopadol Srikieatikajohn

client
Post Quick Company

agency
Ogilvy & Mather / Bangkok

05073D

designer
Neil Powell

art director
Rachael Powell

writer
Josh Rogers

creative director
Neil Powell

client
Powell

agency
Powell / New York

05074D

designers
Simon Newman
Anthony Wolch

art directors
Simon Newman
Anthony Wolch

photographer
Al Peacock

illustrator
Simon Newman

creative directors
Duncan Bruce
Pat Pirisi

client
Static – Music and Sound Design

agency
Publicis / Toronto

05075D

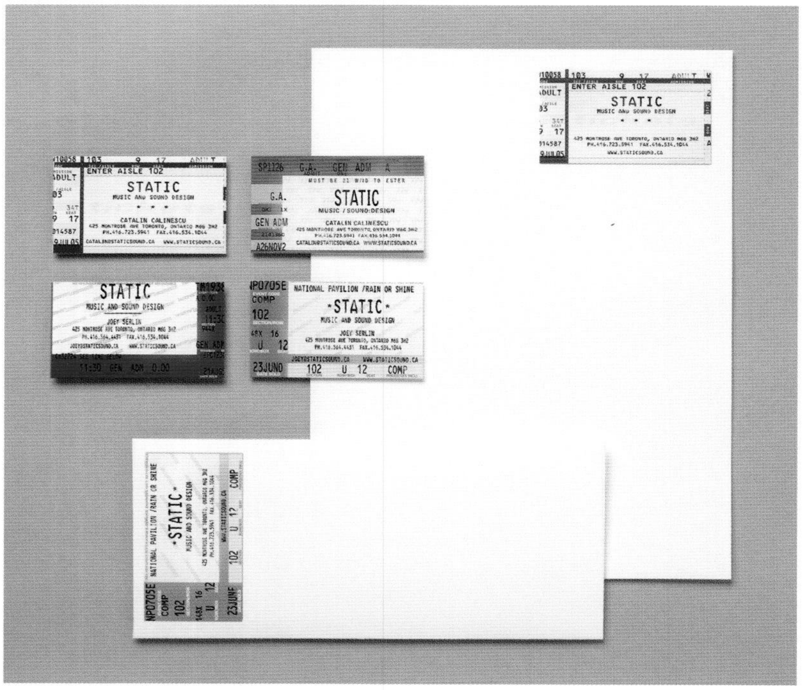

designer
Roger Kennedy

art directors
Dan Cole
Jo Smetham

writers
Dan Cole
Jo Smetham

creative director
Trefor Thomas

client
Betteridges Solicitor

agency
Saatchi & Saatchi / London

05076D

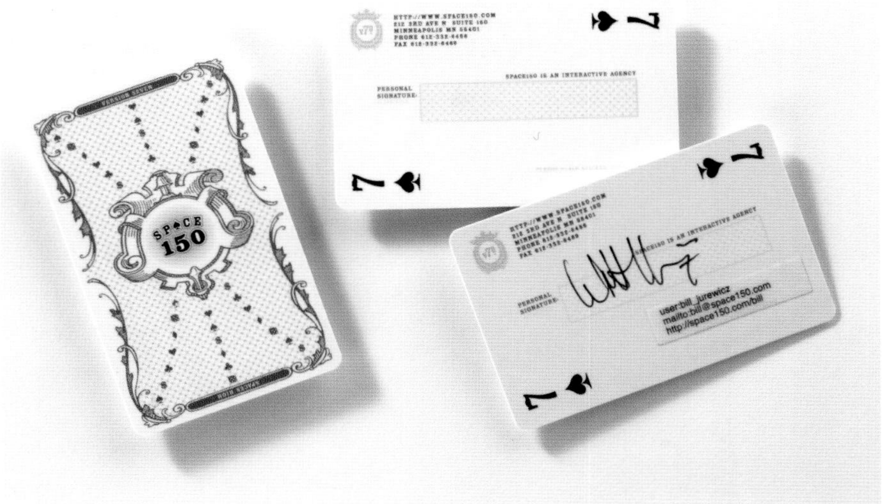

designers
Jeff Johnson
Jason Walzer

art director
Jeff Johnson

writer
Jeff Johnson

illustrator
Jason Walzer

creative director
Jeff Johnson

client
Space 150

agency
Spunk / Minneapolis

05077D

designers
Renata Giovanni
Celina Guimaraes

art directors
Renata Giovanni
Celina Guimaraes

photographer
Peter Baasch

illustrators
Renata Giovanni
Celina Guimaraes

creative director
Nathan Reddy

client
Sowearto

agency
TBWA\Gavin\Reddy / Johannesburg

05069D

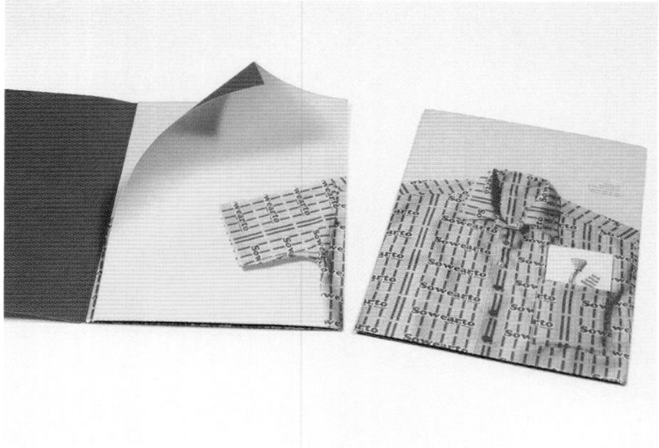

designers
Ben Horner
Michael Hendrix

art director
Michael Hendrix

creative director
Michael Hendrix

client
Tricycle

agency
Tricycle / Chattanooga

05078D

Turner Duckworth San Francisco welcomes you to
our new studio

designer
Shawn Rosenberger

photographer
Wendi Nordeck

creative directors
David Turner
Bruce Duckworth

client
Turner Duckworth

agency
Turner Duckworth /
San Francisco

05079D

BRAND AND CORPORATE IDENTITY DESIGN : LOGO/TRADEMARK

designers
Jesse Kaczmarek
Patrick Miller

creative director
Bill Thorburn

client
City of Minneapolis

agency
Carmichael Lynch
Thorburn / Minneapolis

05080D

art director
Joe Baran

photographer
Joe Baran

creative directors
John Carstens
Marshall Ross

client
Hotel Victor

agency
Cramer-Krasselt /
Chicago

05081D

Five interchangeable logos, applied randomly in signage and communications. Inspired by sea photographs of jellyfish, a recurring theme of the hotel's interior design.

designer
Melinda Beck

art director
Matthew Duntemann

illustrator
Melinda Beck

client
Nick Digital - NOGGIN

agency
MTV Networks /
New York

05082D

designers
Barry Deck
Stella Bugbee
Iwona Waluk

creative directors
Weston Bingham
Barry Deck
Brian Collins
Clark Morgan

client
AT&T Wireless

agency
Ogilvy & Mather /
New York

05083D

designers
Yap Pow Hoong
Jann Lim

art directors
Yap Pow Hoong
Ken Goh
Jann Lim

photographer
Melvin Lee (Untold Images)

illustrators
Monica Lee
Wong Fun Hing

creative directors
Yap Pow Hoong
Kit Ong

client
Alinna

agency
Foote Cone & Belding / Kuala Lumpur

05084D

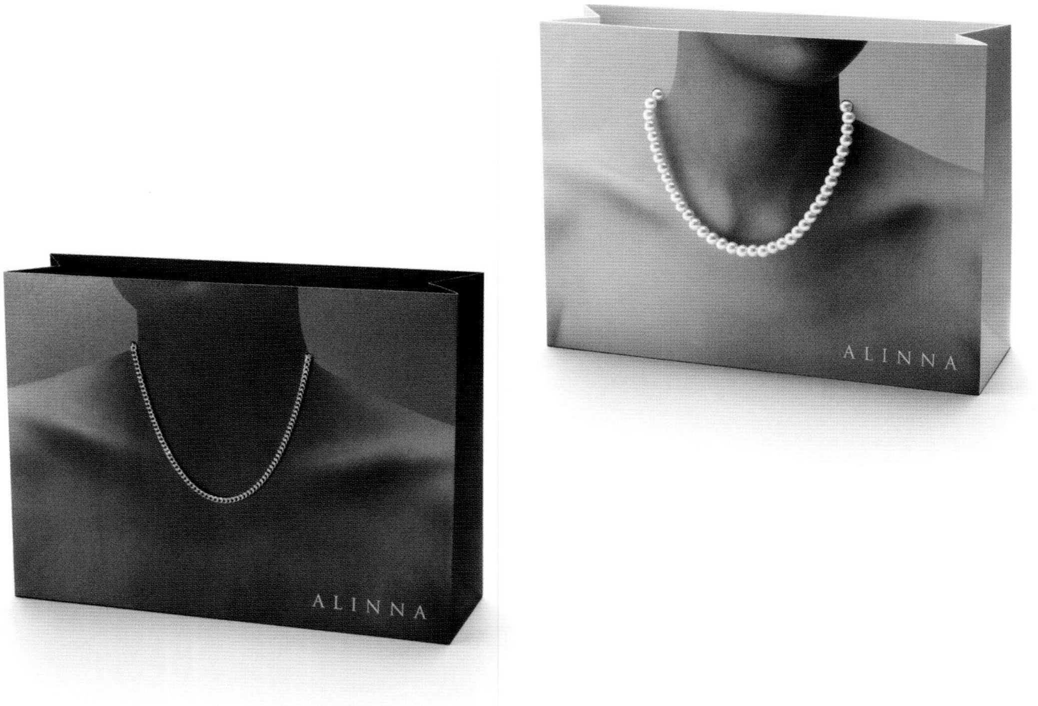

art director
Chie Morimoto

writer
Toshiyuki Konishi

illustrator
Shingo Ono

creative director
Miki Matsui

client
Oorong-sha

agency
Hakuhodo in Progress / Tokyo

05085D

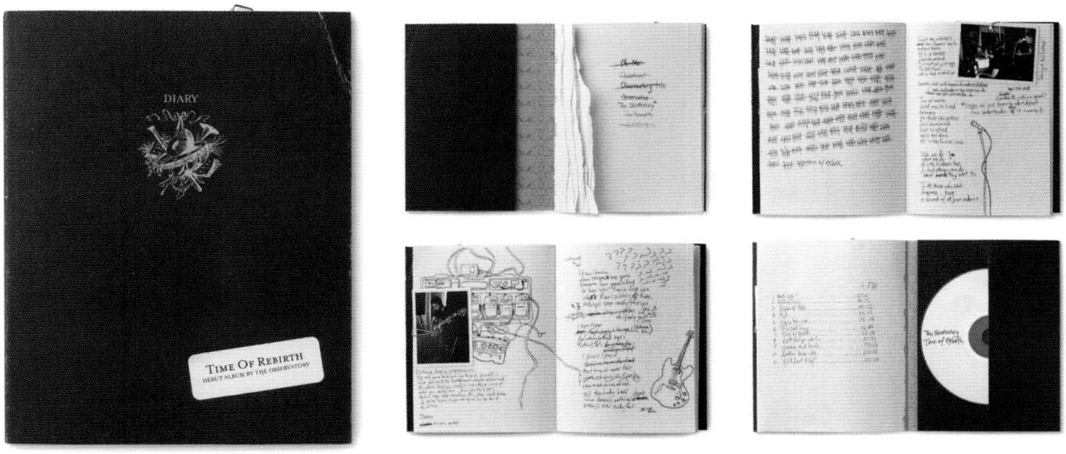

designers
Leng Soh
Pann Lim
Roy Poh

art directors
Leng Soh
Pann Lim
Roy Poh

writer
Leslie Low

photographer
Pann Lim

illustrator
Leng Soh

creative director
Kinetic

client
The Observatory

agency
Kinetic / Singapore

05086D

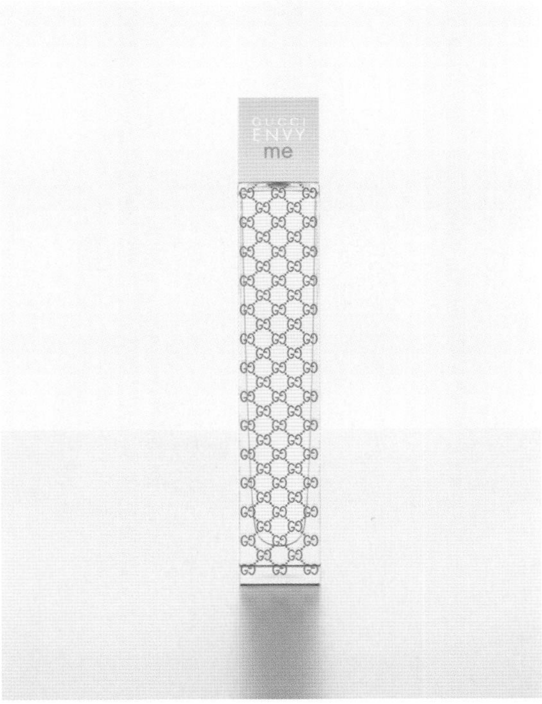

art director
Studio Von Birken

creative director
Doug Lloyd

client
Gucci

agency
Lloyd and Company / New York

05087D

designer
David Turner

creative directors
David Turner
Bruce Duckworth

client
McKenzie River

agency
Turner Duckworth /
San Francisco

05088D

designer
Christian Eager

photographer
Steve Baxter

creative directors
David Turner
Bruce Duckworth

client
Waitrose

agency
Turner Duckworth /
San Francisco

05089D

designers
Todd Piper-Hauswirth
Aaron Dimmel
Jovaney Hollingsworth

art director
Charles S. Anderson

photographer
Aaron Dimmel

illustrator
CSA Images

client
Blue Q

agency
Charles S. Anderson
Design / Minneapolis

05091D

Merit

PACKAGE DESIGN : CAMPAIGN

One Show Design

PACKAGE DESIGN : CAMPAIGN

designers
Todd Piper-Hauswirth
Kyle Hames
Sheraton Green

art director
Charles S. Anderson

writer
Todd Piper-Hauswirth

photographer
Aaron Dimmel

illustrator
CSA Images

client
Blue Q

agency
Charles S. Anderson
Design / Minneapolis

05090D

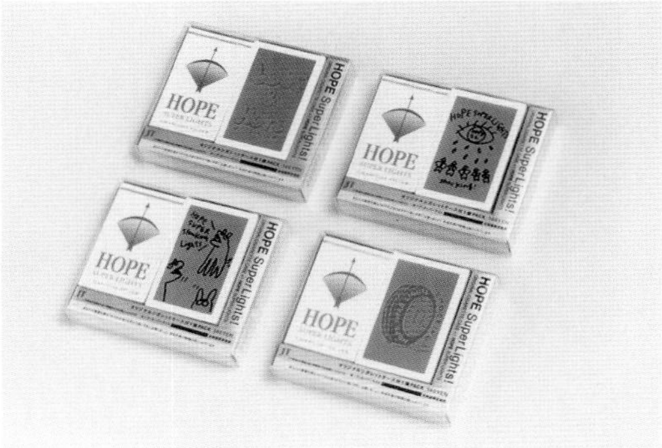

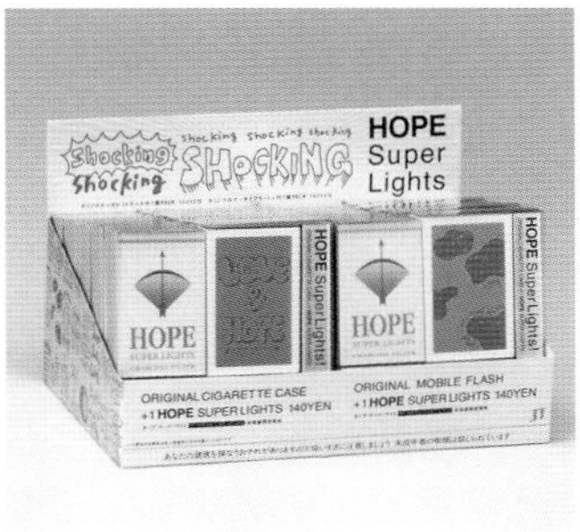

designers
Takeru Kawai
Akitomo Negishi

art director
Koichi Sawada

writer
Yutaka Tsujino

illustrator
Koichi Sawada

creative directors
Koichi Sawada
Megumi Ota

client
Japan Tobacco

agency
Dentsu / Tokyo

05092D

designer
Christian Eves

creative directors
Shaun Dew
Steve Gibbons

client
The Body Shop

agency
Dew Gibbons / London

05093D

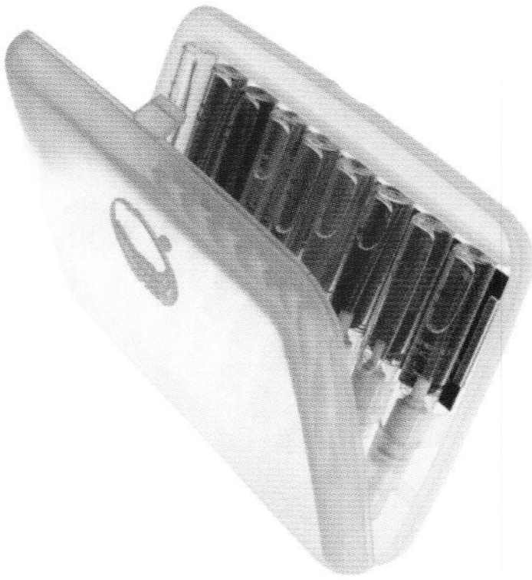

designer
Eymard Angulo

art director
Craig Markou

writer
Jana Peck

photographer
Richard Heyforn

creative director
Dan Pawych

client
Pepsi QTG - Life Cereal

agency
Downtown Partners / Toronto

05094D

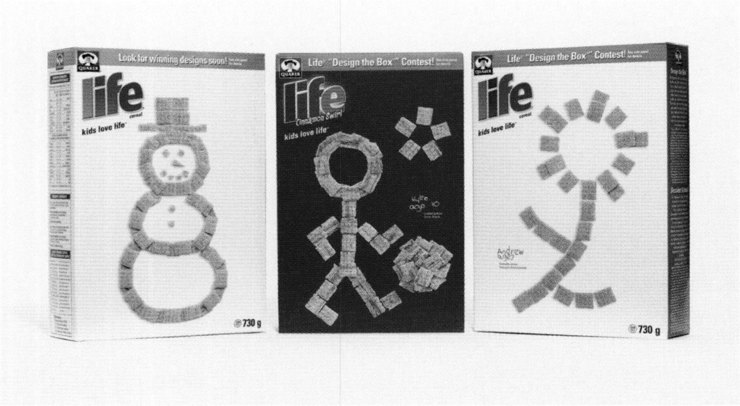

teany
white tea with pomegranate
100% natural 100% nice
16 fl oz
473 ml
ok, i'm trying to write some clever label copy for our white tea with pomegranate cooler, but i am distracted because my cat is trying to disembowel a pen, and my dog is giving me baleful looks from the couch as if to say, 'why do you love your laptop-pet more than you love me?' so, quickly, we wanted a super-healthy anti-oxidant cooler to serve at teany so we put pomegranate and blueberry and white tea and pear juice together and we came up with this drink which we loved and which we drink everyday and which we (being ostensibly altruistic) want to share with you here in this bottle. now i have to go and perform triage on a mutilated pen and shower a pig with love and affection. thanks. — moby (and kelly)

teany
teany
teany
teany
teany

designer
Graham Clifford

writers
Nick Shearer
Guy Barnett
Moby

illustrator
Moby

creative director
Graham Clifford

client
Teany Beverage

agency
Graham Clifford
Design / New York

05095D

FALKSALT
GOURMET
FLINGSALT
FRÅN HAVET
NATURELL
100 GRAM
FALKSALT
GOURMET
FLINGSALT
FRÅN HAVET
CITRON
100 GRAM
FALKSALT
GOURMET
FLINGSALT
FRÅN HAVET
ROSMARIN
100 GRAM
FALKSALT
GOURMET
FLINGSALT
FRÅN HAVET
CHILI
100 GRAM

art director
Mikael Blom

creative director
Anders Kornestedt

client
Hanson & Möhring

agency
Happy Forsman &
Bodenfors / Gothenburg

05096D

art director
Andrew Bannecker

writer
Trevor Sloan

illustrator
Andrew Bannecker

creative directors
Ron Lawner
Woody Kay
Fred Burgos
Craig Coughlin

client
Amacai

agency
Arnold Worldwide / McLean

05097D

SINNER

art director
Fernanda Fajardo

writer
Roberto Kilciauskas

photographer
Marcel Vieira

creative directors
Carlos Silverio
Francesc Petit

client
Lego

agency
DPZ Propaganda / São Paulo

05100D

The most interactive toy.

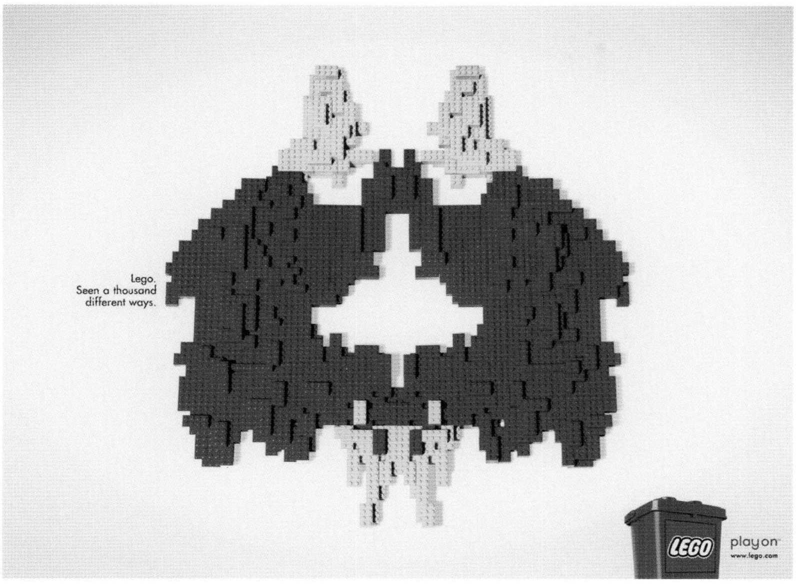
Lego.
Seen a thousand
different ways.
LEGO
play on
www.lego.com

art director
Robson Oliveira

writer
Mauricio Machado

photographer
Lucio Cunha

illustrator
Robson Oliveira

creative directors
Jose Zaragoza
Carlos Rocca

client
Lego

agency
DPZ Propaganda /
São Paulo

05101D

LEGO
The most interactive toy.

art director
Fernanda Fajardo

writer
Roberto Kilciauskas

photographer
Marcel Vieira

creative directors
Carlos Silverio
Francesc Petit

client
Lego

agency
DPZ Propaganda /
São Paulo

05099D

COLLATERAL DESIGN : POSTERS — SINGLE

designer
Go Takahashi

art director
Manabu Mizuno

creative director
Manabu Mizuno

client
Twinkle Corporation

agency
Good Design
Company / Tokyo

05102D

art directors
Matt Dimmer
Alex Lowe

illustrator
Nick Redyoff

creative directors
Tom Cordner
Dan Cerullo
Brad Phillips

client
Detroit Music Hall

agency
J. Walter Thompson /
Detroit

05103D

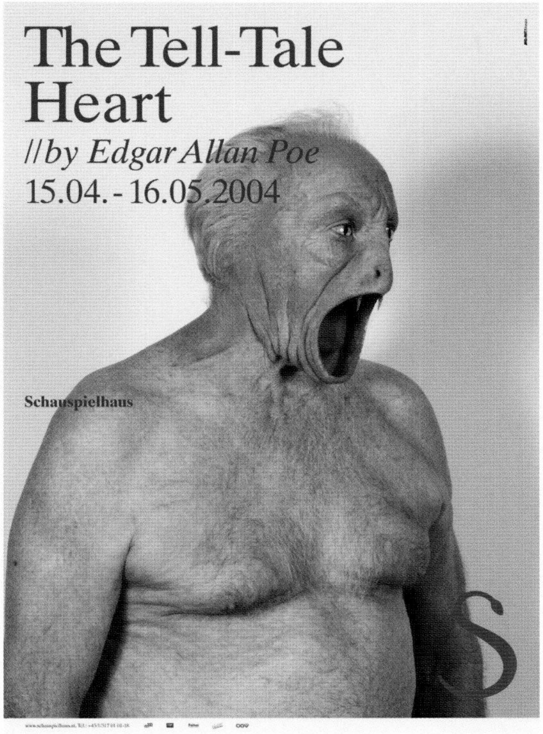

art director
Guenter Eder

photographer
Jork Weismann

illustrators
Stefanie Putz
Philipp Glueck
Albert Winkler

creative director
Andreas Putz

client
Schauspielhaus Wien

agency
Jung von Matt / Vienna

05104D

designers
Thomas Berger
Jim de Barros

art director
Thomas Berger

illustrator
Thomas Berger

creative director
Jeffrey Keyton

client
MTV Design

agency
MTV Networks / New York

05106D

art director
Steve Jockisch

writer
Ben Pagel

illustrator
Steve Jockisch

creative director
Jeff Johnson

client
Tank Goodness

agency
Spunk / Minneapolis

05109D

TANK
GOODNESS
Cold days, warm cookies.

designer
Alex Hammerl

art director
Alex Hammerl

writer
Nathan Reddy

photographer
Michael Meyersfeldt

illustrator
Alex Hammerl

creative director
Nathan Reddy

client
The Think Council

agency
TBWA\Gavin\Reddy / Johannesburg

05105D

10 years of democracy
call for entries national poster competition
think
sappi

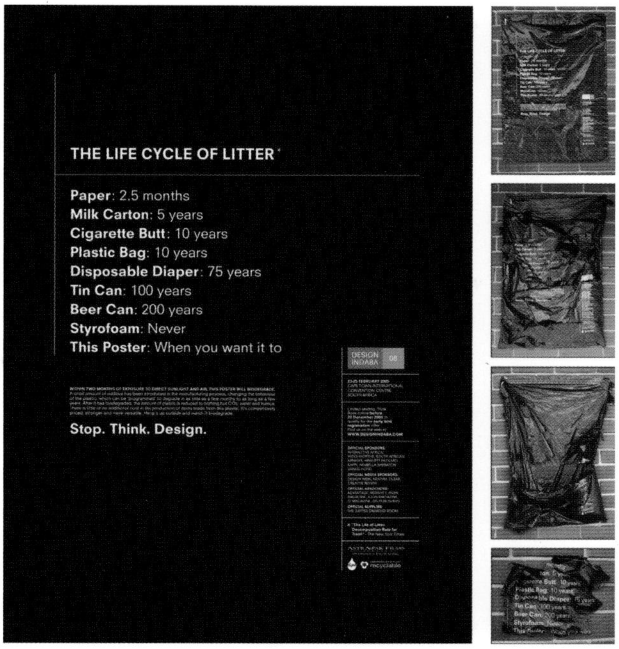
THE LIFE CYCLE OF LITTER*
Paper: 2,5 months
Milk Carton: 5 years
Cigarette Butt: 10 years
Plastic Bag: 10 years
Disposable Diaper: 75 years
Tin Can: 100 years
Beer Can: 200 years
Styrofoam: Never
This Poster: When you want it to
Stop. Think. Design.
DESIGN INDABA 08

art director
Carla Kreuser

writer
Iain Thomas

designer
Carla Kreuser

creative director
Joanne Thomas

client
Cape Town Major Events

agency
The Jupiter Drawing Room / Cape Town

05110D

TIFFANY O'BRIEN
SOLO ART SHOW
Candy Coated
NIGHTMARES
FRIDAY JULY 2 SEED ART GALLERY 205 WEST SIXTH STREET 7PM

art director
Lee O'Brien

illustrator
Lee O'Brien

creative director
Keith Borshak

client
Tiffany O'Brien

agency
The Woodbine Agency / Winston Salem

05111D

COLLATERAL DESIGN : POSTERS — CAMPAIGN

art director
Yukimi Sano

writer
Syoichi Kume

creative director
Yukimi Sano

client
Sesame Street Partners
Japan

agency
ADK / Tokyo

05112D

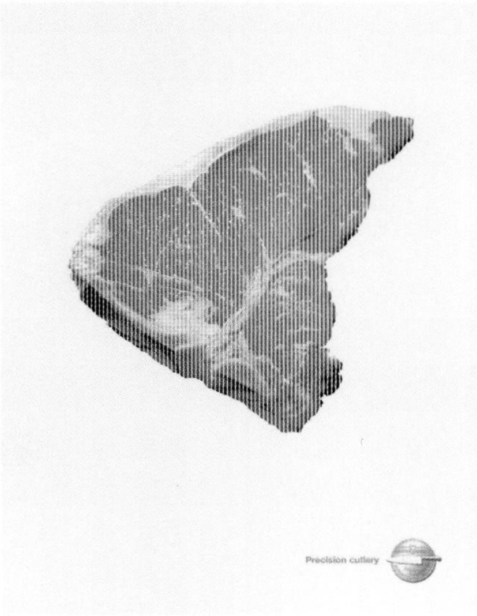

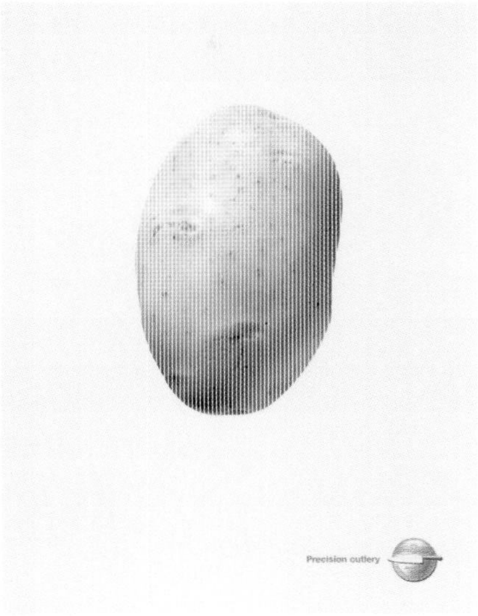

designer
James Clunie

art director
James Clunie

writer
Tim Cawley

creative director
David Lubars

client
Dexter Russel Cutlery

agency
BBDO / New York

05113D

COLLATERAL DESIGN : POSTERS — CAMPAIGN

art director
Mike Hughes

writer
Ed Cotton

creative directors
John Butler
Mike Shine

client
Converse

agency
Butler, Shine, Stern & Partners / Sausalito

05114D

DOGS
a new film by MARK DECENA
now playing at ConverseGallery.com
CONVERSE

FEATHERBALL
A NEW FILM BY
RYAN NELLIS
NOW PLAYING AT CONVERSEGALLERY.COM
CONVERSE

HALF-COURT
a new film by KARLSBERG/NARDINO
now playing at ConverseGallery.com
CONVERSE

JOHN'S
POLKA
A NEW FILM BY
M. STEWART THORNDIKE
NOW PLAYING AT CONVERSEGALLERY.COM
CONVERSE

SPIN THE BOTTLE
A NEW FILM BY ALAN POON
CONVERSE
NOW PLAYING AT CONVERSEGALLERY.COM

堕出来！流出来！就是不能生下来！
不

隧道股份
要在夏季掀起 生育新高潮！

可血流成河，
不准 生一个！

art director
HaiBo Huang

writers
Cecilia Zhu
Kijin Luo

photographer
HaiBo Huang

creative directors
SheungYan Lo
Nick Lim
Bill Chan

client
Long Xi

agency
JWT / Shanghai

05115D

Kinokuniya

Kinokuniya

Kinokuniya

art directors
Chan Lee Shon
Tan Chee Keong

writers
Chan Lee Shon
Donevan Chew
Paul Lim

photographer
Edmund Leong (Untold Images)

creative directors
Chan Lee Shon
Yasmin Ahmad

client
Kinokuniya

agency
Leo Burnett / Kuala Lumpur

05116D

COLLATERAL DESIGN : POSTERS — CAMPAIGN

art director
Marion Bryan

writer
Asheen Naidu

photographer
Michael Meyersfeld

illustrator
Stock

creative directors
Julian Watt
Mike Schalit

client
Simba - Ghost Pops

agency
Net#Work BBDO /
Hyde Park

05117D

Also Awarded:
merit
Exceptional Innovation
in Marketing: Single

Simba
GHOST POPS

Simba
GHOST POPS

Simba
GHOST POPS

art director
Mike Brandt

writer
Jens Ringena

illustrators
André Roesler
Springer & Jacoby Design

creative director
Uli Guertler

client
Raffles Hotel Vier
Jahreszeiten

agency
Springer & Jacoby /
Hamburg

05119D

KIRSCHKERNSPUCKEN IST,
GANZ EHRLICH,
MEISTENS NICHT
GANZ UNGEFÄHRLICH.
ALLES, WAS KINDER
ÜBER GUTES BENEHMEN
WISSEN MÜSSEN – AB MÄRZ 2005
IN UNSEREN BENIMMKURSEN.
Raffles Hotel Vier Jahreszeiten

DIE SERVIETTE
UM DEN HALS DRUMRUM?
TU'S LIEBER NICHT,
DENN DAS IST DUMM.
ALLES, WAS KINDER
ÜBER GUTES BENEHMEN
WISSEN MÜSSEN – AB MÄRZ 2005
IN UNSEREN BENIMMKURSEN.
Raffles Hotel Vier Jahreszeiten

HERUMGEFUCHTEL
MIT BESTECK?
DA IST GANZ SCHNELL
EIN AUGE WEG!
ALLES, WAS KINDER
ÜBER GUTES BENEHMEN
WISSEN MÜSSEN – AB MÄRZ 2005
IN UNSEREN BENIMMKURSEN.
Raffles Hotel Vier Jahreszeiten

PIZZA ISST MAN BESSER:
MIT DER GABEL
UND DEM MESSER.
ALLES, WAS KINDER
ÜBER GUTES BENEHMEN
WISSEN MÜSSEN – AB MÄRZ 2005
IN UNSEREN BENIMMKURSEN.
PIZZA PIZZA
Raffles Hotel Vier Jahreszeiten

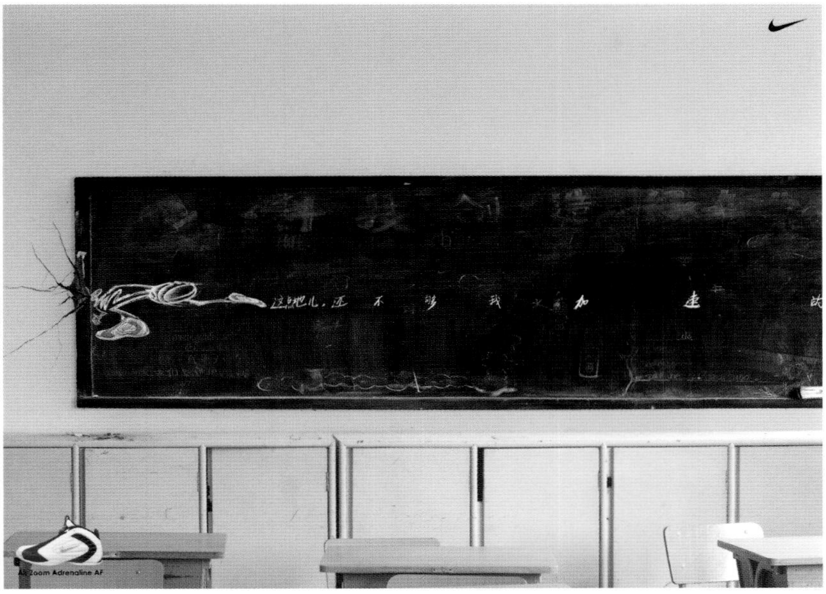

art directors
Gang Hu
Paul Yu
Hai Liang

writers
Thomas Zhu
Liang Zhang

photographer
JianXin Liu

illustrator
Paul Yu

creative directors
SheungYan Lo
Nick Lim
Bill Chan
Gang Hu
Thomas Zhu

client
Nike

agency
JWT / Shanghai

05120D

designer
Joan Jacobs

art director
Joan Jacobs

writer
Livio Tronchin

photographer
Gillian Lochner

creative director
Jenny Ehlers

client
Levi Strauss SA

agency
King James RSVP / Cape Town

05121D

One Show Design

COLLATERAL DESIGN : P.O.P. AND IN-STORE — SINGLE

art director
Sébastien Vacherot

writer
Manoëlle Van Der Vaeren

photographer
Dimitri Daniloff

creative director
Erik Vervroegen

client
Sony Playstation

agency
TBWA\Paris

05123D

Also Awarded:
merit
Consumer Magazine
Color: Full Page: Single

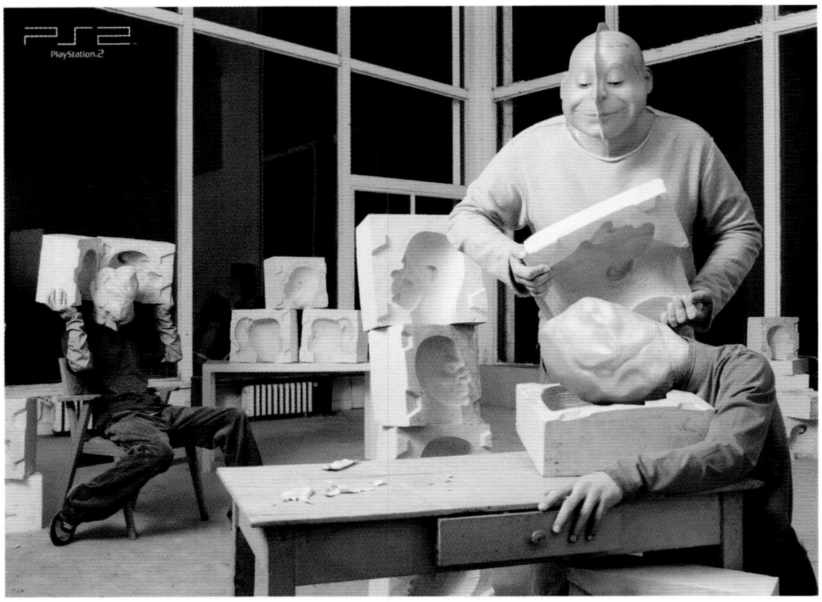

designers
Peng Ji
Fan Ge
Tif Wu
Eddie Wong

writer
Rabbit Shen

photographer
Jun Li - Insight Studio

illustrator
Fan Ge

creative directors
Eddie Wong
Tif Wu

client
adidas

agency
TBWA\Shanghai
(180\TBWA)

05125D

"FOREPLAY?"
For all she puts up with, get her a Donato gift certificate.
DONATO

"I was GONNA CALL!"
For all she puts up with, get her a Donato gift certificate.
DONATO

"I JUST showered TWO DAYS AGO."
For all she puts up with, get her a Donato gift certificate.
DONATO

designer
Daniel Vendramin

art director
Daniel Vendramin

writer
Darren Clarke

illustrator
Dan Page

creative director
Dan Pawych

client
Donato Salons & Spa

agency
Downtown Partners / Toronto

05126D

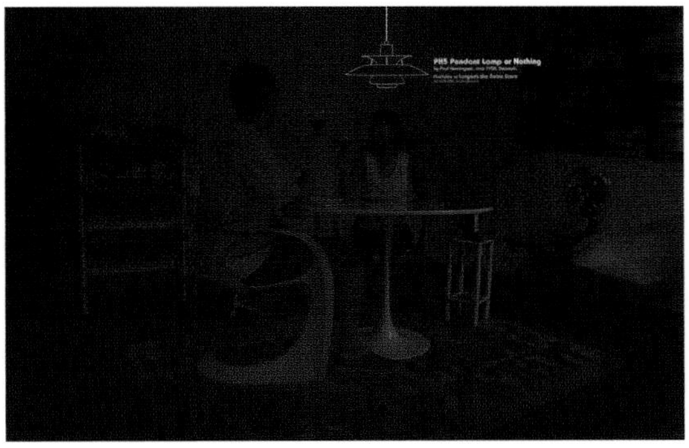
PH5 Pendant Lamp or Nothing

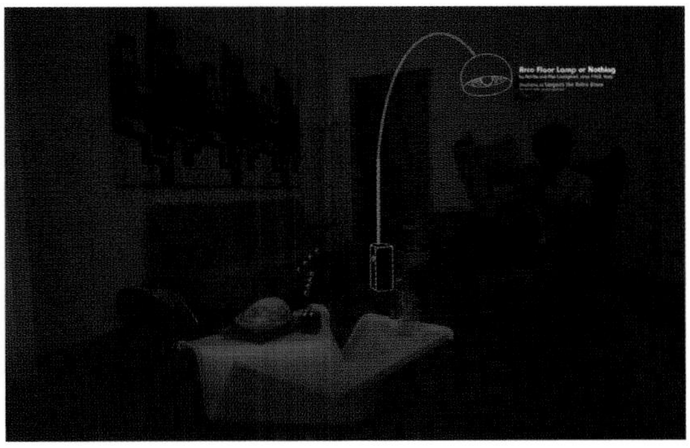
Arco Floor Lamp or Nothing

Panthella Table Lamp or Nothing

designers
Pann Lim
Roy Poh

art directors
Pann Lim
Roy Poh

writers
Roy Poh
Pann Lim
Alex Goh

photographer
Jeremy Wong

illustrators
Pann Lim
Roy Poh

creative director
Kinetic

client
Lorgan's The Retro Store

agency
Kinetic / Singapore

05127D

designers
Kum-jun Park
Jong-in Jung
Joong-gyu Kang
Seung-youn Nam

art director
Kum-jun Park

writers
Joon-young Bae
Eun-ju Ahn
Myoung Hwa Shin

illustrator
Kum-jun Park

creative director
Kum-jun Park

client
601Bisang

agency
601Bisang / Seoul

05128D

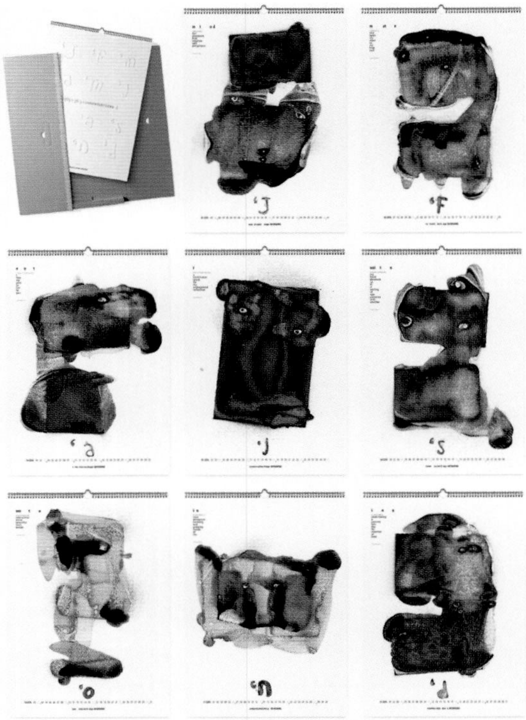

art director
Christoph Steinegger/
Interkool

photographers
Various - represented by
Bransch

illustrator
Interkool

creative director
Susanne Bransch

client
Bransch

agency
Bransch / New York

05129D

394

YOU CAN'T PICK YOUR FAMILY
BUT YOU CAN PICK YOUR FAMILY'S HAIR
Glued hair when final
HAPPY FLIPPIN' HOLIDAYS

YOU CAN'T PICK YOUR FAMILY
BUT YOU CAN PICK YOUR FAMILY'S HAIR
HAPPY FLIPPIN' HOLIDAYS

designers
Milan Bozic
Jim deBarros

art directors
Christopher Truch
Lance Rusoff

writer
Nick Sonderup

photographer
Aaron Ruell

creative director
Jeffrey Keyton

client
MTV Design

agency
MTV Networks / New York

05130D

Merit

One Show Design

ENVIRONMENTAL DESIGN : SINGLE

art director
Mikael Blom

creative director
Anders Kornestedt

client
Centre for Management
of the Built Environment

agency
Happy Forsman &
Bodenfors / Gothenburg

05131D

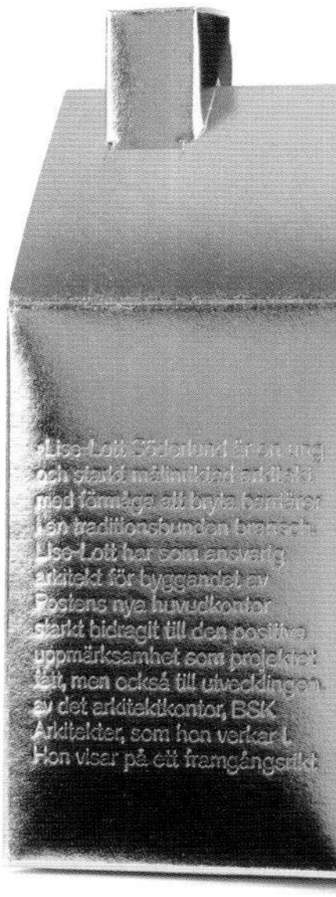

designers
Bertrand Kirschenhofer
Christoph Bielefeldt
Philipp Dörner

art directors
Mark Höfler
Michael Kuhn

writers
Ingmar Bartels
Karsten Lübke

photographer
Sven Glage

creative director
Lars Rühmann

client
ASICS Europe

agency
Nordpol / Hamburg

05133D

photographer
Ryota Atarashi

creative directors
Nikken Sekkei
Lighting Planners
Associates
Living World

client
Kansai Electric

agency
Yoshiaki Nishimura /
Tokyo

05135D

ENVIRONMENTAL DESIGN : CAMPAIGN

art director
Marco Howell

writer
Clarence Bradley

illustrator
Freestyle Collective

creative directors
Bill Pauls
Dave Stanton
Jeff Nixon

client
Cingular

agency
BBDO / Atlanta

05136D

ENJOY
Shiner
BOCK
INDEPENDENTLY BREWED SINCE 1909
Reagan

MAKE MINE A COLD
Shiner Beer
FROM TEXAS' OLDEST INDEPENDENT BREWERY
Reagan

MAKE MINE A
Shiner Light
FROM TEXAS' OLDEST INDEPENDENT BREWERY
Shiner
LIGHT

How 'bout a
COLD
BEER
FROM Texas' OLDEST INDEPENDENT BREWERY

FROM TEXAS'
Oldest Independent
BREWERY
SHINER
est. 1909
Shiner
LIGHT
Reagan

designers
Derrit DeRouen
Craig Crutchfield
Silver Cuellar III

art directors
Derrit DeRouen
Craig Crutchfield
Silver Cuellar III

illustrators
John Kachik
Paul Rogers

creative directors
James Mikus
Bryan Jessee

client
Spoetzl Brewery

agency
McGarrah/Jessee / Austin

05138D

designer
Julie Ruiz

art director
Nancy Mazzei

writers
Traci Terrill
Nicole Morgese
Richard Lufrano

creative directors
Nigel Cox-Hagan
Phil Delbourgo

client
VH1 Off-Air Creative

agency
MTV Networks /
New York

05139D

art director
Erich T. Kloth

writer
Roman Karcher

illustrator
Juergen Heimbach

client
Against Abuse

agency
Scholz & Friends /
Hamburg

05140D

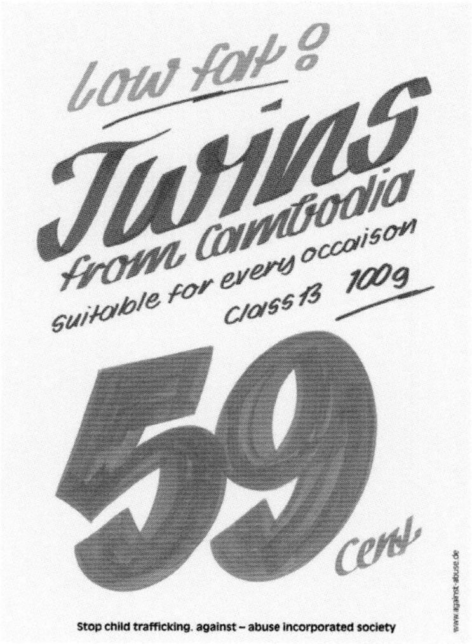

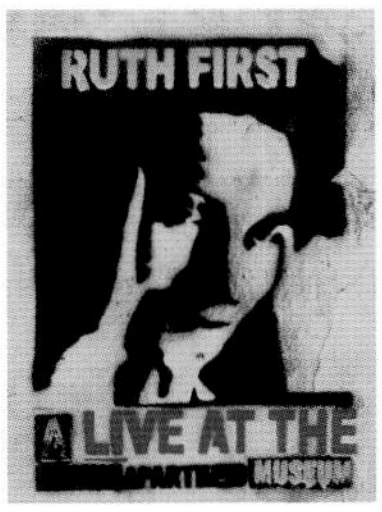

designer
Marike Stapleton

art directors
Marike Stapleton
Bernadette da Silva

writer
Felix Kessel

photographer
Pierre Peters

illustrator
Marike Stapleton

creative directors
Marike Stapleton
Felix Kessel

client
Apartheid Museum

agency
TBWA\Gavin\Reddy / Johannesburg

05137D

designers
Stacy Drummond
Alison Roberto

art director
Stacy Drummond

writer
Nick Sonderup

illustrator
George Bates

creative director
Jeffrey Keyton

client
MTV Design

agency
MTV Networks / New York

05141D

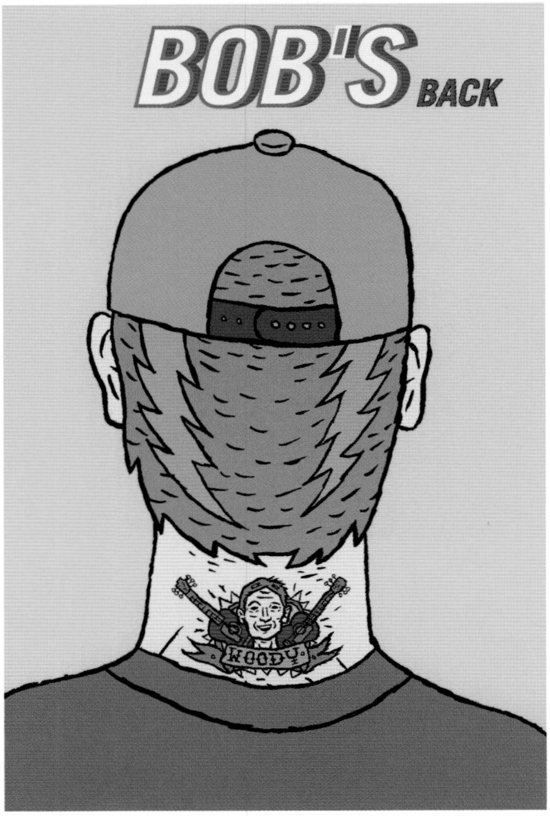

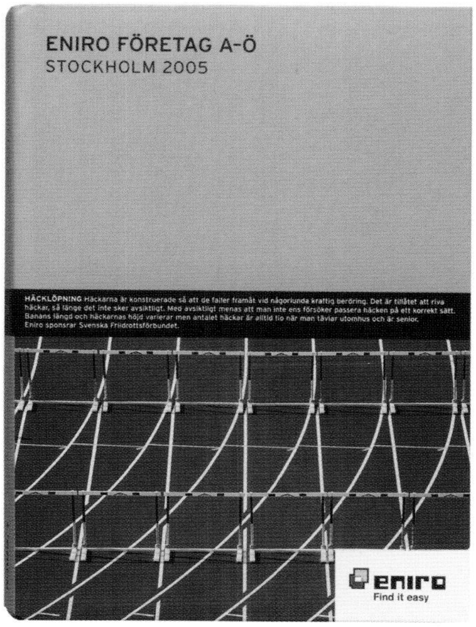

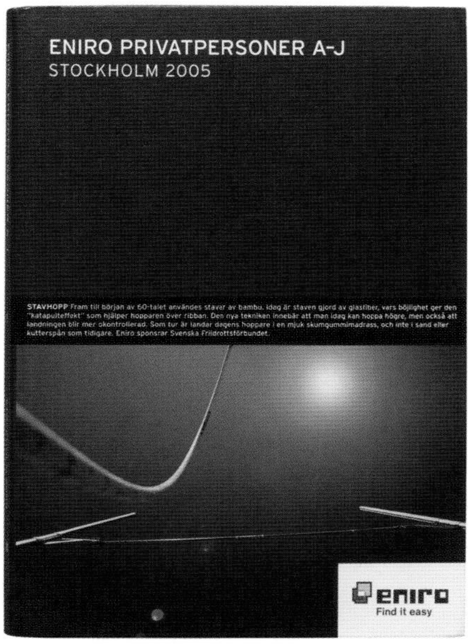

designers
Niclas Hakansson
Camilla Böttiger

art director
Lotta Friberg

writer
Ulrika Kukulska

photographer
Stock

client
Eniro

agency
Ogilvy Design /
Stockholm

05142D

One Show Design

PUBLICATION DESIGN: BOOK JACKET DESIGN

designers
Hee Jeong Lee
James O'Brien
Ana Pavlovic

art directors
Hee Jeong Lee
James O'Brien
Ana Pavlovic

photographers
Kanako Sasaki
Michael Bayer
Lindsey Rome

creative director
Genevieve Williams

client
School of Visual Arts

agency
School of Visual Arts/
New York

05143D

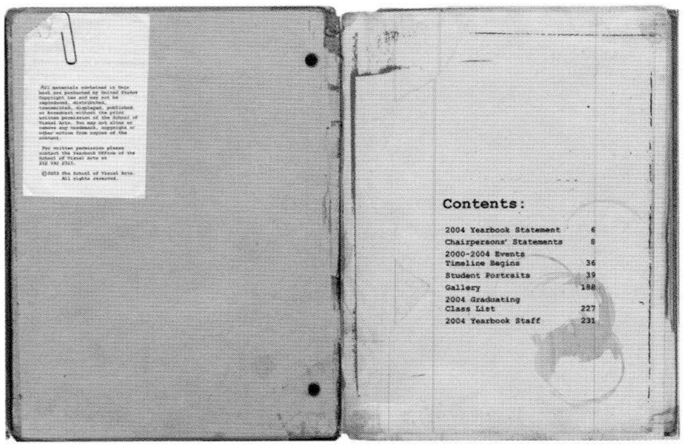

designer
Good Design Company

art director
Manabu Mizuno

illustrator
Keiko Itakura

creative director
Manabu Mizuno

client
Hakuhodo

agency
Good Design Company / Tokyo

05144D

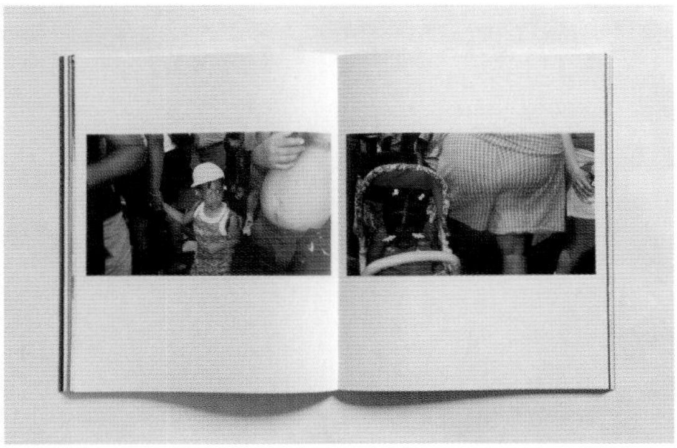

art directors
Hans Seeger
John Shachter

photographers
Richard Burbridge
Liz Chilsen
Eric Claridge
Joseph Costa
Barbara Crane
Jonathan de Villiers
Mitch Epstein
James Franklin
Kathryn Frazier
Andy Gray
Darcy Hemley
John Herndon
Keith Herzik
James Hughes
Michael Jefferson
Magnus Magnusson
Tom Raith
Jamie Robinson
Jay Ryan
Warwick Saint
Melissa Scherrer
Stephanie Serpick
Kipling Swehla
Robert The
Patrick Voigt

client
Big Magazine

agency
Hans Seeger / Wauwatosa

05145D

art directors
Andy Boonthong
Tim McIntyre

creative director
Douglas Lloyd

client
Arena Homme Plus 21
+ 22

agency
Lloyd and Company /
New York

05146D

designers
Gunther Schreiber
Philipp Dörner

art directors
Bertrand Kirschenhofer
Christoph Bielefeldt

writer
Ingmar Bartels

creative director
Lars Rühmann

client
Sportfive

agency
Nordpol / Hamburg

05147D

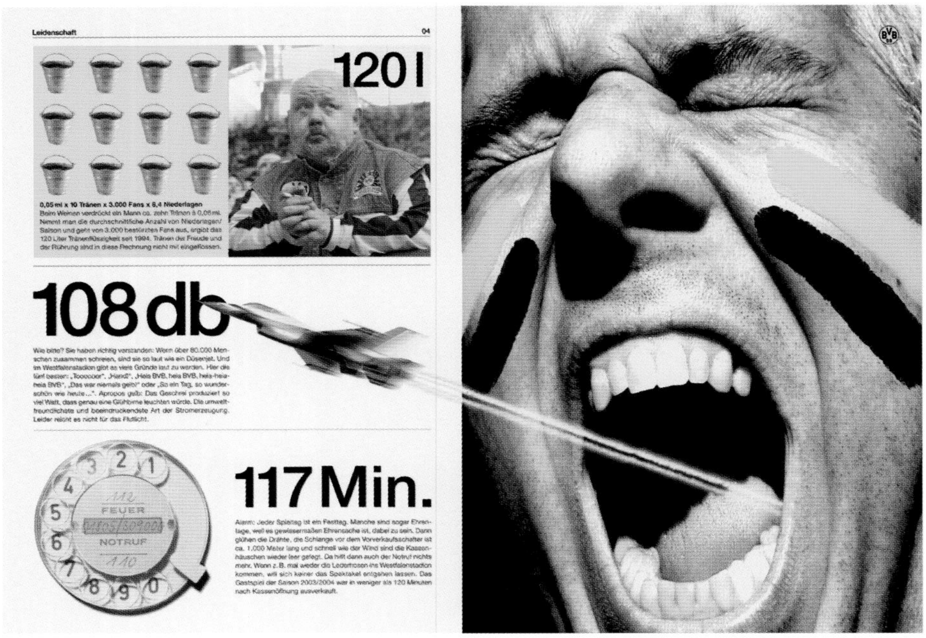

art directors
Tuan Ching
Chris Dixon

writers
Tonice Sgrignoli
Rosemary Lavan

creative director
Brian Collins

client
Ogilvy & Mather

agency
Ogilvy & Mather / New York

05149D

designers
Leigh Okies
Helena Fruehauf
Satian Pengsathapon
Nathalie Hennequin

writer
Tonice Sgrignoli

creative directors
David Israel
Brian Collins

client
Ogilvy & Mather

agency
Ogilvy & Mather / New York

05148D

art director
Gary Amante

writer
Kite Lacuesta

creative director
Merlee Jayme

client
4As of the Philippines

agency
BBDO Guerrero Ortega / Makati City

05150D

THE OFFICIAL
GUNN REPORT™
ADULT DIAPER
2004 EDITION
CONTAIN YOUR EXCITEMENT AS YOU SEE THE WORLD'S BEST ADS –IN PERFECT COMFORT!
IT'S EASY AS 1-2-3!
1 ADJUST
2 FASTEN
3 ENJOY
ASSIGNED TO:
OF:
26 NOVEMBER 2004 • 10:30 AM • GREENBELT 3 CINEMA 3

art director
Dave Dye

photographer
Sean Doyle

client
Campbell Doyle Dye

agency
Campbell Doyle Dye / London

05151D

I'm a Creative Director
I change the odd word and mostly say no.
I'm a Graphic Designer
I'm a Typographer
I think this badge is so predictable looking.
I'm a Writer
Well, a copywriter. But writer sounds more important.
I'm a TV Producer
My role is to... ooh look, there's Frank!
I'm a Art Director
I'm an Illustrator
I wouldn't usually mix with your type socially, but it's good for business.
I'm a Client
I'm a Product Designer
I'm a Planner
My job is an integral part of the creative... No, don't go.
I'm a Web Designer
I'm in I.T.
Somebody dropped out.
Editor
I'm a Student
I'm a Director
I'm a Photographer
You have fabulous cheekbones.
I'm a Ligger
Please direct me to the bar.
I am... well, you know very well who I am.
I'm a Sound Engineer
Yes, there is a reason for all those knobs.
I'm an Account Manager
I'm a Group Head
I'm sorry
I'm at the wrong event.
I'm a Direct Mail Specialist
Your ticket to the 2004 D&AD Annual Launch Party

Blackmail
The heads of New Zealand's leading Creative Directors were retouched on to bodies in compromising photographs.
These photographs were then sent to the Creative Directors in question with a simple threatening note: '... you'd be wise to retouch with us...'

designer
HQ Imaging

art directors
Karl Fleet
Guy Rooke

writers
Guy Rooke
Karl Fleet

photographer
Colenso BBDO

creative directors
Toby Talbot
Rich Maddocks

client
HQ Imaging

agency
Colenso BBDO / Auckland

05152D

designer
Maria Lishman

art director
Maria Lishman

writer
Maria Lishman

creative directors
Rich Maddocks
Toby Talbot

client
Liquid Sound Studios

agency
Colenso BBDO / Auckland

05153D

DIRECT MAIL : SINGLE

designer
Ken Sakurai

creative directors
Joe Duffy
Dan Olson

client
Duffy & Partners

agency
Duffy & Partners / Minneapolis

05155D

art directors
Lisa Careborg
Andreas Kittel

writers
Björn Engström
Emma Zetterholm

creative director
Anders Kornestedt

client
Arctic Paper

agency
Happy Forsman & Bodenfors / Gothenburg

05157D

art directors
Andreas Kittel
Lisa Careborg

writers
Björn Engström
Emma Zetterholm

photographer
Magnus Carlsson

illustrator
Io

creative director
Anders Kornestedt

client
Arctic Paper

agency
Happy Forsman &
Bodenfors / Gothenburg

05156D

art directors
Andreas Kittel
Lisa Careborg

writer
Björn Engström

creative director
Anders Kornestedt

client
Arctic Paper

agency
Happy Forsman &
Bodenfors / Gothenburg

05159D

art directors
Lisa Careborg
Pontus Höfvner

creative director
Anders Kornestedt

client
Hasselblad Center

agency
Happy Forsman &
Bodenfors / Gothenburg

05161D

Also Awarded:
merit
Collateral: Single

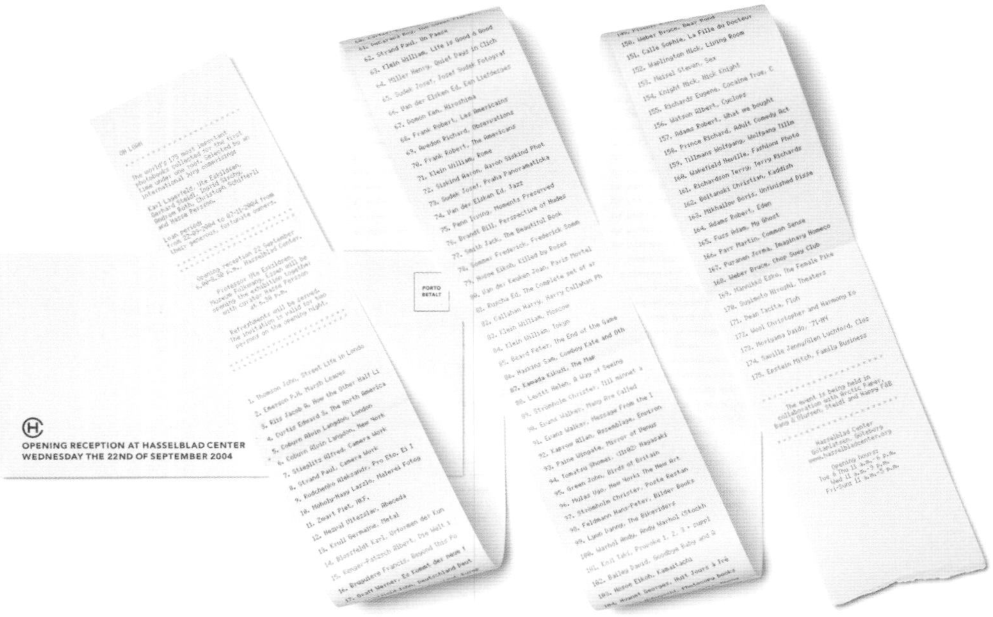

art director
Axel Eckstein

writer
Inken Rohweder

creative director
Alexander Jaggy

client
Tur & Partner

agency
Jung von Matt / Zurich

05162D

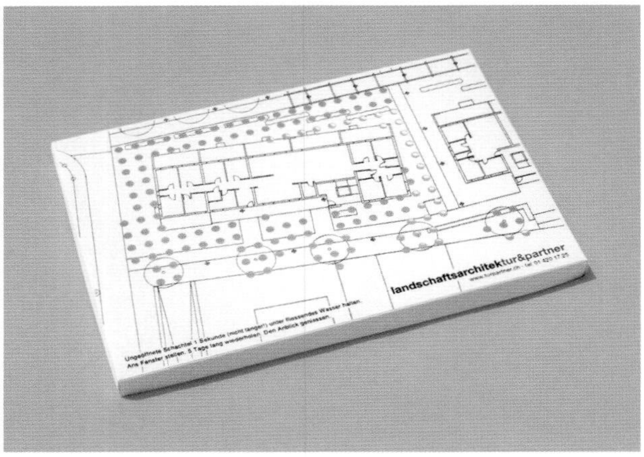

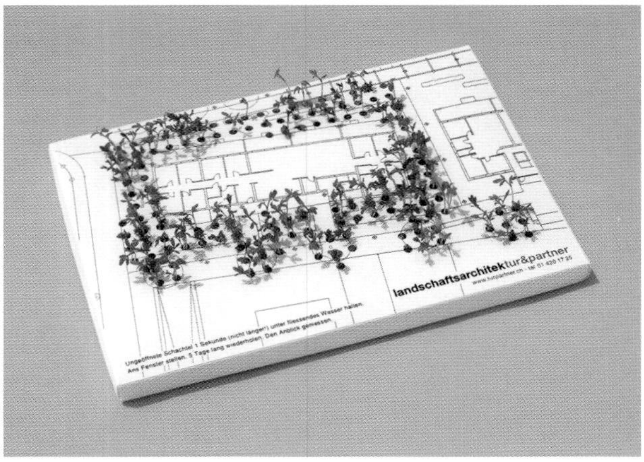

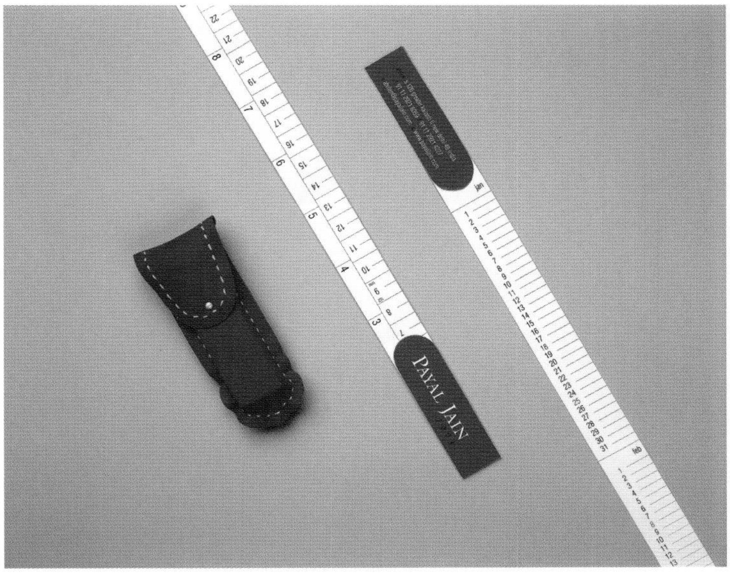

designer
Gaurav Nautiyal

art director
Gaurav Nautiyal

writer
Ranjan Nautiyal

creative director
N. Ramesh

client
Payal Jain

agency
Ogilvy & Mather / New Delhi

05163D

designers
Don Emery
Drew Waiss

writer
Pivot Design

creative director
Brock Haldeman

client
Unisource

agency
Pivot Design / Chicago

05164D

designers
Luke Manning
Karl Wills
Olly Guise
Ryan Wills
Alex Bane
Spencer Buck

art director
Ryan Wills

writer
Spencer Buck

illustrator
Jem Hobbs

creative director
Spencer Buck

client
Science Museum

agency
Taxi Studio / Bristol

05165D

art director
Trevor Williams

writer
Brian Harris

photographers
Heidi Niemala
Gary Sparks
Glenn Gyssler

creative director
Carolyn Hadlock

client
The Delta Faucet Company

agency
Young & Laramore / Indianapolis

05166D

designers
Rafael Grampá
Paula Nobre
Guilherme Marcondes

art director
Kevin Fitzgerald

writer
Kevin Fitzgerald

agency producers
Alex Dervin
Ashley Nixon
Loic Dubois
Martha Smith
Joao Tenorio

production company
Lobo

creative directors
Mateus de Paula Santos
Pete Johson

client
Cartoon Network

agency
Lobo / São Paulo

05167D

BROADCAST DESIGN : SINGLE

agency producers
Alex Dervin
Martha Smith
Loic Dubois
Joao Tenorio

production company
Lobo

creative director
Mateus de Paula Santos

client
Panasonic

agency
Lobo / São Paulo

05168D

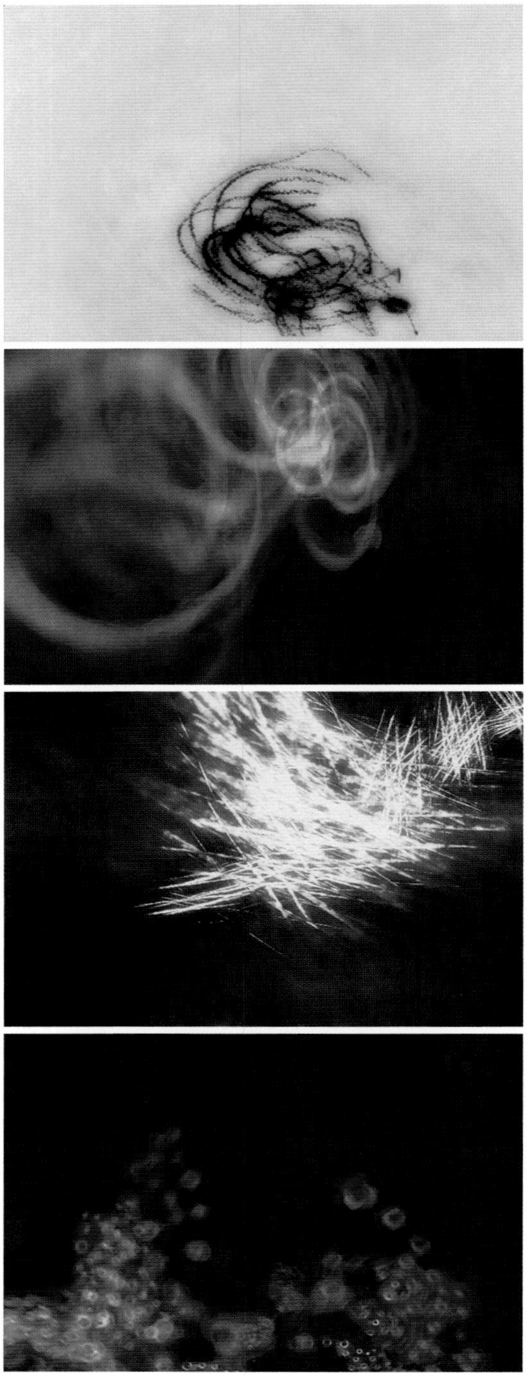

designers
Kip Bogdahn
Lena Beug

art director
Lena Beug

writer
Clay Weiner

producers
Adam Rourke
Owen Plotkin
Dave Skinner
Leslie Legare

creative directors
Jeffrey Keyton
Romy Mann

client
MTV Design

agency
MTV Networks / New York

05173D

art director
Kyle Cooper

agency producers
Josh Laurence
Phyllis Weisband

production company
Prologue Films

director
Sam Rami

creative director
Kyle Cooper

client
Sony Pictures

agency
Prologue Films / Malibu

05174D

art director
Kyle Cooper

agency producers
Phyllis Weisband
Josh Laurence

production company
Prologue Films

director
Richard Longcraine

creative director
Kyle Cooper

client
Universal Studios

agency
Prologue Films / Malibu

05176D

Merit

BROADCAST DESIGN : SINGLE

art director
Kyle Cooper

agency producers
Phyllis Weisband
Josh Laurence/ Prologue

production company
Prologue Films

director
Zack Snyder

creative director
Kyle Cooper

client
Universal Studios

agency
Prologue Films / Malibu

05175D

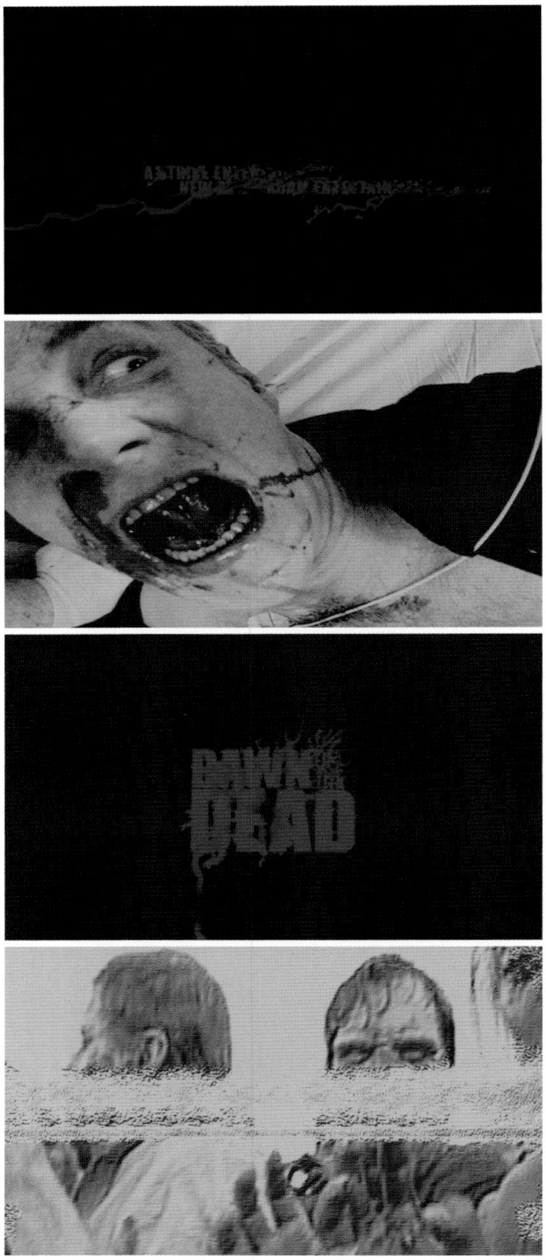

designer
Chye Yong Hock

art director
Chye Yong Hock

writer
Prakash Kamdar

agency producer
Prakash Kamdar

production company
The Upper Storey

director
Chye Yong Hock

creative director
Chye Yong Hock

client
Nokia

agency
The Upper Storey / Singapore

05177D

designers
Takagi Maskatsu
Woog
Shinsuke Koshio
Sunday Vision

art director
+Cruz

agency producers
Arto Hampartsoumian
Bruce D Ikeda

production companies
Wieden+Kennedy
Tokyo Lab
Sunday Vision

directors
Takagi Masakatsu
+Cruz
Sun An

creative director
John Jay

client
Wieden+Kennedy / Tokyo

agency
Wieden+Kennedy / Tokyo

05178D

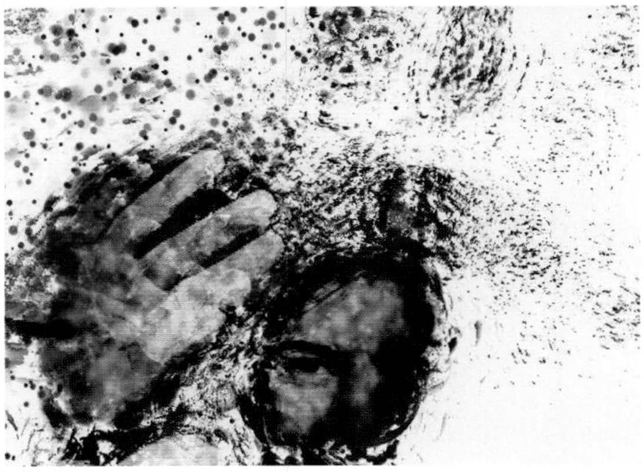

designers
Rafael Grampá
Mario Sader
Paula Nobre
Cadu Macedo
Rogério Marmo
Gabriel Bá
Fabio Moon

art director
Guilherme Marcondes

writer
Matt Fraction

agency producers
Alex Dervin
Martha Smith
Loic Dubois
Joao Tenorio

production company
Lobo

creative directors
Mateus de Paula Santos
Magnotta Michael

client
OLN

agency
Lobo / São Paulo

05179D

One Show Design

BROADCAST DESIGN : CAMPAIGN

designer
Miles Flanigan

art directors
Steve Couture
Jun Asano
Walt Connelly
Ashley Reese

writers
Mark Krajan
Tomohide Endoh
Dante Lombardi

agency producer
Jan O'Malley

production company
Anonymous Content

creative directors
Walt Connelly
Dante Lombardi
Kevin Moehlenkamp
Jeff Huggins

client
Microsoft

agency
McCann-Erickson /
San Francisco

05180D

Also Awarded:
merit
Broadcast Design: Single

merit
Broadcast Design: Single

merit
Broadcast Design: Single

merit
Broadcast Design: Single

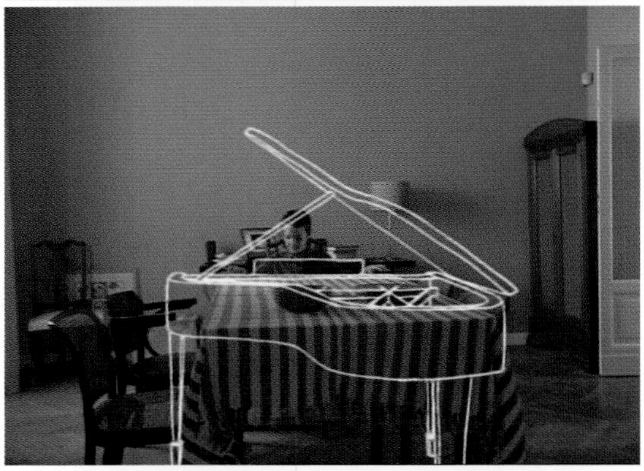

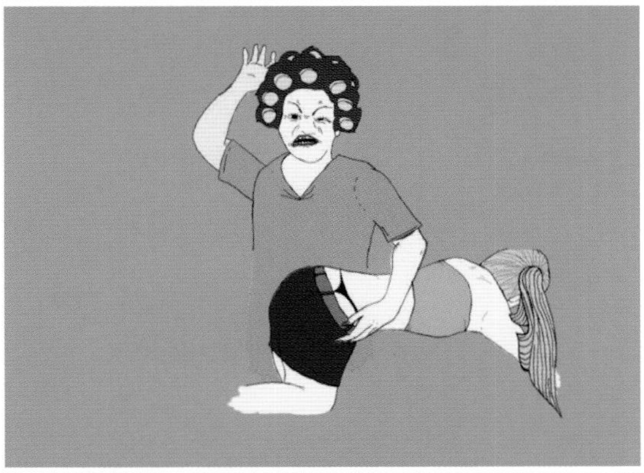

designer
Shilo

art directors
Rodger Belknap

illustrators
Federick Saenz Recio
Kevin Brennan
Alison Roberto
André Stringer

producers
Tracy Chandler
Chaz Windus

production company
Shilo

creative directors
André Stringer
Jeffrey Keyton
Romy Mann

client
MTV Design

agency
MTV Networks / New York

05182D

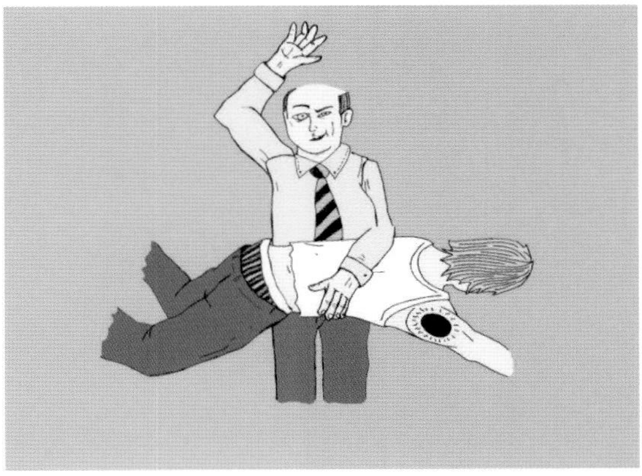

BROADCAST DESIGN : CAMPAIGN

designers
Chie Araki
Hitomi Watanabe
Richard Mather

writer
Richard Mather

creative directors
Jeffrey Keyton
Romy Mann

client
MTV Design

agency
MTV Networks / New York

05181D

426

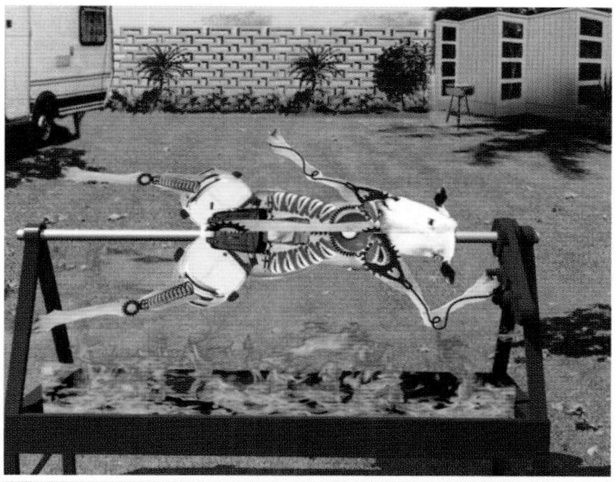

art director
Mariana O'kelly

writer
Annette Nel

agency producer
Caroline Switala

production company
Harmless & Domesticated

director
Carl Addy

creative director
Mike Schalit

client
South African Broadcasting Corporation - RSG

agency
Net#Work BBDO / Hyde Park

05183D

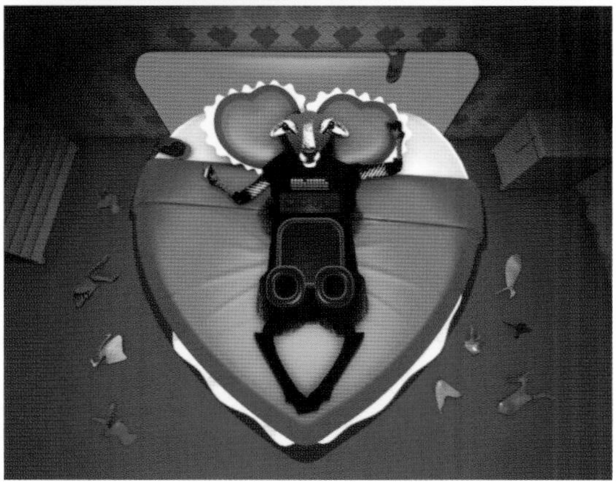

designer
Theresa Tsang Teng

art directors
Theresa Tsang Teng
Tan Kien Eng

writers
Valerie Chen
Tan Kien Eng

photographers
Allen Dang
Wizard Photography

illustrators
Simon Ong
Wizard Photography

creative director
Tan Kien Eng

client
Women's Aid Organisation (WAO)

agency
Arc Worldwide / Kuala Lumpur

05184D

UNFORTUNATELY, EMOTIONAL SCARS LAST A LIFETIME.
BUKIT BINTAN
WOMEN'S AID ORGANISATION (WAO) – "SCARS"

designer
Mitoh

art director
Mitoh

creative director
Michael Hoinkes

client
Dialogue in the Dark

agency
He Said She Said / Hamburg

05185D

Poster
DIALOG IM DUNKELN®
EINE AUSSTELLUNG ZUR ENTDECKUNG DES UNSICHTBAREN
SPEICHERSTADT HAMBURG
BOOKINGLINE 0700. 44 33 2000
BITTE TELEFONISCH RESERVIEREN!
In the light. 1
2 In the dark.
The poster was printed with a colour with glues in the dark, like the security colour for the escape routes in buildings. If the light is on, it charges with light. So it can glue in the dark. By this way, it underlines the idea and sensitive element and experience of the exhibtion where you can only „see" things in the dark.
DIALOGUE in the DARK is an exhibition to discover the unseen. Visually impaired or blind people will show a different world in totally dark rooms. Words and touch will have to replace the function of the eyes. Everyday situations will be experienced in a new way. Familiar things are turned around, things taken for granted will be questioned. You will have to entrust yourself to a complete stranger in order to rediscover your sense of hearing, of smell and your taste all over again. Sight alone seems to guarantee access to the world, we are thinking, speaking and dreaming in pictures. Suddenly the non-visual characteristics are interesting and form the basics for our understanding and enjoyment to integrate into our construct of the world. How paradox – learning to „see" again by not seeing. Out of this tension, DIALOGUE IN THE DARK was born, an exhibition which tries to take as its starting point the ideas and non-visual perceptions of blind people, in order to discover the unseen within and all around us.

MAPLE SYRUP
CUB SCOUT PANCAKE BREAKFAST FUNDRAISER
Sunday February 8, 2004 Serving from 8:30 a.m. - 1:00 p.m.
Our Lady of Grace Church, 5071 Eden Ave, Edina, MN 55436
$5 Donation per person. All proceeds support the Scouting activities of the Pack 102.

designer
Ted Olson

art director
Steve Mitchell

writer
Steve Mitchell

creative director
Steve Mitchell

client
Cub Scout Pack #102

agency
Hunt Adkins / Minneapolis

05186D

27TH ANNUAL
PORTLAND INTERNATIONAL
FILM FESTIVAL
FEBRUARY 13–28

art director
Steve Sandstrom

photographer
Mark Hooper

illustrator
Steve Sandstrom

creative director
Jon Olsen

client
NW Film Center

agency
Sandstrom Design / Portland

05187D

art director
Laura Hauseman

writer
Sanders Hearne

creative director
Bart Cleveland

client
The Atlanta Red Cross

agency
Sawyer Riley Compton / Atlanta

05188D

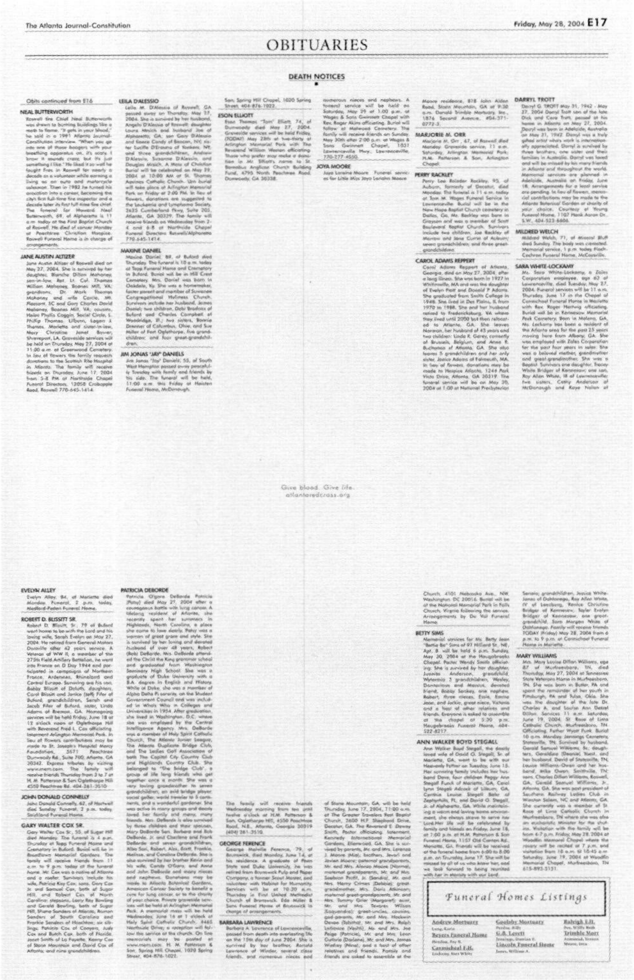

art director
Isabela Ferreira

writer
Pete Figel

creative directors
Mark Figliulo
Dave Loew

client
No Dirty Gold

agency
Y&R / Chicago

05189D

Merit

designers
Diana Tung
Michael Ashley

art directors
Diana Tung
Michael Ashley

writer
Dinesh Kapoor

photographers
Linsay Brown
Matt Trego
James Moslander

creative director
Michael Ashley

client
VCU Adcenter

agency
Arnika / Richmond

05190D

SIXTY
music trends culture life v. 7
EXIT 190
95 SOUTH
Petersburg
EXIT 190
5th Street
Downtown
Coliseum
WEST NORTH
64 95
Charlottesville
Washington

designers
Victor Gómez
Jon Onaindia

art directors
Victor Gómez
Jon Onaindia

writer
Manolo Moreno

creative directors
Uschi Henkes
Manolo Moreno
Urs Frick

client
Bits Sin Fronteras

agency
Grupo Zapping / Madrid

05191D

This action consisted of three different child faces of various ethnic backgrounds: Asian, Black and Indian. The mouth had an opening just were the coin to release the supermarket cart is inserted. Each coin would symbolically feed a child. Under the image you could read: You can feed a child for two days with what you spend renting this cart. Help.

art directors
Pontus Höfvner
Lisa Careborg

creative director
Anders Kornestedt

client
Hasselblad Center

agency
Happy Forsman & Bodenfors / Gothenburg

05192D

designers
Garth Walker
Janina Masojada
Andrew Makin
Eschen & Reid

art director
Garth Walker

writer
Blake Pickering

photographer
Garth Walker

client
Constitutional Court of South Africa

agency
Orange Juice Design / Durban

05196D

PUBLIC SERVICE / NON-PROFIT / EDUCATIONAL : COLLATERAL — SINGLE

designer
Jo-Wayne Peacock

art director
Jo-Wayne Peacock

writer
Spike Kunene

creative director
Conn Bertish

client
Wolanani AIDS Initiative

agency
Saatchi & Saatchi /
Cape Town

05197D

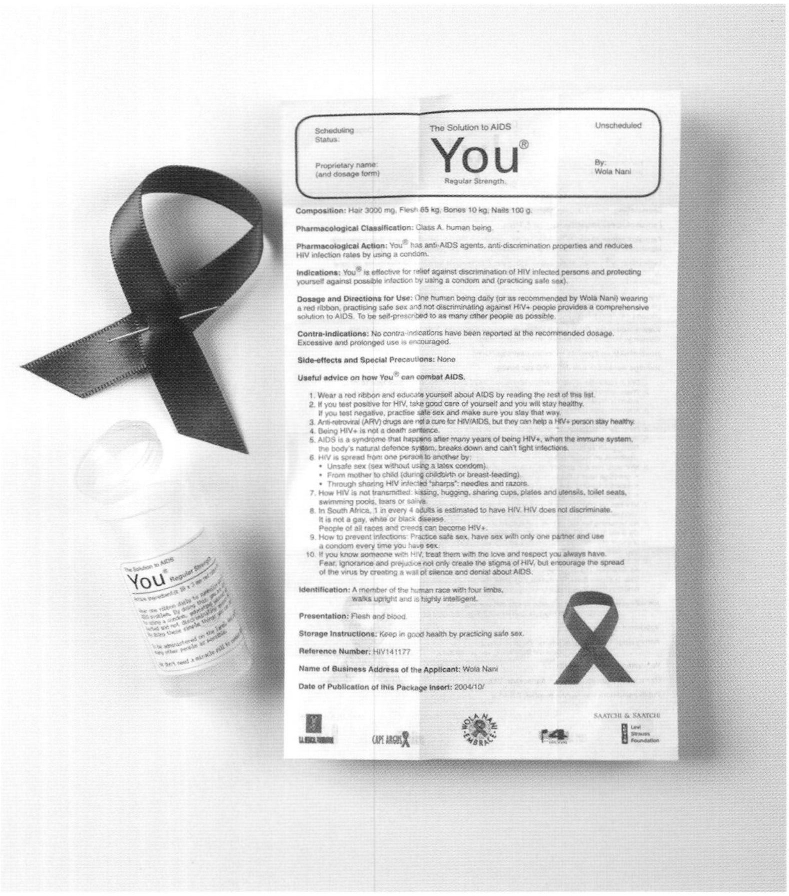
Scheduling Status:
The Solution to AIDS
Unscheduled
Proprietary name: (and dosage form)
You®
Regular Strength.
By: Wola Nani
Composition: Hair 3000 mg, Flesh 65 kg, Bones 10 kg, Nails 100 g.
Pharmacological Classification: Class A. human being.
Pharmacological Action: You® has anti-AIDS agents, anti-discrimination properties and reduces HIV infection rates by using a condom.
Indications: You® is effective for relief against discrimination of HIV infected persons and protecting yourself against possible infection by using a condom and (practicing safe sex).
Dosage and Directions for Use: One human being daily (or as recommended by Wola Nani) wearing a red ribbon, practising safe sex and not discriminating against HIV+ people provides a comprehensive solution to AIDS. To be self-prescribed to as many other people as possible.
Contra-indications: No contra-indications have been reported at the recommended dosage. Excessive and prolonged use is encouraged.
Side-effects and Special Precautions: None
Useful advice on how You® can combat AIDS.
1. Wear a red ribbon and educate yourself about AIDS by reading the rest of this list.
2. If you test positive for HIV, take good care of yourself and you will stay healthy. If you test negative, practise safe sex and make sure you stay that way.
3. Anti-retroviral (ARV) drugs are not a cure for HIV/AIDS, but they can help a HIV+ person stay healthy.
4. Being HIV+ is not a death sentence.
5. AIDS is a syndrome that happens after many years of being HIV+, when the immune system, the body's natural defence system, breaks down and can't fight infections.
6. HIV is spread from one person to another by:
• Unsafe sex (sex without using a latex condom).
• From mother to child (during childbirth or breast-feeding).
• Through sharing HIV infected "sharps": needles and razors.
7. How HIV is not transmitted: kissing, hugging, sharing cups, plates and utensils, toilet seats, swimming pools, tears or saliva.
8. In South Africa, 1 in every 4 adults is estimated to have HIV. HIV does not discriminate. It is not a gay, white or black disease. People of all races and creeds can become HIV+.
9. How to prevent infections: Practice safe sex, have sex with only one partner and use a condom every time you have sex.
10. If you know someone with HIV, treat them with the love and respect you always have. Fear, ignorance and prejudice not only create the stigma of HIV, but encourage the spread of the virus by creating a wall of silence and denial about AIDS.
Identification: A member of the human race with four limbs, walks upright and is highly intelligent.
Presentation: Flesh and blood.
Storage Instructions: Keep in good health by practicing safe sex.
Reference Number: HIV141177
Name of Business Address of the Applicant: Wola Nani
Date of Publication of this Package Insert: 2004/10/
WOLA NANI EMBRACE
SAATCHI & SAATCHI
Levi Strauss Foundation
The Solution to AIDS
You® Regular Strength

designers
Jesse Kaczmarek
Patrick Miller

writer
Riley Kane

creative director
Bill Thorburn

client
AIGA-Minnesota Design Camp 2004

agency
Carmichael Lynch Thorburn/ Minneapolis

05198D

don't trust the experts.
So, whaddya say?
It'll be a great place to sit, hold your hands up to the fire and feel your palms sweat. In other words, good practice for creating bold, groundbreaking design.
designcamp

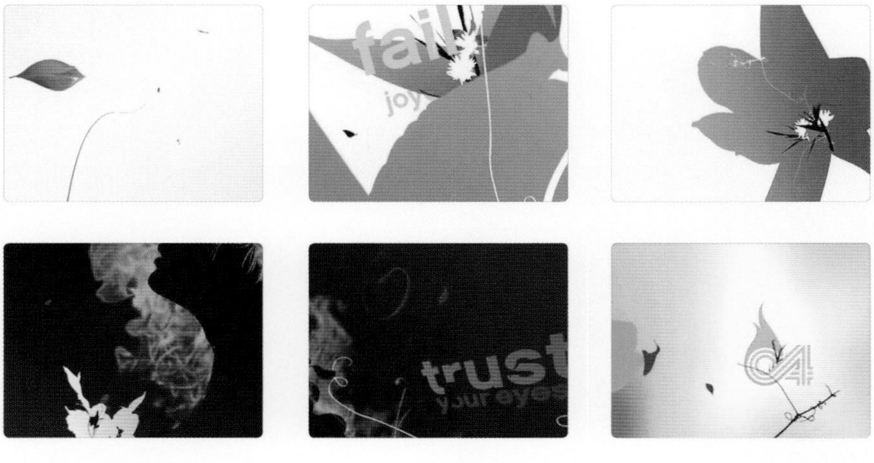
fail
joy
trust
your eyes

Merit

Soldiers of the Future

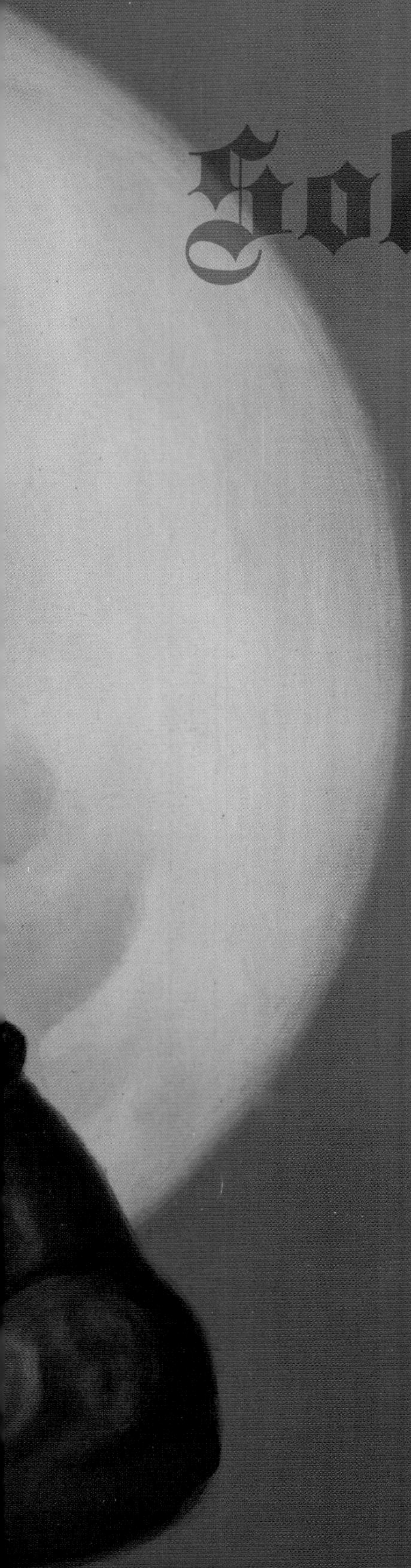

College Merit

art director
Matthew Keats

writer
Matthew Keats

school
Adhouse/New York

CCA04

OUR APPROACH TO RESEARCH AND DEVELOPMENT IS A LITTLE DIFFERENT FROM OUR COMPETITORS. WE CALL IT FARMING.
Domino SUGAR
100% PURE CANE SUGAR

art director
Ron Tapia

writer
Ron Tapia

school
Art Center College of Design/Pasadena

CCA05

DAVID HASSLEHOFF
PRESENTS THE BEST OF
LOUIS ARMSTRONG
VOLUME 1
LESS JAZZ, MORE PIZZAZZ
WHEN
IT'S PURE
IT'S BETTER
SUGAR
Domino
100% PURE CANE SUGAR

Domino
"We'll Always Be Your Sugar!"
SUGAR
Natural
Selection
Domino

art director
Mike Maluso

writer
Mike Maluso

school
The Art Institute of
Washington/Arlington

CCA06

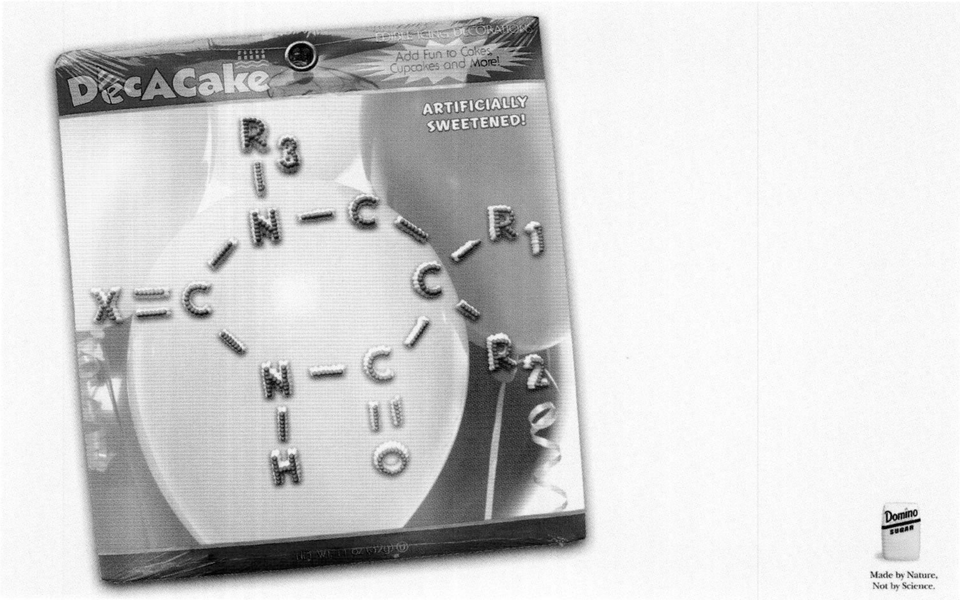
DecACake
Add Fun to Cakes, Cupcakes and More!
ARTIFICIALLY SWEETENED!
Domino
SUGAR
Made by Nature,
Not by Science.

art director
Bryan Carroll

writer
Tiffany Appleton

school
The Book Shop/
Culver City

CCA07

art director
Stephen Chow

writer
Ashley Lyon

school
The Book Shop/
Culver City

CCA08

Splenda is produced by
chlorinating sucrose.
Splendox
Chlorinated Sweetener
ULTRA
Regular
1.41 GAL (180 FL OZ) 5.32 L
Domino
SUGAR
What are you adding?

art director
Nancy Esguerra

writer
Aroon Mukhey

school
The Book Shop/
Culver City

CCA09

PROVEN TO CAUSE
CANCER IN MICE
AT TESTING LABS.
Results still pending for
guinea pigs at coffee houses.
Domino
SUGAR
The alternatives aren't so sweet.

art directors
Bryan Leonard
Lynette Mota

writers
Bryan Leonard
Lynette Mota

school
California State
University/Long Beach

CCA10

art director
Meng Leong Chong

writer
Meng Leong Chong

school
City College of
New York/New York

CCA11

art directors
Braden Belmonte
Heather Barnes

writers
Heather Barnes
Danielle Asmus
Braden Belmonte

photographer
Amy Leonard

school
The Creative Circus/
Atlanta

CCA12

art director
Wesley Wright

writers
Jeremiah Follett
Jenn Hertzig

photographer
Trent Smith

school
The Creative Circus/
Atlanta

CCA13

"If it's good enough
for lab rats, it's good
enough for rug rats."
Domino
There's no substitute.

art director
Jack Bagdadi

writer
Justin Kramm

school
Miami Ad School/
Miami Beach

CCA14

100% pure

art director
Emily Honigsfeld

writer
Megan Stark

school
Miami Ad School/
Minneapolis

CCA15

art director
Janny Yang

writer
Sarah Bergey

school
Miami Ad School/
San Francisco

CCA16

art director
Craig Evans

writers
Scott Mahoney
Ashlea Powell

school
Portfolio Center/Atlanta

CCA17

"On the good ship lollipop
it's a saccharin trip to the
candy shop."
Domino
SUGAR
There is no subsitute for sugar.

art director
Natalie Garber

writer
Natalie Garber

illustrator
Natalie Garber

school
Savannah College of Art and Design/Savannah

CCA18

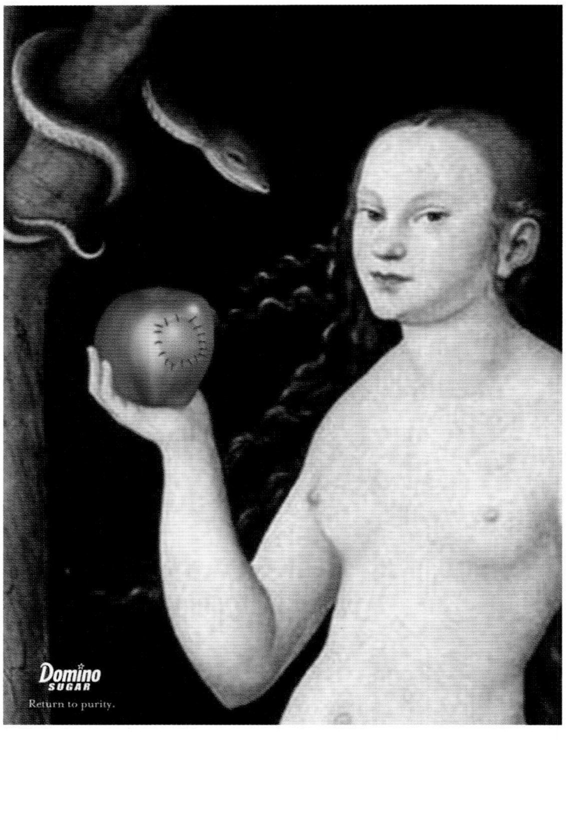
Domino
SUGAR
Return to purity.

art director
Jared Weinberger

writer
Lauren Boyle

school
School of Visual Arts/ New York

CCA19

art director
Saskia Ketz

writer
Santiago Fernandez
Concha

school
University of British
Columbia/Vancouver and
Design Akademie/Berlin

CCA20

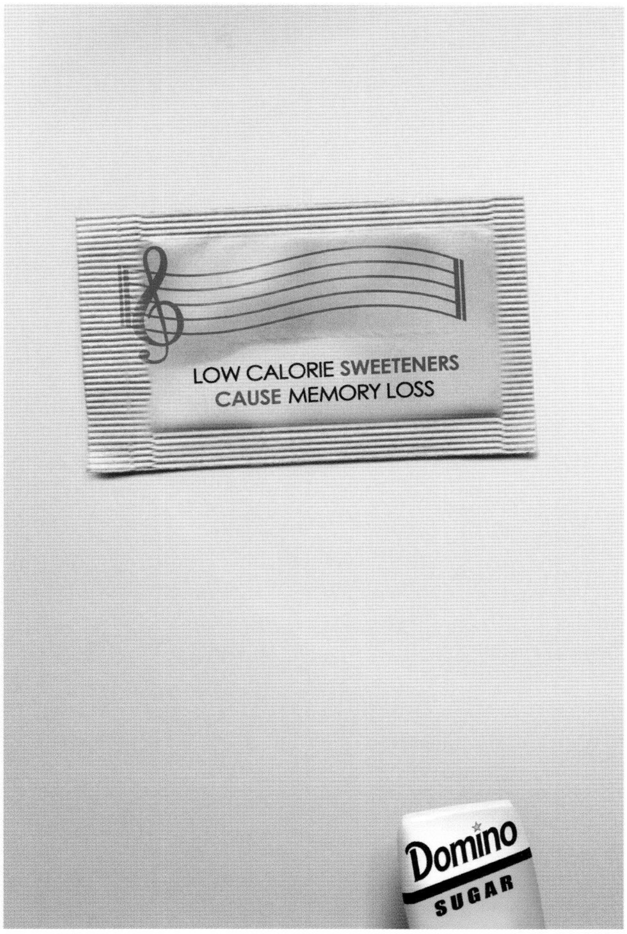

LOW CALORIE SWEETENERS
CAUSE MEMORY LOSS
Domino
SUGAR

art directors
Sara Corenzwit
Mark Griffin
Chad Brophy

writers
Sara Corenzwit
Mark Griffin
Chad Brophy

school
University of Colorado/
Boulder

CCA21

Maybe sugar isn't the reason people need to eat less sugar.

Sugar comes from a plant, not a plant.
pure

art director
Jeremy Boland

writer
Eric Terchila

school
University of Colorado/
Boulder

CCA22

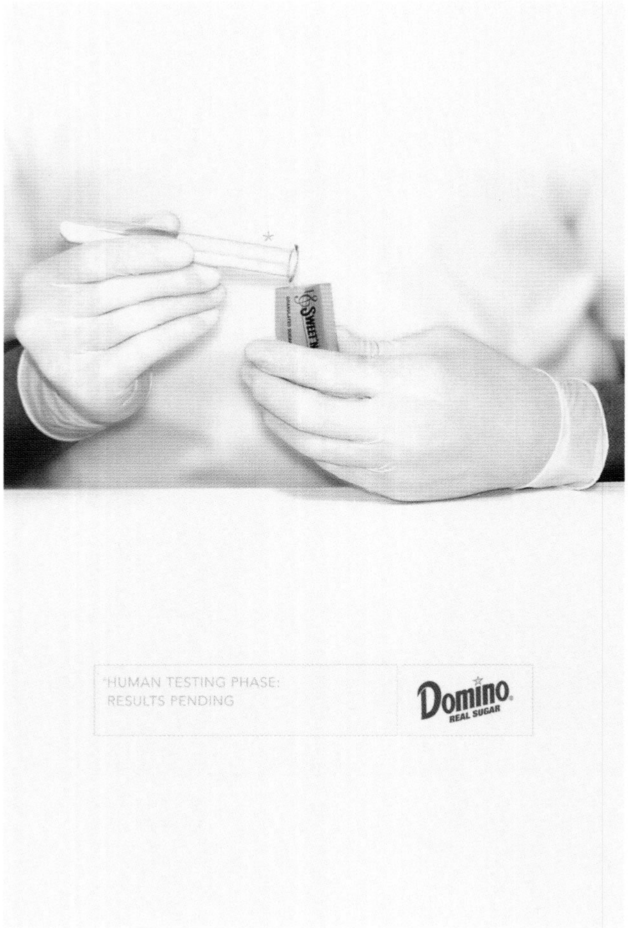
*HUMAN TESTING PHASE:
RESULTS PENDING
Domino
REAL SUGAR

art director
Ryan Stotts

writer
Ryan Stotts

school
VCU Adcenter/
Richmond

CCA23

art director
Kaleena Tucker

writer
Amy Narvaez

school
VCU Adcenter/
Richmond

CCA24

Prove to your ex you can still be friends. Bake him brownies using Equal.
(Equal is made from aspartame which can cause headaches and memory loss. Loser.)
Domino SUGAR
Save it for those you love.

art director
Allison Hayes

writer
Allison Hayes

school
VCU Adcenter/
Richmond

CCA25

Domino
SUGAR
a natural sweetener.

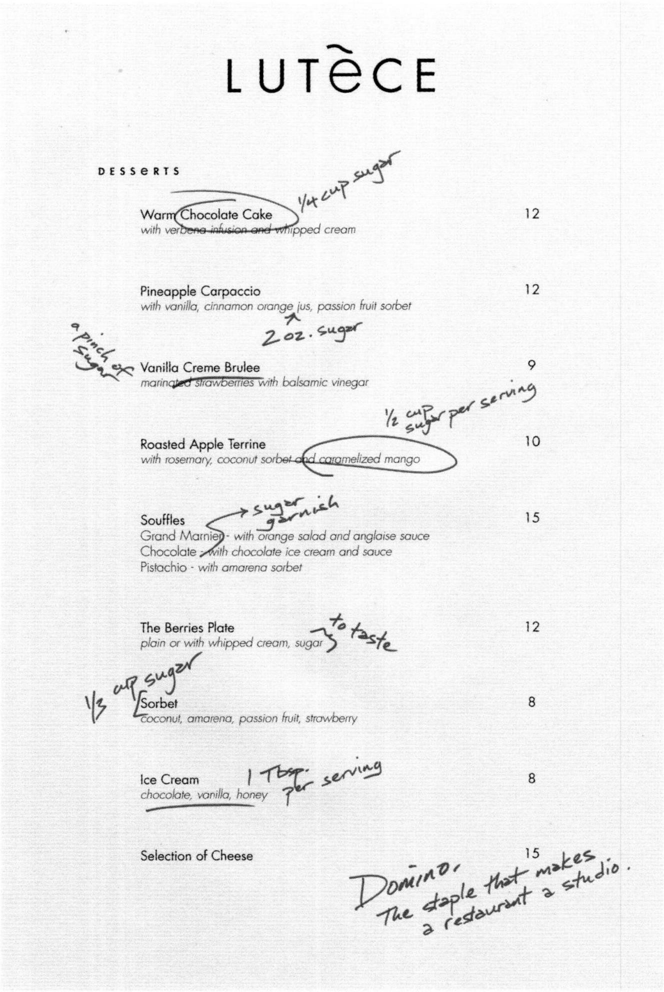

art director
Daniel Burke

writer
Eric Steele

school
VCU Adcenter/
Richmond

CCA26

designer
Chris Bushway

school
The University of Akron-
Myer's School of Art/
Akron

CCD04

When choosing
a sweetener
it should
be obvious.
For the past one-
hundred years,
Domino® Sugar
has been
the choice.
Their all-purpose
sugar is of the
highest quality
and ideal for
baking, canning,
preserving, and
sweetening
beverages.
GRANULATED
BROWN
CONFECTIONERS
[KNOW]TICE
8 oz
1 CUP
6 oz
2/3
4 oz
1/2
2 oz
1/3

designer
Jenny Pearson

art directors
Rachel Kern
Brandon Knowlden

writers
Brandon Knowlden
Jenny Pearson

school
Art Institute of
Pittsburgh/Pittsburgh

CCD05

NO ONE
ASKS FOR
Nutritive Dextose, 3.6% Soluble Saccharin, Cream of Tartar, Calcium Silicate (an anti-caking agent).
WITH THEIR COFFEE.
THINK NATURAL.
Domino
SUGAR
PREMIUM
PURE CANE
GRANULATED

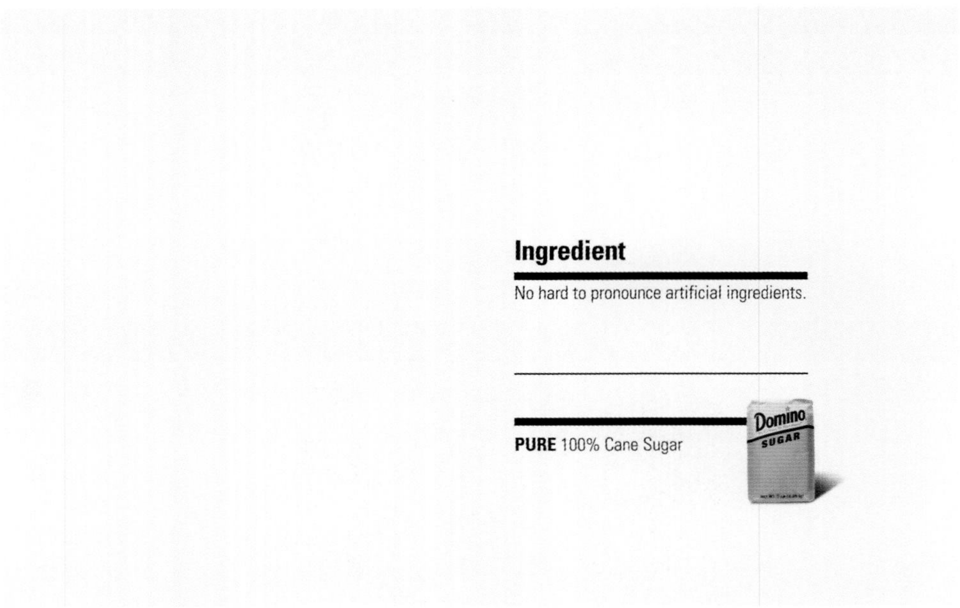
Ingredient
No hard to pronounce artificial ingredients.
PURE 100% Cane Sugar
Domino
SUGAR

designer
Meng Leong Chong

art director
Meng Leong Chong

writer
Meng Leong Chong

school
City College of
New York/New York

CCD06

cancer
SWEET'N LOW
Domino
SUGAR
The real thing.

designers
Taylor Hersh
Anna Olshansky

art directors
Anna Olshansky
Taylor Hersh

writers
Taylor Hersh
Anna Olshansky

school
Fashion Institute of
Technology/New York

CCD07

designers
Jenny Venn
Wallis Osborn

art directors
Jenny Venn
Wallis Osborn

writers
Jenny Venn
Wallis Osborn

school
Fort Hays State
University/Hays

CCD08

LOOKS LIKE YOU'RE
GONNA YAK
ALTERNATIVES ARE UPSETTING. DOMINO SUGAR IS SWEETNESS REVIVED.

designer
Jeffrey D. Guinn

art director
Jeffrey D. Guinn

writer
Jeffrey D. Guinn

school
James Madison
University/Harrisonburg

CCD09

As much fun as
Weed
without the red eyes and paranoia.
Sugar
A Natural High
Domino
SUGAR

designer
Sarah Walker

writer
Sarah Walker

school
Portfolio Center/Atlanta

CCD10

designer
Karen Cassel Bear

school
The University of Akron-Myer's School of Art/Akron

CCD11

COLLEGE COMPETITION — INTEGRATED BRANDING

art directors
Emily Strand
Leo Saito

writer
Jaime Schwarz

school
Miami Ad School/
New York

CCB01

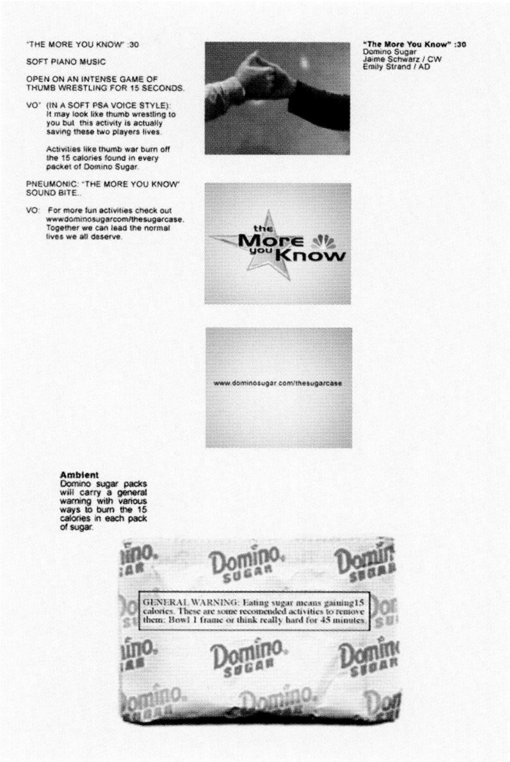
"THE MORE YOU KNOW" :30
SOFT PIANO MUSIC
OPEN ON AN INTENSE GAME OF THUMB WRESTLING FOR 15 SECONDS.
VO" (IN A SOFT PSA VOICE STYLE): It may look like thumb wrestling to you but this activity is actually saving these two players lives.
Activities like thumb war burn off the 15 calories found in every packet of Domino Sugar.
PNEUMONIC: "THE MORE YOU KNOW" SOUND BITE..
VO: For more fun activities check out wwwdominosugarcom/thesugarcase. Together we can lead the normal lives we all deserve.
"The More You Know" :30
Domino Sugar
Jaime Schwarz / CW
Emily Strand / AD
the More you Know
www.dominosugar.com/thesugarcase
Ambient
Domino sugar packs will carry a general warning with various ways to burn the 15 calories in each pack of sugar.
Domino SUGAR
GENERAL WARNING: Eating sugar means gaining15 calories. These are some recomended activities to remove them: Bowl 1 frame or think really hard for 45 minutes.

designer
Michelle Leong

writer
Ashlea Powell

school
Portfolio Center/Atlanta

CCB02

*And to think Randy trusted his wife with his wardrobe.
Submitted by Jerry Schweitzer, Billings, MT. To surrender your tackiest memory, visit dominosugar.com.
domino*

DieHard
CAR BATTERY

museumofsex

Patrick Kelly Scholarship Award

Jason Campbell
School of Visual Arts / New York

Established by EURO RSCG in conjunction with The One Club to honor the late Patrick Kelly, the scholarship is awarded to a student based on the merits of his or her portfolio, essay and teacher recommendations.

This year's recipient of the Patrick Kelly Scholarship Award is Jason Campbell from the School of Visual Arts.

IF YOUR LIFE FLASHES BEFORE YOUR EYES,
WE'VE MADE SURE IT'S NOT THE LAST TIME.
BELL

Illustrators

Rene Borst

Rene Borst
Best of Show; Gold, Silver, Bronze; Judge's Choice

Rene was born on April 17, 1971 in Geislingen-Germany. From 1994-1998 he studied design at the IBKK in Bochum. In 1997, he interned in the USA. Rene paints in mixed media and has developed a high degree of proficiency in depicting images that display a superb illusion of reality. Since using the Wacom Tablet, he has also produced matte paintings and digital art.

mail@reneborst.com
www.reneborst.com

Benjamin von Eckartsberg
Television and Radio

Benjamin von Eckartsberg was born in 1970 and studied Communication-Design at the Fachhochschule in Munich, Germany. He is a member of the Munich-based illustration studio called "Die Artillerie." Since 1993, Benjamin has worked as a freelance artist for publishers, magazines, advertising agencies, movie and TV productions. His clients include BMG, Maxim, ProSiebenSat1, BMW-Group, Ferrero, Goethe Institut, Deutsche Bank AG, Columbia Tristar, Tresor TV-Produktion GmbH, Neue Constantin Film, Living Room Pictures and many others.

benjamin@die-artillerie.de
www.die-artillerie.de
www.eckartsberg-illustration.com

Benjamin von Eckartsberg

Michael Knepper

Michael Knepper
College Merit

Michael was born in the southern part of Germany in 1952. He studied art, design and painting in Trier and then went to Munich where he worked at an advertising agency. Two years later, he worked as a freelance artist. Major jobs over the years were concentrated on magazines such as Stern, Spiegel, Playboy and film/video covers and advertising campaigns for Mercedes, Opel, Adidas, Bayer, Samson, König-Ludwig-Musical, Mustang-Jeans and many others. His latest project involved 15 variations of raven illustrations.

michaelknepper@alice-dsl.de
www.michaelknepper.de

Andreas Marschall
Cover

Andreas Marschall was born in 1961 and started his career as a comic book artist for various heavy metal magazines. He designed film posters, book illustrations and more than 100 album covers for heavy metal and rock bands like Obituary, Blind Guardian, Annihilator, Immolation, King Diamond, Kreator and others. In the '90s Andreas directed over 60 videos for bands like Kreator and Guano Apes and shot commercials and corporate videos. He worked as an editor for feature films and TV series. In 2004 he directed his first feature, Tears Of Kali, a disturbing, dark and stylish work that earned him numerous festival awards in Europe and USA.

amarschall10@aol.com
www.marschall-arts.de
www.tear-of-kali.de

Andreas Marschall

Frans Mensink

Frans Mensink
Print Merit

A professional illustrator since 1988, Frans works worldwide, and thus fully digital from his headquarters in Belfeld, Netherlands, close to the German border. His illustrations, story boards, animatics, animations, comics, cartoons and matte-paintings are all done in Photoshop, only sometimes preceded by old-fashioned pencil sketches. He works for many leading advertising agencies. He has specialized in illustrating people in all shapes, forms and moods, but the occasional monster is not avoided.

fmensink@plex.nl
www.illustrationen.de -

Ingo Römling
Design Merit

Ingo was born in Frankfurt am Main in Germany in 1969. Since 1985, he has worked as a freelance cartoonist and later worked as a cartoonist for a music magazine where he was first introduced to the Macintosh. After studying communication design, he worked as a freelance illustrator and graphic designer for several big advertising agencies and companies. In 1999, he worked as an art director and desktop publisher in an advertising agency. In addition, he made cover designs for independent record labels. Since 2003, he has been working as a freelance illustrator and graphic designer in Frankfurt.

ingo@monozelle.de
www.monozelle.de

Ingo Römling

Timo Wuerz

Timo Wuerz
Public Service; Innovative and Integrated Marketing

You ain't seen nothing yet...

www.timowuerz.com
www.becker-illustrators.com

Index

Index

agencies

A

Abbott Mead Vickers BBDO / London 19, 22, 117, 147, 153, 186, 248, 308

ADK / Tokyo 385

Agency212 / New York 315

AlmapBBDO / Sao Paulo 186

Ambience Publicis / Mumbai 166

and partners / New York 91, 130, 143

Arc Worldwide / Kuala Lumpur 427

Archrival / Lincoln 42

Arnika / Richmond 239, 431

Arnold Worldwide / Boston 42, 72, 266, 273, 338

Arnold Worldwide / Toronto 219

Arnold Worldwide / McLean 379

B

Bartle Bogle Hegarty / New York 97, 313

BBDO/Argentina 187

BBDO/Atlanta 169, 225, 397

BBDO/Bangkok 169, 228

BBDO/Chicago 170

BBDO Guerrero Ortega / Makati City 170, 407

BBDO/Minneapolis 79

BBDO/New York 201, 219, 228, 386

BBDO/ Singapore 32, 139, 147, 212, 220

Berry Bush BBDO / Cape Town 171

BETC Euro RSCG / Paris 277

Bleu Blanc Rouge / Montreal 325

Block / Leederville 239

Blok Design / Mexico DF 356

BMF Advertising / Pyrmont 267

Bozell/New York 224

Bransch/ New York 393

Butler, Shine, Stern & Partners / Sausalito 71, 387

C

Campbell Doyle Dye / London 209, 407

Carmichael Lynch / Minneapolis 76, 171, 187, 199, 213, 255

Carmichael Lynch Thorburn/Minneapolis 369, 434

CC&E Advertising / Guangzhou 41

Charles S. Anderson Design Company / Minneapolis 81, 128, 374, 375

Chemistry / Dublin 6 330

Clarity Coverdale Fury / Minneapolis 255

Cliff Freeman and Partners / New York 295, 296

Colenso BBDO / Auckland 172, 260, 330, 408

Contract Advertising / Mumbai 201, 357

Contrapunto / Madrid 173

Cramer-Krasselt / Chicago 369

Creative Juice\G1 (A TBWA Company) / Bangkok 24

Crispin Porter + Bogusky / Miami 17, 38, 61, 68, 125, 139, 173, 174, 175, 188, 189, 190, 191, 202, 249, 288, 289, 298, 299, 318, 331, 332, 339, 340

D

Daddy buy me a Pony-a 9November Union Company / Cape Town 99, 132

DDB / Berlin 62, 148, 149, 153, 154, 175, 278, 319, 320, 341

DDB Brasil / Sao Paulo 191, 308

DDB / Chicago 326

DDB / Hong Kong 176

DDB / London 8, 66, 155

DDB / Paris 192, 216

DDB / Sydney 289

DDB / Toronto 148

DDB / Venice 53, 123

DDB / Vancouver 42, 45, 213, 240, 243

Del Campo Nazca Saatchi & Saatchi / Martinez 244

Dentsu / Tokyo 376

Dentsu / Singapore 176

DeVito/Verdi / New York 42, 119, 325

Dew Gibbons / London 377

Diesel / Montreal 351

Dorten / Stuttgart 358

Downtown Partners / Toronto 290, 377, 392

DPZ Propaganda / Sao Paulo 177, 379, 380

Duffy & Partners / Minneapolis 76, 409

Duval Guillaume / Brussels 321

E

Element 79 Partners / Chicago 60, 125, 138

Emphasis Media / Bangalore 256

Euro RSCG / Bangkok 50, 137

Euro RSCG / Lisbon 202

Euro RSCG / New York 164

F

F/Nazca Saatchi & Saatchi / Sao Paulo 244

Fallon / London 90

Fallon / Minneapolis 291, 300

Fallon New York / New York 20, 42, 54, 59, 138, 192, 203, 279, 280, 291, 326

Farfar / Stockholm 77

FCB / Cape Town 359

FCB / Johannesburg 193, 325

FCB / London 225

FCB / Paris 268

Foote Cone & Belding / Kuala Lumpur 83, 371

Foote Cone & Belding / Lisbon 16, 116, 137

Foote Cone & Belding / Shanghai 217, 256

Foote Cone & Belding / Singapore 156, 203, 250

Forsman & Bodenfors / Gothenburg 149

G

Germ / Santa Monica 322

Giovanni, FCB / Sao Paulo 18, 188

GJP _ Gee Jeffery & Partners / Toronto 349

Good Design Company / Tokyo 77, 80, 82, 381, 404

Goodby, Silverstein & Partners / San Francisco 281, 281, 342, 288, 309

Grabarz & Partner / Hamburg 9, 89, 115, 204

Graham Clifford Design / New York 378

Grey / Copenhagen 157

Ground Zero / Los Angeles 65, 193, 316, 317

Grupo Zapping / Madrid 431, 351

GSD&M / Austin 257, 309

H

Hakuhodo in Progress / Tokyo 371

Hakuhodo / Tokyo 96, 131, 144

Hakuhodo\TBWA\G1 / Tokyo 105, 204

Hans Seeger / Wauwatosa 404

Happy Forsman & Bodenfors / Gothenburg 74, 108, 360, 378, 395, 410, 411, 432

He Said She Said / Hamburg 104, 427

Herman Miller / Zeeland 350

Huey/Paprocki / Atlanta 220

Hunt Adkins / Minneapolis 104, 428

I

Ideaology / Marina del Rey 292

J

J. Walter Thompson Argentina / Buenos Aires 282

J. Walter Thompson / Detroit 381

J. Walter Thompson / Lisbon 245

J Walter Thompson / London 87

J. Walter Thompson / Sao Paulo 150

Jung von Matt / Berlin 6, 115, 194, 325

Jung von Matt / Hamburg 311, 326

Jung von Matt / Stuttgart 69, 325, 352

Jung von Matt / Vienna 382

Jung von Matt / Zurich 411

Jupiter Drawing Room (South Africa), The / Johannesburg 31

Jupiter Drawing Room (South Africa), The / Cape Town 325, 384

JWT / Manchester 343

JWT / Shanghai 85, 221, 388, 390

JWT / Ho Chi Minh City 229

K

Kinetic / Singapore 73, 79, 128, 225, 361, 372, 392

King James RSVP / Cape Town 73, 75, 127, 390

Kolle Rebbe / Hamburg 23, 118

L

la comunidad / Miami Beach 57, 124

Laurie DeMartino Design / Minneapolis 86, 129, 142

Lemon / Mumbai 361

Leo Burnett / Chicago 95, 194, 205, 292

Leo Burnett / Far East Square 214, 233

Leo Burnett / Kuala Lumpur 158, 388

Leo Burnett / Hong Kong 26, 118

Leo Burnett / Mumbai 150

Leo Burnett / Paris 177

Leo Burnett / Prague 251

Leo Burnett / Sao Paulo 35

Lewis Moberly / London 78

Lloyd and Company / New York 98, 372, 405

Lobo / Sao Paulo 101, 133, 414, 415, 422

Lowe / New York 274

Lowe & Partners / Selangor 209

Lowe / Bangkok 221

Lowe Bull / Bryanston 151, 159, 325

M

M&C Saatchi / Singapore 226, 245, 333

M&C Saatchi / Sydney 168

marcandtom.com / Ossining 329

Marketforce / West Perth 40

Martin Agency, The / Richmond 34, 56, 167

Martin Williams / Minneapolis 269

Matthew Vescovo / Brooklyn 314

McCann Erickson / Kuala Lumpur 66, 352

McCann Erickson / Mumbai 205, 234

McCann Erickson / New Delhi 270

McCann Erickson / San Francisco 423

McCann Erickson / Singapore 234

McGarrah/Jessee / Austin 398

McKinney / Durham 166

Mother / London 49, 344, 362

MTV Networks / New York 102, 103, 134, 283, 284, 293, 370, 382, 394, 399, 401, 416, 424, 425

Mullen Advertising / Winston-Salem 312

N

Naga DDB/Malaysia 178, 229

Net#Work BBDO / Hyde Park 7, 47, 151, 389, 426

Niket Parekh / Mumbai 362

No Luggage / Charlotte 363

Nordpol / Hamburg 334, 395, 405

O

180 Amsterdam (180\TBWA) / Amsterdam 55

Ogilvy & Mather / Bangkok 35, 39, 195, 230, 364

Ogilvy & Mather / Frankfurt 30, 106, 134

Ogilvy & Mather / Kuala Lumpur 231

Ogilvy & Mather / London 67

Ogilvy & Mather / New Delhi 226, 412

Ogilvy & Mather / New York 94, 353, 370, 406

Ogilvy & Mather / Santiago 260

Ogilvy & Mather / Singapore 14, 28, 37, 120

Ogilvy Design / Stockholm 402

Ogilvy & Mather / Taipei 206

Ogilvy & Mather / Toronto 179

Ogilvy / Mexico 179

Ogilvy South Africa / Cape Town 235, 257

Ogilvy South Africa / Johannesburg 325

Orange Juice Design / Durban 432

P

Pivot Design / Chicago 412

Powell / New York 130, 365

Prologue Films / Malibu 417-419

Publicis Conseil / Paris 152

Publicis / Frankfurt 206

Publicis / Kuala Lumpur 235, 264

Publicis Mojo / Auckland 36, 246, 261, 264

Publicis Mojo / Melbourne 93, 180

Publicis / New York 165, 271, 285

Publicis Salles Norton / Sao Paulo 180

Publicis / Toronto 365

R

Radical Media / New York 302

Reed Collins / Chicago 215

Rethink / Vancouver 43, 51, 70, 121, 123, 126, 207, 325, 345

Richards Group, The / Dallas 200, 215

RMG David / New Delhi 335

Ruf Lanz / Zurich 325

Index

S

601Bisang / Seoul 107, 393

Saatchi & Saatchi Australia / Sydney 63, 252, 258

Saatchi & Saatchi / Bangkok 310

Saatchi & Saatchi / Cape Town 325, 433

Saatchi & Saatchi / Johannesburg 231

Saatchi & Saatchi / London 25, 43, 181, 195, 217, 236, 325, 366

Saatchi & Saatchi / Madrid 181

Saatchi & Saatchi / New York 222

Saatchi & Saatchi / Petaling Jaya 237

Saatchi & Saatchi / Singapore 182, 336

Sandstrom Design / Portland 100, 353, 354, 428

Sawyer Riley Compton / Atlanta 429

Scholz & Friends / Berlin 27, 29, 119, 196, 210, 218, 258, 355

Scholz & Friends / Hamburg 196, 399

School of Visual Arts / New York 95, 131, 403

Sedgwick Rd / Seattle 303, 304

Shackleton / Madrid 253, 325

Shong! / Seattle 246

Spearhead / Seattle 238

Springer & Jacoby / Hamburg 21, 64, 84, 88, 99, 117, 129, 160, 232, 262, 323, 389

Spunk / Minneapolis 366, 383

T

10AM Communications/ Singapore 263

Target Marketing / St. John's 326

Taxi / Toronto 44, 121, 324

Taxi Studio / Bristol 413

TBWA\Chiat\Day / Los Angeles 305, 306

TBWA\Chiat\Day / New York 293

TBWA\Chiat\Day / San Francisco 48, 122, 124, 286, 307

TBWA\ESPAA / Madrid 182, 183

TBWA\G1\Champs Elysees / Paris 197

TBWA\Gavin\Reddy / Johannesburg 367, 383, 400

TBWA\Hunt\Lascaris / Sandton 162, 183, 265

TBWA\Japan / Tokyo 65, 126, 141, 207

TBWA\London 58

TBWA\Paris 15, 28, 184, 185, 222, 391

TBWA\PHS Helsinki 247, 259

TBWA\Shanghai 210, 391

TBWA \ Singapore 10-12, 161

Tonic Communications / Dubai 14, 116

Tractenberg Advertising / New York 211

Tricycle / Chattanooga 367

Tugboat / Tokyo 75, 127, 141

Turner Duckworth / San Francisco 368, 373

U

Underground / Chicago 315

Upper Storey, The / Singapore 420

V

Vitruvio Leo Burnett / Madrid 337

W

WestWayne 227, 329

Wexley School for Girls / Seattle 218

Whybin TBWA / Pyrmont 208

Wieden + Kennedy / London 2-3, 46, 122, 135-136

Wieden + Kennedy / New York 185, 198, 294

Wieden + Kennedy / Portland 47, 52, 86, 197, 286, 287, 294

Wieden + Kennedy / Tokyo 101, 346, 421

Wongdoody / Seattle 325

Woodbine Agency, The / Winston Salem 80, 384

Y

Y&R / Buenos Aires 163

Y&R / Chicago 33, 198, 326, 430

Y&R / Singapore 254

Yoshiaki Nishimura / Tokyo 396

Young & Laramore / Indianapolis 413

Young & Rubicam / Kuala Lumpur 152, 223

Z

ZiG / Toronto 51, 326

art directors

A

Acedo, Paloma 181

Aguilar, Victor 253

Aldorf, Frank 311

Alinsangan, Susan 305

Alirol, Jean-Michel 268

Allsop, Nick 8

Almgren, Lovisa 155

Alvarado, Sebastian 260

Alvarez, Ali 90

Amante, Gary 407

Ambrose, Jason 175, 191

Anderson, Charles S. 81, 128, 374, 375

Andersson, Nils 105, 204

Anselmo, Frank 201, 228

Anuncibay, Carlos 181

Arena, Gianfranco 313

Arruda, Saulo 150

Asano, Jun 423

Ashley, Michael 239, 431

Askwith, Dave 181

Assawanapanon, Aniruth 228

Atienza, Jayson 201, 228

Aun, Alex Lim Tye 32, 139, 147, 220

B

Back, Steve 330

Baird, Rob 279

Bamfield, Mark 161

Bannecker, Andrew 379

Baran, Joe 369

Barnes, Justin 67

Bauer, Jorg 352, 358

Belford, Paul 19, 22, 117, 186, 248

Belknap, Rodger 424

Beng, Poh Hwee 217

Benjamin, Jay 258

Berger, Thomas 382

Bergstrom, Nicke 77

Best, Wayne 280

Beug, Lena 102, 103, 134, 416

Bexiga, Pedro 202

Bezuidenhout, Jean-Roux 193
Bhat, Raghu 234
Bhatt, Manish 234
Bianchi, Valdir 188
Bielefeldt, Christoph 405
Bindi, Adrien 292
Black, Dustin 79
Blom, Mikael 378, 395
Bobst, Christian 194
Boettcher, Philipp 30
Bohm, Andreas 153, 175
Bond, Michael 165
Boonthong, Andy 405
Bostad, Anne Max 337
Bottez, Katrien 321
Braddock, Mark 239
Brandt, Mike 99, 389
Brazier, Paul 153
Broden, Mattias 77
Bryan, Marion 389
Bryson, Rick 169
Bubb, Brenton 359
Buchanan, Alan 198
Burnard, Alex 17, 188, 190, 340

C

+cruz 101, 421
Calcao, Tony 175, 190, 191, 288, 298, 299
Callis, Ben 67
Cama, Felipe 308
Campbell, Cosmo 243
Campos, Rodrigo 150
Capel, Brian 158
Careborg, Lisa 74, 108, 360, 409, 410, 411,
Carrasco, Ivan 179
Cass, Mishy 303, 304
Castelau, Vanessa 245
Chaladus, Carol 177
Chalermwong, Jon 24
Chan, Edmond 176
Chantrawan, Passakorn 35
Chen, Claire 37, 120
Chiang, Lii 206
Ching, Tuan 406
Chisholm, Heidi 99, 132
Choo, Chee-Wee 66
Choo, Kenny 26, 118
Chow, Eric 235
Chu, David 210
Chudalla, Thomas 319
Chung, Steven 210
Clarke, Phil 217, 236
Clunie, James 219, 255, 386
Cochran, Steve 172
Cohen, Fern 222
Cohen, Marion 195
Cohen, Nicole 183
Cole, Dan 366
Collins, Reed 215
Combs, Josh 218
Connelly, Walt 423
Cooper, Kyle 417, 418, 419
Copiz, Stefan 288
Corps, Daryl 147
Coulter, Jesse 294
Courtney, Bryan 231
Couture, Steve 423
Covitz, Phil 72, 273, 338
Crooker, Scot 220
Cruickshank, James ce 23, 118
Crutchfield, Craig 398
Cuccinello, David 164
Cuellar, Silver 398
Curtis, Hal 47

D

Darfeuille, Martin 216
Dasari, Ramprasad 256
Dattalo, Frank 170
Davis, Brock 199
Davis, Joel 329
Dawson-Hollis, James 68
DeMartino, Laurie 86, 129, 142
DeRouen, Derrit 398
Detweiler, Curt 197
Devgun, Rohit 335
Dickinson, Kelly 14
Dietrich, Mike 179
DiLallo, Andy 258
Dimmer, Matt 381
Dixon, Chris 406
Dogra, Deepak 226
Doman, Matt 22
Douglass, Dave 44, 121
Driggs, Steve 291
Drummond, Stacy 401
Duntemann, Matthew 370
Dye, Dave 209, 407
Dyer, Leighton 264

E

Eckstein, Axel 411
Eckstein, Vanessa 356
Eder, Guenter 382
Edwards, Geoff 48, 122, 124
Eghammer, Johan 149
Eklind, Anders 149
Elliott, Yan 49
Emmett, Brad 295, 296
Eng, Tan Kien 427
Engelhardt, Justus v. 323
Everitt, Peter 200

F

Fairbanks, Mark 308
Fajardo, Fernanda 379, 380
Fang, Kai 225
Faudet, Michael 289
Favat, Pete 266
Fernandez, Roberto 186
Ferrare, Michael 68
Ferreira, Isabela 430
Fetrow, Mike 255
Fierro, Daniel 244
Fitzgerald, Kevin 414
Fleet, Karl 408
Flores, Lou 167,
Fonferrier, Marianne 185
Forte, Tim 180
French, Gregory 196, 258
Friberg, Lotta 402

Index

Frick, Urs 351

G
Ga, Naoki 28
Gaikwad, Vinayak 166
Gainsford, Kirk 265
Garbutt, Chris 15
Gayraud, Pascale 152
Gehrig, Kim 362
Genell, Jim 194
Gerard-Huet, Jessica 184, 222
Giovanni, Renata 367
Glue Society, The 87
Gomez, Victor 431
Godkin, Gary 208
Goh, Ken 83, 371
Goldblatt, Stephen 288
Gradert-Hinzpeter, Tobias 323
Grais, Ian 51, 123, 345
Green, Oliver 225
Guadarrama, Alejandro 179
Guimaraes, Celina 367

H
Haggerty, Frank 213
Hall, Graeme 66
Hammerl, Alex 383
Hansen, Hans 171
Hardcastle, Tony 22
Harris, Justin 169
Harris, Pat 316
Hashimoto, Shintaro 65, 126, 141
Hauseman, Laura 429
Hayo, Thomas 313
Hendrix, Michael 367
Heng, Eddie Wong Yew 226
Henkes, Uschi 351
Hicks, Johannes 27
Himmler, Helmut 106, 134
Hine, Nick 184
Ho, T T 352
Hobbs, John 97, 313
Hock, Chye Yong 420
Hofler, Mark 395
Hofvner, Pontus 108, 411, 432
Hogrefe, Birgit 262
Hogya, Bernie 224
Hooff, Arnaud Loix van 148
Hoong, Yap Pow 371
Hopfer, Jeff 215
Horowitz, David 283, 284
Howell, Marco 397
Hu, Gang 85, 390
Huang, Ean-Hwa 66
Huang, Hai Bo 388
Hughes, Brian Lee 307
Hughes, Mike 71, 387
Huse, Tim 172, 260
Hyndman, Roy 22

I
Iglesias, Angel 182
Ireland, Philip 47

J
Jacobs, Jan 43
Jacobs, Joan 75, 390
Jangaard, Mikkel 157
Janke, Michael 154
Jaranphairee, Maytinee 364
Jay, John 101, 346
Jenkins, Jayanta 346
Jin, Ang Sheng 263
Jockisch, Steve 383
Johnson, Graham 168
Johnson, Ivan 171
Johnson, Jeff 366
Johnson, Richard 14
Johnson-Pond, Rebecca 330
Jones, Desirre 274
Jones, Kevin 181
Juenger, Nico 206
Juntaratip, Ariyawat 169

K
Kapoor, Puneet 205
Karkhanis, Ashutosh 201
Karow, Bill 287
Karwa, Renu 234
Kaushik, Niranjan 201
Kawaguchi, Seijo 75, 127, 141
Kawamura, Marcus 35
Keister, Paul 190, 249
Keller, Andrew 61, 125, 139
Keon, Matt 225
Keong, Chow Kok 235, 264, 432, 436, 442
Keong, Tan Chee 158, 231, 388
Kian, Khoo Choo 229
Kiang, Tan Yee 178,
Kiao-on, Winna 169
Kim, Derrick 261
Kim, Goh Wee 212, 214
Kirschenhofer, Bertrand 405
Kittel, Andreas 74, 108, 409, 410
Kloth, Erich T. 399
Kluin, Menno 21, 84, 117
Knauss, Jan 89
Koh, Kit 206
Koller, Kevin 332
Konkaew, Korakot 169
Konttinen, Jyri 247, 259
Kooij, Bart 62
Kosel, Tiffany 173, 174, 188, 189, 202
Kotian, Manasi 234
Kreuser, Carla 384
Kuhn, Michael 395
Kumar, Prabhu 256
Kusano, Denison 198

L
Lable, Jeff 193, 317
Laden, Dave 288
Laksanajinda, Gumpon 39, 195
Landry, Jim 255
Larppitakpong, Kittitat 24
Lavola, Minna 247, 259
Law, Thomas 176
Ledeboer, Mareike 196
Lee, Dean 213, 240
Lee, Hee Jeong 403
Lee, Ian 209

Lee, Kevin 221
Leepakpreeda, Wiboon 50, 137
Lees-Rolfe, Michael 235
Lemoigne, Jean-Yves 192
Leong, Kelvin 237
Leps, Stephen 51
Lessing, Gareth 159
Levine, Jason 285
Liang, Hai 85, 390
Lim, Jann 371
Lim, Pann 73, 79, 128, 225, 361, 372,
Lincoln, Luciano 244
Lishman, Maria 408
Livesey, Adam 151
Loke, Jon 233
Loper, Bjorn 148, 149
Lord, Myles 232
Low, Patrick 254
Lowe, Alex 381
Luebke, Kay 29, 119
Lumsiricharoenchoke, Wisit 39

M
Mackie, Todd 148
Maiorino, Chris 201
Mann, Hylton 70, 126
Mapp, Steve 342
Mara, Miguel de 337
Marcondes, Guilherme 422
Markou, Craig 377
Marmol, Mike del 17, 188, 190, 340
Mart, Lorena 173
Martin, Michael 251
Maryon, Dean 55
Mathew, Rahul 205
Mazzei, Nancy 399
McAllister, Cal 218
McBride, Chuck 286
McBurnie, Scott 63
McGinnis, Mark 215
McIntyre, Tim 405
McKenzie, Selena 93
McTear, Tony 58
Medeiros, Marcos 191
Medeiros, Silvio 18
Meng, Tham Khai 37, 120,
Mertens, Melanie 88, 129
Michurski, Bryan 269
Middleton, Ben 344
Mietz, Jamie 14, 116
Miles, Paul 25
Millar, Tom 329
Milligan-Croft, Dave 330
Minczeles, Antoine 197
Mitchell, Steve 104, 428
Mitoh 104, 427
Mizuno, Manabu 77, 80, 82, 381, 404
Mommertz, Christian 30
Montessano, Julian 57, 124
Moore, Josh 246, 36
Moore, Toby 93
Moreno, Carlos 290
Morimoto, Chie 96, 131, 144, 371
Morris, Kat 38
Morrow, Sally 353
Morton, Becca 306
Mosothoane, Teboho 257
Mously, David 6, 115
MUN 178, 229
Musante, Jason 166

N
Nakajima, Hirofumi 65, 126, 141, 207
Nautiyal, Gaurav 412
Nerman, Jenny 351
Newman, Simon 365
Ng, Kris 156
Nobay, David 63
Nolting, Ralf 9, 115
Norman, John 281
Nussbaum, John 342

O
O'Brien, James 403
O'Brien, Lee 80, 384
O'Brien, Steve 316
Ogden, Peter 289
O'Kelly, Mariana 151, 426
Oliveira, Robson 177, 380
Onaindia, Jon 431
O'Rourke, Ryan 286
Ostrom, Andrew 267
Outhwaite, Stuart 344

P
Padhi, Santosh 150
Palmer, Lara 45
Palmer, Rob 281, 342
Parekh, Niket 362
Park, Kum-jun 107, 393
Parker, James 354
Parker, John 17, 167, 332, 339
Pavlovic, Ana 403
Pea, Pablo Gonzalez de la 183, 253
Peacock, Jo-Wayne 433
Pedersen, Doug 363
Peterson, Shereen 95
Pfeiffer-Belli, Michael 175
Pienaar, Peet 99, 132
Ping, Ong Shi 152
Poh, Roy 73, 79, 128, 225, 361, 372
Powell, Neil 130
Powell, Rachael 365
Prada, Nadine 219
Puettmann, Raphael 210

Q
Quinn, Barry 349

R
Rakowski, Amy 211
Rane, Mangesh 361
Rebeschini, Marcus 10, 11, 12
Reed, Ryan 257
Reese, Ashley 423
Regan, Adam 197
Regan, Noah 252
Renen, Nicholas van 183
Renner, Paul 198
Richards, Tom 343
Ritter, Noel 56

Index

Rittirajcomporn, Thana 310
Rodricks, Priti 357
Romeu, Carla 173
Ronachen, Nikolaus 64
Rooke, Guy 172, 260, 408
Roque, Joao 16, 116, 137
Rose, Szymon 160
Ruhmann, Bjorn 334
Rusoff, Lance 394
Russell, Richard 2-3, 46, 122, 135-136
Russoff, Michael 2-3, 46, 122, 135-136

S
Sahre, Paul 95, 131
Sandstrom, Steve 100, 428
Sano, Yukimi 385
Santana, Jonathan 7
Santilli, Dino 292
Santos, Luciano 180
Saralak, Santaya 230
Sasaki, Keiichi 105, 204
Sawada, Koichi 376
Schaffarzcyk, Till 106, 134
Schilling, Sandra 154, 278, 341
Schimmel, David 91, 130, 143
Schreiber, Gunther 334
Schupp, Jonathan 160
Seeger, Hans 95, 404
Seidenberg, Lee 295, 296
Selman, James 287
Sethumadhavan, Satish 205
Shabaz, Ali 32, 139, 147, 220
Shachter, John 404
Sheahan, Molly 20, 59, 192, 203
Shembeda, Brian 95, 205
Shon, Chan Lee 388
Siakimotu, Gavin 66
Sibilla, Vidi 163
Sides, Brandon 72, 273
Siegal, Meghan 72, 338
Sigg, Stephanie 185, 198
Silber, Joachim 69
Silburn, Paul 58
Silva, Bernadette da 400
Simpson, Gavin 152, 223
Sin, David 209
Singer, Brent 162
Slavin, Levi 40
Smail, David 229
Smetham, Jo 366
Smith, Jason 187
Smith, Scott 62
So&Sau 277
Soaeb, Mohammed 270
Soh, Leng 73, 372
Song, Derrick 10, 11, 12
Songsri, Nimit 50, 137
Sooksai, Voarachai 195
Sorensen, Mark 255
Soto, Jon 309
Spett, Matt 60, 125, 138
Spillane, Jeff 309
Spinadel, Cody 34
Staples, Adam 25
Stapleton, John 227
Stapleton, Marike 400
Starkey, Bill 312
Stead, Mark 73, 127
Stechschulte, Paul 188, 191
Steinegger, Christoph 393
Stephens, Geordie 174, 188, 340
Stiller, Mathias 320
Stockmar, Tim 355
Stoller, Aaron 293
Studio Von Birken 98, 372
Sugiuchi, Scott 315
Suknipitapong, Tawatchai 310
Sumedi, Din 182, 336
Swartz, Dave 318, 339
Sweetman, Rob 43, 70, 121, 207, 126

T
Tajer, Pablo 244
Tan, Terrence 245
Tanapatanakul, Thirasak 24
Taroux, Philippe 28
Taylor, Guybrush 324
Taylor, Mark 331
Teng, Theresa Tsang 427
Teng, Vancelee 221
Terwilliger, Jeff 171
Tharp, Storm 197
Thompson, Sean 2-3, 46, 122, 135-136
Thrall, Maari 218
Timonen, Mikko 149
Tindall, Justin 155
Ting, Tricia 72, 273
Toland, Chris 300
Trost, Brad 52
Truch, Christopher 394
Tsujimoto, Tadashi 207
Tulinius, Tomas 204
Tung, Diana 239, 431

U
Urgino, Carl 170

V
Vacherot, Sebastien 391
Valganon, David 181
Vecino, Gonzalo 187
Vendramin, Daniel 392
Vescovo, Matthew 314
Vior, Ricky 57, 124
Vitrone, Scott 293
Vladusic, Alan 165

W
W+K 12, 86
Walker, Garth 432
Wan, Leo 210
Wangpaitoon, Vasan 228
Watson, Ralph 257
Weber, Marco 30
Weiner, Clay 271
Weiss, Volkmar 218
Wibowo, Ivan Hady 234
Wielopolski, Liam 31
Wiggins, Mark 176
Williams, Jeff 294, 302
Williams, Trevor 413
Williamson, Luke 49, 362

Wills, Ryan 413
Wolch, Anthony 365
Wong, Eddie 210
Wong, Karen 223
Wong, Tracy 246
Wood, Bradley 33
Wood, Jason 238
Woolcott, Marcus 54, 138, 291, 280
Wu, Robin 221
Wu, Tif 210

Y
Yang, Jane 26, 118
Yang, Thomas 333
Yap, Henry 237
Yeo, Eric 203, 250
Yi-ping, Liu 41
Young, Paul 147, 186
Yu, Paul 85, 390
Yuan, Maggie 256
Yuen, Jonathan 361

Z
Zhuang, Bamboo 85

clients

A
Absolut Vodka 208
Ad Council 329
Adidas China 391
adidas 48, 55, 65, 122, 124, 126, 141, 207, 210, 286
Adorama Camera 224
Aerolineas Argentinas 282
Against Abuse 399
AIGA-Minnesota Design Camp 2004 434
Akatu Institute for Conscious Consumption, The 35
Alinna 371
Allied Domecq 165
Amacai 379
American Cancer Society/Blue Cross Blue Shield 104
American Legacy Foundation 38, 42, 72, 249, 266, 273, 338
Ameriquest 53, 123
Amnesty International 246, 247, 259
Amusement Creation 195
Anglican Welfare Council 37, 120
Anheuser-Busch 326
Animal ID Promotion Organization 105
Apartheid Museum 400
Apple 305
Aquent 214
Arctic Paper 74, 409, 410
Arena Homme Plus 21 + 22 405
Arnika 239
Ashutosh Parikh 362
ASICS Europe 395
Association of Librarians of the Czech Republic 251
AT&T Wireless 370
Atlanta Red Cross, The 429
Atmosphere PR 75
Auckland City Mission 264
Auckland Regional Council 330
Australian Red Cross Blood Service 267
Axe / Unilever Thai Holdings 221
Axion-Youth banking 321
AXN 336

B
Band Aid Washproof 234
BC Lions 51, 123, 345
BC SPCA 45
Berliner Morgenpost 325
Berlitz 27
Betteridges Solicitor 366
Bic 184
Big Babol Bubble Gum 205
Big Magazine 97, 98, 404
Bisley Office Equipment 23, 118
Bits Sin Fronteras 431
Blood Bank/Charity 265
Blue Q 374, 375
BMW do Brasil 18
BMW Malaysia 220
BMX Rider Magazine 25
Bob & Ronna Real Estate Team 315
Body Shop, The 377
Borders 318
Bradesco Bank 180
Bransch 393
Buenavista 351
Buenos Aires Zoo 244
Burger King 68, 288, 298, 299, 331, 332

C
Cadbury Schweppes-Snapple 295, 296
Campbell Soup Southeast Asia 223
Canadian Film Centres Worldwide Short Film Festival 44, 121, 272
Cape Town Major Events Co. 384
Cartoon Network 414
CDD 407
Centre for Management of the Built Environment 395
Cerebos 152
Chelsea Guitars 164
Chicago Creative Club 95
Chicago Music Exchange 60, 125, 138
CHUM 325
Cingular 169, 397
Citibank 291, 300
City Mission 257
City of Minneapolis 76, 369
Classic Tattoo 166
CNN.com 301
Coco de Mer 195
Companhia Athletica (Gym) 308
Constitutional Court of South Africa 432
Converse 71, 353, 354, 387
Cort Guitar 194
Crest 236
Crystal Group 353
Cub Scout Pack #102 428
Cub Scouts (Viking Indianhead Council, BSA) 255
Culture Curry 361

D
Daimler-Chrysler 228
DDB Canada 213, 240

Index

Delta Faucet Company, The 413
Detroit Music Hall 381
Dexter Russel Cutlery 386
DHL 6, 115
Dialogue in the Dark 104, 427
Diamond of California 309
Dick Gerdes 34
Diesel 101, 133
Distress Centres of Toronto 349
Donato Salons & Spa 392
Dove 94
Dr. Pradumna S. Mamtora 357
Duffy & Partners 76, 409

E
eBay 281, 342
Economist, The 14, 19, 22, 117, 147, 151
Editora Abril 186
Ella Cheong Spruson & Ferguson 212
Energizer 148
Engen 325
Eniro 402
ESPN/Miller Brewing Co. 65
ESPN 185, 198, 294, 316
EUT 178, 237
Evian 277

F
4As of the Philippines 407
Fame Adlabs 201
Fare Start 325
Fatty Golf Open 315
Fenda Seguros 188
First United Mission 243
Focus Ireland 330
Ford 67
Fox Sports Net 307
Frankfurter Allgemeine Zeitung 355
French Paper Company 81, 128
Fundacao SOS Mata Atlantica 244

G
Galatea Spirits 77
Geico 56
General Motors 7
Gillette India 226
Global Alliance 250
Google 339
Gotham Comedy Club 211
GP Battery Marketing 235
Graffiti Exhibition 258
Grand Hyatt Dubai 78
Grande Reportagem Magazine 16, 116, 137
Guardian, The 155
Gucci 372
Guinness 153, 228, 308
Guru Bicycle Corp. 351

H
Hakuhodo 404
Hansaplast 222
Hanson & Mohring 378
Harley-Davidson 187, 199
Hasselblad Center 108, 411, 432
HBO/Soprano's 201
Henkel 153
Herman Miller 350
Herringbone 168
Hewlett-Packard 281
History Channel, The 193, 317
Honda 2-3, 46, 122, 135-136
Hormel Foods Corporation-DiLuso Genoa 79
Hotel Victor 369
House Foods 204
HQ Imaging 408

I
IFAW 262
IKEA 289, 326
In Touch Magazine 219
Indosport (Thailand) 169
INPES Passive Smoking 268
Insurance Corporation of British Columbia (ICBC) 42
Intertool 30
Intown Ace Hardware 220
Irving Oil Limited 326
ITS Travel 69

J
Jackson Walker Law Firm 215
Japan Tobacco 376
Jeep 333
JOS 225
Junge Karriere 194
Justine Drake 359
JWT 87

K
Kansai Electric Power Co., Inc. 396
Kellogg Raisin Bran Crunch 292
K-fee 311, 326
Kingdom Kids 256
Kinokuniya 388
KIRIN Beverage 77
KIWI 200
Konica Minolta Photo Imaging 218

L
Labatt Breweries - Bud Light 290
Land Rover Owners Club 209
Land Rover 179
Laurie DeMartino Design Co 86, 129, 142
Le Barran 192
Lego 177, 379, 380
Levi Strauss & Co. 313, 390
Lion Breweries 172
Liquid Sound Studios 408
Long Xi 388
Lorgan's 392
Los Angeles County Fair 292
Los Angeles Film Festival (IFP) 322

M
M Net 325
Manfrotto 217
marcandtom.com 329
Mark Hooper 100
Masterfoods/Pedigree 162
Maxim 340
McCann Erickson 352
McDonalds 150, 205, 217
McKenzie River Co. 373

Mediawise 269
Mercedes Benz 64, 160, 173, 232, 323
Merrydown 209
Metro 157
Microsoft Singapore 234
Microsoft 423
Miller Brewing Company 33, 326
Miller High Life 294, 302
MINI
10, 11, 12, 173-175, 188, 189, 190, 202, 325
Miracle Creations 361
Mitsubishi Motors 196
MNCASA 255
Modern Digital 218
Molson 17, 190
Monaco 172
Mother 362
Mount Sinai Medical Center 325
MTV Design
102, 103, 134, 382, 394, 401, 416, 424, 425
MTV 271, 283, 284, 293, 314
Muehlehalde Home of the blind Zurich
325
Museum of Flight 325
My Sisters' Place 274

N
National Coalition for Gun Control 258
National Corporation Against Child Abuse
260
National Park Wildlife and Plant
Conservation Dept. 35
National Thoroughbred Racing Association
42, 119
Nebraska Domestic Violence Council 42
Neckar Valley Green Space Foundation, The
352
Ned McNeilage & Linda Knight 239
Neenah Paper 91, 130, 143
New Zealand Blood Service 261
New Zealand Book Council 260
New Zealand Coastguard 36
Nextel 293
Nick Digital - NOGGIN 370
Nike 28, 47, 52, 85, 180, 187, 197,
206, 221, 229, 286, 287, 346, 390
Nikon 229
Nissan 184, 185, 197
No Dirty Gold 430
Noble Education 225
Nokia Corporation 420
North American Coffee Partnership 279
NSPCC 43
NW Film Center 428

O
100 Days 358
Observatory, The 372
Observer, The 344
Office of Road Safety 40
Ogilvy & Mather 406
Olay 181
OLN 422
Onion, The 167
oorong-sha 371
Orange Consumer 49
OroVerde Rainforest Foundation 106, 134
Osram Long Life Bulbs 231

P
Panasonic 415
Parmalat - Everfresh 235
Payal Jain 412
Pentel 159
Pepsi QTG - Life Cereal 377
PetsUnite 158
Pfizer 147, 150
Philips 191
Pie Books 96, 131, 144
Pizza Hut 32, 139, 231
PlayStation2 58, 306
Polar Music Prize 108
Polaroid 196
Polartec / High Country 225
Porsche Cars North America 171
Post Quick Co. 364
POWA 325
Powell Communications 365
Pro Helvetia (Swiss arts Council) 99, 132
Procter & Gamble - Pepto 165
Procter & Gamble 177
Proctor & Gamble - Tide 222
Pulling String 73

Q
Queseras Bel Espaa, S.A. 181

R
Radiology Malaysia 264
Raffles Hotel Vier Jahreszeiten Hamburg
99, 389
Rapala 213
RayTan Florist 83
Reckitt Benckiser 31
Renault 152, 206, 334
Research Surveys 73, 127
Rheingold Beer 130
RSPCA 248

S
601Bisang 393
Salvation Army 245
Samsung 156
Sanyo Shokai 75, 127, 141
Saturn 288
Save The Children 253, 325
SC Johnson & Son 203
Schauspielhaus Wien 382
Schering-Plough 176
School of Visual Arts 95, 131, 403
Science Museum 413
Science World 43, 70, 121, 126, 325
Scruffs 343
Sealy 312
Seattle Magic 238
Sesame Street Partners Japan 385
Shatterprufe Safety Glass 183
Simba - Ghost Pops 389
Singapore Environment Council 263
Sitges Sci-fi and Fantasy Film Festival 337
Smith & Wesson 21, 84, 117
Snickers 186
Soken Electronics 50, 137
Sonovision Recording Studios 193
Sony Computer Entertainment 182, 183
Sony Pictures 417

Index

Sony Playstation 15, 28, 391
Sony 14, 66, 116
South African Broadcasting Corporation - Rsg 426
Southwest Airlines 309
Sowearto 367
Space 150 366
SPCA 254
Sphere 161
Splash Corporation 170
Spoetzl Brewery 398
Sportfive 405
Static - Music and Sound Design 365
Steele Technologies 363
STIHL 216
Subaru 171
Swedish Museum of Architecture, The 360
Sylvania 310

T
3M Trim-Line 207
Taller de Empresa 356
Tamiya Assembly Toys 24
Tank Goodness 383
TAXI 324
Teany Beverage 378
Think Centre 245
Think Council, The 383
Think, Feel, Vote 246
Tiffany O'Brien 80, 384
TIME Magazine 20, 203
TimeWarner/TBS 285
Tourism Victoria 93
Toykar 226
Toyota / Tazz 325
Toyota 63, 182, 325
Travel Channel 198
Tricycle 367
Truthout.org 257
Tur & Partner 411
Turner Duckworth 368
TVI 202
Twin Palms Publishing 227
Twinkle corporation 80, 82, 381

U
UNIFEM 252
Unilever - Dove Beauty Bar 179
Unilever Home & Personal Care - Axe 151
Unilever Home & Personal Care - H/Andy Oven Cleaner 325
Unilever Thai Holding 230
Unisource 412
United Airlines 90
Universal Studios 418, 419

V
VCU Adcenter 431
VH 1 57, 124, 399
Victorinox 233
VIDAK 107
Vier Pfoten e.V. Foundation for Animal Welfare 88, 129
Vim 51
Virgin Atlantic Airways 47
Virgin Mobile USA 42, 54, 59, 138, 192, 280, 291, 326
Virgin 61, 125, 139, 191
Visa Argentina 163
Volkswagen 8, 9, 62, 66, 89, 115, 148, 149, 154, 175, 204, 219, 278, 289, 319, 320, 341
Volvo 149

W
W+K 12 86
Waitrose 373
Walt Disney Studios
Washington Mutual 303, 304
WD-40 176
Weru 29, 119
Western Union Money Transfer 166
Wieden+Kennedy Tokyo 101, 421
Wm. Wrigley Jr. Company/Orbit White 170
Wolanani AIDS Initiative 433
Women's Aid Organisation (WAO) 427
Wong CoCo 79, 128
WWF 39, 41, 256, 335
www.prayas.org 270

Y
Y+ Yoga Center 26, 118
Yamaha 210
YoungGuns 215

creative directors

A
Adams, Tom 38, 42, 72, 249, 266, 273, 338
Adkins, Doug 104
Agost-Carreno, Cesar 260
Ahmad, Yasmin 388
Ahrens, Tobias 64
Alexander, Joe 34
Altmann, Olivier 152
Alvarez, Javier 337
Andeer, Mark 79
Andersson, Nils 105
Anton, Rafa 337
Anuncibay, Carlos 181
Aota, Mitsuaki 204
Areekul, Karanee 230
Ashley, Michael 239, 431
Azuma, Hideki 77

B
Babinet, Remi 277
Baldacci, Roger 38, 42, 249, 266, 338
Baldwin, David 166
Bamfield, Mark 161
Bannohr, Frank 64
Barclay, Sarah 222
Barrett, Jamie 281, 288, 342
Barthuel, Antoine 177
Bassett, Steve 56
Bauer, Jorg 358
Bayala, Carlos 47
Bazarkaya, Toygar 160
Beattie, Trevor 58
Belford, Paul 308
Belford, Paul 19, 22, 117, 147, 186, 248
Bell, Dave 101, 133

Beng, Poh Hwee 217, 256
Benjamin, Jeff 68, 331, 332
Bernardi, Tio 180
Bertish, Conn 325, 433
Best, Wayne 280, 326
Bianchi, Valdir 18, 188
Bijur, Arthur 295, 296
Bildsten, Bruce 300
Bingham, Weston 353, 370
Bogusky, Alex 17, 38, 42, 61, 72, 125, 139, 173, 174, 175, 188, 189, 190, 191, 202, 249, 266, 273, 288, 298, 299, 318, 338-340
Booth, Eddie 26, 118
Borshak, Keith 80, 384
Braddock, Mark 239
Bransch, Susanne 393
Brazier, Paul 153
Brockenbrough, John 312
Brooklyn Brothers 301
Brovelli, Fabrice 277
Brown, Warren 267
Bruce, Duncan 365
Buck, Spencer 413
Bullock, Richard 55
Burgos, Fred 379
Burke, Greg 235, 257
Burnard, Alex 340
Butler, John 71, 387
Byrne, Mike 47, 52, 197, 286, 287

C

Camp, Roger 294
Campos, Fernando 18, 188
Capara, Pablo 163
Cappeletti, Pedro 191, 308
Carstens, John 369
Cerullo, Dan 381
Chan, Bill 85, 388, 390
Chan, Danny 256
Chan, Peter 231
Cheetham, Andy 343
Cheong, Eugene 37, 120
Choe, Edmund 237
Choo, Kenny 26, 118
Chou, Murphy 206
Chudalla, Thomas 175
Clark, Stuart 208
Clay, Steve 235, 264
Cleveland, Bart 429
Clifford, Graham 378
Clint! Runge 42
Clow, Lee 55
Cohen, Ian 218
Colin, Marco 179
Collins, Brian 94, 353, 370, 406
Colonnese, Pablo 282
Condon, John 292
Connelly, Walt 423
Cooper, Kyle 417-419
Cordner, Tom 381
Corr, David 165
Coughlin, Craig 379
Coverdale, Jac 255
Cox-Hagan, Nigel 399
Craigen, Jeremy 8, 66
Crandall, Court 65, 193, 316, 317
Cullen, Matt 14
Curtis, Hal 47, 52, 197, 286, 287
Curtis, Jeffrey 221

D

Dabral, Sonal 231
Dady, Glenn 200
Dasari, Ramprasad 256
Davidson, Tony 2-3, 46, 122, 135-136
Davis, Craig 87
Deck, Barry 370
Delbourgo, Phil 399
Demilio, Chavo 244
Denberg, Josh 194
Desai, Devesh 357
Deshpande, Ravi 361
Detweiler, Curt 197
Devito, Sal 42, 119, 325
Dew, Shaun 377
Dias, Agnello 150
Dias, Luis Silva 16, 116, 137
Driggs, Steve 291, 300
Duchon, Scott 48, 122, 124
Duckworth, Bruce 368, 373
Dye, Dave 209

E

Eckstein, Vanessa 356
Edwards, Geoff 48, 122, 124
Ehlers, Jenny 73, 75, 127, 390
Eng, Tan Kien 427

F

Faudet, Michael 289
Favat, Pete 38, 42, 72, 249, 266, 273, 338
Fernandes, Fabio 244
Ferrer, Dave 170
Figliulo, Mark 33, 198, 326, 430
Fisher, Mark 235
Flintham, Richard 90
Fohr, Daniel 177
Francucci, Atila 150
Fraser, Andrew 155
Freeman, Cliff 295, 296
French, Neil 254
Frick, Urs 351, 431
Frykholm, Steve 350

G

Gadallah, Khaled 14, 116
Gamper, Mario 210, 218
Ganser, Stephan 194, 325
Garner, Mike 330
Gaxiola, Robert 156, 203, 250
Gentile, Jerry 306
Geyer, Andreas 23, 118
Gibbons, Brendan 301
Gibbons, Steve 377
Gins, Guillermo 182, 183
Gley, Ove 311, 326
Godin, Helene 351
Goldsmith, Gary 274
Goodby, Jeff 281, 309, 342
Gotz, Chris 235
Graf, Gerry 228, 293
Grais, Ian 43, 51, 70, 121, 123, 126, 207, 325, 345

Index

Granger, Tony
25, 43, 181, 195, 217, 222, 224, 236, 325
Green, Oliver 225
Green, Sheraton 81, 128
Green, Tim 229
Gross, Mark 326
Grunbaum, Eric 305
Guerrero, David 170, 220
Guertler, Uli 99, 389
Guttesman, Marc 329

H
Hacohen, Dean 274
Hadlock, Carolyn 413
Haeusermann, Dirk 232, 262
Haldeman, Brock 412
Hammond, William 148
Hansen, Hans 199
Harbeck, Matthias 232, 262
Hartsock, Eric 315
Hayo, Thomas 313
Hendrix, Michael 367
Henkes, Uschi 351, 431
Herberstein, Camilla 183
Herve, Alexandre 192, 216
Heuel, Ralf 9, 89, 115, 204
Himmler, Helmut 106, 134
Hin, Tay Guan 214
Hirsch, Paul 194
Hock, Chye Yong 420
Hoffman, Susan 294
Hohmann, Till 323
Hoinkes, Michael 104, 427
Hollingsworth, Jovaney 81, 128
Hoong, Lim Sau 263
Hoong, Yap Pow 83, 371
Hopfer, Jeff 215
Horner, Garry 289
Hu, Gang 85, 390
Huang, Ean-Hwa 66, 352
Huggins, Jeff 423
Human, Gerry 325
Huvart, Lars 106, 134

I
Iglesias, Angel 182, 183
Immesoete, John 326
Israel, David 94, 406
It, Ng Tian 234

J
Jacobs, Jan 195, 224
Jager, Achim 352
Jaggy, Alexander 411
Jaroensuk, Chukiat 50, 137
Jay, John 101, 346, 421
Jayme, Merlee 407
Jensen, Matias Palm 77
Jessee, Bryan 398
Johnson, Ivan 171
Johnson, Jeff 366, 383
Johnson, Richard 14
Johnston, Steve 303, 304
Johson, Pete 414
Joshi, Prasoon 205, 234, 270
Jung, Richard 196

K
Kaloff, Constantin 311, 326
Karkhanis, Ashutosh 201
Kassaei, Amir
62, 154, 175, 278, 319, 320, 341
Kaushik, Niranjan 201
Kavander, Tim 219
Kay, Woody 379
Kearse, John 72, 273
Keister, Paul 289
Keller, Andrew 61, 68, 125, 139, 173-175, 188, 189-191, 202, 288, 298, 299, 331, 332
Kelly, Graham 182, 336
Kensley, PJ 325
Keon, Matt 225
Kessel, Felix 400
Kestin, Janet 179
Keyton, Jeffrey 102, 103, 134, 382, 394, 401, 416, 424, 425
Khow, Subun 169
Kinetic 73, 79, 128, 225, 361, 372, 392
Kleman, Robert 37, 175
Knight, Linda 239
Kong, Stephen 26, 118
Kornestedt, Anders
74, 108, 360, 378, 395, 409-411, 432
Kuhn, Bastian 148, 149
Kulkosa, Nikrom 228

L
Ladd, Brent 309
Laden, Dave 288
Lang, Graham 325
Lanz, Danielle 325
Lawner, Ron
38, 42, 72, 249, 266, 273, 338, 379
Lear, Mike 167
Lee, Kevin 221
Lee, Ruth 26, 118
Lee, Steven 176
Lee, Szu-Hung 66, 352
Leepakpreeda, Wiboon 50, 137
Leick, Stefan 210, 218
Leube, Jan 27, 29, 119, 355
Lewis, Mary 78
Lighting Planners Associates 396
Lim, Alex 158
Lim, Nick 85, 388, 390
Lim, Ted 178, 229
Lima, Eduardo 244
Limpisirisan, Passapol 50, 137
Lindemann, Arno 232
Lindenberg, Ruy 35
Linneu, Joao 150
Lloyd, Doug 372
Lloyd, Douglas 98, 405
Lo, Sheungyan 85, 221, 388, 390
Locke, Linda 214
Loew, Dave 33, 198, 326, 430
Lombardi, Dante 423
Low, Patrick 254
Lubars, David
201, 219, 228, 279, 291, 386
Lucero, Santiago 282
Luckin, Fran 325
Lumsiricharoenchoke, Wisit 39, 195, 230
Lynn, Elspeth 51, 326

M
Mackall, Kevin 283, 284, 293, 314
Maddocks, Rich 172, 260, 330, 408
Madiraju, Shyam 322
Madon, Farrokh 245, 226, 333
Mann, Romy 102, 103, 134, 416, 424, 425
Marshall, Duncan 165, 271, 285
Martin, Fernando 337
Maryon, Dean 55
Matejczyk, John 291, 300
Matsui, Miki 371
Mazur, Sam 315
Mcallister, Cal 218
McBride, Chuck 48, 122, 124, 286, 307
McCarthy, Donna 326
McHugh, Peter 55
McLennan, Rob 151, 159, 325
McLeod, Andy 90
McNeilage, Ned 239
Melo, Duarte Pinheiro De 16, 116, 137
Meng, Tham Khai 37, 120
Merkin, Ari 20, 42, 54, 59, 138, 192, 203, 279, 280, 291, 326
Merrifield, John 65, 126, 141, 207, 210
Meske, Stefan 160, 232
Meunier, Philippe 351
Michael, Magnotta 422
Mikus, James 398
Millar, Tom 329
Miller, Adrian 209
Miller, Steve 309
Milner, Duncan 305
Mina, Basil 251
Mitchell, Steve 104, 428
Mizuno, Manabu 77, 80, 82, 381, 404
Moehlenkamp, Kevin 423
Molla, Joaquin 57, 124
Molla, Jose 57, 124
Mommertz, Christian 30
Montague, Ty 185, 198
Montero, Antonio 173
Montgomery, John 205
Morales, Dan 295, 296
Moreno, Manolo 351, 431
Morimoto, Chie 96, 131, 144
Morris, Brett 193, 325
Morrow, Sally 353
Mortier, Jens 321
Moudry, Thomas 269
Mroueh, Zak 44, 121, 324
Murphy, Tom 326
Myburgh, Gerhard 193

N
Nair, Raj 201, 357
Namouric, Gatan 325
Nanji, Elsie 166
Nelson, Jim 187, 213
Newbery, Bill 219
Ng, Ronald 220
Nixon, Jeff 169, 397
Nobay, David 63, 252, 258
Nobre, Fernando 150
Nolting, Ralf 9, 89, 115, 204
Nonzioli, Juan 253, 325
Norman, John 281

O
O'Connell, Steve 175
Oka, Yasumichi 75, 127, 141
Olf, Bettina 21, 84, 88, 117, 129
Oliva, Toms 173
Olivieri, Sebastin 163
Olsen, Jon 428
Olson, Dan 76, 409
Ong, Kit 83, 371
Orzio, Marty 170
Ota, Megumi 376
Overheu, Sally 274

P
Padhi, Santosh 150
Palmer, Rob 281, 342
Panes, Raoul 170
Paprocki, Joe 220
Papworth, Kim 2-3, 46, 122, 135-136
Park, Kum-Jun 107, 393
Parson, David 257
Paterson, Ewan 8, 66
Patroulis, John 48, 124
Patzold, Patricia 9, 89, 115, 204
Paul, Josy 335
Pauls, Bill 169, 225, 397
Pawych, Dan 290, 377, 392
Pereira, Tony 176
Petit, Francesc 379, 380
Phillips, Brad 381
Pienaar, Peet 99, 132
Pirisi, Pat 365
Plumet, Herv 152
Powell, Eliot 193
Powell, Neil 130, 365
Poynton, Malcolm 67
Praditpong, Prangthip 24
Pross, Martin 258
Proudfoot, Kevin 185, 294
Putz, Andreas 382

Q
Quinn, Barry 349

R
Raffray, Vincent 14, 116
Ramesh, N. 226, 412
Ranchod, Rajesh 231
Raposo, Leandro 282
Rebeschini, Marcus 10, 11, 12
Reddy, Nathan 367, 383
Reed, Ryan 235
Reilly, Rob 68, 288, 298, 299, 331, 332
Renfro, Mike 215
Renner, Paul 185, 294
Ricciarelli, Papon 187
Roberts, Nigel 19, 22, 117, 147, 186, 248, 308
Rocca, Carlos 177, 380
Roddy, Kevin 164
Roope, Nicholas 344
Roper, Tim 318
Ross, Marshall 369
Roux, Yves 79
Rovner, Mike 315
Royer, Ted 235, 264

Index

Ruf, Markus 325
Ruhmann, Lars 334, 395, 405
Ruiz, Miguel Angel 179
Russell, Alan 42, 45, 213, 240, 243
Ryan, Dennis 60, 125, 138

S

Sandstrom, Steve 100, 354
Sano, Yukimi 385
Santilli, Dino 292
Santo, Joao Espirito 245
Santos, Luciano 180
Santos, Mateus De Paula 101, 133, 414, 415, 422
Sasaki, Keiichi 105
Sato, Sumiko 346
Saville, Robert 49, 344, 362
Sawada, Koichi 376
Schalit, Mike 7, 47, 151, 220, 389, 426
Scheven, Burkhart von 6, 115, 194, 325
Schiff, Dave 340
Schimmel, David 91, 130, 143
Schmidt, Julia 258
Schmidt, Matthias 196, 258
Schneider, Don 201
Schneider, Wolfgang 62, 153, 154, 278, 319, 320, 341
Schofield, John 246
Schuman, Danny 60, 125, 138
Schwarm, Christian 358
Seisser, Tod 222
Sekkei, Nikken 396
Serpa, Marcello 186
Sheinberg, Scott 227, 329
Shine, Mike 71, 387
Shiue, Rich 206
Shon, Chan 158, 388
Silber, Joachim 69
Silverio, Carlos 379, 380
Silverstein, Rich 281
Sim, Tanya 239
Simon, Andrew 148
Simpson, Gavin 152, 223,
Simpson, Steve 281
Sinclair, James 67
Singh, Pushpinder 166
Smail, David 229
Smith, Craig 28
Smith, Jimmy 346
Smith, Jud 171
Soares, Alexandre 150
Soto, Jon 309
Spaetgens, Matthias 27, 29, 119, 355
Spiller, Darren 93, 180
Sridhar, K.V. 150
Srikieatikajohn, Nopadol 35, 364
Stanton, Dave 169, 397
Staples, Chris 43, 51, 70, 121, 123, 126, 207, 325, 345
Stapleton, Marike 400
Stern, Thomas 268
Stiller, Mathias 62, 153, 154, 278, 319, 320, 341
Straw, Steve 214, 233
Stricker, Pablo 282
Stringer, Andre 424
Sucharittanonta, Suthisak 169, 220, 228

T

Talbot, Toby 172, 260, 330, 408
Tan, Terrence 226, 245, 333
Tanapatanakul, Thirasak 24
Tang, CC 176
Tao, Lorraine 51, 326
Teixeira, Jorge 202
Teoh, Alvin 229
Thaidumrong, Jureeporn 310
Thirache, Sylvain 192, 216
Thomas, Joanne 384
Thomas, Trefor 366
Thomsen, Axel 323
Thorburn, Bill 76, 369, 434
Tilly, Ahmed 325
Tinning, Andrew 40
Torres, Toni 97
Tranter, Gary 14,
Turner, David 373, 368
Tutssel, Mark 95, 205

U

Ulmer, Goetz 325

V

Valente, Sergio 191, 308
Vaquero, Agustin 182, 183
Vare, Jasun 161
Vega, Guillermo 163
Vervroegen, Erik 15, 28, 184, 185, 222, 391
Vescovo, Matthew 314
Villiers, Francois De 359
Vior, Ricky 57, 124
Vogel, Stephan 30
Vonk, Nancy 179
Voss, Oliver 325

W

W+K 12 86
Waites, Mark 49, 344, 362
Wakefield, Rich 329
Walsh, Stuart 151, 325
Wangpaitoon, Vasan 228
Warner, Paul 162, 183
Warsop, Graham 31
Waterbury, Todd 185, 197, 198, 294
Watson, Ralph 257
Watt, Julian 389
Weber, Timm 21, 84, 88, 117, 129
Weber-Grun, Alexander 148, 149
Wee, Francis 32, 139, 147, 212, 220
Wehrli, Ursus 23, 118,
Welsh, Ben 168
Wenneker, Mark 288
Williams, Genevieve 403
Willmott, Howard 165, 271, 285
Willvonseder, Claudia 206
Witt, Sandra de 265
Wong, Derek 176
Wong, Eddie 210, 391
Wong, Tracy 246, 325
World, Living 396
Worthington, Nick 36, 246, 261, 264
Wright, Bill 17, 61, 125, 139, 190, 191, 339
Wu, Tif 210, 391

Wyville, Jon 326

Y
Young, Al 225

Z
Zaragoza, Jose 177, 380
Zheng, Daming 41
Zhu, Thomas 85, 390
Zou, Leo 41
Zunkeler, Ulrich 23, 118

designers

A
Adewumi, Kristy 100
Akiba, Hideo 78
Akimoto, Yuta 82
Akiyama, Shigeto 91, 130, 143
Anderson, Kristin 100, 354
Anderson, Nate 329
Andrew, Shanin 353
Angulo, Eymard 377
Apparatus, Aesthetic 104
Ashley, Michael 239, 431
Aun, Alex Lim Thye 32, 139, 220

B
Ba, Gabriel 422
Bane, Alex 413
Beck, Melinda 370
Bela, Carlos 101, 133
Benoit, Marie-Elaine 351
Berger, Thomas 382
Bielefeldt, Christoph 395
Bingham, Weston 353
Bloching, Miriam 210
Blumenfeld, Luis 101, 133
Bohm, Andreas 341
Bottiger, Camilla 402
Bozic, Milan 394
Braddock, Mark 239
Brandt, Mike 99
Broadbent, Will 101, 133
Bubb, Brenton 359
Buck, Spencer 413
Bugbee, Stella 370
Burnard, Alex 340

C
Chen, Curtis C. 339
Chisholm, Heidi 99, 132
Ciuraj, Cathrin 355,
Clifford, Graham 378
Clormann, Lorenz 210
Clunie, James 219, 386
Crutchfield, Craig 398
Cuellar, Silver 398

D
Deck, Barry 370
DeMartino, Laurie 86, 129, 142
DeRouen, Derrit 398
Dimmel, Aaron 374
Dorner, Philipp 395, 405
Drummond, Stacy 401
Dull, Andrew 350

E
Eager, Christian 373
Eckstein, Vanessa 356
Emery, Don 412
Enriquez, Vanessa 356
Etzel, Paul 27
Eves, Christian 377

F
Fiebig, Nicole 334
Flanigan, Miles 423
Frick, Urs 351
Fruehauf, Helena 94, 406
Fuwa, Minoru 75, 127, 141

G
Ge, Fan 391
Gehrig, Kim 362
Giovanni, Renata 367
Goh, Ken 83
Gomez, Victor 431
good design company 404
Gramp, Rafael 101, 133, 414
Gramp·, Rafael 422
Green, Sheraton 375
Griffiths, Thomas 353
Grun, Simone 262
Guggenbuhl, Christian 411
Guimaraes, Celina 367
Guise, Olly 413

H
Hakansson, Niclas 402
Hames, Kyle 375
Hammerl, Alex 383
Hendrix, Michael 367
Henkes, Uschi 351
Hennequin, Nathalie 94, 406
Ho, T T 352
Hobbs, John 97
Hock, Chye Yong 420
Hollingsworth, Jovaney 374
Hoong, Yap Pow 371
Horner, Ben 367
Huang, Wei-Hwa 339
Hyodo, Toshihiro 75, 127, 141

I
Imaging, HQ 408
Infahsaeng, Apirat 353

J
Jacobs, Joan 75, 390
Janke, Michael 341
Jaranphairee, Maytinee 364
Jeutter, Andreas 69
Ji, Peng 391
Johnson, Jeff 366
Jung, Jong-in 393

K
Kaczmarek, Jesse 76, 369, 434
Kalil, Diogo 101, 133
Kang, Joong-gyu 107, 393
Karkhanis, Ashutosh 201
Kasuga, Megumu 75, 127, 141

Index

Kawai, Takeru 376
Kennedy, Roger 366
Kirschenhofer, Bertrand 334, 395
Kobayashi, Mari 75, 127, 141
Koshio, Shinsuke 421
Kreuser, Carla 384

L
Lanne, Emil 344
Lee, Hee Jeong 403
Lee, Sin Eng 32, 139
Legare, Leslie 102, 416
Lim, Jann 83, 371
Lim, Pann 73, 79, 128, 225, 361, 372, 392
Lishman, Maria 260, 330, 408
Locherer, Claudia 355

M
Macedo, Cadu 101, 133, 422
Manning, Luke 413
Marcondes, Guilherme 101, 133, 414
Marmo, Rogerio 101, 133, 422
Maskatsu, Takagi 421
Matz, Starlee 353
McArthur, Hamish 222
McCarthy, Suzanne 72
Miller, Patrick 369, 434
Minh, Pham Tuan 229
Mitoh 104, 427
Miyamoto, Hitoshi 105, 204,
Mochinaga, Nobuya 105, 204
Moon, Cindy 338
Moon, Fabio 422
Morrow, Sally 353

N
Nam, Seung-youn 393
Nautiyal, Gaurav 412
Negishi, Akitomo 376
Nerman, Jenny 351
Newman, Simon 365
Nguyen, Loc 229
Nicol, Jonathan 351
Nobre, Paula 101, 133, 414, 422

O
O'Brien, James 403
Okies, Leigh 94, 406
Olson, Ted 428
Onaindia, Jon 431

P
Panchal, Rahul 332, 340
Parekh, Niket 362
Park, Kum-jun 393, 107
Parker, James 354
Pavlovic, Ana 403
Peacock, Jo-Wayne 433
Pengsathapon, Satian 94, 406
Peterson, Shereen 95
Pfennighaus, Max 72, 338
Pienaar, Peet 99, 132
Piper-Hauswirth, Todd 374, 375
Poh, Roy
73, 79, 128, 225, 361, 372, 392, 225
Powell, Neil 130, 365

Q
Quinn, Barry 349

R
Rane, Mangesh 361
Reintz, Martin 77
Richter, Sebastian 355
Rivas, Oscar 340
Rodricks, Priti 357
Rosenberger, Shawn 368
Ruiz, Julie 399

S
Sader, Mario 101, 133, 422
Sahre, Paul 95, 131
Sakurai, Ken 76, 409
Sandstrom, Steve 100
Schabenberger, Stefan 232
Schreiber, Gunther 405
Sega, Nanae 105, 204
Shabaz, Ali 32, 139, 220
Shilo 424
Siegal, Meghan 372, 338
Soh, Leng 73, 372
Stapleton, Marike 400
Stead, Mark 73, 127
Switowski, Joanna 21, 117

T
Takada, Yui 77
Takahashi, Go 77, 80, 82, 381
Tan, Sie-Yang 66
Teng, Theresa Tsang 427
The Ice Box 66
Toesangaun, Saovapa 221
Tung, Diana 431
Turner, David 373

V
Valencius, Chris 72
Vendramin, Daniel 392
Verdon-Smith, Fiona 78
Vision, Sunday 421

W
Waiss, Drew 412
Walker, Garth 432
Waluk, Iwona 370
Walzer, Jason 366
Warne, Jason 338
Williamson, Luke 362
Wills, Karl 413
Wills, Ryan 413
Wolch, Anthony 365
Wong, Eddie 391
WOOG 421, 101
Wu, Tif 391

Y
Yokoo, Misugi 96, 131, 144
Yom, Bill 232
Yuen, Jonathan 361

directors

A
Acord, Lance 55
Addy, Carl 426
Alberdi, Agustin 57, 124
Aldorf, Frank 326
Alshin, Adam
An, Sun 421
Ariola, Dante 313

B
Beletic, Brian 48, 122, 124
Bernard, Evan 60, 125, 138
Bertish, Conn 325
Blanco, Javier 282
Blomkamp, Neill 52
Brink, Matthew 325
Buckley, Bryan 49
Burrows, Steve 315

C
+Cruz 101, 421
Clarke, Peter 42
Cornish, Trevor 51, 123, 345
Craig, Peter 71

D
Downing, Michael 43, 70, 121, 126

E
Elvis, Les 268
Enfield, Harry 61, 125, 139, 332

F
Fogwill, Andy 57, 124
Foulkes, Adam 344
Frankham, David 286, 307
Freedman, Gary 68
Fueter, Martin 325

G
Gerbosi, Dave 326
Gibbons, Brendan 301
Gill, Slade 325
Gillespie, Craig 288, 303, 304, 309
Godsall, Tim 44, 59, 266
Goldstein, Lionel 321
Gordon, Josh 56
Gorman, Jeff 312
Granger, Martin 288, 290, 298, 299
Grey, Greg 47
Guest, Christopher 316

H
Happy 289
Hoagland, Christian 72, 273
Hock, Chye Yong 420
Horowitz, David 283, 284
Hosking, Jim 309

J
Jenkins, Jim 285, 293
Johansson, Ulf 47, 286
Jones, Tom 315

K
Keith, JJ 308
Kleinman, Daniel 58
Kleinmann, Danny 43
Kneebone, Jonathan 68
Krallman, Randy 293
Kuntz, Tom 54, 138, 280, 291

L
Lawrence, Ben 267
Leih, Joe 329
Longcraine, Richard 418

M
Madiraju, Shyam 322
Maguire, Mike 54, 138, 280, 291
Malone, Vince 271
Malze, Marc 334
Masakatsu, Takagi 421
McKeviit, Alastair 71
Meyers, Dave 305, 346
Middleditch, Paul 289
Miller, Peter Darley 306
Miller, Steve 278, 319, 341
Mo, Lab Ky 343
Morris, Brett 325
Morris, Errol 294, 302
Morton, Rocky 331
Murphy, Dominic 274
Murphy, Patrick 317
Murro, Noam 48, 124, 279, 281, 342

N
Nelson, Chris 292

O
O'Reilly, Terry 326

P
Palmer, Chris 287
Perlorian Brothers, The 51
Persson, Lorens 325
Petchsuwan, Suthon 50, 137, 310
Peters, Ole 323

R
Rami, Sam 417
Rogers, Steve 63
Romanek, Mark 288
Clint! Runge 42

S
Sanders, Rupert 48, 124, 288
Schadel, Timo 323
Schlermann, Marc 64
Scott, Jake 287
Sehr, Kai 311
Shane, David 45, 294
Sharda, Ritu 270
Sheridan, Jim 318
Smith&Foulkes 2-3, 46, 122, 135-136
Smith, Adam 344
Smith, Baker 338
Smith, Bart 42, 338
Smith, Chris 295, 296
Snyder, Zack 419
So&Sau 277
Soaeb, Mohammed 270
Speck, Will 56

Index

Stoller, Aaron 293
Strasser, Sebastian 62, 320

T
Tadaro, Frank 292
Tarry, Rob 325
Thomas, Kevin 291, 300
Thrush, Laurence 65
Tikhomiroff, Joao Daniel 308
Traktor 313

V
Vescovo, Matthew 314
Vincent, Scott 269
Viral Factory, The 67
Vogel, Francois 281

W
Weinmaster, Colin 325

production companies

A
A52 317
Adam Rourke 102, 416
Anonymous Content 288, 423
Another Country 326
Archrival 42
Arden Sutherland Dodd 61, 125, 139
ASD 332
Audio Z 325
Avion Films 290

B
B&S Studios 325
Backyard 315
Barbarian Group 331
Bartradio 42, 338
Beith 389
Big Look Productions 315
Biscuit Fiimworks
48, 59, 124, 266, 279, 281, 342

C
Capitaine Plouf 277
Caravan Pictures 267
Chelsea Pictures 60, 125, 138
Chicago Recording Company 326
Circle (Hungry Man) 45
Clatter & Din 325,
Cobblestone 62, 311 320
Colenso BBDO 330
Compana Cinematografica 282
CRC 326
Creative Post 324
Czar.be 321

D
Dave Skinner 102, 102, 416, 103, 134
Deli Pictures 311
Doublehead 326

E
Exposure Films 308

F
Fad New York 314
Food Chain Films 271

G
GGRP 42
Godman 343
Go Film 316
Gorgeous 287

H
Harmless & Domesticated 426
Harvest Films 338
Hastings 325, 326
Headquarters 65
Hollywood 288, 298, 299
Hungry Man 49, 269, 285, 293, 294, 301

I
Independent Media 295, 296

J
JGF Films 312
Jingle Box 325
Jodaf 308

K
Kamen Entertainment 42, 326

L
Landia 57, 124
Large 43, 58
Lobo 101, 133, 414, 415, 422

M
Markenfilm 64
Matching Studio 50, 137, 310
McHale Barone 42, 119, 325
Media Concierge 65, 126, 141
MJZ 288, 303, 304, 309, 313, 313, 331
Morton Jankel Zander 54, 138, 280, 291
Moxie Pictures 292, 298, 299, 318
MTV In-House 283, 284, 293

N
Neelratan 270
Nexus 344, 2-3, 46, 122, 135-136

O
Oceanmonsters 101
Omaha Pictures 48, 56, 124, 288

P
Paranoid Pictures 281
Park Pictures 55
Partizan 274, 309
Pirate Radio 326
Plaza Films 289
Prologue 417-419

R
@radical.media
68, 268, 294, 302, 305, 306, 346
@radical.media Berlin
278, 319, 341
Radke Films 70, 126, 43, 121

Rafa Arnau 325
Redtree Productions 72, 273
Reginald Pike 51
Revolver Films 63
Richard Mather 425
Robot Communications 96, 131, 144
Rosnick Mackinon Webster 326
RSA 287, 292

S
Sehsucht 323
Shell Like 325
Shilo 424
Silbersee Film 334
Smith and Jones 47, 286
Smuggler 48, 122, 124, 286, 289, 295, 307
Sonovision Studios 325
Spy Films 51, 123, 345
Sterling Sound 325
Studio Bellerive 325
Studio Funk 325
Sunday Vision 421

T
The Embassy 52
The Upper Storey 420
The Viral Factory 67
Thomas Thomas Films 291, 300
Traktor/Partizan 313
Triton Films 101

U
Untitled 44, 121, 322

V
Velocity 47

W
Wave Productions 325
Wieden+Kennedy Tokyo Lab 101, 421
Wizz/Quad Productions 277

Z
Zaaz 71

Schools

A
Adhouse / New York 437
Art Institute of Pittsburgh / Pittsburgh 449
Arts Center College of Design / Pasadena 437
Arts Center College of Design / Pasadena 110

C
California State University / Long Beach 440
City College of New York / New York 440, 450

F
Fashion Institute of Technology / New York 450
Fort Hays State University / Hays 451

J
James Madison University / Harrisonburg 451

M
Miami Ad School / Miami Beach 109
Miami Ad School / Miami Beach 442
Miami Ad School / Minneapolis 442
Miami Ad School / Minneapolis 109
Miami Ad School / New York 453
Miami Ad School / San Francisco 443

P
Portfolio Center / Atlanta 443, 452, 453

S
Savannah College of Art and Design / Savannah 444
School of Visual Arts / New York 444

T
Texas A&M University Commerce / Commerce 112
The Art Institute of Washington / Arlington 438
The Book Shop / Culver City 438, 439
The College of Saint Rose / Albany 111
The Creative Circus / Atlanta 441
The University of Akron - Myer's School of Art / Akron 449, 452

U
University of British Columbia / Vancouver and Design Akademie / Berlin 445
University of Colorado / Boulder 445, 446
University of Mississippi / University 111

V
VCU Adcenter / Richmond 446, 447, 448

writers

A
Adams, Tom 188, 298, 299
Adkins, Doug 104
Aguilar, Victor 325
Ahern, Brian 224
Ahn, Eun-ju 393
Akkermann, Nico 62
Alexander, Joe 34
Alshin, Adam 42, 54, 138, 280, 291
Alvarez, Ali 90
Ampe, Peter 321
Andersson, Nils 105, 204
Anselmo, Frank 201, 228
Anuncibay, Carlos 181
Armstrong, Pete 343
Ashley, Michael 239
Askwith, Dave 181
Asmal, Mirjam 99, 132
Atienza, Jayson 201, 228
Aun, Alex Lim Thye 32, 139, 147, 220
Azuma, Hideki 77

B
Bae, Joon-young 393
Bagley, Jason 52
Bakhshi, Ajay 66, 352

Index

Baldacci, Roger 266
Ballard, Dustin 191
Barnes, Derek 197, 286, 302
Barnes, Justin 67
Barnett, Guy 378
Barr, Nancy 97
Barrett, Jamie 281, 288, 342
Barry, Ted 330
Bartels, Ingmar 334, 395, 405
Benjamin, Jay 258
Benzinger, Michael 232
Bertish, Conn 325
Bester, Jake 235
Bhat, Raghu 234
Bhatt, Manish 234
Bielefeldt, Christoph 334
Birkenstock, Linda 269
Blore, Michael 31
Boettcher, Philipp 30
Bohm, Andreas 153
Bonnici, Joseph 243
Bootlis, Paul 180
Botfeld, Kevin 329
Bouchet, Jean-Francois 184, 222
Bradley, Clarence 169, 397
Bradley, Joel 217, 236
Branning, Matthew 15
Brazier, Paul 153
Bremer, Bjorn 148
Breton, Pete 44, 121
Brink, Matthew 151, 325
Brothers, Brooklyn 301
Buck, Spencer 413
Bullock, Richard 55
Byrne, Mike 47, 287

C

+cruz 101
Cade, Nick 292
Callis, Ben 67
Camp, Tom 187
Campos, Fernando 188
Canright, David 200
Carrigan, Andy 198
Carvalho, Thiago 18
Casarotti, Flavio 191
Cassis, Francisco 337
Cavaille, Elvire 177
Cawley, Tim 386
Chan, Danny 217
Chantrawan, Passakorn 35
Charoenwiwatchai, Wirat 228
Chen, Monica 83
Chen, Valerie 427
Cheong, Eugene 37, 120
Chester, Ricardo 308
Chew, Donevan 388, 158, 231
Chiaphanumas, Nutchanun 24
Chiew, Clarence 263
Chitpanvong, Sirilak 39, 195, 230
Choo, Kenny 26, 118
Christmann, Tom 219
Chudalla, Thomas 175, 319
Cianfrone, Bob 190, 249, 289, 331
Clark, Stuart 208
Clarke, Darren 392
Clay, Steve 235, 264
Clement, John 42, 119
Cloete, James 7
Cockeran, Kyle 171
Cohen, Bob 164
Cohen, Ian 218
Cohen, Nicole 183
Cole, Dan 366
Collins, Bryan 207
Collins, Reed 215
Condon, John 95
Connolly, Kara 79
Copeland, Liz 97
Cotton, Ed 387
Crandall, Court 65

D

Dasari, Ramprasad 256
Dasgupta, Malobi 361
Davenport, John 47
DeCarolis, Anthony 42, 119
Deisenhofer, Stephan 210, 218
Delfgaauw, Martien 204
Denberg, Josh 194
Deng, Billy 256
Design, Pivot 412
Detweiler, Curt 197
Devaris, Oliver 168
DiLallo, Andy 258
Dogra, Deepak 226
Doksroy, Kulvadee 39, 195
Doria, Icaro 16, 116, 137
Dorner, Philipp 334
Doyle, Sean 209
Dubois, Fabrice 152
Duchon, Scott 48, 122, 124
Dutton, Chris 220
Dyer, Leighton 264

E

Ebner, Ryan 33
Echlin, Hobey 97
Einhorn, Marc 42, 72, 273, 338
Elliott, Yan 49
Emery, Toria 342
Emmett, Brad 42, 119, 295, 296
Endoh, Tomohide 423
Eng, Tan Kien 427
Engstrom, Bjorn 409, 410

F

Fahrenkopf, Erik 42, 119
Fairbanks, Mark 248, 308
Faudet, Michael 289
Figel, Pete 430
Figueiredo, Marco 245
Finnegan, Annie 72
Fitzgerald, Kevin 414
Fleet, Karl 172, 261, 408
Fleig, Paul 69, 325
Flohrs, Oliver 352
Ford, Chris 288
Fraction, Matt 422
Franco, Sergio 180
Frericks, Daniel 326, 311
Fry, Evan 17, 332, 339

Fujita, Katsuhisa 207

G
Gaikwad, Vinayak 166
Ganser, Stephan 325
Gardiner, Neil 325
Gaxiola, Robert 203, 250
Genell, Jim 194
Germon, Ghislaine De 185
Giachetti, Daniel 42, 119
Gibbons, Brendan 301
Gil, Pablo 244
Gill, Slade 325
Gines, Guillermo 182
Goh, Alex 73, 225, 79, 128, 392
Gordon, Nick 231
Gorman, Heather 309
Govier, Dave 40
Green, Howard 325
Green, Oliver 225
Greenstein, Keith 167
Gross, Avery 95, 205
Group, Assignment 87
Gschwend, Charlie 71
Guadarrama, Alejandro 179
Guillo, Nacho 253, 325
Guttesman, Marc 329

H
Haeussler, Michael 29, 119
Hall, Charles 198
Hall, Graeme 66
Hamann, Rick 60, 125, 138
Harbeck, Jan 194, 325
Harris, Brian 413
Haruo, Luiz 150
Hathiramani, Jackie 72, 273
Hayo, Thomas 313
Healy, Forrest 303, 304
Hearne, Sanders 429
Heartfield, Ian 22
Helfman, Jonathan 315
Henning, Daniel 194
Herman, Christie 209
Hershfield, Bobby 185
Hien, Ngo Xuan 229
Hine, Nick 184
Hirsch, Paul 194
Hollister, Bill 72
Horowitz, David 283, 284
Howard, Mike 42, 338
Hunt, John 286
Hunter, Bernard 165
Huse, Tim 172, 260
Huvart, Lars 106, 134
Hwang, Raymond 306

I
Ignazi, Peter 290
Immesoete, John 326

J
Jachmann, Lina 149, 148
Jackson, Al 225
Jalfen, Martin 57, 124
Jay, John 101
Jeffers, Crockett 307
Jenkins, Simon 14
Johnson, Jeff 366
Jones, Kevin 181
Jung, Jong-in 107
Juniot, Marcio 35
JWT 87

K
Kahler, Florian 323
Kain, Peter 313
Kalleres, Greg 198, 294
Kamdar, Prakash 420
Kane, Riley 434
Kapoor, Dinesh 431, 239
Kapoor, Puneet 205
Kapur, Priti 214, 214
Karcher, Roman 399
Karkhanis, Ashutosh 201
Katzenstein, Rob 167
Kaushik, Niranjan 201
Kay, Ben 147, 186
Kearse, John 72, 273, 338
Kekalainen, Eeva 247, 259
Kelly, Albert 288
Keon, Matt 225
Kessel, Felix 400
Khan, Irfan 349
Khow, Subun 169
Kidson, Dylan 359
Kilciauskas, Roberto 379, 380
Kleman, Robert 10, 11, 12
Kling, Jeff 294
Kluin, Menno 21, 84, 117
Knight, Linda 239
Kong, Stephen 26, 118
Konishi, Toshiyuki 371
Kovac, Maria 97
Krajan, Mark 423
Krallman, Randy 293
Kukulska, Ulrika 402
Kulkosa, Nikrom 228
Kume, Syoichi 385
Kummer, Stuart 27
Kunene, Spike 433
Kung, Giant 206
Kutscher, Ryan 332

L
Lacuesta, Kite 407
Lai, Sally 176
Langlade, Jerome 192
Lavan, Rosemary 406
Lawson, Joe 56
Le, Kevin 178
Lear, Mike 167, 339
Lee, James 213, 240
Lee, Matt 155
Leinweber, David 88, 129
Leroux, Benoit 28
Liebig, Jana 326
Lim, Pann 79, 128, 225, 361, 392
Lim, Paul 388
Lima, Eduardo 244
Limpisirisan, Passapol 50, 137
Linardatos, Andy 51, 123, 345
Lindner, Torsten 355

Index

Linnen, Scott 173, 189, 202
Lishman, Maria 408
Little, Paul 42, 45
Livesey, Adam 325
Loew, Dave 198, 326
Lombardi, Dante 423
Longie, Troy 255
Loo, Calvin 250
Lopez, Nicolas 260
Lourenco, Marcelo 202
Low, Leslie 372
Low, Victoria 352
Lu, Kurt 206
Lubke, Karsten 395
Lufrano, Richard 399
Luo, Kijin 388
Lutzenkirchen, Ulrich 154, 278, 341

M
Machado, Mauricio 177, 380
Madiraju, Shyam 322
Madon, Farrokh 226, 245, 333
Maiorino, Chris 201
Makinen, Tommy 247, 259
Makita, Tomoyuki 96, 131, 144
Malcolm, Clark 350
Manalich, Felipe 260
Manikas, Konstantinos 206
Marchand, Dominique 268
Martinez, Juan Carlos 337
Mather, Richard 425
Mathew, Rahul 205
Mazur, Sam 315
McAllister, Cal 218
McBride, Chuck 286
McBurnie, Scott 63
McCain, Matt 325
McCarthy, Donna 326
McCommon, Mike 309
McKechnie, Andrew 212
McKenzie, Selena 93
McNeilage, Ned 239
McTear, Tony 58
Mendes, Jason 252
Merrifield, John 65, 126, 141
Miao, Miu 41
Middlton, Ben 344
Miles, Paul 25
Miller, Adrian 209
Mitchell, Steve 428
Moby 378
Monroy, Juan Carlos 181
Moore, Toby 93
Moreno, Manolo 431
Morgan, Clark 370
Morgese, Nicole 399
Moroze, Adam 167
Morris, Brett 325
Mroueh, Zak 324

N
Naidu, Asheen 389
Namouric, Gaitan 325
Nandwani, Amit 335
Nantananontchai, Wiparat 310
Nasunee, Juntiga 228
Nautiyal, Ranjan 412
Nel, Annette 426
Nelson, Jacob 149
Ng, Ronald 237
Ng, Victor 233
Nobay, David 63
Northrop, Ronny 38

O
O'Brien, Steve 316
O'Connell, Steve 175
O'Connor, Tom 193, 317
Ogden, Peter 289
Okkararojkij, Sittichai 50, 137
Ong, Carol 170
Ong, Edward 223
Ourlian, Robert 97
Outhwaite, Stuart 344
Owett, Margot 222
Oyasu, Tohru 198, 326

P
Pacheco, Carmen 181
Padhi, Santosh 150
Pagel, Ben 383
Pagel, Florian 323
Panes, Raoul 220
Parekh, Niket 362
Parson, David 257
Parubrub, Richard 312
Patroulis, John 48, 124
Patzschke, Reinhard 9, 115
Peck, Jana 377
Peck, Ryan 291
Pena, Pablo Gonzales De La 325
Perarnaud, Edouard 216
Petch, Andrew 267
Phoon, Herbie 264
Pickering, Blake 432
Pinana, Sara 173
Pinchevsky, Avital 265
Ping, Ong Shi 152
Piper-Hauswirth, Todd 375
Poh, Roy 79, 128, 225, 361, 392
Polcar, Ales 106, 134
Ponte, Alberto 287
Pope, Seymour 36, 246
Poris, Michael 97
Pratt, Leonardo 57, 124
Premutico, Leo 43
Puhl, Eskil 311, 326

Q
Quennoy, Eric 285
Quester, Peter 196, 258

R
Rachford, Chuck 326
Raffray, Vincent 14, 116
Ragan, Kimberley 330
Rakowski, Amy 211
Ray, Gordon 257
Rebalderia, Hernan 244
Reddy, Nathan 383
Rehfus, Mike 97
Reichenthal, Ian 293, 326